# Disorganized Capitalism

DUNDEE

Uni

# Social and Political Theory from Polity Press

*Published*

David Beetham, *Max Weber and the Theory of Modern Politics*
Richard Bellamy, *Modern Italian Social Theory*
Richard Bernstein, ed., *Habermas and Modernity*
Norberto Bobbio, *The Future of Democracy*
Raymond Boudon, *Theories of Social Change*
John Burnheim, *Is Democracy Possible?*
Cornelius Castoriadis, *The Imaginary Institution of Society*
Stanley Cohen, *Visions of Social Control*
Robert A. Dahl, *A Preface to Economic Democracy*
Ferenc Feher and Agnes Heller, *Eastern Left, Western Left*
David Frisby, *Fragments of Modernity*
Harold Garfinkel, *Studies in Ethnomethodology*
Anthony Giddens, *The Constitution of Society*
Anthony Giddens, *The Nation-State and Violence*
W. F. Haug, *Critique of Commodity Aesthetics*
Susan Hekman, *Hermeneutics and the Sociology of Knowledge*
David Held, *Models of Democracy*
John Heritage, *Garfinkel and Ethnomethodology*
J. N. Isbister, *Freud: An Introduction to his Life and Work*
Martin Jay, *Marxism and Totality*
Hans Joas, *G. H. Mead: A Contemporary Re-examination of his Thought*
Harvey J. Kaye, *The British Marxist Historians*
Claude Lefort, *The Political Forms of Modern Society*
Thomas McCarthy, *The Critical Theory of Jurgen Habermas*
Carole Pateman, *The Problem of Political Obligation*
Mark Poster, *Foucault, Marxism and History*
Barbara Sichtermann, *Femininity: The Politics of the Personal*
John B. Thompson, *Studies in the Theory of Ideology*
Sylvia Walby, *Patriarchy at Work*

*A Selection of Forthcoming Titles*

Barry Barnes, *The Basis of Power*
Zygmunt Bauman, *Legislators and Interpreters*
Norberto Bobbio, *What is Socialism?*
Norberto Bobbio, *The Future of Democracy*
Pierre Bourdieu, *Language and Symbolic Power*
Nancy Fraser, *Power, Discourse and Gender*
Anthony Giddens and Jonathan Turner, eds, *Social Theory Today*
Jurgen Habermas, *The Philosophical Discourse of Modernity*
David Held, *Foundations of Democracy*
Scott Lash and John Urry, *The End of Organized Capitalism*
William Outhwaite, *Habermas*
Alan Ryan, *Political Philosophy: An Introduction*
Michelle Stanworth, *Feminism and Sociology*
John B. Thompson, *The Interpretation of Ideology*
Nigel Thrift, *Social Theory and Human Geography*
Paul Willis, *To Labour: The Subjective Side of Capital*

# Disorganized Capitalism

## Contemporary Transformations of Work and Politics

CLAUS OFFE

*edited by John Keane*

Polity Press

© Claus Offe, 1985

First published 1985 by
Polity Press, Cambridge, in association with Basil Blackwell, Oxford.
Reprinted 1986

Editorial Office: Polity Press
Dales Brewery, Gwydir Street, Cambridge CB1 2LJ, UK.

Basil Blackwell Ltd
108, Cowley Road, Oxford, OX4 1JF, UK.

Basil Blackwell Inc.
432 Park Avenue South, Suite 1505, New York, NY 10016, USA.

*British Library Cataloguing in Publication Data*

Offe, Claus
    Disorganized capitalism : contemporary
    transformations of work and politics.
    1. Labour supply
    I. Title      II. Keane, John
    331.12      HD5706
    ISBN 0–7456–0085–9
    ISBN 0–7456–0086–7 Pbk

Typeset by Oxford Publishing Services, Oxford
Printed in Great Britain by Bell and Bain Ltd Glasgow

# Contents

# Introduction

Most of the essays in this volume have been published previously in German, and in a rather wide variety of contexts. They are, nevertheless, bound together by a common analytical scheme concerned with a range of problems usually associated with the discipline of political sociology. Expressed in the most simple and general formula, political sociology deals with empirical relationships between two sets of phenomena: social power and political authority. The dynamic interactions between these phenomena become evident if answers to the following question are sought after: How are relations of social power translated into political authority, and how, conversely, does political authority process and transform these power relations within civil society? In the following introductory remarks, I should like to briefly explore this issue, to situate the following essays within it, and to clarify the connotations of the term 'disorganized capitalism'.[1]

The first object of attention in political sociology is the matrix of social power. This is an attribute not of actors, but of modes of interaction. Not all interactions are relationships of power (in the sense of dependency), but those which are result in the privileging of certain partners in the processes of interaction, and the disadvantaging and exploitation of others. Forms of interaction can be strictly symmetrical (so as to involve no power differentials whatsoever), or they may be affected by power in unsystematic ways. In the latter case, sometimes one category of actors, sometimes another benefits disproportionately from the interaction, while substantive gains remain variable in kind and social distribution. To speak of a *matrix* of social power is to reject such 'pluralist' and 'dispersed' notions of power. It rather implies the thesis, developed most clearly within the tradition of Marxist class theory, that dominant modes of interaction consistently favour one category of actors and result in the systematic exploitation of others.

In 'The Political Economy of the Labour Market', I argue that the institution of the labour market, which treats labour power as if it were a commodity, constitutes the most significant feature of capitalist social structures. It is a power-generating mode of interaction that leads to a relatively stable and consistent matrix of social power, which at the same time also serves as a starting point for the explanation of phenomena of power dispersion. According to classical historical materialism, the labour market consists of a simultaneous and yet self-contradictory process of consolidation and disruption of power, of its crystallization and subversion: the stronger the power holders become, the more their power is challenged and undermined. This dynamic is fundamental to the grandiose scenario of a bipolar struggle between social classes. However, the conflict component of this scenario does not follow deductively from the recognition of the fact of exploitative forms of interaction: even though the market interaction between workers and capitalists is a relationship of power, the rational response of participants in this interaction is by no means restricted to that of engaging in a class-wide collective conflict centring on the abolition of the commodity form of labour power. They might also engage in displaced or limited forms of conflict that produce a secondary dispersion of power: workers can either be compensated partially for the losses they suffer as a result of the exploitative production relations in which they are situated, or they can engage in conflicts among themselves, the outcomes of which in turn determine who pays most for the total costs of this exploitation, as well as who emerges from this trilateral game as the 'winning loser'. Given the possibility (and reality) of such secondary processes of the dispersion of social power, the theoretical anticipation of comprehensive class conflict can be challenged. As a model of the structure and dynamic of relations within civil society it is of doubtful validity. Indeed, there are good reasons why it may be rational for individual actors in a class society *not* to act in reference to classes or in accordance with their class interests.

The model of a multipolar and complex pattern of cleavages, collectivities and conflicts which are constituted by the prevailing modes of social interaction and exchange seems to be particularly relevant and fruitful if we observe the vertical and horizontal cleavages within the work-force of contemporary capitalist societies. One of these lines of differentiation is that between 'productive' and 'service' labour. This structural differentiation within the work-force evidently has repercussions both on the level of social-scientific theories (of 'post-industrial society', for instance) as well as on the level of social and political conflict (e.g. in the 'new social movements'). The complex and partially conflicting theories concerning the growing importance of services in advanced capitalist social structures are explored in 'The Growth of the Service Sector'. An even more consequential cleavage within the working class is the separation of those who actually participate in labour markets (in that they are both employed and exploited) from those who are instead involved in such non-market forms of activity and material subsistence as private households as well as state-organized institutions such as schools, armies or prisons. For the foreseeable future, as I argue in several of the following essays, labour markets in many countries will continue to exhibit a declining absorption potential, thus removing or excluding increasing numbers of potential workers from direct and full-time contact with the supposedly central power mechanism of capitalist society. It is this separation between the employed and the non-employed, and the various and conflicting strategies aimed at solving the problems of the latter, which form the central themes of 'Three Perspectives on the Problem of Unemployment' and 'The Future of the Labour Market'. The reasons why it is also doubtful whether the matrix of social power can still be theoretically reconstructed by reference to the primary categories of work and labour, as has been the intellectual inclination of not only Marxists, but of the whole of the classical sociological tradition, are summarized in 'Work : The Key Sociological Category?'

The second central object of attention in political sociology is institutionalized political authority. An even modestly systematic treatment of state theory is not to be found in the following pages, since I have attempted to pursue this type of analysis in some of the chapters of *Contradictions of the Welfare State*.[2] The social-scientific treatment of state authority seems presently to be suspended somewhere between the Weberian position (which argues that the state has historically performed an unlimited multitude of goals, and can therefore only be studied by reference to the varying *modes* and *means* of performing these functions), and the Marxian project. The latter, in its numerous variants, posits a more-or-less direct, more-or-less open correspondence between the existing matrix of social class power and the form and content of state authority. In reconsidering this controversy, and in attempting to escape its narrowly defined alternatives, I have attempted to think of the modern state as a highly complex agency that performs a variety of different, historically and systematically interrelated functions which can neither be reduced to a mere reflection of the matrix of social power nor considered as part of an unlimited multitude of potential state functions. In order to extend this idea somewhat further, one could draw upon the modern tradition of normative political philosophy to reconstruct both the state's cumulative acquisition of functions and, correspondingly, the criteria of legitimation through which the holders of political authority have attempted to justify their authority as such. A schematic outline of this evolutionary sequence of the functions of legitimate authority would include the following developments.

First, in the early stages of modernity, the key functional problem of the state was the securing of *peace* (whether in the form of the capacity of a political community to secure itself in a hostile *international* environment, as discussed by Machiavelli or instead, or in addition, the capacity to overcome and prevent civil war, which was the prime concern of Hobbes). Second, and in addition to the goal of peace, the institution of 'passive' citizenship rights (*habeas corpus*, private property, the separation of political and paternal authority) was added to the list of normative criteria according to which the legitimacy of political authority was to be judged. That is to say, legitimate political rule was thereafter to be self-restricted, partial rule from which citizens, and hence a sphere of civil society, were to be exempted. This second set of functions corresponds to the liberal and 'negative' notion of *freedom* from state interference defended by such thinkers as Locke and Voltaire. Third, and again building on the two earlier sets of functions, *equality* of rights, including the right to actively participate in the process by which political authority is constituted, became the major standard of legitimacy. It is defended (by Tocqueville,

J.S. Mill and others) through the notion of 'active' citizenship – citizenship understood as the democratic entitlement to political rights. Finally, and as a direct consequence of this democratic interpretation of political authority, a fourth criterion has been added to the universe of legitimate and legitimacy-conferring state functions. This criterion is associated with the state's capacity to manage and distribute societal resources in ways that contribute to the achievement and securing of prevailing notions of *justice*, as well as its apparent prerequisites such as 'economic growth'. This, of course, is the focus of the Keynesian welfare state and its designs for social, economic and industrial policies, which have become prevalent during the course of the twentieth century.

My aim in listing these four consecutively appearing criteria related to the development and legitimation standards of the modern state is neither to demonstrate the comprehensiveness of this list nor to account for the mechanisms which have led to the (self- ) transcendence of political authority from one phase to the next. Both of these important theoretical tasks would require a much more extended theoretical and historical treatment than I can offer here. My intention is simply to call attention to the (limited) variety, the internal complexity and potential inconsistency of functions which have been assigned to the modern state. For this complexity to be maintained, and the manifestation of incompatibilities between state functions to be avoided, adequate institutional mechanisms of intermediation and communication must be developed and maintained. Their function is to regulate the relationship between civil society and its matrix of social power and the state and political authority.

These mediating links and channels of communication between social power and political authority, as well as questions concerning their adequacy for maintaining a dynamic balance between social forces and political functions, have always served as a third object of attention in empirical research and theoretical development in political sociology. One of the models which seeks to explain (and, in some cases, normatively justify) this type of mediation is that of 'organized capitalism'. This model was first introduced by Rudolf Hilferding in 1910, developed by him and other German-speaking democratic-socialist theorists in the 1920s, and finally debated as a potentially useful theoretical concept by modern historians and political scientists.[3] In this model, the competitive market interaction between individual economic actors is seen to be in the process of being superseded by formally organized collectivities of economic action (corporate firms, cartels) and interest representation (trade unions, business associations). To speak of *'dis*organized capitalism' is not to propose an elaborate and coherent counter-model against that of 'organized capitalism'. Rather, my aim is to propose a heuristic perspective that is guided by the following questions: Do the procedures, patterns of organization, and institutional mechanisms that supposedly mediate and maintain a dynamic balance between social power and political authority (i.e. seek to coherently *organize* the socio-political systems of contemporary welfare state capitalism) actually *fail* to perform this function? If so, what are the symptoms, consequences and potential remedies of such failures of the process of mediation?

These questions concerning the failure or inadequacy of the mediating links between social power and political authority are the focus of the essays in the latter half of this volume. 'Interest Diversity and Trade Union Unity' which, as with most of the other essays, draws its empirical references from the society and polity of the Federal Republic of Germany, without limiting its diagnosis to the specific arrangements within that country, examines the validity of the traditional notion of trade unions as the representatives of unified class interests at the point of production. The claim of trade unions to comprehensively represent the interests of wage-dependent persons under capitalist conditions is questioned. The validity of the model of voluntary collective action on the part of interest organizations also serves as the key concern of the essay 'Two Logics of Collective Action'. This tries to link, in an admittedly speculative manner, class theory with the theory of collective action and political organization. The theoretical problem considered here (as in the essay on 'The Attribution of Public Status to Interest Groups') concerns the 'neutrality' of institutional forms and substantive interest content. Only if the means of political intermediation and the channels of communication between civil society and political authority are 'neutral' (in the sense that they permit the effective and non-discriminatory transmission and processing of diverse interests, rather than selectively privileging some interests at the expense of others), can these procedural forms themselves be considered as legitimate or worthy of acceptance. Wherever the adequacy and fairness of these procedures is questioned, the conflict over interests will be supplemented with a meta-conflict concerning the appropriate institutional forms for *processing* and *resolving* conflicts of interest. As a consequence, substantive conflicts are transposed – in ways that are very familiar to any observer of contemporary politics – into constitutional conflicts. At the very least, these conflicts erode the binding and legitimacy-conferring capacity of the institutional forms (e.g. political parties, legislatures, elections) that aggregate, shape and communicate the will of socio-political collectivities.

While the following essays mainly emphasize the asymmetries of representation that are built into voluntary associations and neo-corporatist arrangements, the critical analysis of the deficiencies of existing forms of political mediation (as well as of some of the consequent responses to such deficiencies) could also be extended, for instance, to the mechanisms of competitive party democracy, the mass media, social movements and the electoral system and its collective decision rules, such as majority rule.[4] Problems associated with the latter mechanism are discussed in 'Legitimation Through Majority Rule?' In this essay, I argue that, in order to substantiate claims on behalf of the (apparently self-evident) fairness of the majority-decision rule, one must make empirical assumptions about the social and political structures within which this rule is to be applied. I argue, furthermore, that there are serious doubts as to whether these assumptions are actually satisfied in the political processes of Western liberal democracies.

The essays on voluntary interest associations (trade unions as well as business and employers' associations) and majority rule also attempt to specify a further and related problem of welfare-capitalist democracies: the problem of the *fusion* of those channels of mediation through which actors within civil society act upon political authority, with those channels of communication through which, inversely, the state acts upon civil society. This fusion, or partial reversal, of 'inputs' and 'outputs' and their effects has often been observed in the case of political parties. While their historical roots are certainly to be found within civil society, where they served originally as 'mouthpieces' of the socio-political will of citizens, contemporary political parties often act as organs of communication for governments (when the party is in office) or for party elites aspiring to the office of government.

A similarly pronounced tendency of collective actors to transform themselves into organs of (at least) 'two-way communication' (if not of manipulation and 'non-decision-making') can be observed in the case of certain voluntary associations, which undergo alteration from 'pressure groups' to 'private governments' or 'quasi-governmental' associations. Such tendencies clearly undermine traditional constitutional notions of 'the separation of powers'. More recently, they have been studied from within the 'corporatism' paradigm, a most productive and innovative, if sometimes conceptually muddled development in political sociology, to which (as 'The Attribution of Public Status to Interest Groups' indicates) my own work is indebted.

The inverse transformation – the usurping of 'representative' functions by the executive agencies of the state – has received rather less attention in the literature of political sociology. Not only have 'input' organizations assumed 'governmental' functions; the state executive and administration, whose function is traditionally considered as that of bureaucratically implementing legal rules and decisions (or as that of a 'mouthpiece' of political authority), has also assumed 'representative' functions for actors within civil society. To be sure, clientelistic and symbiotic relations between the 'sponsoring agencies' of the state and particular interest groups in civil society have been studied in a wide variety of empirical contexts. What seems to be less-well studied, however, is the extent to which these 'deviations' from the 'normal' case of bureaucratic, rational-legal modes of interaction have themselves become the normal case, while the Weberian ideal-type of administration has lost most of its counterpart in reality. This, at least, is the (again speculative) conclusion suggested by my last essay in this volume, 'The Divergent Rationalities of Administrative Action'. The welfare state administration, that is to say, has become increasingly sensitive to the parameters of 'feasible' policy-making, as well as to the threats, obstructive tactics and incentives established by powerful actors within the respective segment of civil society within which its administrative organizations operate. This in turn entails the risk of duplicating and amplifying the matrix of social power and of short circuiting the relationship between social power and political authority, rather than constituting the latter as 'legitimate' according to such criteria as peace, freedom, equality and justice through 'fair' practices of mediation.

Throughout these essays, the normative models and empirical self-understanding of the 'official' system of political institutions and procedures of welfare capitalist democracies serve as the 'null-hypothesis' against which violations of received organizational forms of political exchange and communication and the rise of 'deviant' or 'unofficial' political practices are measured. Such notions and rudimentary theories as the centrality of the labour-capital cleavage, the basic homogeneity of interest on the respective sides of this division, the separability of factual power and legitimate authority, the universalistic character of the liberal democratic institutions of participation and representation, the fairness of the majority rule, the viability and neutrality of bureaucratic modes of administration, and the possibility as well as desirability of 'full employment' serve as something like a cognitive map which orients the prevailing perceptions within contemporary capitalist societies. If these assumptions become implausible when exposed to a reality test, this will in turn contribute, at the very least, to the disorganization of not only our mode of thinking about modern capitalism but also, and consequently, to the political disorganization of the patterns of organization of welfare-capitalist democracies themselves.

# 1

# The Political Economy of the Labour Market

Economic crises are defined by the fact that they generate unemployment and underemployment as mass phenomena. Governments and trade unions of all developed capitalist countries agree that the relief of such mass unemployment must be a priority of government policy. The priority given to full employment is even more pronounced for governments of 'welfare states', which are subject to a legal obligation to pay unemployment compensation to a certain extent (earnings-related benefits), as well as to guarantee the financial viability of social security programmes. A further factor directly influencing government policy is that unemployment – and the associated loss of portions of income earned by the population – directly cuts into the revenue side of the public budget and consequently affects the state as a 'tax state'.

The interest of trade unions in full employment is a function of their role as coalitions of the suppliers of labour power. In this role, they pursue three broad categories of interests which can, of course, come into conflict with each other: (i) the interest in the maintenance or increase of real earned income; (ii) the interest in good working conditions; and (iii) the interest in a high level of employment. Very limited strategic means for promoting the goal of increasing employment are, however, available to these coalitions, especially if the criterion of the compatibility of those means with the survival of the trade union organization itself is

Translated by Karen Grislis and Raymond Morrow. This essay was written with Karl Hinrichs and published originally in Projektgruppe Arbeitsmarktpolitik and C. Offe (eds), *Opfer des Arbeitsmarktes – Zur Theorie der strukturierten Arbeitslosigkeit*, (Neuwied/Darmstadt, 1977), pp. 3–61. This translation is based on the thoroughly revised and expanded version which appears in *Arbeitsgesellschaft: Strukturprobleme und Entwicklungsperspektiven* (Frankfurt, 1984).

taken into account. The existence of the organization would be endangered, for example, if in the interest of increasing employment, trade unions offered to sacrifice wages on a scale (or for a period of time) that would render it less than worthwhile, in the eyes of workers, to become or remain union members and to pay membership dues. Conversely, the existence of the organization would also be endangered if a suddenly aggravated employment situation were attributed causally to earlier successful wage demands and, for this reason, turned away (potential) members from the organization.[1] In order to avoid *both* of these organizational and political risks, the trade union interest in full employment consists primarily in attempts to exercise appropriate political pressure on political parties, governments and parliaments. Both the intensity of this interest and the appropriate political pressure, however, varies considerably in historical and comparative terms, depending (among other things) on the respective prevailing type of trade union organization. The more extensive the organizational scope of unions (the extreme case being unified trade unions based on a federation of industry-wide organizations), the stronger the union's political motives and possibilities for advocating employment goals for public policy. For unions tied to political parties or doctrines, as well as for occupational, and company-based unions, this is far less the case.

There is, however, no politically and theoretically agreed upon (and practically applicable) means appropriate to the policy goal of 'full employment'. Even if one begins with the assumption that the restoration of full employment will not be possible without economic growth, and therefore not without an increase in the investment of entrepreneurs, two important complications arise. First, even if the investment propensity of entrepreneurs were to be raised successfully, the resulting effect on employment could very well be insignificant, given the negative employment effect of rationalizing investment (micro-electronics) in many cases ('jobless growth'). Second, even if a positive effect on employment were produced successfully, it remains uncertain whether (and if so, with how much delay) the so-called 'problem groups of the labour market' (see below) would benefit. The contemporary Western European and North American capitalist economies are faced not only with *high*, but also distinctively *structured* unemployment which affects different groups in a highly differentiated manner. In view of this fact, the political problem of the labour market consists not only in a global *increase* in the demand for labour power, but also (and increasingly) in the well-balanced and fair *distribution* of this demand among categories of the (potential) work-force who are affected by labour market risks very differently. In this essay, we should like to clarify theoretically this second problem of the unequal, group-specific distribution of labour market risks.

The need to clarify this problem is made evident by a brief review of three facts. First, there is a characteristic 'lumpiness' in the social distribution of labour market risks. If we look at the pattern of those groups within the work-force that become unemployed more often than average; are unemployed for more than the average length of time; have particular difficulties in even entering into employment relations; are laid off more often; receive below average incomes; are found frequently in restrictive jobs characterized by limited autonomy; and are exposed to exceptional risks of having their physical capacity to work and their qualifications destroyed, we see that these characteristics do not vary independently of each other but, rather, accumulate among particular parts of the work-force. In other words, we find a high degree of overlap between the social groups differentiated according to these separate labour market risks. Second, these features may be closely connected not only with each other, but also with social characteristics that are not 'acquired' (such as education, income, place of residence), but are socially 'ascribed' and connected with certain fixed and internationally unchangeable qualities (age, sex, physical condition, ethnicity). Such ascribed qualities of individuals are of great sociological interest, inasmuch as it is assumed widely that their importance for the distribution of life chances has declined in the process of the modernization of Western societies, and will diminish even further. The third fact significant for the formulation of our problem is that since the 1960s – at least in a series of Western European countries, including the Federal Republic of Germany – a group-specific disaggregation of policies regarding the labour market can be observed.[2] Labour market policies and their legal foundations are no longer directed only at the global goals of employment, qualifications and mobility. Additionally, and increasingly, they seek to positively influence the market situation of specific, often very finely differentiated occupational, sectoral, age, gender and regional segments of the entire work-force.

Taken together, these three facts suggest that the labour market risks are distributed in a highly uneven, sharply structured way, and that this distribution pattern corresponds to 'ascriptive' qualities. This is the case even though (or because?) governmental labour market policy increasingly has at its disposal group-specific packages of measures or instruments of support. In addition, all three facts are in evidence despite (or because of?) the belief, held by many sociological theorists (as well as by the numerous ideologues who rely upon them), that a work- and production-oriented society, one which rests on the basic institution of the 'free' labour contract (i.e. the labour market), leads to the erosion of particularistic features of social life in the framework of universal equality of opportunity and freedom of contract and, furthermore, emancipates market participants from the rigidity and unchange-ability of the conditions of individual existence that was character-istic of pre-market societies. In this manner, a type of 'abstract' standard employee is supposed to be created, whose social position is no longer determined through inherited or ascribed group status, but solely through a *collective* class position and anonymous market processes, on the one hand, and through the strictly *individual* characteristics of achievement and market success resulting from these premises and limitations, on the other. In view of our three facts mentioned above, this model of an abstract and largely homogeneous group of 'employees' (a 'work-ing class'), in which quasi-feudal and other inner principles of group organization are meant to play at best a subordinate or diminishing role, is in need of at least a certain amount of revision. This would especially be the case if it could be shown that the lack of homogeneity of the supposedly normal category of 'the standard employee' is not a remnant and residue of 'pre-modern' social structures but is, in fact, created in the process of modernization itself and caused by its crises. In order to expand upon this thesis, we shall first of all examine the dynamics and social consequences of that most peculiar market, to which we refer usually as 'the labour market'.

## The Labour Market and Other Markets

In capitalist societies the labour market is the main institutional solution to a dual allocative problem that must be solved in all societies: on the one hand, the production system must be supplied with the labour inputs it requires; on the other, labour power must be provided with monetary (income) and social (status) means of subsistence.[3] The labour market solves both of these allocative problems simultaneously, while in non- or pre-capitalist societies we find predominantly institutional forms in which the type and level of the means of subsistence provided to individuals depends on factors other than the individual's contributions to social production. The important point is that the labour market organizes production and distribution as an exchange relationship of wages and labour inputs, and that here, as in all other markets, suppliers and buyers of 'labour' stand opposed. A further similarity is that in all markets the relationship of competition is given: supplier and buyer compete with other suppliers and buyers against whom they must assert themselves if, respectively, their offer is to be successful or their demands are to be satisfied. This relationship of competition therefore also necessitates the pursuit of specific rational strategies of supply and demand. On the supply side, these strategies involve specifying, as fairly as possible, the type, quantity, location and timing of the labour inputs offered, as well as adjusting the price demanded (wages) to the willingness of the demand side to pay. Conversely, for the actors on the demand side, the aim is to reduce the specificity of their demands for the type and quantity of labour needed or, if necessary, to raise the price offered (wages) in such a way that the demand of the individual employer can be satisfied from the available supply (e.g. 'wage-drift' as an internal competitive strategy of individual purchasers of labour). An important adaptive strategy for both sides of the market is for them to free themselves from their respective dependencies upon the other side by putting themselves in the position of finding substitute sources for the satisfaction of this need. The labour market – like every other market – requires both sides to engage in continuous and complementary strategic adaptations. This forced adaptation arising from market relations is often viewed as a powerful source of the social processes of rationalization which are especially reflected in continuous productivity increases.

The arsenal of strategic options associated with the dynamic and the results of market processes is, however, not exhausted by the individual strategies of particular suppliers and purchasers of labour. A further important strategic option for both sides consists in reducing the intensity of the relations of competition on one's own side of the market relative to the intensity of competition on the 'other' side. This occurs primarily through forming coalitions and engaging in other types of collective action. For example, workers come to a mutual understanding by forming a coalition to establish maximum limits for the supply of services or minimum limits for price/wage demands; by not violating these limits, they avoid either continuously outbidding each other with respect to the level of labour offered, or continually underbidding each other with respect to the level of wages demanded. The same effect is sought by hindering access to the market of those potential suppliers who would be prepared or even compelled to violate one limit or the other. Internal solidarity and external (possibly violent) discrimination are thus rational strategies for attaining market advantages on the supply side. The same holds true for the demand side: the purchasers of labour can form an alliance to moderate their internal relations of competition and/or negatively sanction 'more attractive' buyers (e.g. through their exclusion from employer associations). The common principle of these strategies, in short, is the lessening of the intensity of competition in one's own 'camp' relative to the level of competition in the other.

In addition to the techniques of solidarization (coalition formation) and discrimination (exclusion), the same strategically advantageous effect can also be achieved when the intensity of competition in the other camp is successfully heightened, assuming a constant intensity in one's own camp. The purchasers in a market can succeed in doing this when, for example, they are in a position to relatively increase the numbers of suppliers entering the market, or to ensure that attempts undertaken on the supply side to create coalitions or discrimination fail. Analogous possibilities for influencing the intensity of competition are also available in principle to the supply side, which can draw upon a rich and complex repertoire of strategies, both individual and collective, solidarizing and discriminating.

But the various markets – for raw materials, goods, capital and labour – differ fundamentally according to the criterion of whether, and to what extent, buyers and sellers can actually utilize this 'in principle' symmetrical catalogue of rational market strategies. Should one or other side of the market find itself in a position of having exhausted its reservoir of strategic options to a greater extent than the other side, an asymmetrical power relationship would be evident in the market process itself. Of interest to us here with regard to the relationship between the supply and demand sides are the peculiarities of the labour market which make it possible to speak of a differential in the availability of the diverse rational market strategies, and consequently of a power differential in favour of the demand side and to the disadvantage of the supply side.

The peculiarly disadvantaged market and strategic position of the 'commodity' labour power consists in 'the employee always ending up in a position unfavourable to him when concluding a labour contract under free competition'.[4] The first reason for this alleged 'peculiar position' or 'fictive' character of the 'commodity' labour power,[5] is that while it is indeed treated as a commodity in markets, it does not reach these markets in the way most other commodities do. The quantity and quality, place and time of supply of other commodities depend on the expectations of the respective sellers of these commodities concerning their marketability. The entry of 'real' commodities into markets is regulated, or at least codetermined, by the criterion of their expected saleability. This is not the case with the 'commodity' labour power. Even in purely quantitative terms, the rising 'supply' of labour power is determined by non-strategic demographic processes and the institutional rules of human reproductive activity. It is also determined by socio-economic processes which 'set free' labour power from the conditions under which it could maintain itself *other* than through sale in the market. To the degree that labour power is prevented from turning to modes of subsistence outside the labour market (e.g. through utilizing private agricultural land), the labour supply pressing into the market becomes quantitatively inelastic: 'Above all other factors that can otherwise still influence elasticity stands the massive question of physical existence, the question of whether it is possible to remain above water by other means, and for this the distribution of property is certainly of fundamental importance.'[6] An initially important peculiarity of labour power, therefore, is that while it is indeed treated as a commodity in the market, it enters this market for reasons other than those of other commodities. One could thus speak of a structural handicap of labour power in the market, for the supply side has no way of controlling its own volume of supply in a market-strategic manner.

A second handicap of the supply side of the labour market is that labour power, continuously dependent on the supply of the means of subsistence which can only be acquired through its 'sale', is not (or only within very narrow limits) in a position to 'wait' for favourable opportunities. This difficulty is related to the temporal parameters of supply. The inability to 'wait' before selling results from the typical situation whereby labour power does not control the (natural or manufactured) means of production which would allow it to either live on the sale of *products* manufactured from these means of production, or to use these (agricultural) products themselves as a means of subsistence. An essential aspect of the capitalist process of industrialization consisted precisely in destroying these conditions of economic independence (i.e. the self-sufficiency of agricultural and household production), as well as the preconditions of strategically 'waiting' for favourable demand conditions. To the degree that these preconditions are destroyed, the supply of labour power that does not meet with demand is in itself totally 'worthless'. As a result, it is structurally compelled to extensively relinquish its own strategic options, to submit to any presently given conditions of demand, and to accept the going wage it is offered. Labour power also cannot afford to sell its labour for a longer period of time 'for less than its value', that is, at a minimal level of subsistence, even when its long-term market opportunities would be increased by such a self-subsidy. It is dependent upon the *continuous* flow of *adequate* means of subsistence.

For the supply side of the labour market, the existence of its own numbers is a given and strategically invariable quantity; it can additionally be influenced by the demand side, namely, through the strategic utilization of the technological change that sets labour power free and thus expands the potential supply. A quantitative policy related to the supply side becomes possible, historically as well as systematically, only when an authority *external* to the market appears in the form of state social- and labour-protection policies. On the one hand, these policies guarantee the right to coalition formation; on the other hand, they hinder portions of the available labour supply from entering the market (e.g. the prohibition of child labour, the setting of maximum working hours, the standardization of the working day). But at the same time they make available *non-market* means of subsistence (e.g. retirement insurance) to the labour power 'excluded' from the supply side, such that this labour power is no longer forced to offer itself on the market. This means that the strategic options that are otherwise available to the suppliers of other commodities must, in the case of the 'commodity' labour power, be facilitated and guaranteed from the outset through political regulation. Only through the presence of a politically organized unemployment insurance scheme are the suppliers of labour power (at least partially) able to strategically 'wait', instead of directly and immediately accepting each demand, that is, every wage offered.

A third peculiarity of labour power and its limited strategic options is that its own need for subsistence means is largely constant within the framework of a materially and culturally defined 'minimum standard of living'. At any rate, its need is essentially more rigid than the reciprocal need of employers. If wages procure the means of subsistence of workers and if, inversely, the allocation of labour is a means for producing goods and services, an asymmetry between these two relations becomes evident: through the use of technological change, production can very well be maintained even with a fall in labour input per unit of output, while reproduction of labour power can*not* be maintained with a fall of income per household. An asymmetry between the two sides of the market is based on the fact that (at least on average, and in the long term) the buyers of labour can more easily make themselves independent of supply than is the case with the suppliers of labour with respect to the demand side. The purchasers of labour can increase the efficiency of production, but the suppliers cannot increase the efficiency of their reproduction; the latter have only the option of cutting their standard of living as soon as possibilities for 'economizing' on their incomes (e.g. by walking to distant discount stores) have been exhausted.

A fourth handicap lies in the *qualitative* potential for adaptation on the supply side of the labour market. No doubt, both individual suppliers and purchasers of labour are qualitatively 'determined'. Concrete labourers can be combined only with certain functions in the production process (because of their special occupational training and experience, for instance), just as certain concrete machines require specifically skilled operators. What is decisive, however, is the greater degree of qualitative 'liquidity' of capital in comparison with labour. Every unit of capital, whether over the short or long term, passes through a phase of 'liquidity' – a phase of liquefaction into money. At the end of a phase of the capital cycle, the owners of capital are free to decide whether or not they wish to purchase other means of production suitable for combining with labour power (with less or other qualifications) for the next phase in that cycle. Herein lies a qualitative opportunity for mobility that has virtually no equivalent on the side of labour power (where one would have to think of unlimited possibilities of retraining as an equivalent). In fact, and quite unlike capital, the concrete labour capacity that suppliers of labour have to offer does not pass through a phase of 'liquidity', in which it could rid itself of all qualitative determination and, so to speak, start a new life; strictly speaking, capital does not 'age', but rather moves in a circular pattern of constant renewal. Suppliers of labour power, by contrast, can vary the quality of their offer only within very narrow limits, and again only because of such forms of external (political) support as education and retraining.

The only variable through which the supplier of labour power can possibly improve its strategic position in the market is that of the spatial dimension. Accordingly, the historically most important adaptive responses by labour *without* public assistance have taken place in the spatial dimension, through such movements as emigration, urbanization, and commuting. But it is obvious that even in spatial processes of adaptation, which represent the sole dimension in which the supply side of the labour market can employ autonomous strategies against the demand side, labour is forced to make sacrifices. These become evident in the destruction of local family and social relations, but also in specific risks of impoverishment or marginalization, as in the urban development not only of Third World countries, but also in the USA and, increasingly, Europe.

The relative strategic rigidity of the supply side of the labour market, which is evident in the dimensions of the quantity, quality, and timing of supply, and which distinguish this particular market for labour power from all other markets, is paid for above all through relative losses of income. Because the individual seller of labour power – or workers organized as a whole – cannot, for the structural reasons already discussed, employ market strategies, they must compensate for these strategic handicaps through a drop in the rate of pay demanded for labour. Exploitation results from the asymmetrical strategic capacity of supply and demand – even more so in the case of labour power than in the standard market constellation of agricultural production, where farmers can of course strategically vary the type, but not, as a rule, the timing and quantity of their products. Producers are, therefore, often forced to sell their usually 'perishable' products at a price far below their production costs. The example of agricultural production is also instructive, since in both cases only voluntary forms of collective action (trade unions or cooperatives) or public guarantees (guaranteed producer's prices or labour protection and social policies) make it possible to at least partially equalize the power differentials between the supply and demand sides of these markets.

## The Labour Contract Compared with Sale Contracts

The argument so far is that in labour markets – more than in any other market – there is a structural differential between the respective possibilities for the supply and demand sides to employ rational market strategies. This differential – at least under the ideal conditions of a 'pure', politically unregulated labour market – must lead to relations of power and exploitation that can at best be (partially) equalized through welfare-state policy intervening 'unilaterally' in favour of the weaker side of this market. In the discipline of sociology, it is widely held that such a power differential must lead necessarily to continuous social and political conflict, more precisely, to the industrial or class conflict between capital and labour. Such a view cannot, however, be justified conclusively with the arguments developed thus far. For even if one considers this unequal relationship of power as unjustified on political or moral grounds, it could well be a stable, passive, continuously self-reproducing power relationship, whose stability and unalterability the respective parties would, so to speak, become accustomed to in time. A further argument is, therefore, required in order to show that there is a structurally embedded and constantly virulent 'industrial class conflict' in societies with a labour market. We will develop this argument that there are necessary conflictual effects generated by this power differential by comparing labour contracts with those made between the respective sides of other markets (for instance, contracts of sale, tenancy agreements, and so on).

Buyers and sellers in the labour market enter into labour contracts with one another. Labour contracts differ from contracts of sale in that they do not stipulate the *totality* of the relations that arise between the contracting parties. In contracts of sale, the economic relations between buyer and seller are, in fact, fully specified: the contract stipulates what (qualitatively and quantitatively) specified thing shall pass from the ownership of the seller to that of the buyer, as well as under what conditions and at what price. The contract of sale thus reciprocally defines the spheres of disposition of both contractual partners. In complying with the contract, the seller loses every legal and physical power of disposition over the item sold, while the buyer pays the stipulated price. In this respect contracts of sale bring about a precise social disjunction: what was previously under the legal and actual disposition of the one is now placed at the disposal of the other. Herein lies the peace-making and assuring function of contractual rights for both sides. At any moment, it is possible for each person to decide unambiguously for each commodity whether it belongs to this person or not. *Tertium non datur.*

Labour contracts, however, lack a comparable measure of clarity of the kind typical for property and commercial law. Of course, labour contracts do regulate social relations between buyers and sellers: the purchaser of labour agrees to make payments of a specified amount (wages) to the seller for the period of validity of the labour contract. In a normal labour contract (unlike one concerning just a specific and limited task, such as translating a book) the work performed in return for the payment of wages is not fixed, however, but simply circumscribed more or less precisely and more or less indirectly. When, for example, an electrical contractor engages an employee, the labour contract does not specify that a fixed number of cables be laid or switches installed in a certain amount of time; rather, the employee is engaged only 'as an electrician'. In this manner the seller of labour power is generally obliged to perform tasks of a certain type (defined according to job specification, occupational description, etc.) within an enterprise at fixed times and in the framework of that enterprise's rules and organizational relationships. The labour contract, in other words, has the character of just a contractual framework. The concrete, quantitatively and qualitatively speci-fied operative work activities are not the subject of the contract, but merely the formal *conditions* under which entrepreneurs can use labour power for concrete purposes that are from the outset not fixed precisely, and indeed could not be fixed in advance.

Contrary to first appearances, this is even true of piece-work: the 'normal' production of $x$ pieces per time unit is a standard which itself is not a constituent element of the labour contract. Rather, it is something which can be varied in the framework of an on-going employment relationship through technological and organizational changes, shop-floor negotiations, conflicts, and so on. The contractual indeterminacy of the concrete output which an employee is expected to produce is a completely unavoidable characteristic of labour contracts because concrete business conditions (like the situation concerning orders and other details of future labour processes) are not yet fixed or known. (By virtue of this indeterminacy within the labour contract, the employer is assured of a certain freedom to utilize labour power, a leeway which is claimed as a 'right of management' and which enables the employer to order concrete work assignments on an *ad hoc* basis.) The intensity of work activity also cannot be fixed contractually, but only indirectly circumscribed (e.g. by specifying the number of working hours per day, but not production per hour).

The typical indeterminacy of the labour contract with respect to the type and quantity of work to be rendered by the employee is not just related to the insufficient predictability of the need for concrete operative work activities in the course of the production process. It is also related to the fact that a detailed, legal specification of the employee's activities could not in fact be enforced even in the (atypical) case of strictly uniform, routinized work tasks. It could not be enforced because the employer does not purchase an item with a specific, measurable or estimable use value, but 'living' labour power that actually remains under the control of its owner – the worker – even after it has legally passed into the sphere of disposition of the purchaser – the employer. The use-value an enterprise extracts from labour power is quantitatively and qualitatively tied to the subjectivity of the worker, to his or her willingness to work, and so on. The type and quantity of work activity rendered by the employee as a partner in the labour contract cannot, therefore, be legally specified in the way, for instance, the performance characteristics of a machine can be specified and made the subject of contracts of sale. 'A . . . peculiarity of the "commodity" labour is that only rarely can it be purchased without at the same time bringing the person of the seller into a certain dependency.'[7] The fundamental Marxian concept of 'living' labour power and Marx's insistent characterization of the wages system as 'wage slavery' also refer to this fact. This means that the enterprise that buys labour power is dependent on the purchased 'object' maintaining its subjectivity and being prepared in some measure to work 'on its own' and cooperate in the labour process. It would prove to be either 'technically' impossible or highly uneconomic and counterproductive for employers to force upon employees legal claims for performances which are specified in detail. Wherever the subjectivity of workers, their motives for working and their autonomous control of their work activity *could* be dispensed with, the enterprise would install machines or other material means of production. If it purchases 'living' labour power, however, it thereby indicates that it (still) is not possible on technical and organizational or profitability grounds to do away with the 'subjective' factor of labour power, which is, however, at the same time always a potential source of disturbance. The management of an enterprise cannot itself set in motion like a machine the labour power it has purchased. Labour power necessarily remains under the actual control of its 'seller', from whom it cannot be separated (as is the case with commodities and transferred property titles). It would, therefore, be totally futile, even counter-productive, to attempt to entirely 'regulate away' the autonomy of the worker by fully detailing legal claims for specific work activities, because it is precisely the limited autonomy left to the worker which makes the utilization of 'living' labour power attractive to businessmen.

On the other hand, this unavoidable recognition of a measure of autonomy and subjectivity brings with it the risk – from the perspective of the purchaser of labour power – that it will be used for purposes *other* than those of the enterprise, especially those which are in the employees' interest and which enable them to avoid over-exertion in the work process. This means that there is a double control mechanism inherent in the framework of the labour contract, an overlapping of spheres of disposition that cannot be separated legally. The interest of employees in defending their autonomy, the physical integrity of their labour power and their skills conflicts with the entrepreneurial interest in maximum economic utilization of the 'purchased' labour power, whose productive use-value is by no means assured by the worker merely showing up at the work-place and remaining there for the duration of working hours (as is specified in the labour contract). This inescapable conflict – or, at least, a conflict which cannot be controlled by legal forms – can certainly be channelled through organized surveillance, control, instructions, supervision, and accountability, even though it cannot be prevented *as* conflict. For the enforcing of claims upon labour performances, for the appropriation of 'work' from 'labour power', conditions that have been secured initially and abstractly only through the labour contract, the employer is always dependent on the medium of *organization* which cannot, of course, fully guarantee that the labour process will function without conflict.[8]

If one wanted to imagine contracts of sale modelled on that social relationship characteristic of labour contracts, one would come up with the following somewhat fanciful analogy. The exchange of commodities for money would require that, through the payment of an 'admission fee', the purchasers secure access to the seller's stock of commodities for a specified period of time and observe specified general rules; there they would be entitled to take as many, and as many different types of, commodities as they could. The owner of these commodities would need to prevent 'excessive' decimation of his inventory through the use of physical force, through appeals to the social conscience of the clientele, and through other suitable defence measures, thereby ensuring that something remains for future buyers. Only if the exchange of goods for money proceeded in such a fashion would the fundamental difference between the types of economic relations established by the labour contract and contracts of sale be overcome. In such an exchange relationship, however, the peacemaking function of property and contractual rights would also be destroyed, inasmuch as this function consists precisely in unambiguously and compulsorily demarcating spheres and rights of disposition. In place of the legal transaction would appear a sequence of legally unqualified acts of appropriation or defence. The contract of sale would (in exactly the same way as actual labour contracts, which provide enterprises with access to the utilization of labour power) institutionalize conflict, and not the social peace of *'suum cuique'*. Unlike regular contracts of sale, the labour contract creates a sphere in which contrary claims are brought to bear on labour power, and in which similar rights must be brought into actual balance with each other. 'There is here, therefore, an *antinomy*, right against right, both bearing the seal of the law of exchanges. Between equal rights *force* decides.'[9] Here, by the way, the parallels with the previously mentioned supplier of agricultural products also come to an end. While it is certainly an open question whether the subordination of farmers to the market for agricultural products will serve as a triggering mechanism for political conflicts or other forms of collective action, their relationship to their partners on the other side of the market is nevertheless determined by contracts of sale. In the relationship between employee and employer, by contrast, there is an inevitable conflict-generating moment, in which the spheres of interest of both sides can only be defined vaguely in the framework of the labour contract, and consequently must be brought into an at best unstable balance through continuous advances and setbacks on both sides.

## The Labour Market and Other Organizational Forms of Human Labour Power

Even in societies where the production of goods and the distribution of income are essentially directed by the institutions of the labour market and the labour contract, by no means all individuals are in the labour market or in contractually based labour relationships. Not all individuals who do not own the means of production actually appear on the supply side of the labour market, as the example of children demonstrates. It is also quite plausible to assume that the *total* subjugation of all propertyless individuals to the wage-labour relationship would soon bring the institution of the labour market to an end. The reproduction of the capacity for work would be prevented if the labour market were a 'cover-all' institution; it would consequently destroy itself. The niches, free spaces and buffer zones – beginning with the family – in which those who are indeed propertyless but not wage labourers live, are socially established through cultural and political norms which more or less permanently determine which persons living in which conditions are not required (or allowed) to offer their labour power in labour markets. There is no past or present society where, over a long period of time, more than half of its members have invested their labour power in money-mediated relations of exchange. The contractual exchange of labour power for money income is not an historically, but also always a quantitatively, limited phenomenon. The question therefore arises as to the type of relationship which exists between the organizational model of wage labour and other, simultaneously practised forms of the utilization and alimentation of labour power.

In order to classify precisely the resident population of an area at a given point in time in terms of its relationship to the labour market, the following typology is useful.

I    The '*inactive*' segments of the population. This includes all those groups whose life activity can either not be labelled as 'work' (e.g. children, the chronically ill, the retired), or who, when they 'work', do not obtain their means of subsistence as *compensation* for their work, but instead from legal titles and support claims that are not based on labour contracts (e.g. housewives, students). Their labour power is thus not treated as a commodity, but is employed in accordance with culturally and legally defined obligations, and provided with means of subsistence through support claims drawn upon private or public 'households' (including, e.g., prisons). This category of 'inactive' persons differs from the organizational principle of the labour market because its productive function is not regulated by labour contracts, but through status rights and obligations. A sub-group of this segment of the population is the category of 'hidden unemployment' (or the 'silent reserve', as German labour market statisticians used to call it). It is defined by the fact that its members *would* enter a labour contract if an appropriate demand for their labour power could be anticipated. But since such a demand does not exist, a potential supply of labour power does not, in fact, enter the labour market (housewives who stop looking for part-time work because they cannot find any, or students who anticipate employment problems and therefore continue their education, are cases in point). In such cases, a supply of labour power which is without any prospects of employment can remain outside the labour market because it can have recourse to the family system or to public institutions.

II  Following the conventional statistical definition, there are also those individuals 'in' the labour market who are not presently involved in a contractual work relationship, but who either actively seek such a relationship by looking for employment themselves, or in any case are 'available' for work. These persons are subsumed under the category of the registered *unemployed,* to whom claims for insurance benefits or public transfer payments are granted on the condition that they are willing to respond to demands for their labour power and, if possible, to enter into an employment relationship.

III  This category of those who are 'in' the labour market can in turn be distinguished from the *category of the actually employed,* whose continuous exchange of labour power for waged income takes place in the framework of a labour contract. As long as the labour contract continues, both contracting partners refrain from taking advantage of the option of terminating the contract that is constantly available to them; thereby they insulate the existing labour relationship against the labour market. This insulation of the labour relationship is only very conditional, however, since the awareness that the option of termination is available to the respective contractual partners looms over the labour relation as structural condition, substantially codetermining the on-going exchange of wages and services on both sides.

IV   Finally, there is a group of working people who are clearly not in the labour market, though for wholly different reasons than the first-mentioned group. This fourth category consists of those who are *'independent'* or *'self-employed'*. Because of their possession of means of production with which they can combine their labour power, persons in this category do not need to *sell* their labour power but, rather, can offer the results of this combination (goods or services) on the market. While they work for the purpose of securing income, this is not 'contractual income' paid in compensation for the labour power made available, but 'residual income', whose amount is *ex ante* indeterminate, and results from the difference between profits and costs. The 'self-employed' are exempted from the 'pressure to sell' their labour power because they possess means of production. Their role in the labour market is confined to the fact that they may or may not exercise their own market demand for labour power.

These four social forms of organizing labour power provide a complete classification schema; every individual in a society can at any time be assigned clearly to one of these categories. Yet the inclusion of individuals within any one of these is obviously not determined through their free choice alone. Rather, there are a series of objective functional relations between these categories, and these relations determine the relative size and composition of each of these groups in relation to the labour market.

We have seen that those belonging to the second and third categories of our classification schema directly or indirectly 'take part' in the labour market, while those in the first and fourth categories find themselves in situations in which their own labour power is not governed by the mechanisms of the labour market. Now, how is a transition from categories I or IV to categories III or II made possible? One mechanism of transition consists of previously independent suppliers of goods and services having to drop out of the market as a consequence of competition in commodity markets and, lacking alternative economic possibilities for survival, thereby emerging as suppliers of their own labour power in the labour market. In this sense, the rate of migration from the fourth category into the third or second is determined by the processes of innovation and concentration and crisis-related developments within commodity markets. Completely different mechanisms govern the transition from categories I to III or II and vice versa. Here, the main mechanisms are cultural norms and legal regulations that establish the temporal and personal limits for participating in the labour market and, most importantly, exempt individuals with certain characteristics from participation under certain conditions. Beyond this, the rate of migration from the first category to the third (or second) is regulated by the anticipated chances of employment for newcomers: the less these chances are perceived, the greater the tendency will be to reproduce labour power at least temporarily through support from (private and public) budgets, instead of through its (uncertain) sale in exchange for earned income. However, since the budgets (of private domestic households as well as the public outlays on social policy and social security) which provide the support for individuals who do not participate in the labour market are in turn dependent on the amount of individual or collectively earned income, the rate of pay secured individually or on the average plays a decisive role in determining the absorption capacity of the first category. This results in the familiar and only apparently paradoxical 'inversion' of labour supply. In contrast to all other commodities, the supply of labour power tends to *rise* when the demand (and wages) fall, because under these conditions the possibility of *not* participating in the labour market becomes increasingly impractical for economic reasons.

The relative size or rate of movement between categories II and III is influenced, finally, by such economic determinants of the demand for labour power as the development of demand on goods markets, or labour-saving technological change. The relationship between the employed and the unemployed also depends on the spatial and qualitative flexibility of the suppliers of labour power. Legal and wage regulations also play a role in this respect. They determine for whom and under what conditions a transition from categories III to II (unemployment) is possible (e.g. the protection against termination and rationalization, or the limited possibilities for dismissal in the civil service), as well as for whom, under what conditions, and for what period of time remaining in category II is permitted and made economically bearable (factors such as the payment of wage compensation benefits to the unemployed, as well as the criteria according to which unemployed people can be forced to accept inferior or lower-paying jobs relative to the ones they have lost or were trained for).

It is, therefore, in general not the case that the individual is able to freely choose between his or her belonging to one of the four categories, or to migrate freely between them. Most importantly, the possibility of surviving outside of the labour market with means of subsistence made available by private or public budgets is influenced by the social distribution of property and by processes that take place in labour or commodity markets. To be sure, not every individual is always exposed *directly* to the dynamics of the labour market. Nevertheless, the labour market is a power relationship that touches, permeates and envelops *all* forms and spheres of social life. The labour market is, thus, a social *power* relationship because it exerts a structural, contractually organized pressure on labour power which is, as long as it is left to itself, totally 'valueless'. The labour market thereby allows the structurally limited adaptability of the 'commodity' labour to work to the advantage of the demand side, which realizes this advantage within the framework of inherently 'incomplete' labour contracts and by means of organization and managerial domination.

Having outlined the participants, as well as the rules of the game and the options these rules provide for individual participants in the labour market, we now wish to examine the typical strategies and the respective consequences that are pursued or provoked by sellers and buyers who operate in the labour market within the framework of these rules.

## Strategies of the Supply and Demand Sides

In spite (or out of ignorance) of the strategic handicap mentioned above, individual suppliers can endeavour to adjust as flexibly as possible to demand, and in this way try to secure advantages over fellow suppliers. They would then, for example, strive to maximize the differences between their own, individual offer and the offer of as many other fellow suppliers as possible, so as to minimize the risk of their being substituted. If this succeeds, they would obviously protect themselves against the danger of other suppliers outbidding their offer and being given preference. The same effect can be achieved through the individual dropping of the price offered (wage underbidding) or through raising the level of individual efforts offered. Such an individualization and specialization of supply must naturally be adjusted strictly to the requirements criteria of the demand side itself.

On the demand side, the contrary interest certainly dominates – the interest in overcoming excessively 'specialized' needs and, consequently, of not being dependent on any quasi-monopolistic suppliers.[10] Technical and organizational measures can contribute to the development of an 'ideal situation' on the demand side, at which point 'anyone could be replaced by anyone'. This would be the case when buyers, instead of being dependent upon qualified and specialized labour, could make do with labour that was equipped with merely 'minimum qualifications'.

A higher degree of specialization of labour supply is only innocuous and ultimately even welcome for the buyer when it simultaneously diminishes the suitability of labour power for alternative jobs with other buyers. The market position of the supplier would then not be fundamentally improved through specialization; on the contrary, it would be 'over-specialized', and would thus lose the option of playing off different buyers.[11] The ideal situation for the individual suppliers would be to develop such characteristics of quality in their offer that would allow them to credibly advance an offer which is as unspecific and yet as usable as possible. In this way, they would be largely immunized against both the pressure of competition from other suppliers and the danger of dependency on a single buyer.

Such strategic calculations can be concretized and illustrated by way of a series of observable patterns of activity in the labour market. For example, (future) employees must strive to make their labour power 'scarce' and thereby competitive by acquiring a *qualification* profile with the highest possible or most diverse applicability. In this way, the competitive pressure of other suppliers is averted and the stability of demand assured. The *occupational structuring* on the supply side of the labour market splits this into a multitude of partial markets,[12] between which relations of competitive supply are practically interrupted. The precondition of acquiring qualifications, as for the occupational structuring of the labour supply, is that state authorities make available corresponding possibilities for education, facilitate access to these possibilities, and institutionalize images and descriptions of occupations around which both sides of the labour market can orient themselves. Left to their own devices, individual workers cannot vary the quality, but at best only the quantity (temporal duration) or intensity of their work efforts in order to 'out-compete' their fellow suppliers.

Success in the competitive struggle among suppliers may also lead to the displacement of other suppliers through (in the extreme case, violent) discrimination based on such ascriptive categories as age, gender, nationality, thereby bringing about not an occupational but (for example) an ethnic or racial structuring of the labour market. Such solidarization for the purpose of generating discrimination ('social closure') is a strategy of competition that is not entirely dependent on governmental and political assistance; rather, it can build on existing role and status-ascribing norms and ethnocentric views of society and exploit these in the interest of collective status.

A further mode of strategic behaviour on the supply side of the labour market or in the framework of already existing labour contracts consists in individual employees consciously relinquishing the option of moving between companies, thereby demonstrating a loyalty to 'their' enterprise in the hope that they will be given preferential treatment within the enterprise whenever decisions regarding promotion and relocation are made. Conversely, it can also be a rational marketing strategy for labour to willingly and resolutely bear the material and non-material costs that are associated with extremely high rates of regional, temporal and occupational mobility between enterprises.

To what extent, and in what combination, these strategies are pursued empirically cannot be examined here. Common to each of them is the attempt to compensate as far as possible on the *individual* level for the *collective* power differentials which exist between the opponents in the labour market. The room for manoeuvre generally open to successful individual supply and search strategies is, however, in turn defined by the demand side. The demand side can generate conditions (e.g. through technically and organizationally effective changes or the lowering of its

qualification requirements) which an individualized and specialized supply strategy can scarcely expect to escape. Far more
promising are those out-flanking and equalizing *political* measures
and legislation which reduce the necessity for individual labourers
to adapt (e.g. work and termination protection) and/or increase
their capacity to adapt (e.g. through 'active' labour market policies
with programmes for retraining and continuing education). Taken
together, these measures can partially level out the power
differentials in the labour market. The problem with such
programmes, protective legislation and measures, however, is that
they must come from a 'third' side – state authorities – whose
possibilities for adopting and implementing such measures are
often and paradoxically influenced negatively by the very employment crises they are supposed to ameliorate.

*Between* individual and political strategies lie those of a
'corporate' or associational type. The recourse to such group
strategies, through which particular advantages can be obtained
by certain groups of employees and defended against others
increases, we suspect, to the degree that *individual* strategies of
competition on the supply side become hopeless and *political*
strategies for equalizing labour market political power simultaneously cannot be implemented. The recourse to acquiring or
defending 'corporativist' (in the Italian sense) status advantages in
the labour market takes the form of a displacement of the power
differential between supply and demand in the labour market to
the *supply side itself,* that is, as an overcoming of the power
differential between the supply and demand sides through the
establishment of a *new* and derivative power differential between
strategically better- and worse-placed groups of suppliers of
labour. Examples of this strategy of redistributing the advantages
and disadvantages for groups on the supply side of the labour
market (discussed under the rubric of 'social closure' since the time
of Max Weber)[13] can be found not only in American industrial
unions,[14] or in tendencies in the Italian trade union movement
referred to as '*corporativismo*', but even in industrial and unified
trade unions in the Federal Republic of Germany.[15]

Furthermore, organized trade union coalitions always display a
dual tendency of building up 'internal solidarity' only to the degree
that they practise 'external exclusion'. Before the potentially
coercive strategic advantages of *collective* action can be realized,

those competing suppliers who cannot be included in the
framework of solidarity (because of their special situation in the
labour market, or the individual supply strategy they have chosen)
must be driven out or eliminated through sanctions; examples of
those excluded are the wage under-bidding 'strike breakers', as
well as the overproductive 'rate-busters' who 'ruin the piece-rate'
for the others. The worse the average income and employment
situation of employees, the greater their difficulty in building up
the measure of solidarity required for successful collective action;
the 'temptation' of slipping into short-term and 'egoistic' survival
strategies is then especially great. But the problem of protection
against 'cheap labour' also exists generally for trade union
organizations, whether it be against labourers who find themselves
forced to accept substandard wages because of their particular
position, or against those (e.g. housewives) who are not 'dependent' upon a full and normal wage, and receive only 'supplementary' income from waged employment. As a rule, successes
in overcoming this problem of trade unions defending themselves
against competition from other suppliers of labour depend on
their acquiring recognition and support from either the political
side (e.g. through the guaranteed, universally binding character of
wage agreements, limiting the access of foreigners to the market)
or directly from the side of the employer ('closed shops').

The greater trade union successes have been in the past, the
greater the present demand for the means required for intimidat-
ing, disciplining or excluding the action of those unable or
unwilling to observe the norms of solidarity. Every successful
wage agreement expands the room for others to operate below the
contracted wage norms or above the agreed-upon performance
norms, because the conditions to do so become more 'tolerable'. In
this respect, and quite apart from the employment and political
dangers which the demand side conjures up (and by the use of
which it can counter the wage-bargaining successes of the trade
union), every success impairs the prospects for success in the next
round of bargaining. Another example of this connection between
the successes and risks of collective action is the negotiated
'exchange' of wage gains for employment losses (occasioned by
rationalization), as is particularly the rule in American company
unions. The consideration of such mechanisms suggests a sobering
conclusion: the primary front on which the supply coalitions of

employees struggle is not that of the 'primary' power differential, that is, the 'class front' between supply and demand in the labour market; instead, this struggle is located at the front of the 'secondary' power differential, at which the *distribution* of income, working conditions and employment opportunities *within* the totality of employees is decided.

A second function of trade unions consists in standardizing and generalizing the existing equilibrium in the global conflict between supply and demand. Thus the relations of exchange between wages and work performed are fixed for a specified time period and for specified categories of employees through wage agreements, that is, they are limited 'downwards'. This, too, does not decisively alter the 'primary' power differential between the two sides of the labour market. Rather, it only transforms the unregulated, continuing conflict into one that is centralized and carried out periodically. In addition, it transforms the labour market from one of a 'bazaar' type (in which individual items are offered for prices negotiated *ad hoc*) into a regular 'market' in which, due to standardized prices and predictable offers, economically rational comparisons and decisions in fact become possible.[16]

## The Emergence of 'Problem Groups' as the Result of Supply- and Demand-Side Strategies

The considerations developed thus far can be summarized in the thesis that the position of every individual employee in the labour market can be understood as the combined result of two factors: the average global power differential that exists between the supply and demand sides of the labour market, which represents a 'primary' power differential; and the group-specific differences in the opportunity of employees to none the less practise successful strategies of adaptation within the framework of this primary power differential ('secondary' power differentials). At one extreme, the spectrum of different positions in the labour market is thus defined by highly privileged employees who, because of the type of demand they are faced with and their own strategic chances and modes of activity, find themselves in a favourable market situation in which they can protect themselves successfully from the pressure of substitution by other suppliers. At the other extreme, this spectrum is limited by the disadvantaged position of those employees who are defencelessly exposed to the pressure to adapt exerted by the demand side, as well as to the pressure of substitution exerted by competing suppliers, and who therefore must accept unstable employment relations, low wages, restrictive working conditions, and so on.

The question now arises as to why the individual probability of successful self-assertion in the labour market is obviously not distributed according to chance, but rather clearly depends on 'ascriptive' characteristics, which lead to marked differences of position in the labour markets of supply groups defined by age, gender, health status and ethnicity. The key to explaining the differential access of ascriptively defined groups of employees to 'successful' strategic options is not to be found in any quality of labour power or its use-value for the production process that depends on such characteristics as age or gender. The emergence of 'problem groups' in the labour market cannot be explained by some physical 'inferiority' of their labour market bid, but only by the fact that their chances of 'marketing' their otherwise 'equal' bid have been worsened by political and normative factors. The role-specific impairment of opportunities to adapt in the labour market must, therefore, be explained in relation to institutional mechanisms, not by the 'natural' qualities of those who hold these roles.

In observing the strategically disadvantaged labour market position of women, youth, older employees, the disabled and foreigners, it is initially striking that these groups are all bearers of characteristics that are also used on a cultural and political level for the definition of those segments of the population which are 'granted access' to life forms outside of the labour market (category I).[17] Connected with these characteristics are institutionalized claims, options and expectations that disallow continuous participation in the (domestic) labour market. For the members of these groups a (limited) period of non-participation in the supply side of the labour market counts as normal and legitimate, as is also the case for the 'independent' members of category IV whose access to their own means of production also allows them to avoid participation in the labour market and employment. The recourse to constituting ascriptive categories is the means by which industrial capitalist societies try to institutionally overcome a dilemma, namely, that they cannot possibly force the *entire* population into direct participation in the labour market, while at the same time they cannot make generally available the option of non-participation in the labour market (and thus dependence on means of subsistence external to it). If the latter option were available, a 'mass exodus' from market relations – which are also power relations – would have to be reckoned with. To overcome this dilemma within the framework of a social order structured by the organizing principle of the labour market, these societies are dependent upon criteria of exclusion or exemption from the labour market that must have two qualities: (i) they may not be freely chosen individually and thus potentially usable as a means of strategic withdrawal from the labour market; and (ii) they must be selected in such a way that the 'exempted' portion of the population of category I is not in a position to place 'excessive' demands and politically effective expectations about its need for the means of subsistence on the production and occupational system. Both of these criteria correspond to the institutions located on the outer limits of the labour market, in which we regularly find special relations of force and control which deprive people of the resources for collective action and thus prevent them from realizing their economic or other interests: family systems, schools, prisons, social security programmes, armies, hospitals, and so on.

Apart from the special case of children, the overwhelming majority of the members of category I 'housed' and provided for in this way cannot actually be prevented (often not even legally) from putting their individual bids to work into the labour market. These criteria and institutions for a life outside the labour market thus represent for these groups of people an available option, a role that serves as an alternative to their labour market participation; they enjoy the licence to conduct a life outside of the labour market. But it is precisely the reverse side of this status of potential membership in category I that reveals the disadvantages and strategic handicaps of participating in the labour market (by moving into categories II or III). It is clear that the labour market cannot absorb 'everyone'; that would only lead to its self-destruction. It is equally clear that the option of leaving the supply side of the labour market cannot be granted to everyone at any time; this would also destroy its capacity to function or, at least, its power relationships. It is also clear, finally, that the objective and ascriptive facts that authorize non-participation in the labour market can only be defined as options and not as levers for effectively 'banning' labour from the (black) labour market. Thus the problem arises that substantial portions of the population are contingently related to the labour market: while they *can* participate, they can also exercise their option of *non*-participation. With respect to the labour market they are characterized by a 'broken' social identity. Their conduct always appears to themselves (and to their market partners) in the light of the alternative role to which they can always switch for rationally justifiable reasons. One motive for switching from category III (or II) to category I is that one can escape the burdens and strategic disadvantages to which one is exposed in the labour market. Limited chances for doing just this doubtless arise under conditions of economic crisis, including even the option of moving into category IV ('new self-employment'). Motives also exist for the contrary movement – from category I to category III – inasmuch as the special relations of force and control, as well as the restricted possibilities for subsistence offered by institutions outside the labour market, exert a constant pressure to participate in the labour market.

It is our central thesis that with the development of the welfare state the option is made available to increasing segments of the population to locate their individual mode of subsistence either within the labour market or in institutions external to it. The problem of persons 'enjoying' this option is not that of having too few, but 'too many' choices. For, under many circumstances, this option is a highly ambivalent 'Greek gift': not only does it burden the personal identity of individuals with a potential dual role, but it also leads to the impairment of their strategic possibilities for action *in* the labour market. Women, foreigners, youth, older employees and the handicapped are themselves faced with a structural problem of an insufficiently defined conception of what their 'normal' form of social existence actually is – a problem the physically able, native-born male employees of middle age, who do not 'enjoy' the option of non-participation in the labour market, never encounter. In what follows, we will limit ourselves to the attempt to trace those implications for the strategic position of workers in the labour market that result from ascribed alternative roles assigning them the option, yet not the 'normality' of labour market participation and employment.

To begin with, the fact that certain groups have licensed possibilities (and perhaps also the motives) for a mode of subsistence outside the labour market plays an important role in the strategy of the demand side of the labour market. Every hiring of an employee entails fixed costs for the enterprise; among these are the costs of recruitment, training or familiarization with the job, as well as the costs associated on average with the risk that the newly engaged employee will not perform successfully in the job. For the employer, these costs take the form of an investment that becomes profitable only after a certain time. Up to this point, there is a risk that the newly-employed will quit or will not satisfy the expectations placed on him or her. This risk of employing workers, which in the final analysis is traceable to the fact that the hired labour does not 'belong' to the employer like a purchased item whose technical use-value can be precisely evaluated, can only be reduced by offering contractual agreements and other incentives to prohibit the fluctuation of those employees whose costs of recruitment, familiarization and training are especially high. Conversely, this risk can also be reduced by recruiting groups for which the risk of fluctuation is especially high – because of the fact that on the basis of their ascriptive characteristics the option is attributed to them of living *outside* of formal employment – exclusively into jobs where the costs incurred by the enterprise for recruitment and training are particularly low.

The distribution of jobs according to ascriptive criteria that, for the employer, indicate the turnover risks, is from his/her point of view a wholly rational strategy. This is more so the greater the range of alternative options a prospective employee is seen to have. It means, conversely, that the young, those just commencing an occupation, (younger) women, foreigners, immigrant labour and older employees are treated preferentially as 'candidates' for those jobs for which the recruiting enterprise is not dependent on the hired labour power completing costly processes of familiarization and qualification, continually absorbing new knowledge and experiences, and orienting itself to remaining in the enterprise for a long period of time or to a life-long 'occupational career'. Because of the insufficiently defined, 'fuzzy normality' attributed to these ascriptively defined categories of employees, they are given preference for jobs for which qualifications can be acquired quickly, which entail less than average costs of recruitment, and in which the pressure for substitution is high, the wages low, the chances of advancement slim, and working conditions restrictive or characterized by a high degree of direct control – the 'shit-jobs' that 'anybody can do'.[18] The analogy with the capital market is obvious: assets that can be withdrawn at short notice secure a far lower rate of interest, although of course the uniqueness of the labour market phenomenon that we are trying to understand is that the right to choose a longer-term and therefore more 'profitable' form of investment is denied certain 'investors'. It is at least plausible to expect that if this mechanism is perceived by those affected by it, it will lead, in a circular fashion, to a decline of their subjective hopes and expectations of strategically asserting themselves in the labour market, and to a strengthening of their subjective orientation to their respective 'alternative role'. This is especially likely under generally unfavourable labour market conditions: the pattern is reinforced by the hiring practices it gives rise to.

Beyond the level of the *individual* recruitment decisions made by the actors on the demand side of the labour market, the strategic implications associated with the business risk that labour power could escape or withdraw into ascriptively attributed alternative roles are also evident on the *organizational* level. Firms differentiate the structure of their labour force, such that jobs for the 'regular work-force' are sharply delimited from those of the 'marginal work-force' (which has a higher turnover rate that is relatively less damaging to the enterprise).[19] The larger the ratio of marginal workers (who are by definition cheaply, and with no friction, replaceable) the less management is forced to concede to wage demands of its employees, since the substitution pressures to which those employed in the 'marginal work-force' are exposed are greater. Furthermore, a thoroughly 'counter-intuitive' but none the less rational exploitation of welfare-state protection guarantees becomes evident in the hiring policy of employers. The firm's employment policies anticipate (and, at least implicitly, refer employees to) the availability of social and political 'safety nets' outside the labour market for certain employees (such as the old and health-impaired, disabled, housewives and mothers and, in part, youth). These policies in turn reorganize the jobs of those 'favoured' by these safety nets in ways that do, in fact, tend to make it comparatively attractive to them to actually exercise their non-employment options. The more options there are provided by the welfare state, the more a firm can afford to impose rigorous demands upon the beneficiaries of such options. For the firm, this has the advantage of creating a more-or-less sizeable group of 'bad' jobs that can be terminated or refilled without difficulty in case of fluctuating demand. Aggravating political conflicts associated with such jobs are also less likely and at any rate less consequential to the firm than conflicts arising out of the comparatively 'indispensable' positions among the 'regular work-force'. Consequently, the quantitative ratio of the regular work-force to the marginal one, along with the corresponding level of segmentation, must be seen as strategic variables which management can manipulate in order to be able to adapt to changing conjunctural conditions. Hence, under conditions of low growth rates, many large enterprises seem to have discharged their marginal personnel and are operating instead with a regular work-force which can be deployed flexibly (with respect to tasks and working hours), such that the burden of unemployment is predominantly imposed upon the marginal workers.[20]

That certain groups of employees are viewed and treated in the light of a 'second best' reserve role attributed to them (their switching to this reserve role always being anticipated as an eventuality) is not only a crucial feature of the recruitment policies, as well as the division of labour, of enterprises. It also determines the activity of representing employees' interests in the 'works councils' (*Betriebsräte,* in the Federal Republic of Germany). Experience of the recession shows that in the case of dismissals, for which the endorsement of the works councils is required, the councils are always particularly willing to compromise, if those to be fired belong to groups whose temporary or permanent elimination from the labour market is held to be 'acceptable' to the victims of dismissals (because, for example, they are considered to have the option of retreating into the role of a housewife, or into early retirement). Conversely, those groups who anticipate not withdrawal from the labour market (category I), but rather unemployment (category II) as the most likely consequence of dismissal, can mobilize the greatest degree of solidarity and readiness to resist. This difference in conflict behaviour indicates that company (and, equally, trade union) representation of the interests of employees is also oriented subtly to the ascriptive difference between 'regular', 'normal' or 'nothing-but' employees, on the one hand and, on the other to those marginal employees who, if need be, 'can do something else', and on behalf of whom one therefore hardly needs to 'head for the barricades'.[21]

Businesses are thus not only attentive to 'reserve roles' for the sake of a risk-conscious allocation of the 'human capital' which is invested in every time an employee is hired. They are also especially interested in labour power of this type because an above-average rate of exploitation can, as a rule, be imposed upon these relatively defenceless categories of workers within the legally unregulated 'struggle for wages and performance' (see above). Labour power of this type can in any case achieve comparatively little in the way of advancing its interests, working conditions and income by refusing or withholding its services (or by threatening to engage in such actions). This is because the ability of a firm to substitute labour is, as a rule, greater than the chances of these groups' members finding other employment. The dependency of workers upon the particular job they have, with relatively inferior 'exit' options *in* the labour market, is most clearly evident in circumstances where a dual role is not merely a possibility that must be anticipated, but already a constituent element of the actual situation. The best and most well-known example is the actual double burdening of many women by occupational activity and domestic responsibilities. 'Working housewives' are typically deprived of some of their capacity to adapt to market opportunities and can only deploy their labour power within narrow spatial and temporal limits. The same impairment of strategic options in the labour market arises for moonlighting farmers and those who have to work at home. The supply strategies actually available to older employees are also restricted, not primarily because they are physically or psychologically incapable of performing jobs which are too demanding for them but, rather, because their proximity to the age of retirement leaves them no further opportunities for individual strategies such as the acquisition of special skills which otherwise would improve the marketability of their labour power.

Ascribed alternative roles *outside* the labour market impair the strategic options and alternatives that can be exercised *in* the labour market. In all these cases, the relative and particular poverty of alternatives facing the groups of employees mentioned – the spatial, temporal and training factors that leave them 'tied down' and 'inflexible' with regard to certain relations of employment – condemn them to having to accept particularly unfavourable working conditions and particularly low incomes. The part-time labour markets for working housewives (for instance, in the retail trade) are well-known examples of this. Given the position of the demand side in all this, one could speak of 'demand power', or quasi-monopsonistic relations of blackmail that are further secured by the fact that those who are negatively affected are rarely disposed, objectively and subjectively, to organized opposition and trade union activity (see below). As a consequence, the particular strategic handicaps of certain groups of employees – handicaps such as age, disability, but also the status of being an apprentice or an immigrant – provide enterprises with special advantages. The fact that the choices of these employees are systematically constrained can be used to assign jobs and work loads to them that 'regular' employees would reject as unacceptable.

It remains to be explained why such non-occupational, ascriptive principles of organization on the supply side of the labour market, and the consequent hardening of the differences among various groups' labour market opportunities, meet with so little resistance from those who suffer as the disadvantaged 'victims of the labour market'. For it is also conceivable that the most disadvantaged groups of employees might strive politically to overcome their strategically disadvantaged position, thereby adjusting their special negative status closer to that of 'normal' employees. Such a tendency, which is often postulated from positions based on class theory, is most unlikely, however. This is due to the existence of a constellation comprising those already referred-to objective opportunities, the attitudes of those 'stigmatized' by a dual-role definition, interests and strategies on the demand side, as well as biases within the process of shop-floor interest representation, a constellation which contributes to a hardening of the differences mentioned above.

For many members of these disadvantaged groups, their ambiguously defined normality as employees and their orientation towards an alternative role necessitates from the outset that the income they currently seek in the labour market assumes the form of a temporally restricted 'supplementary income', upon which they do not and cannot rely as an enduring source of support. Examples of participation in the labour market which is (at least intended to be) just a temporary one include younger working women who orient themselves to the possibility of a 'break' in their career for having a family; foreign employees who intend to return to their country of origin and its economic opportunities; and moonlighting farmers who often only enter the labour market seasonally. For members of such groups of employees, the level of interest in such factors as employment, career, mobility, income and 'good' working conditions is lower than for 'normal' employees, and for wholly rational reasons. This is the reason why they are often considered by employers as having more than average 'patience' and a 'capacity to withstand stress'.

This central orientation towards a way of life outside the labour market means that, with respect to the willingness to organize and engage in conflict, the expenditure of time and energy that would be necessary for the individual or collective struggle for better working conditions is either objectively not possible or subjectively does not seem worthwhile, since the eventual successes could be enjoyed only for a short time. It is, therefore, also not surprising that we find among the members of these groups a degree of union organization that is far below average – a fact that is reinforced by the 'discriminating' strategies of employee organizations themselves. These groups' interest in trade unions is usually 'palmed off', organizationally speaking, on to comparatively uninfluential special committees, lectures and conferences (e.g. on women, youth, immigrant workers) that are relatively isolated from the bodies and officials that formulate and define the 'collective interest' of the work-force. Accordingly, it is not just 'traditional prejudices' (to be overcome through appeals to 'solidarity') on the part of union leaders and the core working class on whose support they rely, which contributes to an imbalanced process of interest representation of employees. It is equally a rational perception and strategic orientation on the part of those core groups to consider and treat marginal workers' interests differently from their own interests, and to practise strategies of social and organizational 'closure' against them.

## 'Problem Groups' and State Labour Market Policy

One could of course suppose that, as a form of democratic political authority standing outside the labour market, state policy is capable of not only weakening but effectively equalizing the overall power imbalance *between* the supply and demand sides, as well as the secondary group advantages and disadvantages within the supply side that result from this imbalance. If this were indeed done, such power-balancing intervention would only create a condition of material freedom of contract that is considered to be a normal prerequisite of the functioning of other markets. Yet it would also lead to a surprising outcome: a consistent equalization of the strategic market options on both sides of the labour market through public policy would not mean an exchange of labour and capital unhindered by power factors and marked by a 'weapons parity' between both sides. Rather, it would mean the more or less abrupt *end* of this exchange itself. The elimination of power and blackmail from the relationship of exchange between capital and labour would in effect destroy the interest of the demand side in continuing to engage in 'exchange'. If, on average, the individual employer were as dependent on the employee as is true in the reverse direction and if, on average, the individual labourer could switch to other modes of employment or modes of subsistence as easily as being replaced by competing offers of labour power or machines, then the element of superior market power on the demand side would not only be dissolved, but management would also thereby lose any rational motive for employing labour within the framework of labour contracts.

Under such conditions, the anticipated equilibrium wage would be too high for it to be rational to hire employees at all. Paradoxically, the consequent levelling of the power advantage of the demand side of the labour market would, for the first time, both transform it into a labour *market* in the strict sense, while at the same time undermining it, exactly because the incentive would be lacking, on one side at least, for even operating in this market. It is precisely this dilemma within which every state (as well as every trade union) policy is caught: while it works for the levelling of the power differential, it must also fear the more-or-less extensive 'renunciation of contracts' by the demand side that is to be expected as a response to successful attempts to neutralize labour market power. Our point is thus not to deny the willingness of state policy to level the power relations inherent in the labour market. Rather, it should be recognized that precisely when a solution is sought and effectively realized by the state, problems result that are tolerable neither from the point of view of the 'favoured' nor from the point of view of the state's own interests. State policy (as well as trade union wage policy) is thus faced with a problem of 'optimization', in which the power differential prevailing in the labour market can neither be left unregulated nor reorganized in a way that would cause the labour market itself, along with its corresponding power differential, to disappear.

So, what political instruments are available for modifying and regulating the power differential prevailing in the labour market, as well as the power differential between the positions of groups in the labour market, while at the same time preserving the power differential which is the operative premise of the 'system of wage labour'? Figure 1.1 provides a systematic classification of these political instruments along three dimensions. The first distinguishes between the strategies of 'inclusion' and 'exclusion'. By inclusion we mean transfers of individuals from categories I or IV to categories II and III; exclusion denotes transfers in the opposite direction. Second, labour market policy interventions can be distinguished according to whether they operate by means of positive sanctions (incentives) or negative sanctions (disadvantages and penalties). Finally, labour market policies can be analysed according to whether they intervene on the supply or demand sides of the labour market.

|  | *Positive sanctions (incentives)* | *Negative sanctions (penalties)* |
|---|---|---|
| *Exclusion* |  |  |
| Demand side | 1a | 1b |
| Supply side | 1c | 1d |
| *Inclusion* |  |  |
| Demand side | 2a | 2b |
| Supply side | 2c | 2d |

*Figure 1.1   Strategies of labour market policy intervention*

The following list of policy examples is only illustrative, and is far from exhaustive; some of the measures are actually currently employed, while others are presently only being considered or debated.

1a    Early retirement schemes (as they permit employers to lay-off otherwise protected workers).

1b    Prohibition of child labour and of employing illegal immigrant residents.

1c    Paid maternity leave, i.e. general benefits claims for mothers of infants (e.g. for one year); incentives to encourage immigrant workers to return home; start-up and other subsidies for the self-employed and small business.

1d    Temporal extension of compulsory school attendance; lowering the threshold of wage income pensioners can earn without affecting their old-age insurance benefit claims.

2a    Wage-cost subsidies paid to employers of newly hired workers; short-time allowances.

2b    Penalties for employers who fail to employ a prescribed quota of disabled workers; establishment of maximum working hours; protection against unfair dismissal.

2c    Retraining; continuing education; moving allowances.

2d    The income and skill levels of jobs unemployed workers are expected to accept (or otherwise lose their unemployment benefits); suspending the universally binding character of standard wages negotiated between unions and employers.

By the social and labour policy strategy of 'exclusion' (sanctions 1a–d) we understand the totality of state laws, institutions and measures that regulate the legal claims and material living conditions of individuals who are neither employed nor unemployed. These strategies seek to reduce the supply of labour by defining and providing, for certain persons and certain time periods, the conditions of legitimate non-participation in the labour market. They are either exclusionary regulations that come in the form of prohibiting the hiring of certain categories of persons, or providing means of subsistence for sub-groups of the population like housewives, the infirmed and the retired who are then expected to refrain from competing on the over-crowded supply side. The social-policy significance of such regulations is that they both make impossible special labour relations in which the power differential world manifest itself in extreme and (in relation to given norms) unacceptable ways, and relatively weaken the global power relationship that is premised upon the surplus of labour supply. State policy cannot, however, arbitrarily augment the absorptive capacity of institutions and forms of life guaranteed and subsidized outside the labour market. The limits of this 'negative' labour market policy result from the limited fiscal and institutional viability of such institutions outside the market as the family, schools and social security programmes. Through the strategy of 'exclusion', the total quantity of labour market and employment risks can only be 'organized away' under conditions of growing and ultimately intolerable fiscal difficulties, which are evidently onerous both in terms of rising expenditures as well as declining revenues of state and social security budgets. From the fiscal point of view, the most attractive alternative is the self-supporting family household, which is, therefore, often recommended as the ideal form of 'accommodation' for women, youth and the elderly, whose labour-power must be prevented from appearing on the market. What hinders this solution is clearly the fact that, without massive state subsidies, as well as infrastructural and institutional outlays, the family household today appears able to perform this function to only a strictly limited and diminishing degree.

In view of the present and likely future acute volume of labour market imbalances, this traditional exclusion strategy of labour protection and social security is being exhausted for fiscal reasons. As a provider of means of support and as a sphere of non-market activity, the household is also largely exhausted and could only be reactivated for this function through massive welfare-state transfer payments (and against considerable political and cultural opposition). The transfer of members from categories II and III to the domain of economic independence (category IV) – sometimes considered as a means of relieving the labour market supply – is also restricted by its very limited absorptive capacity, which could only be enlarged through equally heavy demands on state budgets for small-business subsidies, and so on. If the 'relative surplus' parts of the population were to be excluded from the labour market and 'taken off the street' in a way that neither directly nor indirectly increased the burden on the public budget, then this could only be done through recourse to forms of forced labour, their transfer to 'total' institutions or their open neglect.

Whether, and to what extent, state policy is tempted to rely on such solutions that clearly negate the 'freedom' of wage labour, depends in part on the extent to which the second type of strategy is employed – that of actively integrating labour into the market. By strategies of inclusion (sanctions 2a–d), we understand all those labour market, social and educational policy measures that seek to change the supply conditions of labour power in such a way as to increase its chances of finding employment that otherwise would not materialize, or to maintain employment that would otherwise disappear. Such strategies of inclusion can concentrate on the qualifications of the labour offered (education, further training, occupational flexibility), its spatial distribution (subsidization of regional mobility), the effective price offered (wage-cost subsidies), or the temporal conditions of labour and, hence, the level of labour volume supplied (stipulation of maximum working hours). Also included among these strategies is legal protection against dismissal for certain groups of employees (at least in so far as the risk of dismissal for other groups of employees is not directly or indirectly augmented to the same extent), as well as 'humanization' measures that seek to prevent the premature exhaustion of labour power, and thereby to protect its supply position.

Attempts to implement these variants of the strategy of inclusion are marked by a series of characteristic difficulties. This is true independently of whether they rely on positive or negative sanctions or whether they approach the problem on the supply or demand sides of the labour market. With regard to positive incentives on the demand side (sanction 2a), the integration effect which can be achieved is highly uncertain (*ex ante* as well as *ex post*) because there is no guarantee that these employment subsidies paid to employers are actually used for *increasing* employment, and not simply 'appropriated' as premiums for recruitment that was planned anyway. The integrative effect of measures directed at the demand side that operate by means of negative sanctions (2b) cannot be viewed any more optimistically. This is evident in the example of regulations regarding expectant mothers and older employees, youth-labour protection, mandatory employment quotas for the handicapped, and other regulations aimed at maintaining the labour capacity or employment prospects of particularly disadvantaged groups of employees.

Certainly, it is true that such measures limit the entrepreneurial freedom to shape working conditions and to terminate work relationships, and that they threaten infractions of such regulations with penalties or fines. None the less, effective employment regulations can hardly be enforced in this way. The reason for this is that these penalties are so mild (and must be so due to the wide variation of individual conditions of business) that there is no effective pressure to comply with norms; or it is because employers remain at liberty not to hire employees who would be protected in special ways if they were employed. Protective legislation which is supposed to secure the quality or continuity of employment for specific jobs or categories of employees consequently often turns out to be in effect disadvantageous from the point of view of the intended objective, because they impede the creation of jobs or the hiring of employees to which protective regulations would apply. Employees with such 'special privileges' become unattractive for the demand side, and the effect that can result from such regulations is correspondingly ambivalent.

Another variant of these strategies of inclusion operates with positive incentives for the supply side (2c). Included here are special measures for encouraging individual occupational training and regional mobility. The means through which these aims are to be realized are material incentives with a fixed time limit, or the compensation of disadvantages. It is doubtful, however, whether the motivating effect of these positive incentives is generally sufficient to stimulate greater flexibility and mobility and, especially, whether the 'right' target groups of employees (those who would actually improve their chances of finding a job in the labour market or remain within it through increased mobility and flexibility) are actually influenced by this motivating effect. Experience shows – understandably – that public funds that are made available for occupational training and retraining are claimed disproportionately by those employees *least* affected by training-related employment risks. With respect to geographic mobility, the effectiveness of this type of measure is also rather limited, inasmuch as the considerable material and non-material costs that can be associated with severing the complex of life-world relations with a given geographic place are difficult to compensate for with subsidies and compensation payments, and also often subjectively too great for those who, in agricultural and structurally weak regions, have completely rational and even economic reasons for not leaving their local context.

If these three types of inclusion strategy (positive and negative sanctions on the demand side, positive sanctions on the supply side) are on the whole relatively ineffective and unreliable, then pressure is placed on the fourth, and remaining variant, the application of penalties on the supply side (2d). These consist of attempts to expose the employees actually affected by employment risks to an increased 'adaptive pressure' through legal threats and other negative sanctions, thereby increasing their willingness to adapt to the conditions forced on them by the labour market. The instruments for reliably bringing about this result include shortening the length and amount of unemployment benefits, a more rigorous definition of jobs that must be accepted by the unemployed even though they may not correspond to their previous skill and income levels, a suspension or relaxation of the protective functions of labour law, and waves of political as well as media denunciations of the unemployed as 'work shy'.

To the extent that state labour-market policy utilizes this fourth variant of strategies of inclusion, it of course loses its quality as an 'autonomous' policy that corrects and balances the power relations arising in the labour market. It even becomes active in removing institutional obstacles and 'rigidities' that hinder the exercise of market power, thereby amplifying the latter. It becomes an agent of the market-pressures to which workers are exposed, thus abandoning its pretensions of neutralizing the general and specific power relations prevailing in the labour market.

# 2

# The Future of the Labour Market

Every society is confronted with the problem of institutionally resolving a twofold task. On the one hand, the labour power of human individuals must be distributed among concrete production processes and activities; on the other, the fruits of this labour must be distributed to the employed, and, via public and private expenditures, to the 'legitimately' non-employed. Capitalist market systems have 'solved' this twofold problem through the institution of a 'market' for the 'commodity' labour. This solution implies the existence of 'free' wage labour, that is, the commodification of labour power ('wage labour'), as well as its release from normative, compulsory or property-based ties to a specific mode of its utilization. A free labour market exists when and only when workers (following Marx's familiar dictum) are free in the double sense that 'as free persons they can dispose of their labour power as their own commodity' and 'are short of everything else necessary for the realization of their labour power'.[1] A labour market presupposes propertylessness in two senses: the worker can neither be tied to an owner like a material component of production, nor control property and thus his/her own chances of securing an existence outside of the labour market.[2] Labour can neither *be* the property of another nor *possess* property.

Following Marx and Weber, the consensus today is that the institutionalization of such a market for labour is the central characteristic of capitalist market systems. If the viability of such

Translated by Karen Grislis and Raymond Morrow. This is a shortened and revised version of a paper originally co-authored with Johannes Berger. It was first published as 'Die Zukunft des Arbeitsmarktes. Zur Ergänzungsbedürftigkeit eines versagenden Allokationsprinzips', *Kölner Zeitschrift für Soziologie und Sozialpsychologie*, special issue 24 (1982), 348–71.

systems rests on the functional efficiency of the labour market, the question arises whether – and within what limits – the labour market is capable of fulfilling its anticipated function. In response to this question, we shall discuss three cumulatively acting types of functional disturbances that are characteristic of the labour market. These show that the labour market is of questionable effectiveness in coping with the long-term double-allocative problem conferred upon it in capitalist societies. Our thesis is that the labour market has had only limited success as an allocative principle for labour power, and will scarcely be in a position to sustain itself as the dominant principle for resolving this double-allocative problem for the conceivable future of economic, social and technological development. If this argument is valid, an evolutionary imperative will emerge which could culminate in the replacement or, more likely, a supplementing of the labour market as the dominant principle of allocation. We also consider this alternative of supplementing the labour market, and examine the preconditions and functions of an arrangement of institutions in which the labour market coexists with various non-market allocative principles.

## The Failure of Labour Markets

Formed in the course of capitalist development, the dominance of the labour market as the reigning allocative principle for organizing human productive activities and distributing the means of human subsistence can obscure the fact that it is anything but a 'self-evident' mechanism. It was Polanyi who made researchers aware of its 'extreme artificiality'. 'No Society', Polanyi remarked, 'could stand the effects of such a system of crude fictions' (treating labour, land and money as commodities) 'even for the shortest stretch of time unless its human and natural substance as well as its business organization was protected against the ravages of this satanic mill.'[3]

For Polanyi, the labour market is a 'satanic mill' because its institutionalization extends the principle of market self-regulation to living labour. Organizing social life through the market mechanism has not only the effect of normatively neutralizing the allocation of labour, thereby violating the values and traditions of workers; it also has a 'systemic' aspect of providing a solution to a basic societal steering problem. For Polanyi, the burden of justification for the subjugation of labour power to the market mechanism had to be assumed by these latter functional arguments. Though the labour market may be 'satanic', its various defenders since Adam Smith argue that it is, nevertheless, also uniquely 'efficient', and hence promises a level of economic welfare that can compensate for this suffering.

From the perspective of economic theory, the labour market is considered as an ordinary commodity market. As a commodity-money relation, it is, like any market, characterized by two opposing flows: households pass productive labour outputs into enterprises (the 'real' flow) and obtain monetary income from enterprises (the 'monetary' flow). The labour market supplies private enterprise and state institutions with labour power, and households with income. The superior economic performance of a labour *market* is obvious within the framework of this model. In comparison to traditional societies, the contingency of acquisition of the labour market is raised to a high level. The recruitment of labour power is supposed to depend upon 'free choice' and is, therefore, not restricted by normative obligations of assistance or the feudal (*ständische*) ties of labour to the land. From the perspective of households, the evolutionary innovation of the labour market consists in the fact that individual reproduction is not guaranteed through traditional rights and obligations, but rather depends entirely upon the success of individual transactions on the labour market. This circumstance pushes the labour force toward a maximum work intensity and willingness to conform.

In the competitive model of the labour market, the price mechanism coordinates the multitude of decisions which are reached independently of each other by those who are supplying and demanding. The allocation of resources (in this case, labour power) occurs solely through individual decisions in response to price signals. The variation of the wage rate forms the strategic variable by means of which the supply of, and demand for, labour power is brought into balance. At the point of equilibrium, all resources are utilized efficiently, that is, each portion of labour power is expended such that it produces the highest economic return, and there is only 'voluntary' unemployment. This claim concerning optimal efficiency in the allocation of labour power to jobs is linked with the (limited) assertion of the justice of the allocation of income to labour. Justice is seen to consist not in the outcome, but in the process of allocating income through exchange based on free individual decision. A further efficiency-inducing advantage follows from the legally regulated disjunction of wage demands (of workers) from control over the product of work by employers: the production process itself is shielded from possible interference and demands on the part of employees and can thereby follow the exclusive dictates of rational capital accounting and profit-oriented initiative.[4] A complete separation between the spheres of the 'household' and 'business' take place, and their mutual exclusion within civil law ensures social peace, as well as economic efficiency.

The decisive question in the study of labour market phenomena is whether this competitive model can be considered as even an approximate representation of the normal reality. Our contention is that for three general reasons it is inappropriate to look at the labour market from within the assumptions of a classical or neo-classical model of a competitive market which efficiently and/or justly solves the double-allocative problem. These reasons are based not upon externally induced 'disturbance factors' but, rather, upon factors which are inherent within the social system and the labour market itself. These cumulatively acting factors, which play a key role in setting limits to the market-based allocation of labour power include the following.

I  Specific features of the nature of the 'commodities' exchanged in the labour market. These features necessitate that labour power can only be a commodity in a fictional sense, i.e. constantly refuted through the practical operation of labour market processes; the labour market cannot function without a *coercive* implementation of the fiction that labour power *is* a commodity.

II  The *strategies* pursued by actors in the labour market and by the state. These culminate in a 'closure' of the labour market – its cartelization, weakening and price-insensitive regulation – thus rendering the competitive model highly unrealistic.

III  Historically accrued changes in the economic, political and cultural parameters of the 'work-centred society'. These changes, which have become manifest since the mid-1970s, and have subsequently dominated labour market and social policy debates, make it appear increasingly questionable whether conditions will emerge or be politically created (at least within the foreseeable future and in sufficient scope) so as to ensure that market mechanisms distribute labour power to work tasks and, conversely, satisfy the consumption needs of individuals (as claimed in the competitive model) from wages derived from employment.

The essential elements of these three points will now be considered.

## I  *The fiction of commodities*

Polanyi introduced the distinction between 'genuine' and 'fictive' commodities.[5] As with property and money, labour power must be considered a fictive commodity for three reasons.

First, unlike genuine commodities, it is not created for the purpose of sale in a market; genuine commodities are generated, in both quantity and quality, according to their expected saleability in the market-place. The decision to produce the fictive commodity labour is not reached in market-oriented enterprises but, rather, in families and other agencies of socialization where motivations are largely distinct from that of marketability. Imbalances in the labour market do not, therefore, lead to the immediate revision of the quantitative and qualitative 'production decisions' for labour power. The criterion of marketability stands directly opposed to the variety of cultural bonds in which persons socialized within a family stand. 'To allow the market mechanism to be the sole director of the fate of human beings . . . would result in the demolition of society.'[6]

Second, labour power differs from conventional commodities because of its marked variability and plasticity. What the procurer of labour purchases in the labour market is not 'labour' but, rather, labour *power*. The question is always the extent to which labour power is transformed successfully into labour actually performed. The variability and plasticity of labour is the reason why Marx termed money-capital spent on the purchase of labour power 'variable' capital. The employment contract is clearly determined only with respect to pay, whereas the specifications for concrete work tasks – the circumstances of labour exertion, work intensity, etc. – remain relatively underdefined. This gap of indeterminacy is closed in the firm through managerial authority ('command of labour'). Maintaining a certain indeterminacy of the employment contract is very much in the interest of management itself, since otherwise each time the concrete work task changed, a new work contract would have to be made.[7] It is precisely this very loose specification of the duties and goals for which labour is utilized that offers the purchaser the possibility of being able to vary the use of labour power *qualitatively* according to shifting managerial requirements. It also allows the purchaser to *quantitatively* alter the utilization of labour power, up to the similarly shifting boundary where managerial surveillance and control meets with the effective resistance of the workers. Consequently, a form of labour power which was (like a commodity) fully determined and unchangeable with respect to its use-value characteristics would be much less suited to industrial production than 'living' and 'variable' labour power.

Third, the 'commodity' labour power is not clearly separable from its owner. Consequently, the purchase of labour power lacks that clarity of the legal transfer of titles which otherwise characterizes market exchange.[8] In this respect, labour power lacks the quality of being able to pass completely, through exchange, from the sphere of disposition of a seller into that of a buyer. Every buyer of labour power must rely on the 'participation' of the worker since, on the one hand, that buyer cannot exclusively control the purchased commodity, and, on the other, the utilization of labour power is linked inextricably to the cooperation of the owners. The worker must also *want* to work; the fundamental problem of every company or organization consists accordingly in inducing the worker, as the subject of labour power, to this cooperation.

## II   *Restrictions of the market*

Just as the specific qualities of 'living' labour impose certain
barriers upon its transformation into an ordinary commodity, so
strategies pursued by actors in the labour market also prevent the
market form of perfect competition from prevailing in the labour
market. Two conditions must be satisfied in order to realize
perfect competition: (i) quantitative adaptation of output and
(ii) free access to the market. The former is satisfied as long as
households and enterprises have no other choice but to adjust the
goods and services they wish to buy and sell to the prevailing
prices. We can term this the 'principle of the excluded strategy'.[9]
Wherever a choice of strategy exists, competition is not perfect. By
a strategy we mean a way of acting that (a) aims to intervene in the
environment ('success-oriented action') and (b) builds into its
calculations expectations regarding the behaviour of at least one
other actor. We find four sites in the labour market where
competitive action based on simple quantitative adaptation of
outputs can be displaced – and actually has been displaced,
historically and empirically – by strategic action: either capital
secures strategic possibilities for acting *vis-à-vis* other units of
capital or labour power; or, analogously, labour power secures
strategic room for manoeuvre *vis-à-vis* other suppliers of labour
power or capital. Examples of these strategic options are presented
in figure 2.1.

|  | Organization | |
| --- | --- | --- |
| Actor | *Capital* | *Labour* |
| Capital | Monopolization of markets | Segmentation of the labour market |
| Labour | Formation of trade union associations | Acquisition of skills and qualifications |

*Figure 2.1*

All four of these strategies – monopolization, segmentation of the
labour market, formation of trade union associations, and the
acquisition of skills and qualifications – have the common feature
of transforming the market from an open into a more-or-less

closed social relationship. The formation of trade unions and the acquisition of skills are, for instance, strategies through which workers seek to limit competition with respect to their employers and other workers, respectively.

A further barrier to the application of the commodity fiction to labour is the fact that the role of supplying labour power in the market is not the only role of workers, even where their reproduction occurs through the labour market. Workers belong to the political and cultural system of society as enfranchised citizens and as interpreters of their social condition who stand within a specific cultural tradition. The labour market is, therefore, never as insulated against the impact of other 'systems' or 'spheres of life' as is the case with markets in which 'genuine' commodities, which are nothing *but* commodities, are exchanged. Much like trade unions, state social policy also develops as a reaction against the threat posed by the surrender of individual existence to the effects of the labour market. It can be understood as a series of politically enacted and culturally legitimated measures which are supposed to protect labour power from the risks to which it is exposed by the exclusive rule of market mechanisms. As new as the labour market is as a social institution, the self-protection of society from its consequences commences almost simultaneously with the institutionalization of labour markets.[10]

### III  Contemporary functional disturbances in the labour market

Since the mid-1970s, Western industrial societies have been confronted with new problems which are referred to through such phrases as the breakdown of the post-war settlement, the end of Keynesianism, limits to growth, and the erosion of the work ethic.

In the *economic* realm, an unprecedented phase of the accumulation of capital came to a close in the mid-seventies. The 25 years of economic prosperity after the end of the Second World War were more the exception than the rule of capitalist development. In part, this boom in prosperity depended upon the exploitation of factors created by the war, and in part the boom was produced by a political and economic constellation which can be described as a model of social partnership based on a productivity-oriented wage policy. A series of developments influenced by the supply and demand for labour power provide every reason for believing that the 'years of plenty' are now over:

1   The international competitive position of so-called 'high income economies' is weakening for reasons that are not connected primarily with the advance of the developing countries, but rather with the multinationalization of domestic capital. 'Multinationals are now able to combine some of the lowest wages in particular countries in the world with the highest kind of technological efficiency in production.'[11]

2   The domestic market for a range of durable commodities relevant for the economic cycle (cars, household appliances, radios, television sets) is showing signs of saturation, such that in these markets only replacement needs will have to be satisfied in the long-run. Today there appears to be no industrial product like the automobile that would satisfy mass needs and trigger corresponding waves of investment which would materially reinforce a new long wave of the economic cycle.[12] To be sure, stagnation arguments, which are based on the assumption of need satiation, have a rather speculative character; because of the flexibility of needs, the boundaries of demand satiation are correspondingly wide. On the other hand, it cannot be overlooked that the economic boom of the post-war period was produced by a need for consumer goods whose present satiation – at least in higher income brackets – gives rise to less consumption-centred sets of preferences.

3   Additional pressure on the labour market results from demographic factors. For instance, according to estimates of the *Bundesanstalt für Arbeit* (Labour Market Agency) in the Federal Republic of Germany, the potential domestic labour force in the Federal Republic will have grown to just under 25.5 million people by 1990 – one million more than in 1975. An ebbing of labour market problems arising from the unfavourable age-structure of the population can only be expected at the beginning of the 1990s. In principle there is, of course, the possibility of countering an increase in the proportion of the

population who are dependent upon earning wages by politically influencing their participation rate. But there is every reason to believe that the chances of success of this kind of political manipulation of the rate of participation in work through a policy of excluding senior citizens, immigrants, women and others have already been exhausted in the course of bringing the last crisis (1974–6) under control.

4   For the coming period, the most important factors determining the relationship of supply and demand in the labour market, namely, labour supply (as measured by numbers of employees and work-time), labour productivity and the demand for final goods, are likely to remain in an unfavourable constellation. In direct contrast to developments in the fifties, and even the sixties, the rate of increase of labour productivity in the seventies is *above* that of production, with the consequence that labour power made redundant by technological advances is no longer employed in the course of expanding production. Technological change thus becomes an endogenous source of unemployment.[13] In principle, forms of political control of technological choices that reduce the speed of technical advance, prioritize capital-saving over labour-saving technologies, and cushion the consequences of technical advances on employees, are of course conceivable. Their feasibility is, however, obviously limited by pressures of international competition. Economic research institutes in the Federal Republic of Germany forecast an average annual rise in labour productivity of 3–4 per cent for the 1980s. An increase in production that would, in the medium term, bring the labour market into balance would have to be at least 6 per cent – a figure that seems neither attainable through the application of political-economic strategies nor desirable or realizable from an environmental point of view.

A second acute set of labour market problems originates in the *political* shift away from Keynesianism as well as the increasing political significance of the ecological problematic. In the Federal Republic of Germany, there has been a change in economic policy – although not as abrupt and powerful as in Britain or the USA – from a demand-oriented Keynesianism to a supply-oriented strategy.[14] The political core of this reorientation entails the state disengaging itself from the responsibility for full employment that it had previously assumed for political reasons. Conservative arguments as to why an employment policy based on the stimulation of demand is ineffective are used to justify the new economic policy. It is said that the price of Keynesian deficit-spending policy consists in intolerable levels of state indebtedness and the intensification of inflation. Keynesian deficit-spending, it is claimed, must be utilized in the long run to be effective, and because of the consequent increase of state expenditures it undermines its own success.

Yet, quite independent of the question of whether or not the state adopts a commitment to full employment, and whether there are political means for reaching this goal with sufficient certainty, a continuation of full employment policy would encounter new political obstacles from the increased sensitivity of the public to questions concerning the protection of the natural environment. Ecological questions gain a direct political dimension by being declared political issues by quantitatively relevant groups of the population. A policy of maximizing employment is, therefore, faced with the problem of implementing demands for the creation of jobs in partial conflict with ecological demands.

Finally, a change of work-related values has been observed in the cultural system of some Western societies. The desire for more leisure time competes with the goal of raising incomes; criticism of the rigid schedule of working hours is growing; and occupational activity is no longer at the centre of the lives of growing proportions of the population. The view that 'work' is good and 'idleness' is bad is undergoing alteration (the 'erosion of the Protestant ethic'). This theme is of course not without precedent. Already Lafargue[15] has wondered about the 'strange mania' that ruled the working class in all countries with a capitalist civilization: the 'love of work, the raving mania for work that culminates in the exhaustion of individuals and their descendants'. Instead of 'struggling against this spiritual aberration', Lafargue insisted, 'the priests, economists and moralists have pronounced work holy'. (One could add, so also have Marxists.) This criticism could always be effectively suppressed in times when real economic development supported confidence in growth. Under the changed economic conditions which have existed since the mid-1970s, and as a result of the welfare-state socialization of labour market risks, this criticism gains a topicality and explosiveness that can hardly be expressed through the neutralizing term 'value change'. The decline of acquisitiveness and the rise of post-acquisitive attitudes toward work within segments of the working class do not seem to express a merely incidental change of values which will be reversed by the next boom. Rather, this manifest change of attitudes reflects, at least among the so-called 'post-industrial new middle class', the increased fragility of an ethos of acquisitiveness specific to capitalism, the observance of which has led industrial capitalist societies closer to the natural and social limits to growth.

At first sight, it is not evident why altered valuations of work should aggravate labour-market problems. Rather, we might expect that a lower evaluation of work would provide some relief for the labour market. The altered appreciation of work does not, however, apply to work in a diffuse sense, but rather concerns the work roles provided by the system of employment. In principle these roles can encounter mounting resistance, either because demands rise or because the quality of jobs further deteriorates.[16] This resistance will of course have no significant influence on the volume of labour supply as long as possibilities for reproduction *independent* of the labour market are not guaranteed through the provision of appropriate economic, political and cultural resources. What can be expected, however, is an erosion of the cultural foundations, and hence the acceptability, of the labour market as the dominant pattern of allocating labour power as well as of distributing income.

## Towards a 'Mix' of Allocation Mechanisms

That the labour market has evidently become a less than adequate system for simultaneously solving the production and distribution problem provides no grounds, of course, for indulging in feelings of triumph inspired by theories of crisis or breakdown. For an alternative logic of utilizing and maintaining labour power (upon which Marxist crisis theory has always relied implicitly) is not in sight; on the contrary, something more like structural helplessness predominates.

This perspective is striking if one is prepared to understand the historically exhausted model of the labour market as not exclusively an arrangement that, in view of the power imbalance between supply and demand (i.e. labour and capital), is in essence exploitative, a relationship of intimidation and blackmail in which 'alienated' labour is subsumed by capital. One must *also* take seriously the (always limited) 'emancipatory' aspect of the model of 'free' wage labour. In this model, labour power at least possesses the formal (contractual) freedom to escape given and fixed specific forms of utilization and, thereby, the freedom to elude the force of normative and authoritative restrictions associated with this specific form of utilization. The 'practical contingency' of labour power with respect to the contexts of its deployment and reproduction is, to be sure, a bourgeois-liberal achievement, whose limited though valid meaning is illustrated strikingly by the demands of both the old and new women's movement for emancipation from the patriarchical family regime through free and equal access to the labour market. At any rate, the theoretical trivialization of this liberating labour market potentiality would lose sight of its emancipatory moment, and hence would deprive us of standards by which the relapse into 'pre-bourgeois' models of the utilization of labour power – whether in the direction of forced labour or 'community' subsistence labour within a rigid estate or family framework – could be judged as regressive. The looming obsolescence of the labour market thus also in a way threatens the substance of some formal freedoms, such as occupational choice and the freedom of coalition formation. To illustrate this point, it is only necessary to refer to the (partly reactionary, partly careless) mental gymnastics that occasionally arise today with respect to the possibilities of 'removing' portions of labour power from the labour market and placing them outside the market – be it by following the example of forced labour or by 'off-loading' them into the household and family spheres.

The indeterminacy of combination within the labour market, the contingent relation between worker and job, guarantees not only a measure of formal (though in fact always limited) freedom for suppliers of labour power, but also freedom of choice for those on the demand side of the labour market. This condition works to the advantage of the *efficiency* of the production process. The fact that employment relations are reduced to nothing more than that makes it possible to organize the selection process around the specific criterion of 'suitability'. It further allows this criterion to be applied in principle to an unrestricted number of workers and in each case to choose the most 'suitable' from among them. Other coordinating arrangements for labour power (for example, family systems, which are not based on universal access and the principle of functional specificity) could not provide such a high 'allocative efficiency', because either the horizon out of which choice is made is narrower and/or the criteria by which it is made are broader.

The following *constructive* formulation of the problem emerges from these considerations: If the labour market increasingly fails as a 'cover-all' principle for the coordination of labour power and jobs because of the three categories of deficiencies discussed above, through which kind of institutional mechanisms could the measure of formal freedom of choice of labour markets constituted by *contract* (as opposed to political coercion or normative obligations) be conserved or even extended, without an absolute decline in allocative efficiency?

We proceed on the assumption that this measure of freedom of choice can in future no longer be preserved or assured *in* the labour market and that, instead, a choice must be offered *between* different principles for allocating labour power and income, of which the labour market is only *one* principle. In the future, a growing proportion of the population in age-groups capable of productive work will have to be provided with an income by means of something other than the 'sale' of their labour power. Today, in view of declining rates of growth, continuing productivity increases and longer life expectancy, this assumption seems to be a safe one. The question that remains is simply whether, given the declining absorptive capacity of the labour market, the circle of those 'entitled' to participate (or, conversely, those to be excluded from productive work because of social criteria such as age, qualifications, sex, family status or place of residence) should be factually or even legally defined as belonging or not belonging to some 'legitimate' work-force, or whether it is not more desirable and practical to open up the boundary between the labour market and other forms of useful activity and income claims in such a way as to allow it to be traversed in both directions by *all,* according to their respective prevailing preferences.[17]

The latter kind of solution would attempt to simultaneously establish different principles of coordinating labour power and income and successfully maintain their coexistence. It would not abolish the labour market as an allocative principle, but compensate for its evident deficiencies by inserting *other* principles of utilizing and supporting labour power, without any one of them being elevated to the status of a 'normal' or 'dominant' model. This conception of a *horizontal combination of distinct organizing principles* supposes that the emerging labour market and employment problems cannot be solved all at once through some kind of global or total solution but, rather, only through a 'mixed structure' in which quite heterogeneous modes of expenditure and material subsistence of labour power of production and distribution exist simultaneously without interfering with each other.[18]

## Labour Market Policy Choices

We wish now to turn from the more normative level of the desirable 'institutional design' of the political economy of labour to the empirical level, and to consider which types of strategies for overcoming the current crisis of the labour market can be distinguished in present-day economic and socio-political debates.

The following typology offers a point of departure for considering a combination of possible solutions to the problem. Together these represent a 'policy-mix' of the form just mentioned. The basic ideas of present-day discussions about labour-related and socio-political strategies can be presented in a simple four-cell matrix, whose two axes distinguish, respectively, 'individual' and 'institutional' strategies, as well as the policy objectives of labour market 'inclusion' and 'exclusion' (see figure 2.2).

Cell 1 denotes 'conservative' or neo-liberal economic strategies for reviving and activating the market mechanism as a way of controlling labour power. This cell corresponds to current government policies in Britain and the USA, and partly to the recommendations of experts in the Federal Republic of Germany. These strategies amount to a reactivation of the pressure on

| Level of intervention | Strategies | |
|---|---|---|
| | *Inclusion in the labour market* | *Exclusion from the labour market* |
| Individual | 1 For example, strengthening the pressure on labour to adjust and be mobile | 2 Transfer payments for 'inactive' categories of persons |
| Institutional | 3 Industrial civil rights | 4 Institutional and material protection of work outside the labour market |

*Figure 2.2*

individual workers to conform by removing the 'anti-competitive' mechanisms within the labour market, including, if possible, the power of unions to control labour supply and state social policy. The theoretical and political protagonists of this strategy promise a reduction of labour costs and thereby a strengthening of the capacity and inclination for capital investment. From this, in turn, the goal of full employment, guided by the labour market, is supposed to be realized in the medium-term future. The most important objections to this strategy are directed, on the one hand, against the underlying assumption that the pressure exerted on employees (a quantitative and qualitative increase in labour supply, coupled with wage policy 'restraint') would in fact significantly increase business willingness to invest.[19] On the other hand, there are objections to the supposition that this market-mediated healing process could be pushed through *fast* enough so as not to incur the political resistance of trade unions or parties attached to welfare-state policies. These latter objections emphasize that, for democratic political systems at least, the patient is not likely to live long enough to experience the healing effect of the therapy prescribed, or that before successful healing takes place the doctor will likely be infected by the illness, and thus be unable to continue providing therapeutic treatment.[20]

Let us accept for a moment the premise of the neo-liberal doctrine that the principle of market allocation of labour power and earned income is only capable of functioning as long as the power potential of the supply side, its institutional status privileges and immunities from adaptation, do not go beyond a certain point. It still, however, seems unrealistic to assume that if this point has already been passed, it will be possible – within the framework of a political system based on some freedom of associative action and competition between political parties, and within the required time period – to reduce the power of those supplying labour and thus, in fact, to restore the market mechanism. This uncertainty arises because employees, who by definition have no alternative in market society but that of selling their labour power, are likely to struggle hard for the defence of political guarantees of status and social-policy protection against market coercion. Employees, or rather their organizations, would no longer be dependent on this hard-nosed defensive strategy if they could switch to a way of activating their labour power and securing income *outside* the market mechanism. In this respect, it could even be argued that the functional precondition of a smoothly functioning 'pure' labour market (i.e. one which is not blocked by power formations) is the presence of a non-market social sphere into which people can move freely and thereby work and live without being subjugated exclusively to the laws of the labour market. This point can be expressed in an inverse way: it is precisely the *totalization* of the labour market which makes this socio-economic principle of organization susceptible to market-distorting power formations, which in turn can be eliminated only under the most extreme forms of state violence employed against labour, as illustrated, for example, by the Pinochet regime in Chile.

Cell 2 represents the traditional social policy idea of releasing individuals from labour market participation because of specific individual characteristics and their legal eligibility for public transfers or insurance benefits. The most important criteria for determining eligibility for such benefits include the phases of life before and after an occupational career, as well as unemployment, disability and illness. There is certain paradox in this form of coping with the problem of work and income distribution. From the 'micro-perspective' of the (potential) benefit recipient, a *substitutive* relationship exists between earned income and its replacement (even if only partial and temporary) through transfer income. From the macro-perspective, by contrast, there is a *complementarity* between these two factors because, as is well known, the extent to which existing *unemployment* (or other instances of need) can be supported via transfer income depends on the volume of current *employment*. This means that, beyond a certain point, the failure of the labour market diminishes the flow of income to those who cannot participate in the labour market. The whole system functions on the assumption that either the demand for benefits from individuals outside the labour market is always relatively small in relation to the income generated through the labour market, or that 'high' levels of this demand will at best be a short-lived exception. In order to guarantee some degree of fiscal balance within the welfare state and social security systems, the criteria of eligibility for transfer income or insurance benefits (e.g. age or medically certified illness) must be defined in 'objective' terms so as to prevent their deliberate actualization by recipients. Moreover, negative incentives are usually built into the social security available to those not participating actively in the labour market.

These negative incentives (benefits lower than earnings, means-tests, contributions to services through individual fees, etc.) are supposed to minimize the incidence and length of demands on the welfare state and thereby motivate individuals to work. They are meant to guarantee that the volume of transfer payment claims – which must be met by public or para-fiscal means – never assumes an order of magnitude which would result in the feared downward spiral (of shrinking employment, consequent increases in financial and insurance costs, whose imposition upon employers and employees leads to a further decline in employment, and so on). In short, the viability of the social security arrangements depends on the relative stability of the labour market. The risks and needs generated by the latter can only be compensated by social security arrangements as long as they remain limited in number and duration.

A further characteristic of the socio-political strategy of individual exemption is that it solves only one of the two problems that a *functioning* labour market would solve – that of the distribution of income – but not that of the allocation of labour power. This may seem unproblematic since (according to cultural definitions and conventions) minors, pensioners, the sick and unemployed either cannot or should not or may not 'work' in any case. Consequently, the problem of providing 'work' to those who are not employed does not arise. The situation would be different, however, in the case of a statutory or contractual *reduction of work time*, the possibility and desirability of which has recently become a central issue in labour market policy debates. In the event of a shortening of the average effective working week to, say, thirty-five hours, it is plausible to assume that the portions of time removed from the sphere of work would not be transferred exclusively to the regeneration of workers' capacity to work. In this case, the question would arise as to which criteria and standards of rationality should be applied to the use of those portions of lifetime which are not absorbed by employment and the necessities of keeping one's self employable. The established system of social security has no answer to this question. A response to it could only be found in policies based on the use of free time, which are at present only in their infancy.

The basic idea of the strategies represented in cell 3 emerge out of this dilemma confronting the strategy of individual exemption: that a not insignificant (and, in the near future, perhaps greatly increased) portion of total social labour power is being 'absorbed' neither into the labour market nor into institutionally recognized and regulated spheres outside the labour market. These strategies depicted in cell 3 can be summarized as the *institutional* reform of the labour market. Their substance is the gradual and limited 'constitutionalization' of employment relations, whose realization, quality and duration are subject increasingly to norms and claims that result neither from the private decisions of individual parties to labour contracts nor from collective bargaining agreements but, instead, from publicly regulated 'labour policy' and the 'industrial citizen rights' it confers. This highly ambivalent strategy, discussed under the rubric of 'juridification' (*Verrechtlichung*),[21] shows that, in the Federal Republic of Germany at least, its important components are the legal establishment of rights of employees to representation and negotiation (through factory and staff councils) *vis-à-vis* management. This strategy also includes the welfare-state goal of securing full employment through state economic policy, all of the legislation concerned with industrial safety and protection against unfair dismissal, the 'right to work' (whose legal consequences remain unclear),[22] the political programme of 'humanizing work', and so on. Through these policies and programmes, state power assumes a certain measure of responsibility for (a) creating a 'sufficient' number of employment opportunities, as well as (b) ensuring that the utilization of labour power takes place *within* the framework of existing employment relations, and in accordance with technical, organizational and social conditions that prevent the premature and/or massive removal of labour power from the production process, as well as help secure peaceful class relations.

The limits of such attempts to politically and legally transform contractual labour market relations through the guarantee of the basic status rights of 'industrial citizenship' are, however, readily self-evident. They derive from the fact that the crucial precondition for making all of these labour-related status rights effective (private investment and the consequent decision to actually employ workers) is ignored by the legal reform of industrial relations; this precondition can only be *presupposed* as the spontaneous result of market processes. Because of this, the problem of publicly securing and creating employment opportunities is reduced to a problem of acceptance: within the framework of their *own* strategic market calculations, investors must either tolerate certain limitations upon their freedom of personnel management or recognize that state policy initiatives work to their own advantage, and are, therefore, worth complying with positively. Conversely, the greater the consequent burdens of state policies – which are no longer modifiable by contract since they are established by legal regulation – the more will investors react hesitantly to investment opportunities in the market. At least, a strong tendency toward capital-intensive 'jobless-growth' strategies will become manifest. The safer and more institutionally protected employment is made for employees, the less attractive it will become for investors to employ still more workers. The advantages for the employed thus forms risks for employment, because of the rational market strategies of investors and employers.[23]

## The Informal Sector

The three basic alternative strategies discussed so far are evidently similar in that, considered together, they are capable of providing solutions to the structural problem of allocating labour power and income within more-or-less narrow and uncertain limits, the violation of which leads to 'explosive' or 'depressive' developments. Consequently, consideration must be given to the possibility and probability of a complex combination of partial solutions – a combination in which the relative and limited capacity of each of the three strategies is utilized without at the same time lapsing into 'overdoses'. The *possibility* of such a combination obviously depends on whether the relationship between the development of production and the development of productivity actually leads to a volume of employment which can, in turn, serve as an adequate basis for this 'patchwork' strategy. The *probability* of actually realizing this strategy clearly depends on whether the relationships between governments, parties and trade unions exhibit negotiation mechanisms and institutions of social exchange, with the aid of which 'insufficiently complex' (monistic or doctrinaire) solutions can be avoided. Currently, there is little reason to expect an optimistic response to either of these questions concerning the possibility and probability of a 'policy-mix' adequate to the problem. This could change, however, to the extent that it becomes possible to rely more heavily upon a fourth strategic option (cell 4).

This option refers to the institutional construction and provision of forms of activity outside the labour market. These perform the function of coordinating labour power with concrete labour tasks, as well as partly furnishing labour itself with means of subsistence not derived from buying and selling labour power. In the past, the most important of these non-market arrangements included work performed in the household, and self-employed entrepreneurial economic activity. Household labour differs from wage labour in that it is normatively regulated, highly immobile and lacks a quantitive equivalence between work performed and income obtained. Self-employed economic activity also differs from wage labour in that (among other things) it is oriented to the demand for goods and services (and not to demand for labour power), and is compensated not through contractual wages but, rather, through residual profit. No detailed discussion is required to establish the normative and empirical reasons why these two important institutions – which in bourgeois society have always functioned as partial solutions to the allocative problem discussed in this essay – are nowadays incapable of relieving the over-worked organizing principle of the labour market. The 'employee society' has largely rendered obsolete the economic preconditions, as well the culturally sanctioned motives, for economic independence and activities performed within private households. It must, therefore, be asked whether functional equivalents of the household and independent entrepreneurial activity can be identified or constructed, and whose development and promotion could positively reduce the scale of a problem which can no longer be dealt with adequately through the labour market and its complementary socio-political institutions.

This point can be explained by briefly considering some important data and trends within the European Economic Community from 1960 to 1975.[24] During this period, the percentage of the civilian working population compared to the total population decreased on average by 2.6 per cent to 40.6 per cent. This is explained by the extension of the period of formal schooling, as well as by increased life expectancy and earlier retirement. The percentage of the work-force engaged in dependent employment rose in all EEC countries. The only exception was Britain, where the percentage (the highest in the EEC) decreased from 92.6 to 92.2 per cent; elsewhere, the level was between 80 and 86 per cent, except in the lowest cases of Ireland (70.8 per cent) and Italy (72.4 per cent). At the same time, there has been a low level, and persistent decline, of the percentage of self-employed in the total work-force. During the same period, moreover, the proportion of women who were employed increased in almost every EEC country; this trend was especially evident among married women, which permits the conclusion that there is a declining quantitative 'absorption potential' of the household and family spheres.

Every attempt to reconstruct or invent modes of work corresponding with the forms of activity of household labour or self-employment encounters a series of difficulties. A 'complete' solution to the problems which are indeed solved by the labour market, namely the utilization of labour power and its provision with means of subsistence, is only evident in the case of the independent entrepreneur (the agrarian village subsistence economy, which is only marginally incorporated into the commodity economy, can be ignored here). In the case of household labour, by contrast, we have a form of work which indeed specifies tasks for labour power, but which does not directly supply that labour power with its means of subsistence. Rather, these provisions are normally secured through the income earned by household members participating in the labour market.

This raises a question: How is the direct distribution of material means of subsistence and services (procured monetarily or non-monetarily) to such forms of productive and useful activity that we find in the private household to be actually organized? This is rather pertinent because as a rule it cannot be assumed that self-employment outside the labour market, especially in 'alternative enterprises', is capable of a level of productivity which permits successful competition with 'normal enterprises'. This is because alternative enterprises typically suffer from limited capital and/or a modest allocative efficiency of its personnel. Where such difficulties are not to be found within the 'informal sector', their absence can normally be explained by (a combination of) three factors: (i) the subsidizing of goods and services offered in the market through a sub-cultural clientele willing and able to pay 'sympathy prices' (for example politically oriented small publishers, ethnic restaurants and artisanal enterprises); (ii) an enforced or ideologically justified reduction of the material level of reproduction to a level far below normal civilized standards (evident, for example, among 'informal' junk dealers and rural communes); and (iii) illegal business practices, such as procuring money and materials through theft, the extensive use of child labour or illicit labour, including the associated practices of intimidation and extortion, tax fraud, the receipt of stolen goods, drug-dealing, and so on. The 'entrepreneurial' variant of the 'new autonomy' can, therefore, be approximated only in so far as the serious risks associated with these three factors are accepted, or when transfer payments provided through the framework of state social policy (see cell 2) are tapped successfully (and mostly illegally, for example through a combination of unemployment benefits with income derived from 'black' labour) as a source of support.[25] The 'common consciousness' of the 'employee society' usually reacts to these symptoms by objecting to 'drop-outs' who take advantage of the generosity of the welfare state in a parasitic manner.[26]

By contrast, the variants of informal labour oriented to the model of household labour (rather than to that of the independent small entrepreneur) make claims to a thoroughly legal and institutional, and not simply individual, basis of support. Included here are forms of assistance, care, counselling and nursing which are located *between* the sphere of domestic 'self-provision' (which has frequently become inadequate or is completely absent) and that of state or communal assistance. The initiators of such expanded 'household labour' organized on the basis of self-help rely on the compelling argument that they can offer psycho-social services much more efficiently and effectively than the political-administrative agencies which are (or at least should be) institutionally responsible for these services. From this argument is derived an often justified claim to institutional support from the public purse. Such self-help initiatives see themselves 'as decentralized, accessible and visible alternatives to processing problems in special areas of social policy', and they rely upon the 'problem-solving competence of those cooperatively involved in the family, neighbourhood and city district'.[27]

## The Formalization of Informal Activity?

There are three reasons why both the 'quasi-entrepreneurial' and the 'quasi-household' variants of informal, non-market and non-contractual labour appear to be a promising, indeed necessary, object of efforts to organizationally and materially encourage and develop the informal sector, that is, to formalize it in the shape of 'new forms of self-employment' and 'new household-centred work'. The first of these reasons is related to the obviously increasing objective possibility and subjective willingness of many people to engage in forms of activity that differ markedly from the normal model of wage-dependent work. This development, whose extent and socio-structural distribution remain largely unresearched, may be the result of increasing scepticism, particularly among the younger generation, regarding the prospects, satisfactions and rewards offered by work in the labour market, as well as the product of cultural transformations ('changes in values'). A shrinking portion of the population is bound temporally and motivationally to the model of the labour market. This fact alone creates space for orientations other than those of a successful career and a secure income. There consequently emerges a 'supply pressure' on 'informal' activities, a pressure which is often linked to political motives and to an interest in the realization of new, 'alternative' forms of life.[28] This supply pressure is today no doubt constrained by the high degree of economic and legal uncertainty, and its further development is impeded by the risks that would accompany the shift (which individuals frequently sense to be irreversible) to the sphere of informal activities.

The development of an analogous 'demand pressure' for services and (certain) goods that can be produced more effectively and/or cheaply through informal activities constitutes a second reason for its importance. One example is provided by the structurally induced growth of demand for psycho-social services, which cannot be provided for by the relatively declining 'self-help capacity' of conventional household units (nuclear families and, increasingly, single people). Other examples include the area of housing construction, repair and services activities, as well as the field of aesthetic production and entertainment. In each case, there is a yawning gap between the capacity of households to care for themselves and the price-level or quality offered by the market; this gap is no longer filled by traditional forms of neighbourly and familial assistance and their corresponding nets of 'connections' and it, therefore, becomes increasingly visible as an unsatisfied sphere of demand.

A third reason in support of our thesis that there are favourable structural preconditions for 'formalizing the informal sector' is the persuasive labour market policy argument that it is becoming increasingly improbable that 'full employment' can be re-established and maintained under politically and economically realistic conditions. As a direct consequence of this condition, state labour market and employment policies have focused upon the *supply* side of the labour market or, more precisely, upon reducing the volume of supply appearing in the labour market. In this situation, every possibility of relieving the labour market from an increasingly chronic over-supply of labour power must be welcomed. The question which remains, however, is whether the reduction of supply is economically and politically discriminatory, and results in deportation, deprivation of rights and impoverishment or whether, instead, it preserves the formal self-determination and freedom of choice in the labour market, even possibly augmenting them. It is likely that the less there are material and legal sacrifices associated with opting out of participation in the labour market, the more policies designed for relieving its supply problems will have quantitatively significant effects. This, in turn, presupposes that the sphere of 'informal' labour is economically and organizationally developed, and revalorized as an institutionally recognized 'normal case' of useful activity, which can be freely chosen and then again given up, just as is the case within the labour market.

If considered together, these three arguments concerning the supply and demand for forms of activity external to the (private and public) labour markets and labour market policy considerations, prompt a series of complementary objections. These deserve attention in so far as they indicate the likely political resistance to the realization of the above proposals. First, there is the sceptical question concerning the nature, intensity, durability and controllability of the *motives* that regulate the supply of self-organized, non-market activity. The suspicion discernible in this question – that the 'ideological-moral energy' (Scharpf) on which these motives could feed is not sufficiently available in societies of our type – can of course be invalidated neither axiomatically nor through empirical 'snapshots' but, ultimately, only in the course of controlled socio-political experiments. That such experimentation could be successful is suggested by the negative observation that the 'ideological-moral energy' of the market economy – an energy which leads workers to work and employers to act entrepreneurially – is itself showing symptoms of exhaustion. It is this widespread motivational rejection of life-long dependence upon labour for income in the market which prompts the search for alternatives and solidaristic 'sources of energy' for social labour. The question which then remains is whether 'institutionalization' accompanied by a minimum of formal responsibilities, controls and demands would hamper rather than enhance the capacity for solidaristic, self-organized activity, given that such institutionalization would stimulate fears of being co-opted and smothered.

As far as the demand or *need* for non-market, self-organized services is concerned, objections directed at the quality, and especially the uniformity and intensity, of the care of clients must

be reckoned with. Deficiencies arising from the deprofessionaliz-
ation or debureaucratization of caring services are at least
conceivable. The force of this kind of objection must, however, at
the very least be assessed with reference to the yawning qualitative
and quantitative gaps in the care presently provided by
professional-bureaucratic forms of services.

Finally, it can be anticipated that there will be objections to the
suitability of institutionalized non-market forms of activity for
relieving pressure upon the supply side of the labour market and
accommodating the interests of public labour market policy.
These objections derive from sectional and status groups –
especially the independent middle stratum of professionals, as well
as trade unions representing public sector employees – and are
directed against the possibility of a competition of supply
developing, a possibility which must be resisted in the interests of
not only their clients.[29]

As serious as these (and the previously mentioned) objections
may be for a realistic assessment of the chances of politically
institutionalizing 'informal' types of activity, they can be reduced
analytically to the problem of a quantitatively and, above all,
qualitatively adequate definition of domains of non-market and
self-organized activities. Even a serious and realistic appraisal of
these objections reveals a paradox of the present situation. There
exists supply as well as demand, and there are over-riding
political-administrative interests concerned to coordinate supply
and demand (for reasons of employment policy, the quality of
social services and fiscal prudence), and yet there are no accepted
*forms* of non-market activity through which these needs and
interests could be accommodated. The problem is that these forms
would have to be capable of being freely accepted or rejected, that
is, entered into neither compulsorily nor under pressure from
economic necessity. Furthermore, a managerial method of *programming* goals and conditions of activity would have to be
designed. This programming could not be left to public or private
'employers' but would, instead, have to synthesize elements of the
normative obligations typical of household labour with quasi-
'entrepreneurial' independence and 'autonomy'. The legal design
of the programming and remuneration of informal activity could
be patterned (among other ways) on the fiscal and legal models of
individual, institutional or project-related support (such as

scholarships, subsidies, granting of tax preferences to charities, etc.) which could be justified politically on the grounds of 'clearing the labour market' or 'unburdening the state'.[30] A final problem associated with identifying and establishing such institutional forms is that activity outside the labour market – as well as outside the traditionally understood spheres of 'household labour' and 'self-employment' – would need to be compensated on the basis of claims whose nature and amount could neither be interpreted as 'prices' for services performed nor as transfers of the social-welfare type.

These forms of social labour, which are characterized by freedom of entry and exit, by considerable autonomy in the programming of activity, as well as by non-discriminatory and legally guaranteed rights to income, could be built upon more traditional forms of activity that we find in cooperatives and voluntary associations. Naturally, a formal recognition and protection of the informal sector is no more a panacea than the other three strategies considered earlier in this essay. Furthermore, it has been quite beyond the scope of the considerations presented here to forecast a definite course of development of the labour market, even on the basis of certain normative criteria. The most that can be said about the 'future of the labour market' is summarized in the negative thesis: the labour market can no longer be expected to continue performing the role that it formerly did during the post-war decades. This means, to speak positively, that the basic socio-economic problem of 'allocating the mechanisms of allocation' is once again becoming topical and that there is, therefore, a chance of supplementing and expanding the existing repertoire of allocative mechanisms by institutionalizing 'informal' modes of useful activity.

# 3

# Three Perspectives on the Problem of Unemployment

In the Federal Republic of Germany, there is a good deal of disagreement among leading political groups, economic decision makers and scientific experts concerning both the future of the labour market and the role of labour in society in general. This disagreement bears on three relevant points: (i) the prognosis of likely future *development;* (ii) the *policy* most suited to this development; and (iii) the *criteria* and *objectives* which determine whether, in fact, a development can be judged as positive or, indeed, desirable.

In this discussion, the first of these three points is the least controversial. Quite a number of contemporary publications in the Federal Republic feature the famous graph, developed in 1982 by the Federal Labour Agency's Institute for Labour Market and Vocational Research, which depicts labour market trends for the years 1965 to 2000. This graph provides clear enough proof: even on the basis of quite unrealistic economic assumptions (an average annual real growth of 4–5 per cent in the 1980s) and equally unrealistic, as well as hardly desirable political circumstances (a drastic reduction in the number of immigrant workers), a situation of full employment could not be achieved until 1995 at the earliest. Until that time, the graph suggests, we will have to learn to cope with (increasing) mass unemployment as a permanent way of life. Simple mathematical calculations indicate that the systems of social security (and some areas of public policy) will simply collapse under the effects of such a level of unemployment. Assumptions and expectations about a similar fate for the system

Translated by John Keane. This is a slightly revised version of 'Perspektiven auf die Zukunft des Arbeitsmarktes', *Merkur,* 5 (1983), 489–504.

of political institutions and certain elements of the political culture seem hardly less plausible. Given the overwhelming convincing power of the economic, financial and demographic data and projections, differences of response to the question, What will happen if nothing happens?, are relatively minor and generally of a cosmetic kind.

These differences of opinion become more marked, however, when the following two questions are asked: How can full employment be re-established? Is full employment really desirable? It is interesting to note that the disagreements which arise out of these questions cut across the politico-economic blocs of both the political party system and the labour market. Questions about the political feasibility and desirability of a full employment market economy clearly touch on the foundations of the social order – to a degree unprecedented in the Federal Republic since the early fifties. They also bear on the two-sided allocation problem with which all societies have to grapple: the distribution of human labour power to work tasks, and the distribution of the outcome of this labour (monetary income, as well as the goods and services which it can buy) to workers and their household members. In what follows, I will attempt to systematize the various intellectual and political responses to this two-sided allocation problem, as well as to analyse the resulting difficulties which confront each approach. The keywords 'orthodoxy', 'realism' and 'third way' will facilitate this, although they serve only as preliminary delineations of the respective positions.

## Orthodoxy

'Orthodoxy' is an apt description of that position which embraces the proven wisdom of the past, judging this knowledge to be generally capable of indicating paths leading to the future, even under exceptional circumstances of crisis. From a philosophical point of view, any orthodoxy is founded on the confident assumption that one can rely upon the accumulated experience and reference knowledge of the past or at any rate that there is no equivalent substitute. This self-confidence feeds upon simple phrases and suggestive imagery. Consider the following example:

'Today's profits are tomorrow's investments are the jobs of the future' (Helmut Schmidt). Such stock phrases not only function as convenient interpretations of the past; they also stimulate optimistic expectations about the future. They stabilize the hegemonic political order and insulate it against doubts or challenges. They construct a disciplined perception of what is normal and what can be expected. Finally, these kinds of phrases reinforce the self-confidence of elites and the patience of non-elites. Even though there may be many doubts about the empirical validity of what is considered normal, it remains difficult to synthesize these doubts into a coherent image of normality of a *different* kind. Orthodoxies thus acquire a counter-factual validity immune to the facts, to the point where they can become zealously blinded to all consequences, a disposition which Max Weber called an 'ethics of conviction' (*Gesinnungsethik*).

Serious objections can be raised today against the orthodoxy associated with Schmidt's postulated correlation between profits, investments and jobs. These objections can be quickly enumerated and corroborated by studying the pages of any of the better daily newspapers, and by drawing up a list of common questions. First of all, concerning those 'profits of today', the following queries arise: Are these profits really being generated? If not, how can they be supported politically – through a Keynesian strategy or by supplying a 'favourable framework' for investors? In both cases, it must be asked: Are governments successful in obtaining a political mandate for themselves, and for how long? What happens if the 'upturn' in economic growth comes, but turns out to have no bearing on employment levels, taking place, as it were, behind the backs of the working (or rather non-working) population? Then, concerning 'tomorrow's investments': Will they be real or financial investments, and abroad or at home? Are there real markets for these investments? Which quantities of investment can be expected in view of the rapidly growing capital productivity (micro-electronics)? Would not the large excess capacities which currently exist first have to be filled before additional investments can take place? Finally, about those 'jobs of the future', where could they possibly be created, and in which quantities? Will these investments not have a rationalizing effect by further eliminating jobs? While a really convincing theory of the secular stagnation of industrial growth probably does not presently exist, a careful and honest response to all these questions would make it clear that exactly this type of theory is needed today.

Another standard argument of economic and socio-political orthodoxy is that wages are too high and that 'everybody' (i.e. employees and the welfare state) is living beyond their means. To address this problem would be to generate full employment as a logical consequence. 'If someone sells oranges at too high a price,' remarked an opinion pollster, turned political economist, recently, 'and cannot find any buyers as a result, it would seem strange to maintain that oranges had run out.' From this point of view, the claim that there are too few jobs would seem equally bizarre. It is easy to detect the error implicit in this example of the high-priced oranges. Whilst the production and marketing of oranges can perfectly well be synchronized with expected demand (which can in turn be adjusted through the price mechanism), this is not so for the supply side of labour markets. The number of workers in search of employment is not the result of calculations about the 'saleability' of available labour power in the market. As most economists are well aware, there is 'no supply function of labour power that could be determined on the basis of utility calculations of workers alone' (R. Hickel). In other words, workers in a capitalist society do not have the option *not* to sell their labour power, and neither do they have the option of living on an income that results from a market-clearing price. This means, contrary to the market-clearing equilibrium price of commodities, that there is not one definite equilibrium wage but three (usually different) wage equilibria. This is because, first, a wage is in equilibrium if it can satisfy all those needs of households which are regarded as socially necessary and legitimate. Equilibrium exists, secondly, if all workers find employment and, thirdly, if the sum of the output of 'wage goods' is equivalent to the total wage income generated by the economy. The point is, however, that there is no *global* equilibrium between these partial equilibria. Any reference to *the* equilibrium wage therefore verges on demagogy.

In almost every capitalist country, economic indicators covering the period 1968–79 confirm the conclusion that capital has fared worse in the struggle over distribution. This development may be welcomed (as delaying an otherwise imminent under-consumption crisis) or regretted (as a cause of the present-day crisis of under-accumulation). Nevertheless, no therapy follows from this diagnosis. It is hardly possible to adopt Margaret Thatcher's anti-union measures which, in any case, have so far not resulted in a single success at the level of employment. The fact that the politico-economic orthodoxy expresses disapproval of the fact that workers' organizations (when and where they *can*) attempt to squeeze out as many 'compensations' as possible in return for the 'negative utility' of labour performed is, in itself, quite astonishing. For this kind of behaviour conforms, after all, not only to the liberal doctrine of the egoistic-rational maximization of utilities but also, in particular, to the classical economic view of labour as a 'grief', as the complete opposite of 'amusement' (A. Marshall). The suggested therapy of 'wage cuts' is also unconvincing, for the simple reason that the distributive gains of labour against capital since the late 1960s have undoubtedly been, for labour, a victorious battle in a war which it has not *won*. It is in fact capital, which is presently reconquering its lost political and economic territory, which is about to win that war over distribution.

The orthodox position utilizes similar arguments to criticize the alleged hypertrophies of the welfare state, which is said to be in need of restriction or even progressive dismantlement. In alarmist tones, neo-liberal policy makers demand that the wheel of the welfare state must be stopped. If this were in fact to be achieved, the results would be highly ambiguous. Economically speaking, this dismantling of the welfare state would abolish a buffer which functions as a demand stabilizer. Politically speaking, the abolition of the welfare state would eliminate a mechanism which has served to secure social peace and stability in the Federal Republic and elsewhere. It would be an experiment whose costs would be extremely high, and whose outcomes would be quite uncertain.

The orthodox position – which seeks a restoration of full employment as soon as possible, and by the drastic reinvigoration of market mechanisms if necessary – is also inspired by claims concerning possible product innovations and unsatisfied needs for goods and services. The claim is that there exists a virtually unlimited growth potential for marketable goods and services. Certainly no sceptic is likely to counter this view with a theory of the *global* exhaustion of demand for industrial goods. It can nevertheless be asked, with reference to West European markets, What is to be produced and marketed? The effects of demand saturation cannot be overlooked in this context. They tend to reduce the absorption capacity of the market to the level of a demand for replacements. Moreover, durable consumer goods are more and more imported from Third World and semi-developed countries where they can be produced, in the long run, at lower costs. Further saturation effects emanate from phenomena described by Fred Hirsch as the 'social limits to growth'. The use-value of many goods declines the more they are used commonly: the fewer cars on the roads, for example, the greater the use-value of one's own car. As long as the present income distribution remains intact – making it more egalitarian no doubt runs completely counter to the premises of orthodox political economy – new markets can be opened up neither by supplying new social strata with existing products nor by stimulating consumption among existing consumer groups. New markets could be achieved only with predominantly *new* products. In order to achieve anything like that stimulation effect upon growth and employment (as was the case in the past, for instance, with automobiles, synthetic fibres and other substances, as well as television and other entertainment electronics), new products would nowadays have to display some rather unlikely overall properties. Namely, they would have to be capable of mass consumption, their production would need to be *both* labour-intensive and capital-intensive, while neither their raw materials nor their use or disposal could legitimately give rise to further economic, health or ecological problems.

Thinking up possible products which would satisfy all these economic and use-value criteria is an entertaining party game. More often than not, this kind of game ends with its participants giving up, simply because, aside from a few technological utopias (individual air travel, TV-telephones, etc.) they cannot think of anything that would not violate the raw materials or ecology criteria (which would be the case with goods such as disposable textiles or furniture), and whose production would, at the same time, allow for high rates of capital absorption (a condition that is absent, for instance, in the production of long-lasting cars and almost all services). It is hard to imagine new industrial products which are designed for mass consumption, and which could trigger a future wave of growth and employment.

This conclusion is confirmed indirectly by the fact that today the growing sectors of industrial production, as well as those considered to have a high growth potential, are predominantly those in which purchasing decisions do not rest with the consumer, but are in the hands of state policy makers. Markets for new products are unlikely to be created by industrial enterprises researching the needs of individual consumer-households and offering them the corresponding products. New products are developing primarily through state planning and guarantees for (the biggest portions of) development costs and product sales. The armaments industry probably comes closest to this 'industrial utopia of an economy without customers' (K. Novy). But the same process, interestingly, is evident in those politically created 'markets' in areas of infrastructural investment, such as transport, new communictions media and, especially, energy. The shared characteristic of these politically guaranteed markets for industrial products – which may also include products geared to environmental protection, hospitals, schools and the police – is that (not unlike the situation in many markets for agricultural products) they seek to reduce the risk of producers' sales being jeopardized by consumers becoming saturated or desiring changes in existing patterns of consumption. A further advantage of this state investment and state-sanctioned 'authoritative consumption' is that markets for private complementary goods (e.g. highway construction equipment, heating and reception devices in energy and communication systems) are often opened up at the same time.

On the other hand, however, a characteristic feature of these 'markets' is that state policies will from here on have to assume responsibility for the *positive* use-value (as well as harmlessness) of the products and systems of an increasingly socialized, compulsory consumption of civilian (and other) technologies and investments. The 'politicization of industrial production' (H. Kitschelt) is a two-sided process. On the one hand, there is the desire of stagnating industries to obtain politically guaranteed sales while, on the other are the protest politics of new social movements who form themselves into an 'anti-productivist' alliance in defence of humane, peaceful, ecological and other values. Industry's call for politically secured markets is certainly pressing enough. According to the 1982 annual report of the Confederation of German Industry (BDI): 'Where the market is incapable of resolving questions about acceptance – such as can be the case with large-scale technological projects – it must be up to the politicians to make the decision, and not to shirk their political responsibility by postponing the decision or foisting it on to courts or experts.' No lesser sense of urgency is displayed in the reactions triggered so far by the strategy of quasi-public reindustrialization. This urgency is expressed in the widespread recent protests against 'administrative reindustrialization' projects, whether in the form of energy (nuclear reactors), transportation (airports, inner-city highways, canals) or mass communications and the mass surveillance of citizens made possible by new communication and information technologies. These reactions have definitely altered the internal balance of power in the Federal Republic and, in this respect, they have certainly rendered questionable the orthodox supposition that industrial markets are virtually inexhaustible in their potential.

The assumption that growth and full employment are unquestionable values in themselves or, at least, indispensable conditions of progress, completes the orthodox vision of a path of development leading into an industrial future. I do not wish to enter here into a normative discussion of this particular assumption. It is probably an empirical fact that a large majority of German *citizens* would prefer growth and full employment rather than their opposite, although this is not likely to play an important role. Rather, the decisive question is, What guarantee, if any, is there that the strategically relevant *collective* actors – governments, employers, unions – do indeed perceive the 'collective goods' of growth and full employment as their prime objectives and, on the basis of such consensus, are prepared to undertake 'joint action' that would lead to a new phase of industrial growth? Again, the evidence on this point is ambiguous. A growth and full employment priority is perhaps most unequivocally endorsed within the state apparatus because, in order to satisfy the state's own financial, economic and political interests, state policy makers must address problems of growth and employment. Of course, the same financial and economic interests of the state itself are simultaneously opposed to an active employment policy that would have to be implemented *within* the public sector. On the employers' side, it is true that there is a rational interest in growth. Employers' interest in full employment is, however, at best a conditional one, especially since, in spite of many predictions, mass unemployment has so far not sparked off any organized socio-political conflicts endangering capital, and is unlikely to do so in the future. No doubt, employers' associations often publicly express an interest in reducing the high rate of youth unemployment, which they fear will turn considerable proportions of entire age-groups into permanently unemployable 'drop-outs' from society. Otherwise, employers are openly advantaged (and little disadvantaged) by one of the *causes* of unemployment (namely, the introduction of labour-saving innovations), as well as by its continued existence. For employers can externalize the social costs of unemployment almost completely, by unloading these costs on to the unemployed and other third parties.

While this situation could be changed only by means of costly (and therefore at this stage hardly realizable) reforms of the ways in which the welfare state is financed, the advantages that employers can and do derive from unemployment are enormous. At the plant level, employees' anticipation of the possibility of being laid off results in a marked improvement in rates of sick leave, work discipline and of personnel turnover. At the level of wage negotiations, wage increases have clearly shown a downward trend and, as a rule, are presently below the rate of inflation; this means that any possible increases in labour productivity can accrue to employers without additional (wage) costs. In this connection, finally, the political arena is likely to be the most decisive for employers, given that a high rate of unemployment exerts a continuously strong pressure on any government to pursue policies in accordance with its own financial and electoral interests, policies which benefit the 'investment capacity of capital' and thus lend at least some credence to the goal of generating new jobs. Overall, then, these advantages of unemployment to employers make it seem rather improbable that there is any effective positive interest in full employment among the representative economic associations of capital.

The position of the trade unions appears to be quite different and entirely unequivocal. Is it not the case that their most basic interest is in a strong demand for labour power and high growth rates, simply because it is upon these factors that any future scope for negotiations over distribution depends? To answer this question positively does not mean *a priori* that unions have also developed (or even could develop) the institutional structures to serve as effective 'vehicles' for these interests. In fact, the opposite is suggested by the extraordinary difficulties which have accompanied trade union attempts to formulate a unified plan for generating employment by reducing work-time. Quite apart from whether a reduction in work-time *would* actually lead to additional employment, it would be obtainable only at the cost of a (relative) wage cut offered by the unions. This means that individual employees would have to sacrifice a proportion of their present (or future) income in order to extend their (uncertain) help to an indefinite number of the (presently or future) unemployed.

This sacrifice requires more than 'solidarity' (which in itself is difficult enough to achieve); it requires altruism, and that is something for which interest associations, generally speaking, are very poorly suited. This is especially true of trade unions, because in each individual member's case the personal gain which could be derived from this sacrifice of income (possibly a few additional hours of free time per week) is not equally attractive for everyone at the already high level of 'leisure time allowance' that has been achieved. There is an additional reason: the prospective beneficiaries of this sacrifice of income – the unemployed – do not themselves (or only nominally) belong to the very trade union organization that would be required to commit its members to additional wage sacrifices (and at precisely a time when real wages are shrinking in any case). For these reasons it appears unlikely that, caught in this difficult strategic situation, the unions have the institutional structures and necessary political power as well as the interest to bring about full employment.

Given these difficulties, could it not be that the orthodox view of industrial society (an orthodoxy oriented towards the core values of growth and full employment) is deluding itself about the institutional foundations of those allies on which it would have to rely for the realization of its ideas? If this is indeed the case, then the orthodox view would be left with little more than the experiences and proven theories of the past and, possibly, a blind confidence in their future validity. It would, however, lack the economic, technological, political, moral and institutional conditions and resources necessary for the projection of this past into the future.

## Realism

Such suspicions, at any rate, are raised by the 'realist' opponents of orthodoxy, who appear to be quickly gaining ground, particularly in both major parties of the Federal Republic of Germany – the CDU and the SPD. I am using the term 'realism' (without any positive evaluative overtones) to describe positions which soberly try to accept new facts, to discard old interpretations, hopes and expectations, and to acquire a fundamentally new orientation whenever 'reality' appears to demand it. In contrast to the orthodox position, the realist approach is concerned with questions about socio-political values, and the criteria of progress. 'Realists' think in terms of discontinuities and breaks, and they give little credit to supposedly timeless theories and principles.

What, then, is the verdict of the realistic approach on the future of work and the labour market? In the first place, there is a general readiness to abandon a seemingly futile resistance to economic 'facts'. Consequently, it is suggested that state policy should cease aspiring to the impossible, such as political guarantees of (the restoration of) full employment. Whereas the premise that the state should actively secure full employment has been the supporting pillar of the 'mixed economy' and of 'modern capitalism' (A. Shonfield) on both sides of the Atlantic since the Second World War, it is now admitted and even proclaimed by the 'realists' that full employment can no longer be guaranteed politically. This is not only because the Keynesian instruments have become blunt, but also because there are no *alternative* ways of achieving this goal. The new realism is just as unsympathetic as the old orthodoxy to the trade unions' struggle for wages and more employment, although their respective motivations are quite different. The orthodox position fears that trade union power might block the path leading back to full employment, whereas the realists argue that this path does not exist anyway, and that this insight cannot be heeded generally until the unions are forced to overcome their false notion of a well-managed growth and full-employment version of capitalism. Similar criticisms of the illusory 'productivism' of the labour movement can be heard from left groupings – including from within the non-union faction of the Social Democratic Party.

The labour market policies of the realist approach contrast sharply with the orthodox position. Whereas the latter aims at an *integration* of the unemployed into an at least stable army of employed (however this may be brought about), the realist position thinks more in terms of *excluding* labour from the market, that is, reducing that part of the population which is in fact (or would like to be) gainfully employed. The favoured candidates to be discarded from the ranks of the supply side of the labour market are well known. First in line are immigrants, followed by women (particularly married women workers), older workers and young people. A 'flexible' reduction of the paid working time of the latter three groups is also envisaged.

There is some sociological realism in this strategy, in so far as it interprets the present stage of society's development (in the words of the prominent CDU politician, Späth) as a 'transition phase', during which 'industrial society will have to mature into a post-industrial information society'. The obvious follow-up question about what is to happen to this 'rejected' labour power, and how it is to be secured economically and socially, receive a number of different responses. The simplest solution would be to let the problem solve itself and, since necessity is the mother of invention, to hope that people will practise the 'art of coping' (Späth). In so doing, they would at the same time help institutions over a 'rough period'. 'The freedom of action which people create for themselves by way of alternatives and the shadow economy provides the institutions with additional time for self-transformation and self-adaptation,' as another well-known CDU thinker, Kurt Biedenkopf, has put it.

Another tendency recommends that family policy provide, so to speak, the redundancy payments to (female) labour power withdrawn from circulation – payments to be made if not exactly in money then in the symbolic currency of 'social recognition'. The foundation of this tendency is clearly to be found in those Catholic groupings within the CDU that have a strong commitment to social policy. Thus, one reads in recent policy document of the Catholic Labour Movement (KAB) that it is necessary to redefine the overly 'narrow' understanding of work as gainful employment, and that all unpaid services rendered in education, care and nursing, as well as housework and the holding of honorary offices

D

should be recognized as 'meaningful' and 'socially useful' and, therefore, also worthy of inclusion in GNP calculations. This demand overlaps to a certain extent with a third variant, one which is concerned with the 'cost-saving' integration of 'rejected' labour power into state-organized social services. The most fervent exponent of this idea is the Berlin Senator for Social Affairs, Fink, and in this he is supported by Späth. According to them, 'it is possible to make up for the loss of teaching hours, to reach security planning targets ahead of time, to keep nursing costs within limits and to speed up environmental programmes with the help of the unemployed of the transitional period'. It is clear that this tendency is thinking of relatively unskilled, inferior and socially insecure auxiliary services which, in addition, may not even be entirely voluntary, and which are to be remunerated on a wage scale that permits further savings or staff cuts within the state sector. Among these trains of thought, which seem to originate from a mixture of 'black' and 'green' political motives, some blue-liberal patterns can also be detected, as for instance in Dahrendorf's discovery that individual self-development and 'freely chosen activity' (which is remunerated intrinsically, rather than through wages) are made possible by the 'disappearance of the working society'.

The problem of growing unemployment, however, will hardly be solved quite so cheaply. Quite apart from the fact that it seems cynical to simply portray the process of a blind and spontaneous 'dualization' of society (its division into job-holders and 'the superfluous' who must practise the 'art of coping') in such glowing terms, there are a number of facts which refute the 'realism' of the realists' calculations. First, and contrary to what might be supposed, low growth rates by no means lead 'automatically' to a drop in the proportion of the population which is gainfully employed (i.e. to a reduction of the sum of self-employed, salaried employees and unemployed workers as a percentage of the total population). As a statistical comparison of the OECD countries indicates, it is rather the countries with the *lowest* growth rates (Denmark, Sweden, the USA) which, in the seventies, experienced the most marked *positive* changes in their work-forces (i.e. in their shares of the formally employed, self-employed or unemployed in the total population). (The exception was Britain, where there was a slight reduction in the relative size of the work-force.) This is by no means puzzling: the less work is available and the more existing conditions of employment are threatened, the greater are the economic pressures on wages and, consequently, the fewer individuals and households there are who can afford – despite their ever worsening job prospects – to abandon, in part or in whole, their (intended) participation in the labour market. In this respect, any strategy of pushing 'superfluous' groups on the supply side of the labour market out of the market would have to deal not with spontaneous, parallel tendencies of withdrawal (e.g. retreat into the family) but with the fierce resistance of those who are by no means prepared to have their labour power banned from the market. Such resistance is likely to grow exactly at the point when overall demand for labour is depressed.

The second point to be emphasized is that there is no direct statistical correlation between the labour market activity rate (the share of the gainfully employed in the total population) and the rate of unemployment. It is wrong to assume that, in order to secure 'full' employment, all that has to be done is to invent social 'spaces' outside the labour market for those not absorbed by it, or to 'pension them off' in a variety of ways. This assumption is false, because very high labour market activity rates are accompanied by low unemployment rates (in Japan, the ratio is 47.2 per cent to 2.2 per cent) just as, conversely, low activity rates coincide with high unemployment rates (in the Netherlands, the respective figures are 34.5 per cent and 10.2 per cent). This suggests that the unemployed do not tend to 'flee' the labour market (and have little chance of doing so), and that those who live outside employment are not those for whom unemployment would be the most likely alternative.

Third, as a consequence of recent warnings by feminists and others, attention has been focused on the fact that the 'realist' strategies of eliminating certain categories from the labour market are aimed directly – *after* immigrant workers and *before* older ones – at women. It can be said that women are the last historical wave of immigrants into the labour market, where (for this as well as for other reasons) they have secured proportionately few of the central, secure, highly placed jobs which are relatively immune from rationalization processes. There is a very close correlation between the labour-market activity rates in the Western industrialized countries and the proportion of women among their gainfully employed populations. If these countries are compared on the basis of these two indicators, the result is two almost identical rank-orders, commencing at the lower end of the scale with Spain, where 46 per cent of the 15–64 age-bracket is employed or formally unemployed and the proportion of women in the labour force is 28.5 per cent and, at the other end of the scale, Sweden, whose respective figures are 78.9 per cent and 46 per cent.

At the same time, and as has been mentioned earlier, a certain widely held view of the social role of the family as an institution (a view reinforced perhaps by a simultaneous concern with population policy) gives rise to the suggestion that the family system should be considered a suitable place where parts of the female labour force could be transferred and accommodated. Quite apart from the fact that egalitarian and feminist values are likely to continue to mobilize considerable resistance to such plans, their implementation is also impeded by the problem that the structural absorption capacity of not only the labour market, but *also* of the family as an institution is strictly limited, and is bound to be reduced further still. Consider the not atypical case of a small family, who lives in a large city and has a modern, well-equipped household and service facilities within easy reach. How, in this case, would it be possible to tie the housewife's labour power to household and family duties for more than a relatively short 'family break' within the female life-cycle especially when, at the same time, rising rents and consumption expenses generate an urgent need for income (if only in the form of 'supplementary income', as women's wages are often referred to both by their husbands and employers)?

Finally, there is a fourth point: the 'realist' position (not unlike many 'green' proposals in this respect) has a tendency to considerably and blindly overstate the unemployment absorption capacity of self-organized, independent forms of activity (*Eigenarbeit*), a type of 'freely chosen activity' which is supposed to take place outside of formal employment conditions. Here, again, it is easy to imagine the playing of a party game, whose disappointing outcome could be quite instructive. The brainstorming about personal or household-based 'useful activity' might well begin with 'do-it-yourself' activities which (in the purchasing of tools, for example) often consume more earned income than they help to save. Suggested 'extra-employment' activities might range from possible alternatives to formal salaried work (games, education, political and aesthetic activity, social work, club activities) to moonlighting and neighbourhood assistance. A closer examination of such proposals readily reveals that all of them encounter three problems; each of these has to do with problematic distribution effects which typical households or individuals can overcome only within very strict limits and to a highly variable degree. The scope actually available for 'autonomous' activities is typically constrained, first, by a shortage of material resources (such as physical space and other facilities); second, by a lack of personnel qualifications, discipline and psychological dispositions; and, finally, by the absence of institutional structures which could guarantee minimum levels of efficiency and continuity, as well as security of expectations and control among their participants.

The evidence suggests that, wherever 'outside' material and institutional support, accepted voluntarily, is not forthcoming, self-managed projects, autonomous initiatives among the unemployed and self-help organizations provide few grounds for optimism. The question raised recently by some left-wing German Social Democrats, 'Can work be invented?', cannot therefore be answered with euphoric references to the beauty of 'freely chosen activity' or to the bliss of 'self-exploitation' (Dahrendorf). It can be answered, if at all, only with a negative thesis: work cannot be 'invented' individually or autonomously by those people who are then supposed to do it. Rather, people have to be provided with the appropriate institutional and material resources which would *enable* them to carry out their self-chosen activities. Any other solution would likely amount only to a camouflaging of the violence, misery and hopelessness of an economy of lifeboats, in which there would always be too few seats.

## A Third Way?

If, as a consequence of these considerations, the 'orthodox' perspective of integrating (at some uncertain time in the future) the labour supply through market forces appears unconvincing, and if the 'realist' proposal for absorbing 'excessive' supplies of labour elsewhere and outside the labour market seems neither feasible nor desirable, then the scenario is depressing indeed. Neither the labour market, nor the institutions and spheres of activity capable of relieving pressure on the labour market, have an adequate absorption capacity. As a consequence, the social mechanisms which are designed for allocating labour power to work, as well as for distributing the returns to labour power from work, no longer function properly. Since there are no viable alternatives to *'working'* and *'living'* from work, however, 'surplus' labour power continues to accumulate, to a great and ever increasing degree, in exactly that place where there is no use for it: on the supply side of the labour market. Thus, the welfare-state institutions designed for supporting the unemployed, the not-yet-employed and the early-retired are faced with continuous fiscal problems, and the foundations are laid for an at least latent conflict between, on the one side, employees *and* employers who are burdened, respectively, with increasing tax contributions and rising social security taxes and, on the other, the unemployed.

This fiscal imbalance results from the operation of the traditional structural principle of social security – the fiscal linking of social security revenues to employment – that appears to have outlived its usefulness. On the revenue side of the security system, it is the level of total wages that determines the volume of funds available for social security transfers. On the spending side, a similar linkage derives from the fact that *claims* to benefits depend upon the length of prior gainful employment; moreover, the *level* of benefits is also dependent upon the former income derived from that gainful employment. Until now, attempts were made to simultaneously maintain both types of linkages between employment and social security, while their quantitative relationship was adjusted under conditions of crisis: the social security system was stabilized by levelling rising social security taxes on the one side, and by speading benefits more thinly, on the other. Increasing percentages of the sum total of wages were collected in the form of contributions, in order to compensate for the diminishing percentage of income-substituting transfers for the growing number of people entitled to these benefits.

This procedure makes a lot of sense as long as unemployment can be regarded as a temporary and quantitatively limited phenomenon. The more unrealistic this premise becomes, the greater the resort to the emergency solution – which is actually contrary to the basic idea of mandatory social 'insurance' – of stabilizing the various branches of social security with subsidies from general tax revenues. Inherent in this kind of fiscal emergency measure (although this remains implicit) is a welcome violation of the principle of 'equivalence', according to which the income of the non-employed must be linked to the (individual and collective) income of those who are gainfully employed. If this linkage of the income of the non-employed to the total income of the employed were to be severed successfully (in respect of entitlement, the level of benefits and previous income earned on the labour market), then a great deal more would be achieved than simply solving the problem of permanently overburdening the system of unemployment insurance. An egalitarian basic insurance scheme of this kind would have the status of a citizenship right to a basic income (instead of being an entitlement to benefits in exchange for contributions paid), and it would at the same time constitute a serious step in the direction of effectively relieving pressure on the supply side of the labour market. *All* strata and groups of those who are (potentially) gainfully employed – and not only housewives and other women – would be able to choose, if the question arose, whether they wished either to seek employment or, instead, to forgo gainful employment; under these new circumstances, the latter option would even become tolerable in financial terms.

If this step were to be taken, the hitherto existing ties between income and work performed, a characteristic feature of market societies everywhere, would be partially broken, and the norm of equivalence which serves as a criterion of social justice (as well as of economic efficiency) would be undermined deliberately. Initially, such steps would have to be justified not so much by invoking old socialist ideals; rather, they would need to be justified with reference to the fact that the chances of earning a wage on the market have dwindled greatly, and will remain so low that they will be insufficient, even in developed welfare states, to cover the income needs of the population. The old principle which insists that those who do not work shall not eat, only makes sense as long as there *are* adequate opportunities to acquire the necessaries of life through work. If this ceases to be the case, it is obvious that, in order to satisfy citizens' needs, the returns upon work need to be distributed in ways other than that of the exchange of labour for earned income and the social security and family systems based on that exchange system. Whoever rejects these implications would have to demonstrate either that there is some truth in the 'orthodox' perspective on how to restore full employment, or that the 'realist' perspective leads to more than simply a 'dualization' of society, that is, to the displacement and impoverishment of large groups of labour. As I have attempted to demonstrate above, both the 'orthodox' and 'realist' positions are faced with serious difficulties which prevent them from justifying either of these two possibilities.

It is, of course, easy to predict the political reactions which would be generated by this proposal for uncoupling income claims from work performed. Critics would quite easily be convinced of the likely reduction of pressure on the labour supply, so much so that they would foresee an 'excessive' flight of labour power out of the labour market – which would be seen as placing excessive demands on the system of guaranteed income or 'national dividends'. The appropriate reply to this criticism would be that the differential between the guaranteed minimum income and the income generated on the labour market could easily be fine-tuned to prevent such consequences, should they indeed become intolerable from the point of view of democratically agreed-upon considerations of macro-economic efficiency. In addition, such undesired consequences, often referred to as 'disincentive-to-work' effects, could be limited by means of qualitative improvements of jobs and working conditions. Those who remain sympathetic to the orthodox perspective might even see some beneficial consequences from this proposed uncoupling of income and work, for if finances for the guaranteed income fund were generated from a tax-base different from that of the volume of actual employment, then this would mean that employers would no longer be able to 'rid themselves' of the social costs of unemployment by shifting them on to the public at large. In other words, employers themselves would have to recognize that redundant labour power and jobs rationalized out of existence still entail costs. This adjustment of the basis of calculation of the business firm might even have some employment-securing effects.

Today, these kinds of considerations concerning the need for fundamental reform can often be observed just below the surface of everyday political discourse. The limitations of the ideas presented here concerning a 'third way' of solving the labour market problem consist not in the fact that they 'go too far' but, rather, that their proposed solution remains incomplete. This is true in two respects. First, it cannot be assumed, as a matter of course, that a monetary income guaranteed independently of gainful employment and distributed, as a citizenship right, to those sectors of the population who do not participate in the labour market, would actually be sufficient to satisfy their life needs beyond a civilized subsistence level, especially if the costs of maintaining the fund for 'national dividend' payments were to be kept within economically justifiable limits. Second, and even if this problem were to be overcome, only *one* dimension of the labour market problem would have been solved constructively. The labour market problem has *two* dimensions – the distribution of the means of subsistence to labour power *and* the allocation of the capacity to work to socially useful work tasks. This means that even a materially satisfactory strategy of allowing labour power to 'lie fallow' by means of generous social policies would not only be economically inefficient; it would also fundamentally violate the human need for meaningful, useful and purposeful activity.

This second aspect of the labour market problem could only be solved if the separation of claims to monetary income from the sphere of gainful employment were accompanied by the reciprocal partial uncoupling of useful activities from the nexus of monetary remuneration. If this were achieved, monetary income would not only no longer depend upon work performed in the labour market; the 'means of life' would cease to be provided *exclusively* from money, but also in part *directly* from self-organized, independent labour (*Eigenarbeit*) – the allocation of whose results would not be mediated by monetary wages and purchases. This solution to the second aspect of the labour market problem has nothing whatsoever to do with an economically and socially 'regressive' utopia of an economy of 'small communities' providing *exclusively* for themselves.

During recent years, the research and programmatic discussions concerning the 'informal economy' and the 'dual economy' (for instance, J. Huber and J. Berger in the Federal Republic of Germany; J. Gershuny, R. Pahl and J. Robertson in Britain; and A. Gorz in France) have clarified the extent to which (and the conditions under which) people can supply themselves with goods and services without having to purchase them, even in advanced industrial societies. This type of informal or 'decommodified' provision of benefits consists of use-values which can substantially supplement and improve the level of material well-being that individuals and households attain through monetary income. The informal provision of goods and services has the additional advantage of ensuring that those parts of the labour potential which cannot be accommodated in the labour market are utilized in a self-determined way, and are not condemned simply to passivity. Of course, advocates of the informal economy have not always made it clear that a blind, *laissez-faire* process of dualization and a type of a consciously designed dual economy which is *politically* justified and reinforced are diametrically opposed models. In the first process, those sectors of the population remaining outside the sphere of contractual labour are somehow supposed to cope, survive and help themselves; at the same time, they are meant to accept – in a manner ranging from approval to indifference – moonlighting, petty crime and the grossest forms of exploitation and self-exploitation as facts of life. In contrast, in the second model, that of a politically instituted dual economy, the goal is to institutionally recognize, promote, secure and extend the limited sphere of informal, self-organized independent labour and, at the very least, to subject it to the same criteria of social justice which claim validity in the formal employment sector of society.

It is this opposition between a blind process of spontaneous 'dualization' of society and a dual economy based on a political programme which is bound to cause a parting of the 'black-and-green' and 'red-green' tendencies, which presently appear to be engaged in a semi-public contest of ideas concerning the future of work and the labour market. Fully developed organizational models are to be found within neither tendency. And it is difficult to say whether the continuing labour market crisis will help stimulate imagination and political inventiveness, or instead breed fatalism and cynicism and relegate increasing parts of the working class to 'marginal' conditions of subsistence. Crises are always ambivalent, in that they either *increase* or *paralyse* a system's learning capacity. Paralysis would prevail if either the stubbornness of 'orthodoxy' or the 'realist' position, aptly described by Fritz Scharpf as 'cheerful resignation', were to remain dominant.

# 4

# The Growth of the Service Sector

According to a development hypothesis often advanced since the 1930s, the proportion of 'service labour' in the total volume of social labour in industrial societies is increasing continuously. This is considered to be of crucial importance for labour relations and the conditions of work, as well as for the distribution of social power and the structure of political domination. In the history of sociology, the origins of this development hypothesis can be traced back beyond the inter-war period, for instance, to the studies of Lederer on the growth and social significance of the white-collar class, to Karl Renner's concept of the 'service class', or even to Marx's well-known *Grundrisse* speculations on the rise of an 'automation society', in which human labour power would progressively abandon material production, and assume the functions of 'watching and controlling' production.[1]

The following, predominantly optimistic, expectations are associated with this development hypothesis. The hope is

1   that since service workers no longer directly utilize tools and material objects, but instead manage symbols and treat people, the strain on the individual worker will be eased;

2   that human capacity for labour will be improved through new and intensified training of those skills and faculties typically associated with service activities, that 'higher' welfare

Translated by John Keane. This essay was written for a research project on the development of service labour, conducted at the University of Bielefeld during 1977. An earlier version was presented as a lecture at the University of Essex, England, in November 1981.

claims will be satisified, and that economic and administrative functions will be rationalized;

3   that in spite of enormous productivity increases in the realm of material production, the service sector will be capable of absorbing surplus labour power from that realm, thereby preventing crises of unemployment;

4   that industrial conflict generated in the sphere of material production will be reduced, even eliminated.

Considered together, these expectations have often imbued the sociological prognosis of the expanding-service-sector hypothesis with a socio-political message – what Fourastié calls a 'great hope'.

In an empirical-prognostic as well as normative-evaluative sense, there is today every reason to reconsider this complex network of forecasts, hopes and programmes associated with this development hypothesis, and to revise its assumptions in more complex and cautious directions. In an empirical-prognostic sense, this reconsideration is prompted by the rapid development of information and control technologies and their associated organizational systems, as well as by allegations about the overloading of state budgets because of the spread of 'unproductive' employment.[2] Not only is the prospect of further growth in the total volume of service labour being called into question; it is also viewed as a mixed blessing. From Max Weber's pessimistic analysis of the proliferation of administrative bodies within the state and economy, a tendency which he considered to be linked closely with capitalist modernization, to present-day (conservative and 'alternative') normative criticisms of bureaucracy, the professions and large-scale organizations, there is a noticeably increasing aversion to the production, consumption and power relations of 'the service society' – an aversion, ironically, which appears to have its social base within the new class, that is, among the cadres, staff and apparata of the 'service class' itself.

The following considerations do not develop a prognosis of the overall development of service labour and its consequences. Nor do they seek to develop an inventory of the socio-political and cultural standards for evaluating this development. They concentrate only on the available theoretical hypotheses and formulations for explaining the growth of service labour and the service sector. The question concerning whether (and according to which measurement procedures, in which countries, and for what time periods) a quantitative growth of the service sector has in fact taken place cannot, therefore, be discussed here; in agreement with the entire literature and data on this subject, it is assumed that this question has already been answered in the affirmative.

### Problems of Measurement

In this connection, attention should be given, at least in passing, to the considerable problems associated with all three of the mathematical determinants (numerator, units of measurement and denominator) of the quotient (the 'service-sector ratio') whose increase is under discussion here. This holds, first of all, for the denominator, about which it can be asked: What is the universe of social labour by reference to which the shape of service labour is measured? Normally, this is taken to be contractual employment performed within national economies. This immediately prompts the objection, however, that the expanding share of service labour, when measured in this way, may in fact be connected with the internationalization of material production, and hence the evident overseas transfer of the production of non-services. In turn, this suggests the need to rely upon supranational economic systems as the crucial denominator for deciding the service-sector ratio. Such a high level of aggregation nevertheless conceals the fact that service labour is traditionally an urban phenomenon, concentrated in metropolitan areas.[3]

Difficult questions also arise concerning the units of measurement of service labour. For instance, should they be the economic output of various types of business, the size of different occupational categories, the actual content of jobs, or even the quantities of labour time spent on services? Finally, should the numerator include only service activities performed in the shape of *gainful employment,* or should it also include housework and autonomous, private labour? In the latter case, the concept of work, and its delimitation from 'non-work', would become controversial. In the former, the suspicion could not be eliminated that what is being measured is not the growth in the share of service labour, but the commodification of labour formerly performed within the domestic household. Which of these explicit or implicit decisions about measurement techniques is made heavily depends, in general, upon such pragmatic research considerations as the availability of data. The everyday experience of social research also confirms that the most powerful indicators are at the same time least often found in official economic and social statistics and, therefore, require the greatest efforts of data collection. This is why it may be assumed that a decision in favour of one of these measurement techniques biases the findings concerning the size of the growth (or perhaps even the decrease) of services in a society in a given period. In view of these methodological problems, the following discussion of the hypothesis advanced for explaining the growth of service labour carries the proviso that, at least with respect to its size, this growth is indeterminate, and a methodological artefact of the measurement techniques which are utilized.

### Definitions

When estimating the service-sector quotient of a society, as well as its quantitative development, the basic theoretical concept of service labour is, of course, crucial. Within the literature on the 'tertiary' or service sector, however, the concept of service labour is in general very poorly defined; it is used as a residual category comprising all those types of work (in the sense of contractual employment) or work organizations that cannot clearly be classified as either 'primary' (extractive) work or 'secondary' (productive) work. In cases where the characteristics of service labour are in fact stated explicitly, we find that (as soon as we leave the level of *specific* activities, organizations and professions, and instead consider service labour as a whole) almost exclusively negative attributes predominate. Service labour produces *non-*material outcomes, which *cannot* be stored or transported. Service labour is *not* – or, at least, is *less* – susceptible to technical and organizational rationalization when compared with goods-producing labour. The productivity of service labour *cannot* be measured and, hence, its standards of productivity *cannot* be controlled. Service labour is *not* 'productive' (in the sense of both classical political economy and Marxism); and so on. These negative definitions developed in the field of labour economics find their counterparts in the discipline of sociology. Here, service workers are conventionally termed 'middle class', which implies that they are neither classifiable as 'upper' nor as 'lower', or else they are categorized as 'new' middle class, which simply indicates that they do *not* belong to an 'old' middle class. Equally uninformative is the concept of post-industrial society introduced by Bell; this designates a social system which is 'other than' or 'no longer' industrial, that is, one in which service labour is the prevailing type of work. The only exception to this rule of negative definitions of service labour is the well-recognized characteristic that clients must be 'present' and 'co-productive' in most service activities, a point which has been emphasized recently by, among others, Herder-Dorneich.[4]

In order to deliberately avoid the unsatisfactory practice of defining service activities as a residual and negative category, the attempt has been made to develop a positive sociological concept of service labour, focusing on the social functions which can and must be performed by service activities.[5] This concept is based upon the idea that service activities are always oriented to the maintenance of 'normal conditions' within a society or among its parts, that is, to the task of defending and preserving the differentiated elements of the social structure, as well as mediating between them. The problem of 'normality' which service labour is concerned to resolve has, therefore, two aspects. On the one hand, the *particularity,* individuality, contingency and variability (of the situations and needs of clients, students, patients, passengers) must be preserved, respected and acknowledged. On the other hand, service labour must ultimately bring about a state of affairs which conforms to certain *general* rules, regulations and values. Hence, one criterion of the quality of service labour is that it neither suppresses the individuality and situational specificity of a 'case' in favour of a rigid reference norm nor, conversely, attributes an importance to particularities such that the normal conditions anticipated by third parties are not realized. This characteristic task of service labour is perhaps best grasped through such concepts as 'synthesizing', 'mediating' or 'normalizing' labour.

This definition of service labour, presented here only in basic outline, draws attention to processes of individuation and differentiation, on the one hand, and coordination and standardization requirements on the other. Service labour can be deemed successful if it effects a balance between these two aspects. This equilibrium can only be achieved by *mutually* adjusting the 'specificity of the case' and the 'generality of the norm'. Only *one* side of this adjustment process is covered if it is stated, for instance, that the task of a physician is to cure patients, or that the job of a sales-person is to sell goods. However correct this may be, it is also true, conversely, that the recognized standards of 'successful treatment' or 'selling', as well as the specific means of reaching those ends, must be concretely determined in relation to the specificity of the case. It is always necessary to simultaneously normalize 'the case' and individualize the norm.


## Services as 'Work'


What is striking is that the synthesizing function of service activities is executed in the form of *work,* and not through personal rule or cultural tradition. In so far as the concept of work implies the *schematization* of actions according to its means and ends, there is an inconsistency built into the concept of service *work.* Contractual employment becomes more 'rationally' organized the more clearly its outcomes are defined and fixed. The more this happens, the less there is room for discretion concerning the utilization of technical equipment and labour time and, hence, the greater the degree of control over labouring activities, the less the scope for articulating the conflicting motives of workers, and the more the environment of the labour process (e.g. the flow of materials) becomes uniform and standardized. Because of the immanent rationality of service activities, outlined above, the situation is quite different in the sphere of service labour. Here the anticipated outcome of action is often more likely to be achieved the less means and ends are specified in detail, the more there is scope for interpretation and manoeuvre, the less the personal motivation of the service worker is subject to external control and, hence, given greater opportunity to respond *ad hoc* to the particular features of a particular environment which in principle cannot be standardized without producing counterproductive consequences. Service labour is, therefore, always located at the intersection of two rationalities: (i) the rationality of 'industrial economy' based on contractual employment, which entails the detailed specification of means and ends, direct vertical control over work activity, little scope for manoeuvre and high levels of standardization; and (ii) the rationality of 'mediation and conciliation' typical of service activities, which require room for manoeuvre precisely in order to respond as services to specific situations.

These brief reflections, which need not be illustrated further in this context, suggest that all types of service labour – the most general social function of which has been designated as that of 'synthesizing' or 'normalizing' – are subject to a double dilemma, or to the permanent problem of balancing and resolving two dilemmas. Service activities must, however, deal with the dilemma between norm and 'case', which can be resolved neither through complete standardization nor through complete individualization if the synthesizing function of these services is in fact to be carried out. Services are 'adequate' in so far as they adequately take into account both components, whose relationship is more or less undefined and must, therefore, in each case be decided by 'responsible' *ad hoc* interpretations. This first dilemma occurs at the *personal* level of service provision, and it must be resolved through the reliance upon normative orientations, experience, professional ethics and specific interaction competencies and social skills. On the other hand, at the *organizational* level, there is a second dilemma, which results from the fact that service activities are performed as contractual *work*. When this is indeed the case (as in the provision of education through work-based organization and not through families or peer-groups), the criteria of rationality of the organization (effectiveness, efficiency, control, standardization of its relations with the environment, etc.) clash with the autonomy and flexibility requirements engendered by the first-mentioned dilemma. This problem has often been described and analysed as a structural dilemma between bureaucratic and professional orientations and mechanisms.

The question concerning the factors contributing to the growth of the share of service work in the total volume of work (however it is measured, as discussed above) can be subdivided into two questions. First, how can the increase in the volume of service activities be explained? Second, which factors account for the fact that a (perhaps constant) volume of services is increasingly provided through *formal* and specialized service *work* (and not, for instance, through household work or autonomous, non-market labour, self-help, or a combination of productive and service functions within the same work role)? In other words, is *service* labour or service *labour* on the increase? This distinction is of special interest since Gershuny, in several of his influential writings,[6] has advanced the prognostic thesis that in industrial capitalist societies the (increasing) need for services will more and more be satisfied by all kinds of 'self-service' activities, thus leading to a decrease in the share of service *work*. Corresponding normative concepts, designed to serve as guidelines for a reorganization of services in general and of the social services in particular, have also been widely advanced and criticized.[7]

Accordingly, it cannot be assumed that an increasing volume of service labour involves, or corresponds to, an increasing *need for services*. On the contrary, increasing volumes of service labour may well reflect a rising demand for formal employment or the strategies of service workers defending their supply-side interests. These latter hypotheses are illustrated in the right-hand column of figure 4.1, which serves as a point of reference for the following examination of the various attempts to explain the development of service work. The 'Need/demand' column, by contrast, refers to approaches which assume that the growth of service work can be

|  | Need/demand | Labour market supply |
|---|---|---|
| System integration (equilibrium conditions) | 1 Increasing need for control because of rising complexity | 2 Absorption of structurally increasing labour market surplus |
| Social integration (action orientation) | 3 Changes in demand of private households due to rising income | 4 Changes of preference and autonomous power of service suppliers to define needs |

*Figure 4.1 Schematic representation of major explanations of the development of the service sector.* (The numbers correspond to the following sections of the text.)

explained by the rising need for service activities, and hence for the specialized fulfilment of their 'synthesizing' and 'normalizing' functions. Figure 4.1 is organized vertically in accordance with Lockwood's well-known and fruitful distinction between predominantly 'system-integrative' and predominantly 'social-integrative' approaches.[8] It therefore distinguishes between approaches that proceed mainly from the equilibrium and control problems of social systems, and those that concentrate on the development of social norms, institutionalized needs and interests.

## 1 Systemic requirements

The first cell in the above figure refers mainly to arguments that provide a functionalist explanation of the growth of service labour, which is viewed as resulting from increasing 'systemic' needs for services. These requirements consist of a quantitative component indicating the volume of the 'required' regulative functions, as well as of a 'specialization component' which specifies the differentiation of the specific work and occupational roles assigned to these functions. The requirements are viewed, in turn, as rooted in certain changes in the social structure of developed, industrial capitalist societies.

The central point in this functionalist explanation is that the increasing requirements of control and coordination are a consequence of increasing complexity. The division of labour, structural differentiation and pluralization can only be 'tolerated', and the corresponding gains in economic and administrative efficiency only utilized, in so far as a parallel and compensatory process of 'mediation' is developed. This requires planning, coordination, regulation and control functions. The essential idea is identical with that developed in Galbraith's model of the 'techno-structure'. A modified form is found in numerous contributions to the theory of the state which concentrate especially on the causes of the growth of public services. This basic thesis that the division of labour and societal differentiation 'must' be compensated through coordination and 'mediating' labour is so elementary and well known that it will not be elaborated here. It is, in any case, confirmed by economic historians, who consider the expansion of the tertiary sector as a precondition and concomitant of the industrial revolution:

> It was the expansion of such intermediate services as banking, discounting, accounting and wholesaling which was such a notable feature of the industrial revolution. . . . What was novel during the industrial revolution was the expansion of a group of activities which we now call services, activities which had been of minimal importance in pre-industrial economy. It was the expansion of the non-agricultural and the non-industrial sector – the service sector – which created the most significant break with the past with the onset of industrialization in the advanced economies. . . . The services which expanded most obviously with economic growth were transport, distribution, finance and government. . . . Industrialization could not have occurred, or would have occurred more slowly, had there not been an expansion of social overhead services like transport and education, and of intermediate services like retail and wholesale trade, which were necessary as productive activities became more specialized. . . . Viewed in longer perspective, since the beginning of industrialization, the growth of services had closely followed, and sometimes preceded, the growth of industry.[9]

Of greater interest are several additional arguments which shed light upon the relationship between specifically *capitalist* processes of modernization and the growing volume of 'necessary' synthesizing and mediating labour. Capitalist economic and social structures are those which combine the principle of profit-directed *investment* with a market in 'free' wage labour. These two components can be considered in turn. The profit principle implies an extensive normative neutralization of the entire realm of economic activities, that is, the exclusion of every criterion of the success and appropriateness of action except that of economic profitability. In this respect, the profit principle is synonymous with an extensive 'deregulation' and the destruction of traditional/normative mechanisms of control and coordination – a fact well characterized in the Marxist thesis concerning the 'anarchy' of capitalist production.

> The substitution of gratuitous, non-professional services with monetarized professional services is a characteristic feature of the increasingly social character of capitalist production and the dissolution of traditional social structure it reinforces. . . . [The reason] why this substitution tendency and the growing needs for

*new* social services are objectively necessary include: the emergence
of the nuclear family and the decline of household size; urbanization; increasing participation of women in the paid work force;
changes in the age structure of the population as well as changes in
the patterns of disease towards chronic-degenerative and psycho-
somatic types; increased demands for spatial, occupational and
regional mobility; a rise in qualification and educational requirements; and so on.[10]

These considerations reinforce the functionalist argument that
the repertoire of 'pre-modern' control and regulation mechanisms,
which are destroyed by the emergence of capitalist society, must be
reconstructed (e.g. in the form of a legal-administrative state
apparatus) if capitalist society is not to collapse under the weight
of its own 'anarchic' modernizing tendencies. Profit-oriented
production for an anonymous market requires services which
mediate buyers and sellers. In a spatial sense, these services include
commerce, transportation and communications and, in a temporal
dimension, they encompass the facilities provided by the banking
system (commercial credits).[11]

In an economy based on profits, economic actors are in a
competitive relationship, in the sense that their economic existence
is endangered constantly by other competitors in the market-place.
It can be assumed that the continual risk of falling victim to the
'creative destruction' of competition induced the internal
bureaucratization of business firms, the development of formal
capital accounting and, later on, the growth of specialized and
various types of administrative staffs, whose most general task is
to provide the individual economic unit with strategically utiliz-
able information about the type and extent of its competitiveness,
thereby reducing the risk of being victimized by its competitors.
Following Max Weber, these considerations serve to explain why
it is precisely that an increasingly 'socialized' market society
requires not only a state apparatus which regulates the whole
society, but also leads to the internal bureaucratization of
individual business firms.

The second component of the concept of capitalism, the
emergence of a labour market and the corresponding treatment of
labour power as a commodity, also serves as a starting point for
explaining the expansive dynamic of service labour. Labour power
differs from all other commodities. It is a highly artificial

'commodity' which cannot be separated from its owner and, therefore, can be 'sold' in only a very metaphoric sense. This is why, unlike all other commodities, labour power entering the productive process cannot be readily 'transferred' to its buyer in exchange for money. Within the framework of the labour contract, rather, it must be 'won over' or 'extracted' from its owners with the aid of specific arrangements and against the ever-present possibility of their resistance. Within the modern business firm, such extraction is attempted through instruction, control, training and supervision of the labour process. It can, therefore, be said that the structural element of wage labour and the labour market requires special types of conflict-regulating service labour which appear, for instance, in the form of personnel administration, a specialized type of labour power which is employed for the purpose of dealing with conflicts inherent in the commodification of human labour power. These services designed to regulate conflicts between wage labour and capital at the level of the single business firm are paralleled at the level of the whole society by a profusion of control, compensatory and regulatory functions, which are performed in the modern welfare state by specialized state agencies and private associations.

Additional light is shed on the connection between the unique dynamics of capitalist modernization and the growth of socially 'necessary' service labour if we enquire into the causes of the differentiation of the mediating and synthesizing service functions, that is, their assignment to specific work-roles concerned exclusively with these functions. It is, of course, possible to think of a mode of regulating the complexity of a market society – whereby service functions would be performed not by specialists, but as an element of every work-role – 'as a part-time activity by most adult members of society'.[12] Apart from the specialized functions of law, religion and medicine, the services of pre-industrial societies were to a considerable degree performed in a 'diffuse' manner. This kind of 'diffuse' allocation of service tasks, however, is for various reasons unlikely under capitalist economic and social conditions:

a   If such a diffuse institutionalization of service functions were to be realized, it would require a form of socialization and acquisition of competences based on a stable fund of traditional norms. Such a shared and reliably imparted repertoire of traditional knowledge and competence has, however, been undermined and dismantled gradually during the course of the capitalist modernization and mobilization process, which even affects the sphere of household services. Traditional knowledge and competence has been replaced by scientifically grounded control competences (e.g. juridical, medical, pedagogic and technical skills) which, accordingly, can only be performed by specialists, that is, by a small number of service functionaries who have been formally trained as professional workers.

b   A reason for the performance of service functions by specialists is the high probability that a *diffuse* provision of service functions might always result in conflicts of interest – which arise through market competition and from the potential antagonism between labour and capital – over what is understood as the requisite 'normal conditions'. These conflicts must be prevented through the creation of jurisdictional monopolies which assign specific functions to 'office holders' or to members of certain status groups.

c   A diffuse organization of service functions would clash with the rationality of capitalist modernization because a combination of 'productive' and 'normalizing' tasks within one and the same work-role would impede increases in the efficiency and productivity of labour, which is promoted precisely by the continuous schematizing and standardizing of work tasks. As the extreme case of Taylorism indicates, increases in the productivity of labour depend upon eliminating all elements of individual discretion.

The range of functionalist arguments reviewed here unanimously suggest that in capitalist societies there is an increasing functional need for services, which must necessarily be allocated through specialized work-roles or 'service jobs'. An attempt has also been made here to reformulate and sharpen the general argument about complexity, so as to highlight the unique features of the profit-directed economy and the market allocation of the 'commodity' labour power. We have observed that the expansion of service labour represents a compensatory counter-tendency;

service labour reduces the deficit of control which results from the 'privatization' or 'normative neutralization' of capitalist economic activity, and satisfies the constantly emerging needs for mediating functions of all kinds (such as commerce, communications, police and military protection, law, banking, insurance). What is characteristic of the argument that focuses on the systemic requirements generated by growing complexity is that, in contrast to theories of 'post-industrial society', and revolutionary models of social development, it views the expansion of tertiary functions as a counterpart, and even in part a precondition, of the capitalist-industrial mode of production.[13] This is seen to be so for three reasons. First, competition poses permanent threats to economic survival, and, therefore, forces individual firms to establish service staffs which pursue the strategic goal of perceiving, absorbing and preventing such threats. Second, the opposition of wage labour to capital demands constant efforts to regulate and control conflict at both the organizational and state levels. Third, the provision of service functions within the framework of capitalist social structures is only conceivable as a structurally specialized form of jurisdictional monopoly.

## 2   Employment deficits

Each of the above arguments postulates a rising systemic need for functionally specialized service labour, but the second type of argument is also located at the level of 'system integration' and is concerned with the supply-side of the labour market. In simplified form, the thesis of this argument is that in developed industrial capitalist societies there is a structural, if latent, surplus of labour because the increase of production lags behind the growth in productivity. Since the suppliers of labour power, who are without property, can neither return to the primary sector nor enter the world of the economically self-employed, this surplus labour power is transferred continuously to the tertiary sector. The service sector thus contributes to the level of system integration mainly through its latent, and not manifest functions. These latent functions consist in the allocation of work tasks to surplus labour power under the manifest pretext, so to speak, that there exists a need to which this labour responds. This argument is usually illustrated by referring to the state-provided 'social services', which are seen to have the double effect of withdrawing from the market the labour power of service workers themselves as well as their clients.

> Capitalism is entering the new historical phase of *disaccumulation* in which the wage labour system is contracting and the accumulation of variable capital . . . is coming slowly to a halt. . . . The extension of production independent of an extension in variable capital, of measured labour time, represented the first signs of a new system for organizing work and increasing productivity. . . . A new social system is required to guide individual choices and integrate them within aggregate choices at the family and community level. . . . Social policy, represented most concretely in the development and extension of new social services for the individual and new planning modes for the city, region and nation, thus emerges as the new integrating and stabilizing force for people and communities.[14]

The connection between the growth of services and the diminishing rate of capital accumulation (and the corresponding decline in the ability of the industrial labour market to absorb surplus labour power) has been emphasized ever since the 1960s by American Marxist authors such as Baran and Sweezy. The 'law of the surplus class' formulated by Nicolaus develops this theme in the light of the expanding role of science and technology as an independent productive force: 'As less and less people are forced to produce more and more, more and more people are forced to produce less and less.'[15] His discussion of this 'law' results in the following conclusion:

> What does happen, under capitalism, to the mass of people who are released from direct, productive labour by the advance of productivity? . . . There must be an increase of unproductive workers (because) an increase in the surplus product requires an increase in the number of people who can afford to consume it. Surplus production requires surplus consumption. The capitalist system is based on the extraction from the labouring class of more commodities than that class is permitted to consume; the system would collapse if there were not also a class which consumed more than it produced.[16]

This 'unproductive' new middle class includes not only workers who perform services which are essential for the administration and control of the accumulation process. It also includes those workers who do *not* make any 'required' functional contribution and are only integrated *pro forma* into work-roles, contributing merely (by means of the income allocated them) to the maintenance of the circulation of commodities.

The inability of the secondary sector of the economy continuously to absorb the available volume of labour power can be due to the replacement of labour by capital under conditions of stagnating or relatively declining output and/or to international economic relations (commodity imports or the export of capital, for instance). In response to the latter of these two tendencies towards under-employment, not only will there be a statistical increase in the proportion of service activities in total employment but, it may also be assumed, a more or less politically managed structural transformation in favour of service-intensive types of economic and employment structures which are, to an extent, 'protected against external influences'. Hansen expected the expansion of the tertiary sector to compensate for the gaps in employment which, he assumed, would result from the stagnation of industrial growth.[17] By contrast, Bacon and Eltis have drawn upon the case of Britain to analyse the vicious circle in the type of industrial policy that typically arises out of stagnation tendencies:

> insufficient real capital formation in the goods-producing sector → unemployment → lowered flexibility of institutionally fixed (nominal) wages → excessive growth of the public service sector → a further decline in real capital accumulation, and so on.

Such a crisis-ridden structural transformation leads in every case to the *absolute* expansion of the tertiary sector. This is because, in services, clients must always be 'present' and because their output is neither storable nor transportable; consequently, 'goods can mostly be exported, while services, however, must be provided within the respective country itself.'[18] This point is confirmed, conversely, by the example of the Federal Republic of Germany, whose economy until the mid-seventies was marked by its high exports ratio and high 'demand for labour power within the industrial sector, as well as by a comparatively very small service sector in absolute and relative terms.[19] Interestingly enough, however, this small service-sector ratio has entailed no serious 'control' or 'coordination' deficits when compared with countries with a substantially higher service-sector ratio, as one would be inclined to predict on the basis of the first explanatory hypothesis discussed above. The option of a systematic 'tertiarization' of the economic structure also comes to the fore under conditions (e.g. in overcrowded metropolitan areas) where industrial growth is economically possible but is viewed negatively, for reasons of environmental and regional policy.

The thesis that services substitute for inadequate. industrial employment is certainly more relevant (at least with respect to industrial societies) for explaining *prospective* economic and employment policy programmes than for accounting *retrospectively* for structural shifts that have taken place already.[20] Nevertheless, and in contrast to the 'system requirement' argument discussed in the previous section it is clear that the (future) expansion of the service sector can well be interpreted exclusively or mainly from the point of view of its 'absorption' of an otherwise non-absorbable supply of labour power. This is confirmed dramatically by the well-known fact that the mass unemployment in large Third World cities assumes the form of 'hidden unemployment', that is, unemployment disguised behind services of various kinds:

> The current growth of the tertiary sector in developing countries is often negatively evaluated. Tertiarization . . . is considered a sign of maldevelopment. It is argued that the relative growth of services is unhealthy because it reflects the lack of economic development, as population pressures induce people to leave the unproductive primary sector. They migrate to the cities but cannot be absorbed in the . . . manufacturing sector.[21]

At the analytical level, this supply-side-oriented explanation also contrasts sharply with the 'system requirement' argument. Whereas the latter infers the growing volume of service labour from the 'requirements' of the (capitalist) accumulation process, the supply-side approach explains this growth as a mechanism for 'absorbing' those workers who, although not needed directly or indirectly in the accumulation process, are required merely in order to stabilize the circulation of commodities through their role as consumers. The practical utility of this line of argument is evident in all those employment policies which call for an expansion of the service sector primarily with the intention not of contributing to some 'necessary' functions, but of *preventing unemployment* by harnessing the ability of the service sector to absorb surplus labour power. The suggestion that the service sector may assume a stop-gap function in employment policy, or that it will, in any case, perform this function because of its 'autonomous' tendency to grow, generates strong opposition both within the business community,[22] and from those concerned with basic choices in economic policy.[23] In both cases, the emphasis is on considering public and private services, as well as the growth of production- and consumption-related services, as complementary to the growth and dynamics of the secondary sector, rather than as a solution to the problems which this sector fails to resolve.[24]

The contrast between the two explanations considered so far is weakened considerably by the fact that the concept of 'functional requirement' (which lies at the centre of any purely functionalist argument) is quite unclear. Defenders of the second explanation of the growth of services as a mechanism of absorption would be quite at liberty to suspect that a considerable portion of the 'needs' which are nominally provided for by their respective services are, in fact, thoroughly fictitious. Much of the conservative critique of bureaucracy and the welfare state amounts to the claim that even though workers within these apparata and agencies are deluded into believing that their efforts are of some 'utility', they in fact do nothing but justify their own parasitic income claims. From the standpoint of the first explanation, even the most implausible service functions can be declared functionally 'necessary'. It must be added that, when viewed in terms of the *outcome* of labour, the simple absorption of individuals into employment may be functionally irrelevant and yet – when viewed from either a Keynesian or a social worker's perspective – it may contribute to the fulfilment of stability requirements, inasmuch as undesirable consequences would otherwise result if these individuals ceased to participate in commodity markets and work-centred forms of social life. In this sense, it may be argued that service employment creates social order not because of the effects of its *outputs* upon the economy and economic organizations, but because it regulates and disciplines the motivations and aspirations of the employed, that is, conditions their *inputs* into social life.

Apart from the lack of clarity in the concept of functional requirement – a problem which in any case cannot be resolved at the level of system integration itself – the two explanations are, in fact, complementary. Whereas the first argument postulates the *necessity* of an expansionary development of service activities, the second indicates the *possibility* of the system in fact complying with this necessity. Considered together, both suggest a type of inter-sectoral compensation theory, which argues that the supply of labour power which *must* be absorbed into service functions corresponds to the supply of labour power released by growing labour productivity and/or stagnation within the secondary sector, and therefore cannot be employed anywhere else but in the service sector. This type of theory, however, begs questions concerning the mechanism for quantitatively coordinating both developments, as well as the appropriate pace of mutual adaptation. Furthermore, a trouble-free process of 'post-industrialization' or 'tertiarization', as a result of which a growing portion of the employed population would be withdrawn from their role as 'direct producers' and instead become 'watchers and controllers of production' (Marx), appears to be wholly improbable because of the high costs entailed and the lack of acceptability or legitimacy of the underlying norms for determining the demand for service labour.

The need for all types of service labour (much more than is the case for other types of labour) cannot be deduced from technical production functions, but must be decided on the basis of conceptions of need and criteria of normality which are *normatively* justified and always contestable. Whereas it is always possible (at a given level of technology) to specify rather precisely the quantities of raw materials and labour power required for manufacturing a certain product, the 'need' for service labour can rarely be determined with approximately the same precision. Hence, for example, how much police activity is necessary for maintaining an 'orderly' and 'normal' metropolitan traffic system cannot be determined precisely through technical calculations, but only by way of a political process which is contingent upon conflict, controversial estimates about the effectiveness of the service labour in question, as well upon the willingness of clients to make the necessary monetary sacrifices. It follows, therefore, that a purely systemic approach, one which is based on 'objective' needs, functional requirements, stability and equilibrium conditions, is of limited use in analysing the dynamics of the service sector. It also follows, conversely, that it is very important to also consider these dynamics from the perspective of social integration, that is, from the standpoint of the norms, interests and preferences of both the consumers or clients of service labour and service workers themselves.

### 3   Changing demands

The best-known explanatory hypothesis, which also presently dominates scientific debate on the dynamics of development of the service sector, focuses on the changing pattern of consumption of private households. This hypothesis combines three particular arguments

a     As a consequence of increases in productivity within the secondary sector, there is a rise in the average real income of private households.

b     As real income rises, durable consumer goods become subject to saturation effects, and the demand for services consequently increases.[25]

c     By its very nature, the production of services is less susceptible to rationalization than the production of goods; consequently, growing demand for services combined with the above-average labour intensity of service production results in continuous increases of service employment.

Originating in the studies of Fisher, Clark and others,[26] this 'three-sector hypothesis', as it is often called, has been subject to a number of empirical and theoretical criticisms, related to each of its three sub-arguments. To begin with, even if productivity increases in the secondary sector result in a rise in average real income, the changing pattern of consumption depends not only on the *level,* but also on the *distribution* of income.[27] Even if changing income levels do lead to the alteration of consumption patterns, the service sector may not profit disproportionately from the additional demand.[28] Even when plausible psychological theories ('Engel's law', 'Gossen's first law')[29] or sociological assumptions are taken into consideration,[30] the needs of private households are not necessarily directed towards services in direct proportion to rising productivity in the industrial sector and rising real income. For it is quite conceivable that a growing *need* for services is not reflected in a growing *demand* for services in the market but, rather, in a strengthening demand for durable consumable goods (e.g. automobiles, household appliances, entertainment electronics) which make it possible for private households to supply themselves on the basis of 'self-service'. As Gershuny has demonstrated convincingly,[31] such a trend 'from services to goods' will likely take place wherever the growing needs for purchasable services result not only in a greater supply of services but also in disproportionate price increases in those services.[32]

A further problem encountered by the 'changing demands' hypothesis is that the demand pattern of private households, which this hypothesis supposes changes in accordance with either rising income and changes in needs or saturation effects, accounts at most for only a part of the (absolute) growth of service employment. This is so for two reasons. First, the growth in the overall volume of service labour consists, to a great extent, of *public* services that are not determined directly by private households within the market-place.[33] Second, if the development of that portion of GNP made up of private *consumer spending* on specific services is compared with the shares of the *output values* of the corresponding service industries in the overall value of economic production, it indicates that, even for commercial services, the demand of private households accounts for only a small share of the growth of the service sector.[34] This becomes clear if we take into account the possibility that the demand for commercial services (provided, for example, through banks, insurance companies as well as restaurants and hotels) need not consist exclusively or even predominantly of private household demand. At least, 'in all branches of the service sector, the development of private consumer spending on services diverges from the growth in production of these same branches of the service sector'.[35] Changes of demand (and productivity trends) also fail to explain the differential growth of employment within the various branches of the service sector; gains and losses in employment are to be found among service branches with increasing as well as decreasing demand, and among those branches with both high and low productivity.[36]

Even if both the arguments concerning rising income and changing demand pattern were acceptable, the growing demand for services by private households (or even the public sector) would result in an increase in the relative size of the service *sector* (measured by *employment* shares) only if the third argument, claiming a structural lag in productivity of services, were also valid. This latter assumption has been seriously questioned by Voss and others.[37] For the employment-expanding effects of additional demand for services could conceivably be offset and neutralized by rapid developments in labour-saving technologies within the service (and self-service) industries.

Regarding the problem of the *change of wants* consequent upon rising income (a problem presented in the technical literature as one of declining or rising income elasticity in the demand for goods and services respectively), an important distinction must be made, irrespective of the above-mentioned problem that the growing need for services may not necessarily be expressed as market demand, but as either the self-provision of private households or as the state provision of services. The importance of this distinction, outlined below, becomes evident in Hönekopp and Ullmann's following list of some of the standard arguments concerning the alteration of wants:

> It can be assumed . . . that the demand for services will continue to increase proportionately for the following (and other) reasons:
>
> – expenditures on health, culture and entertainment will increase with the development of the age structure pyramid;
>
> – with the emergence of the nuclear family and the concurrent increased participation of women in the paid work-force, there is a growing demand for household services;
>
> – the advancing mechanization of households entails more repair work;

- the demand for leisure industry products increases due to the reduction of work-time;

- as the economic and social structure becomes more complex, more money is spent on such services as tax consultation, legal advice, banking and insurance;

- similarly, consumer spending on market-provided (non-state) services such as occupational retraining and correspondence and language courses may increase as a consequence of rapidly changing occupational requirements.[38]

What is striking about all these arguments is that they are unclear about whether we are confronted here with a change of wants and preferences of private households or whether, instead, we are dealing with political, organizational, technical and health-related *external conditions,* whose alteration would necessitate an increasing utilization of services in order to satisfy otherwise unchanged wants. If the latter were the case, then the argument would amount only to a disguised variant of the complexity-and-control hypothesis underlying approach 1. The dynamic factors accounting for the expansion of services would consequently not be rising income, the change of wants and productivity increases, but structural developments (such as urbanization, technical and occupational change, the declining role of the family, the erosion of cultural traditions) which subject individuals to a state of increasing 'service-dependence'. However difficult it may be to decide between these alternatives in particular cases, and however much this decision affects the justification or discrediting of socio-political criteria of goodness and of progress, it should not for that reason be relegated to the shadowy realm in which questions are declared to be largely unanswerable and, therefore, abandoned to arbitrary opinion. Having said this, however, it is revealing that a recent critical discussion of the three-sector hypothesis concludes with a simple complexity argument, which is both consistent with the basic idea underlying approach 1 and reveals the continuing lack of clarity in the changing-demands hypothesis:

It is possible that the above-average growth . . . of services is explained by an additional factor: the increasing opaqueness of the economic, taxation and legal systems, which induces business firms, private households and the state to resort to specialized service enterprises, thereby generating new markets for service enterprises.[39]

## 4 Supply-side interests of workers

A fourth approach explains the dynamics of the service sector by referring to empirical changes in the supply-side activity of labour power, and thus to its altered preferences regarding career choice and career switching, as well as to the organizational and structural power resources which reinforce these preferences. In this approach, it is assumed that:

a    the type of job held by actors on the supply-side of the labour market is not only an 'exchange-value' expressed in income, but also a 'use-value' founded on the positive and negative experiences and activities associated with the labour process itself;

b    compared with its counterpart in the industrial sector, the use-value of service sector labour is systematically greater, whether measured 'objectively' or in terms of the subjective expectations and perceptions of workers;

c    workers have at their disposal individual and collective strategies which enable them to increasingly take advantage of the benefits associated with work in the tertiary sector.

According to Pollard, 'job content, job satisfaction, work as a consumer good as well as a cost, have played a major part in our recent history. . . . Our hypothesis is that the trend towards white-collar and service employment is substantially boosted by the desire of ever larger numbers of people to work in them.'[40] A clear-cut preference for service labour is to be found especially among (potential) women workers: '(Women) represent the growth element in those (service) sectors. Thus, in Great Britain, the number of male commercial clerks rose by about ⅓ million and the number of female clerks by 2½ million in the course of the 20th century. In the period 1931–1961, 70% of the total increase

in the female labour force went into offices (Offe's brackets).'[41]
The underlying thesis is that the 'quality elasticity' of the female
labour force is high, due to the reduction of family size, increasing
mechanization of the household, combined with rising average
real income and the breakdown of traditional sex roles. It is
implied that women workers respond more strongly to the type
and content of jobs than to rates of remuneration. A similar
tendency is indicated by the occupational goals and patterns of
occupational choice of young people, whose entry into the labour
market for the first time is linked with an (unrealistically) high
preference for service activities. This is consistent with assumptions about the general 'humanizing' effects of service labour:

> If one accepts that industrialization has led to a depersonalization
> of labour, then the expansion of services provides the opportunity
> of reversing this trend, since the direct contact with the client to
> whom service is provided, as well as the necessity of responding to
> the client's personal demands, are features much more common in
> service industries than in any other sectors of the economy.[42]

The objection that this optimistic expectation is by no means
confirmed by empirical findings in the sociology of work can only
be noted here although,[43] of course, even an erroneous or
exaggerated expectation of more 'humane' conditions of work in
the service sector might have a real effect on the supply behaviour
of labour. The expectation that job security is greater within the
service sector also has a certain theoretical plausibility. This
applies not only to the domain of the civil service, but also to
services (such as clerical work) performed within organizations; in
both cases, the employment of white-collar workers is not so
directly affected as blue-collar workers by variations in the market
success of the enterprise. Finally, there is some evidence that the
'attraction of middle class life style',[44] usually associated with
service labour, represents a type of symbolic exchange-value, and
that the relative attractiveness of service labour is also partly a
reaction to the perceived unattractiveness and direct physical
stress of 'productive' labour in the secondary sector.

These points serve to indicate supply-side preferences for
employment within the service sector. The argument remains
incomplete, however, unless it can also be shown that the supply

side is readily able to *realize* these preferences. This seems at least possible in the case of the professions, the civil service and services performed within organizations. As is known generally, professional services (provided by physicians and lawyers, for example) are characterized, even when they are organized on a quasi-commercial basis, by their discretionary power to broadly determine the type and volume of services offered to supposedly incompetent clients. Suppliers of professional services thus control a considerable part of the 'demand' for their services. It must be added that not only professionals in large public and private organizations, but service workers in general, contribute to the achievement of specific organizational goals in ways which often cannot be objectified or controlled. Not only is their contribution not expressed in a marketable unit of economic value; the nature of their contribution is such that it can often be defined negatively, namely, as the 'prevention' of disorders and irregularities. There is consequently a broad area (concerning the definition of the 'required' volume or type of service labour) within which the qualitative and quantitative supply-side interests of service workers can more freely develop compared with the sphere of manufacturing labour which is, as a rule, linked more directly to the market. This is especially true of service activity and 'normalizing' work, where not only the instrumental actions oriented to a pre-given goal, but also the goal itself are largely subject to the independent definition and control of service workers according to the circumstances of the particular case under consideration. The same point applies generally to the professions, and especially to elites administering public services, as has been argued by Schelsky, Illich and others.[45]

All things considered, these observations give rise to a general picture in which one of the most important attractions of service activities consists in the fact that both their use-value and their material compensation are better protected against external controls (whether of consumers in the market or superiors within formal organizations) and can, therefore, be utilized and expanded much more so than those in the secondary sector. This structural power of the supply-side of the service sector can be considered a key explanation of this sector's growth. The power is reinforced financially by the fact that the staffing costs of service activity are either provided through the state budget or, within private sector organizations, they are considered as progressively escalating 'overhead costs'. Both funding arrangements would appear to de-emphasize 'cost-awareness' and to render permanent and detailed efficiency controls both impractical and possibly even counter-productive. The legitimacy of the power of the service-sector supply side is also enhanced by its ability (and regular attempts) to conceal its own interests through reference to, and exploitation of, the arguments associated with explanations 1, 2 and 3. The demands of public-service trade unions, for example, are routinely justified through phrases which point to their compatibility with the common good and the interests of clients.

This 'determination of demand by the autonomy of the supply side' is typical for most of the service sector which is not strictly commercial. The extent to which it can develop is, of course, influenced by the strategies of professional associations, trade unions and political parties, all of which organize service workers or adopt them as their political clientele. Assumptions about an *unlimited* expansion of the service sector certainly cannot be justified in either a retrospective-analytical or a prospective-programmatic sense. The most important barriers against the imposition of needs by service organizations or by the status interests and politics of service workers can only be enumerated here. There are three such barriers capable of limiting the self-serving dynamics of the service sector:

a    The economic or budgetary limits which *impede* a further growth in the quantity of labour absorbed by the service sector.

b    Further mechanization, rationalization and rise in productivity of the service sector would obviate its further growth, even if 'demand' or 'needs' remained constant.

c    A 'saturation' or even 'over-saturation' of the demand for service sector products cannot *a priori* be excluded as a possibility, and would lead to a decline in demand or to the alternative satisfaction of demand through such new forms of service provision as 'self-help'.

## Some Questions for Further Research

This essay's attempt to provide a systematic overview of the main features and weaknesses of the four major sociological explanations of the growth of the service sector leads, first of all, to a negative conclusion: each of these approaches is less than convincing as an overall explanation and, hence, each must prove its relative worth in confrontation with the other competing approaches. Especially important in this regard is the problem (illustrated by the vertical columns in figure 4.1) of whether (a portion of) the growth of service labour can be attributed to objective 'requirements' or subjective wants and needs for services or whether (perhaps in addition to this) the growth tendencies of the service sector are better explained by the need to employ surplus labour and by demands for the extrinsic and intrinsic compensations which can be gained from service labour. It can be assumed that the adequacy of each of the four approaches will depend also upon which particular fields and types of service labour are under consideration. A comprehensive explanation of the development of service labour – one which simultaneously considers the systemic, organizational and micro-sociological dimensions – will only be achieved, however, if answers to the following four questions are combined. First, which stability and equilibrium problems are encountered by complex social systems, and to what extent can they be said to require certain types of services? Second, for which reasons is labour power harnessed to the performance of services, that is, why are services provided in the form of contractual employment, and why is this labour power not employed in tasks other than services? Third, what role is played by the demand of customers and clients in shaping the quality and quantity of services provided through markets or political decision-making processes, and to what extent is the development of these services determined by such demand patterns? Finally, to what extent can the providers of services determine the goals and conditions of service labour (and therefore the quantity and quality of services), and which economic constraints and organizational mechanisms serve as effective limits upon these discretionary powers?

# 5

# Work: The Key Sociological Category?

The classical traditions of bourgeois as well as Marxist sociology share the view that labour is *the* fundamental social fact. They construe modern society and its central dynamic as a 'work society'.[1] Certainly, *all* societies are compelled to enter into a 'metabolism with nature' through 'labour' and to organize and stabilize this metabolism so that its products guarantee the physical survival of their members. One could, therefore, disregard the concept of a 'work society' as a sociological triviality in so far as it refers to an 'eternal natural necessity of social life' (Marx). Before that is done, however, it is important to clarify the specific role which labour, the division of labour, the working classes, work norms, the organization of labour and its corresponding concept of rationality, play in classical sociology.

The purpose of sociological theorizing may in general be summarized as the examination of the principles that shape the structure of society, programme its integration or its conflicts, and regulate its objective development and its image of itself and its future. If we consider the answers given between the late-eighteenth century and the end of the First World War to questions relating to the organizing principles of the dynamics of social structures, we can safely conclude that labour has been ascribed a key position in sociological theorizing. The model of an acquisitive

Translated by John Keane. An earlier version of this essay was first presented as a paper to the opening plenary session of the Twentieth Convention of the Deutsche Gesellschaft für Soziologie, Bamberg, October 1982. It is here translated from the version later published as 'Arbeit als soziologische Schlüsselkategorie?', in J. Matthes (ed.), *Krise der Arbeitsgesellschaft?* Verhandlungen des 21. Deutschen Soziologentages in Bamberg 1982 (Frankfurt, 1983), pp. 38–65.

bourgeois society preoccupied with labour, propelled by its rationality and convulsed by labour conflicts is – notwithstanding their different methodological approaches and theoretical findings – the focal point of the theoretical achievements of Marx, Weber and Durkheim. Today, the question is, Can we still preserve this 'materialist' preoccupation of the sociological classics?

Before critically examining this question, I should like to briefly mention three points which led classical social scientists and political theorists to consider labour as the touchstone of social theory.

1  The overwhelming sociological experience of the nineteenth century was the establishment and rapid quantitative growth of labour in its *pure* form, that is, labour which was separated from other social activities and spheres.[2] This process of differentiation and purification made it possible for the first time ever in history to 'personify' labour in the social category of 'the worker'. This process includes the separation of the household and the sphere of production, the division between private property and wage labour, as well as the gradual neutralization of the normative obligations in which labour had been previously embedded. 'Free' labouring activity separated from feudal ties, regulated by the market, and no longer oriented immediately to concrete use but driven by the 'whip of hunger' (Max Weber) of the structural compulsion to earn a living is, so to speak, the raw material of the theoretical constructions of the sociological classics.

2  The old hierarchy between 'vulgar' and 'noble' activities, between those that are merely useful or necessary and meaningful life-expressions (a hierarchy crystallized in most European languages in such concept pairs as *ponos/ergon, labor/opus,* labour/work and *Mühe/Werk*)[3] was levelled, even reversed, in the wake of the victory of theological reformation, the development of the theory of political economy and the bourgeois revolution. Already in the Saint-Simonian utopia of a diligent, industrial society, not only was wealth to be increased but, above all, the domination of the unproductive classes was to be abolished and society thereby pacified at the same time. The sphere of market-mediated acquisition was either sanc-

tioned theologically and endowed with an ethical status (as
Weber argued), or accorded the imperious status of 'Moses and
the prophets' (Marx) through the 'compulsion to accumulate'
induced by the capitalist mode of production itself. Only
Durkheim sought to prove that the secularized and immanent
counter-pressure of this process leads to the emergence of an
organic solidarity, to a corporatively ordered bourgeois society,
in which the division of labour functioned as a new source of
social ('organic') solidarity and integration.[4]

3   Proletarianization of labour power and the moral unleash-
ing of acquisitiveness driven by the industrial use of this labour
power leads to the dominance of purposive rationality, whose
two components are distinguished more clearly in Marx than in
Weber. These components include the *technical* rationality of
the pursuit of ends in the interaction between humanity and
nature, and the calculating *economically* rational pursuit of
ends by interacting economic actors (analysed by Weber
through the example of rational capital accounting). In Marx
there is an obvious theoretical-strategic reason for contrasting
these elements through the conceptual distinction between the
processes of 'production' and 'valorization'. This distinction
permits the construction of a developmental scenario in which
each process is incompatible with the other; the economic
rationality of the competing units of capital becomes a 'fetter'
upon the 'technical' productive forces. This antagonism is
dissolved in the struggle for a social formation in which the
technical rationality (but no longer the economic rationality) of
capital prevails. For classical Marxism, social political and
cultural relations and systems are products (notwithstanding the
theoretical willingness to take 'reciprocal effects' into account)
and ultimately dependent accompaniments of material production and its two sides – the processes of 'production' and
'valorization'. Marx and Weber agree that the strategic rationality of capital accounting and the uncoupling of labour from all
immediate household and use-value criteria, from the rhythm of
hunger and satisfaction, is the main driving force behind the
'formal' rationalization of capitalist societies. The immediate
processes of labour and production are organized and regulated
according to the dictates of *this* rationality, whose functionaries
are the bureaucratic staff of capital.

Severed from the household and traditional forms of association, and deprived of political protection, wage labour was linked to the capitalist organization and division of labour, as well as to the processes of pauperization, alienation, rationalization and organized and unorganized forms of (economic, political and cultural) resistance inherent within these processes. All these developments consequently became the obvious pivot around which social-scientific research and theory formation rotated, and from which emanated all subsequent theoretical concern with social policy, family and moral systems, urbanization and religion. It is precisely this comprehensive determining power of the social fact of (wage) labour and its contradictions which today has become sociologically questionable.

## The Decline of the 'Work-Centred' Model of Social Research

This thesis can be confirmed by glancing at the thematic concerns and the more-or-less tacit assumptions and relevant viewpoints governing contemporary social science. From this vantage point, one finds ample evidence for the negative conclusion that labour and the position of workers in the production process is *not* treated as the chief organizing principle of social structures; that the dynamic of social development is *not* conceived as arising from conflicts over who controls the industrial enterprise; and that the optimization of the relations of technical-organizational or economic means and ends through industrial capitalist rationality is *not* understood as the form of rationality which heralds further social development.

To illustrate this negative conclusion I shall cite a few preliminary indicators. While the significant sociological studies of industry and work conducted in the Federal Republic of Germany in the 1950s still emphasized the industrial situation of workers, in the hope that this would indicate the future development of the organization of work and of the socio-political orientation of workers, in numerous contemporary studies the work situation appears rather like a dependent variable of the state-initiated 'humanization' of work and social and labour policies. From the outset (and in an entirely plausible way), the sphere of work is treated as 'externally constituted', while industrial sociology is confined mostly to a special branch of applied policy research.[5]

Sociological inquiry into everyday life and the life-world also represents an obvious break with the idea that the sphere of work has a relatively privileged power to determine social consciousness and action. To some extent the opposite approach is even taken, whereby the experiences and conflicts engendered by labour are viewed as a consequence of interpretations acquired outside work.[6] The limitation of the 'work-centred' paradigm is also emphasized by sociological analyses of electoral behaviour and political activity in general. These lead, for instance, to the conclusion that socio-economic status variables are less adequate predictors of voting behaviour than, say, church denomination and membership. Similarly, the national and international conflicts and ideologies of the Second and Third Worlds appear to increasingly escape such categories of 'modernization theory' as production, growth, economic and technical-purposive rationality, scarcity and distribution. In the industrial capitalist societies of the West, too, the predominant social and political conflicts often cut across the distributive conflict between labour and capital emphasized by the concept of social labour. Furthermore, policy-oriented social research in industrial capitalist societies appears to be predominantly concerned with social structures and spheres of activity which lie at the margins, or completely outside the realm of work – domains such as the family, sex roles, health, 'deviant' behaviour, the interaction between state administration and its clients, and so on. What is also interesting is the decline of attempts to comprehend social reality through the categories of wage labour and scarcity within the tradition of historical materialism, where efforts to revise and supplement 'work-centred' models of social reality now predominate.[7] Traditional stratification and mobility studies, which sought to grasp the 'crucial' structural parameter of social reality in variables such as occupational status and prestige (including income-based educational status and consumption levels), have also had to undergo revision in the direction of greater attention to variables such as gender, age, family status, health, ethnic identity, and collective rights and legal claims.

In view of these impressions of the state of contemporary social-scientific research, it is perhaps not too risky to claim that the rigid (analytic as well as political-normative) defence of work- and income-centred social models and criteria of rationality is today a preferred theme of conservative social scientists, whereas social scientists indebted to the tradition of historical materialism or critical theory today frequently reject these models and categories even more decidedly than did the classical theoretical and empirical works of the Frankfurt school in favour of a focus on a 'life-world' to be defended against economic and/or political encroachments. On the other hand, these impressions and observations also suggest the need to consider the objection that the themes and conceptual preferences of social science within any particular conjuncture need not necessarily tell us anything reliable about changes within social life itself. These impressions may simply reflect the confusions of a social-scientific understanding which prematurely fails or despairs when confronted with the classical sociological task of locating the point of origin of the structure and dynamics of society in work, production, property relations and rational economic calculation. If that were the case, a sociological theory of the transformation of its object domain – and not merely the empirical classification of changing themes and perspectives – would be required which then could provide us with a more solid explanation of the reorientation of research interests along the lines discussed above. This in turn would stimulate the following questions: Are there indications of a decline in the objective determining power of labour, production and acquisition for social conditions and social development as a whole? Is society objectively less shaped by the fact of work? Is the sphere of production and work losing its capacity to determine the structure and development of the larger society? Can it be said, notwithstanding the fact that an overwhelming part of the population are wage-dependent, that work has become less central to both individuals and the collectivity? Is one thus entitled to speak of an 'implosion' of the category of work? In the following section, I shall concentrate upon three points which could justify a positive response to such questions.

## Sub-Divisions in the Sphere of Work

The first set of misgivings regarding the centrality of work surface as soon as one seriously takes into account its vast empirical heterogeneity. That a person 'works' in the formal sense that he/she is 'employed' is a fact that has, until now, applied to a constantly growing segment of the population. Nevertheless, this fact has less and less relevance for the content of social activity, the perception of interests, life-style, and so on: to discover that someone is an 'employee' is hardly surprising and not very informative, since relative expansion of dependent wage labour coincides with its internal differentiation. This differentiation can no longer be comprehended adequately by the traditional concept of 'the division of labour' as soon as it also encompasses the distinction between those who are subject to the division of labour, and those who are not, or are to a much smaller extent.

Despite this differentiation and diversity of the social reality of work, the assumption of its unity and internal coherence is normally made by reference to five sociological arguments: a) the common criterion of the wage dependence of (propertyless) labour power; b) the subordination of this labour power to the organized control of management; c) the persistent risk of discontinuities in workers' earning capacity because of either subjective factors (e.g. sickness, accidents) or objective ones such as technical and economic change; d) the indirect homogenization of work that results from the presence and representational monopoly of comprehensive trade union associations;[8] and e) the collective pride of producers, a consciousness that reflexively expresses the labour theory of value and posits labour (in the words of the *Critique of the Gotha Programme*) as 'the source of all wealth and all culture'.

Whether, and to what extent, these supposedly homogenizing attributes can be preserved against the objective diversification of social labour remains an unanswered question. But it seems more doubtful the more particular work situations are marked by a wide variation in income, qualifications, job security, social visibility and recognition, stress, career opportunities, communication possibilities and autonomy. Symptoms of increasing heterogeneity raise doubts about whether dependent wage labour *as such* can still have a precise and shared significance for the working population and their perceived social and political interests and attitudes. These symptoms raise the possibility that work has in a sense become 'abstract', such that it can be considered only as a descriptive statistical category, and not as an analytical category for explaining social structures, conflicts and action. Whatever the case, it is clear that the multi-dimensional processes of differentiation which have been convincingly demonstrated in numerous studies of the segmentation of the labour market, the polarization of worker qualifications, as well as the economic, organizational and technical transformation of working conditions, render the fact of being an 'employee' less significant and no longer a point of departure for cultural, organizational and political associations and collective identities.

In the earlier phases of industrial capitalist development, of course, the formation of a collective identity based on labour as the source of all social wealth was anything but obvious. It may be that the unintended contribution by capital to solidarity, namely, the massive concentration of homogenized and standardized labour power in the organizational form of large-scale industrial production (as analysed by Marx) helped to unite workers objectively as well as subjectively. Labour market conditions and, hence, the vertical and horizontal mobility of work have, nevertheless, always confronted workers at the level of *interests*, with the 'magic triangle' – the always-partially incompatible goals of increasing wages, securing employment, and improving working conditions – as well as with the dilemma, situated at the level of *means*, between the individual or collective pursuit of interests, between 'struggle within the wages system' and 'struggle against the wages system'. The continuing internal differentiation of the collectivity of wage workers, as well as the erosion of the cultural and political foundations of a work-centred collective identity, have amplified these dilemmas of contemporary forms of wage labour to the point where the social fact of wage labour or wage dependency is no longer the focus of collective meaning and social and political division. With respect to their objective and subjective contents of experience, many wage-earning activities have hardly more in common than the name 'work'.

One might be tempted to criticize this conclusion as premature and subjective, and to object that it is the essentially identical logic of capital valorization that both rules over, and fosters the growing variation in, the forms of work. The persuasiveness of this objection seems to me to be limited. For the numerous fractures in the allegedly unified and 'form-determined' wage labour (as well as their impact upon individuals, organizations and political action) are so evident that they cannot be theoretically trivialized. During the 1970s, four such fractures occupied the centre of attention in the sociology of industry, work, stratification, and class-theory. First is the distinction between primary and secondary labour markets, as well as between internal and external ones. Second, it has become clear that to a large and growing extent the production of goods and services takes place outside the institutional framework of formal and contractual wage labour, that is, in areas where workers are not 'employees', but members of families and households, compulsory institutions such as armies and prisons, or of a semi-legal or criminalized underground economy. Third, Marxist sociologists especially have focused on the vertical split within the ranks of wage-workers and on the growth of 'intermediary' or 'heterogeneous' class positions (E.O. Wright), in which dependence upon wage income coincides with some share in formal authority. Finally, sociologists of work have emphasized the differences between 'productive' and 'service' forms of labour.

This last point, upon which I shall concentrate here, has become the basis of macro-sociological accounts of the emerging 'post-industrial service society' (Bell). While one can subsume the greatest part of work performed in the 'secondary' (i.e. producing industrial goods) sector under an abstract common denominator – that of technical-organizational productivity and economic profitability – these criteria lose their (relative) clarity when work becomes 'reflexive', as it does for the most part in the 'tertiary' sector of service work. In industrial capitalist societies, the continuous and steady increase in the proportion of social labour employed in the production of services indicates that scarcity and efficiency problems, which determine the rationality of the production of industrial commodities, are supplemented with problems of order and normalization which cannot be dealt with adequately by means of the technical and economic mastery of scarcity, but rather require a separate rationality of service labour.

An essential feature of all 'reflexive' service labour is that it processes and maintains work itself;[9] within the service sector, production is conceptually and organizationally based. In both private and public enterprises, activities such as teaching, curing, planning, organizing, negotiating, controlling, administering, and counselling – that is, the activities of preventing, absorbing and processing risks and deviations from normality – are overwhelmingly wage-dependent, just as is the case with the industrial production of commodities. These service activities are, however, different in two respects. First, because of the heterogeneity of the 'cases' that are processed in service work, and due to the high levels of uncertainty concerning where and when they occur, a technical production function that relates inputs to outputs can often not be fixed and utilized as a control criterion of adequate work performance. Second, service work differs from productive work in the lack of a clear and uncontroversial 'criterion of economic efficiency', from which could be strategically derived the type and amount, the place and timing of 'worthwhile' work. Such a criterion is absent because the outcome of numerous public services, as well as those performed by 'employees' in private sector firms, is not monetary 'profit' but concrete 'uses'; they often help to avoid losses, the quantitative volume of which cannot easily be determined precisely because they *are* avoided.

As far as the technical rationality of service work is concerned, its non-standardization must to a great degree be accepted and replaced by qualities like interactive competence, consciousness of responsibility, empathy and acquired practical experience. In place of the faltering economic-strategic criteria of rationality, one finds calculations based on convention, political discretion or professional consensus. The rationality criteria developed for the use and control of labour power in capitalist commodity production can be transferred to the 'production' of order and normality by service work only within narrow boundaries, and then only through a characteristic reduction in the degree of 'formal' rationality. This means, conversely, that while the sphere of (public and private) service labour is by no means 'liberated' from the regime of formal, economic wage-based rationality, it becomes a separate but functionally necessary 'foreign body' which is externally limited (but not internally structured) by that economic rationality. It is this differentiation within the concept of work that seems to me to constitute the most crucial point supporting the argument that one can no longer talk of a basically unified type of rationality organizing and governing the whole of the work sphere.

The growth of mediating, regulating, ordering and normalizing service labour can, thus, scarcely be interpreted through the model of a 'totalization' of the rationality of work based on the technical-organizational and economically efficient production of commodities by wage labourers. It may, instead, be interpreted through the model of the 'return of the repressed', in the sense of an increase of 'second-order problems' and 'complexity costs' which have accumulated as a result of the mobilization of wage labour; from this standpoint, these problems and costs now require mastery through service labour of various types (e.g. education, therapy, policing, communications) if 'order' within a society based on formal-rational acquisitiveness is to be preserved. The normatively based 'substantive' rationality which had been successfully repressed in productive work and in the transformation of labour power into a marketable 'commodity' resurfaces, so to speak. Indicting the repression of 'substantive' rationality in the sphere of wage labour, it takes the form of growing numbers of service workers and professionals, whose special task is that of institutionally securing social existence through a special type of work.

The ambivalence and independence of this type of social labour derives from the fact that it is an 'indispensable foreign body'. It secures and standardizes the preconditions and boundaries of a type of work to which it does not itself belong. While it functions as a 'watchman and regulator' (Marx) of work and the process of valorization, it is also partially freed from the immediate discipline of an acquisitive social rationality, and from its corresponding achievement and productivity restraints. As an agent of the conscious synthesization of social systems and processes, the service labour of the 'new class' challenges and questions the work society and its criteria of rationality (achievement, productivity, growth) in favour of substantive, qualitative and 'humane' standards of value.[10] In 'post-industrial' societies the subdivision of 'workers as a whole' into 'producers' and 'producers of production' therefore undermines not merely the structural unity of social labour and its governing rationality. It also challenges the rationality standards which guide (and possibly limit) the socially mediated exchange with nature. This line of conflict is evident today in numerous cultural and political tensions between public-sector workers (as well as part of the service staffs of the private sector) and the protagonists of the model of the work society within the old middle class and the industrial working class.[11]

It seems to me highly inconsistent, from a sociological point of view, to simply denounce the 'new class' and their 'new hedonism' as a foreign body without at the same time reflecting upon its functional indispensability. This polemical attitude today obscures and brackets questions concerning the genesis and growth of the structural and cultural influence of the service-providing 'new middle classes' within an acquisitive work society which produces functional gaps and experiences deficits of order, security and normality. If the surveillance, regulation, securing, and pro-gramming of social processes provided by the new middle class is a requirement generated by these functional gaps, and if these services (which are certainly not limited to the state sector) can only become fully functional when they are relatively autonomous and mobilized against the imperatives and restrictions of wage labour, then it is absurd to denounce, in the name of rationality and the ethos of an 'intact work society', those functional groups which can only service this work society by assuming a standpoint which is 'reflexive' and structurally and culturally in tension with this society. Viewed in this way, we are today confronted with a sociologically explainable ambiguity in the concept of work. This ambiguity is of great consequence for the basic conceptual scaffolding of sociology, as well as for the consideration of the ambiguous and contradictory rationality criteria crystallized in the relationship between 'efficient production' and the 'effective maintenance of order'.

## The Decline of the Work Ethic

A second set of doubts about the centrality of work is connected with the subjective valuation of work within the working population. What significance does wage labour have for the mode of life and consciousness of dependent wage-earners in general? Which orientations and motives do they develop concerning spheres of work and economic activity? What is paradoxical in this regard is that while an ever-greater part of the population participates in dependent wage labour, there is a decline in the extent to which wage labour as it were 'participates' in the lives of individuals by involving and shaping them in distinctive ways. This *decentring* of work relative to other spheres of life, its confinement to the margins of biography, is confirmed by many contemporary diagnoses. Dahrendorf, for example, describes the end of an era in which 'work has been the radiating power of life by binding together all the other aspects of its social construction.'[12]

Sociologically speaking, there are two principal mechanisms which could ensure that work plays such a central role in the organization of personal existence: (i) at the level of social integration, work can be normatively sanctioned as a *duty* or, (ii) at the level of system integration, it can be installed as a *necessity*. In the first case, work is the pivotal point of a correct and morally good life; in the second, it is the mere condition of physical survival.[13] The frequently claimed loss of centrality and subjective relevance of work – the proposition under consideration here – would consequently have to be demonstrated and explained by means of factors and developments which render either or both of these mechanisms inoperative.

To begin with, the convincing power of the idea of work as an ethical human duty is probably disintegrating not only because of the erosion of religious or secularized cultural traditions. Nor is it weakened solely because of the growth of a consumer-centred hedonism, whose propagation ruins the moral infrastructure of industrial capitalist societies.[14] The obligatory power of the work ethic may have been additionally weakened by the fact that it can only generally function under conditions which (at least to some extent) allow workers to participate in their work as recognized, morally acting persons. It is quite uncertain whether, and in which areas of social labour, this precondition is today being satisfied.[15] In so far as they are modelled on the pattern of 'Taylorization', processes of technical and organizational rationalization appear instead to result in the elimination of the 'human factor' and its moral capacities from industrial production.[16] From the standpoint of business strategy, it is completely rational to make the production process as independent as possible of this 'human factor', especially since it can always produce uncertainty and disturbance. However, to the extent that the structural preconditions, and the autonomous space, for 'moral' orientations to work are 'rationalized away', these orientations can be neither expected nor demanded. Together with the frequently observed degradation and deskilling of work,[17] the subjective dimension of work – the cluster of obligations and claims associated with 'producer's pride' and its social recognition – is also undermined. Max Weber regarded the calling of work as a precondition of wage labour and the 'spirit of capitalism'. Nowadays, his prognosis that 'rational life-conduct based on the idea of the vocation' will define our lives 'until the last ton of fossilized coal is burnt', [18] is likely to be disputed.

An additional reason for the moral depreciation and declining subjective significance of the sphere of work is the disintegration of the milieux of life which are organized in accordance with the categories of work and occupation and complemented by family tradition, organizational membership, leisure consumption and educational institutions. Today, as Michael Schumann remarks, the socio-cultural 'localization of the context of proletarian life is radically in decline.'[19] The attempt to interpret the life context as a whole in terms of the centrality of the sphere of work is also increasingly implausible because of the time structure of work and its location within the biography of persons. A biographical continuity between what one is trained for and what one is actually doing as a job, as well as an occupational continuity within one's work-life, may today already be rather exceptional. Moreover, the proportion of work-time in people's lives has been declining considerably; free time has also expanded and appears likely to increase further, which means that parallel experiences, orientations and needs other than those based on work are becoming more prominent.[20] Discontinuity in work biography and a contracting portion of work-time in one's life may reinforce the view of work as one concern 'among others' and relativize its function as a touchstone of personal and social identity.[21] To the extent that the experience (or the anticipation) of unemployment,[22] or involuntary retirement from working life, increases,[23] the more the effect of moral stigmatization and self-stigmatization generated by unemployment probably wears off because, beyond a certain threshold (and especially if unemployment is concentrated in certain regions or in certain industries) it can no longer be accounted for plausibly in terms of individual failure or guilt. In light of the present economic data and forecasts, it does not seem at all unrealistic to expect a drastic decline in the absorption potential of the labour market in the foreseeable future; these conditions are likely to reduce still further the average periods of work as a proportion of lifetime, or instead foster the growth of a large 'marginalized' sector of the population outside of the sphere of gainful employment.[24]

Taken together, these circumstances make it seem improbable that work, achievement and acquisition will continue to play a central role as a norm which integrates and guides personal existence. Nor does it seem likely that such a reference norm could be politically reactivated or reclaimed. Recent attempts to 'remoralize' work and treat it as the central category of human existence must therefore be considered as a symptom, rather than a cure, of crisis.

Greater significance might, therefore, be assigned to the second of the mechanisms distinguished above for conditioning people's attitudes toward work – regulation through the positive incentive of the rewards acquired through work and/or the negative incentive of hardship which is to be avoided by working. These mechanisms correspond to the morally neutralized 'instrumental' relation to work described by Goldthorpe. As above, however, I should like to specify a few of the obstacles which also appear to block the effectiveness of this mechanism.

First of all, recent studies in economic psychology indicate that the motivating effect of wage income operates asymmetrically.[25] The individual and (even more so) the collective rise in income does not increase (or increases only insignificantly) the sense of welfare or collective satisfaction, and may well even lead to its diminution. 'The marginal utility of money is different for the reduction of dissatisfaction and the production of satisfaction.'[26] In other words, the motivating effect of alterations in income, at least at a relatively high income level, only appears negatively, as a punishing effect. 'Commodities, and the income to purchase them, are only weakly related to things that make people happy: autonomy, self-esteem, family felicity, tension-free leisure, friendships',[27] while 'satisfaction with non-working activities contributes more than any other factor to life satisfaction.'[28] Speculations about the positive motivating effects of increasing income may, therefore, lose much of their plausibility, at least at the levels of wages and saturation with consumer goods attained in Western Europe.

If positive and negative changes of income have only limited incentive effects on the quantity and quality of work efforts, then this applies even more so if one compares income with the subjectively experienced 'disutility' attached to work. In industrial sociology, a series of findings suggest the notion of a widening gap between the perceived increases of work disutility, on the one hand, and the perceived decline in the intrinsic satisfaction and income derived from work, on the other. During the 1970s, labour power has generally become sensitized to (and critical of) the physical and psychological stresses of work and to its associated health hazards and risks of deskilling. This has resulted in increased union activity over working conditions, and has (outside the unions) even occasionally stimulated questions about whether the struggle *for* improved working conditions must be abandoned as hopeless, and replaced with a struggle *against* work in its industrial form. Above all, this sensitivity has won 'diplomatic recognition' in the form of state programmes for the 'humanization' of work. All this is reinforced by a growing sensitivity to the *social* and *ecological* costs of production, including those not necessarily concentrated at the work place and in specific enterprises. It is an open question whether this development can be explained more by the increasing violation of *constant* demands concerning the quality of work or by the *increase* of such demands (that is, with reference to 'the defence of needs' or to 'rising demands'). What is clear, nevertheless, is that these demands remain mostly unsatisfied. Should the growing sensitivity among large sections of the work-force to the negative utility of wage labour coincide with a decline in the (sensed) use-value of its products, then one could probably expect a growing loss of subjective relevance of wage labour or a declining acceptance of its physical, psychological and institutional conditions. Perhaps symptomatic of this possibility is the fact that the traditional union call for an effective 'right to work' – a demand which nowadays already has a pronounced utopian ring about it – is widely (and with a certain resonance) criticized as not going far enough, and thereby rephrased as a demand for the 'right to useful and meaningful work'.[29] Further evidence of this possibility is provided by the trade union discussion, which arose during the latter half of the 1970s, about the need for a 'qualitative' form of growth which explicitly problematizes the concrete 'use-value' of both the inputs and outputs of the labour process.[30]

The *reduction* of income may of course have a disciplining effect on workers' dispositions. Persuasive arguments against the likelihood of this outcome have, however, been raised even by neo-liberal economic theorists. It is pointed out that the basic principle (espoused by both the Apostle Paul and Josef Stalin) that 'whoever does not work, should also not eat' is not strongly institutionalized in liberal welfare states. This means that, to the degree that the immediate feedback between *individual* work and *individual* income is dissolved into *collectivized* relations and sanctioned by welfare-state institutions and legal claims, as well as by large enterprises and collective wage bargaining, there inevitably develops a classic problem of collective goods – that of uncoupling actions and their consequences on the level of individual actors. Using this argument for a critique of the welfare state, it can be said that the individual's escape from the (ideally) market-imposed compulsion to work is no longer automatically punished and that, conversely, individual efforts are judged to be no longer 'worthwhile' because their returns would be swallowed up by fiscal and para-fiscal burdens. On the contrary, it even becomes rational for the *employee,* who has contributed individually to collective insurance systems,[31] to claim more benefits than he or she has paid for, thus acting as a 'free-rider' of the welfare state; it also becomes rational for the *investor* to 'wait' until the anticipated dose of economic and political subsidies and allowances reduces the level of risk to almost zero. Conservative critics of the welfare state expect critical developments to emerge from such welfare-state arrangements because they subvert the foundations of the rationality of exchange processes and its norm of equivalence. The logic of such critical developments consists in the fact that the objective *conditions* for the stability of the economic system cannot any longer be transformed sufficiently effectively, reliably and quickly into subjective orientations of individual actors. Within the largely irreversible framework of the welfare state and competitive democracy, an adequate level of individual responsiveness to systematic crisis tendencies could only be expected if there existed an effective moral infrastructure of norms of solidarity and obligations to work. Such norms and obligations are thought to be indispensable to effectively prevent both the 'free-riding' encouraged by social policy, as well as the strategic postponement of investments that is made possible by interventionist economic policies.

Whether attitudes towards work can be 'remoralized' is highly doubtful, for the reasons mentioned above, as well as because a reciprocal social-ethical obligatory commitment by *investors* cannot be realistically supposed within the framework of the existing economic order. Equally unrealistic (and often admitted as much by its protagonists) is the proposal of neo-liberal critics of the welfare state to 'reindividualize' the exchange relations of labour and capital markets by cutting back the state's generalized responsibilities for the social and economic well-being of society. Such a radical cure through a return to 'individualism' and 'market regulation' would possibly seriously endanger the relative social harmony of the work society, which historically was achieved only through a state-guaranteed system of collective distribution and security. In this system, there can be little reliance on individualism and the direct disciplining and legitimating effect of economic distress as one of the integrating means of society. This point is, by the way, especially confirmed within recent Marxist analyses, which emphasize that the reserve army mechanism has lost its general efficacy due, among other factors, to the increasingly 'heterogeneous' character of social labour (discussed above).[32]

A strengthening of universal acquisitiveness or a diminution of wage demands and expectations about the quality of work is also hardly to be expected as the result of the experience of long-term mass unemployment and under-employment. This, again, will especially be the case when unemployment is concentrated in certain neighbourhoods, cities, regions, economic sectors, age- or ethnic groups. Instead of stimulating the acquisitiveness of individuals, such situations evidently lead those adversely affected into fatalistic withdrawal or to collective self-interpretations which hold the state's economic, labour market and social policies responsible for such marginalized and negatively privileged groups. The evidently increasing significance of 'ascribed' barriers that block entry into the labour market in general, or into its preferred parts, by definition makes it impossible to overcome these barriers through individual adaptation. Even where such adaptiveness is not logically excluded, the willingness to adapt is empirically distributed in a paradoxical way: efforts for retraining and regional mobility are disproportionately made by those groups of employees whose labour market position least compels them to retrain and relocate, while it is precisely those who are least mobile in terms of residence and skills who are the most severely threatened by the possibility of unemployment.

Such paradoxical features of the labour market are evident in Britain, Italy and North America, and stimulate the forecast that, wherever structural unemployment is concentrated, sub-cultures based on an impoverished 'informal economy' or 'shadow economy' could develop; the members of these sub-cultures are likely to be at least passively hostile to the values and legal rules of the 'work society', and could easily form themselves into a sub-proletarian 'culture of unemployment', a 'non-class of non-workers' (Gorz). In the Federal Republic of Germany, there are also indications of an emerging 'divided society' marked by a productive core and an expanding fringe of supported poor.[33] Gerhard Brandt, for example, distinguishes between a 'simple' polarization of the wage-earning population, a polarization which could be described through such traditional sociological categories as skills and autonomy, and an 'expanded' polarization taking place between the core regions of the work society and 'unskilled and permanently unemployed or irregularly employed people.'[34]

Overall, these briefly summarized social-scientific findings and reflections concerning the subjective relevance and organizing potential of the sphere of work point to a 'crisis of the work society'. A highly developed industrial capitalist society guided by a highly developed welfare state evidently tends to exclude increasing portions of social labour power from participating in the sphere of wage labour. Nor does this society have at its disposal the cultural resources or economic sanctions necessary for stabilizing the subjective centrality of the orientation towards work, achievement and wages through cultural norms or the mute compulsion of market processes. Not only has work been objectively displaced from its status as a central and self-evident fact of life; as a consequence of this objective development, but quite contrary to the official values and legitimation patterns of this society, work is also forfeiting its subjective role as the central motivating force in the activity of workers.

## Toward a Revised Sociological Theory of Structure and Conflict

If it is true that the contemporary forms of social activity usually designated as 'work' have neither a common rationality nor shared empirical characteristics, and if work is in this sense not only objectively formless but also becoming subjectively peripheral, then a question arises: which sociological concepts of structure and conflict are appropriate for describing a society which, in the sense understood here, has ceased to be a 'work society'? If social consciousness should no longer be reconstructed as class consciousness; if cognitive culture is no longer related primarily to the development of the productive forces; if the political system has ceased to be concerned primarily with guaranteeing the relations of production and managing distributive conflicts; and if, finally, the central problems posed by this society can no longer be answered in terms of the categories of scarcity and production, then, clearly, there is a need for a conceptual system which could help to map out those regions of social reality not completely determined by the spheres of work and production.

An elaborate theoretical proposal which is anchored in the history of sociological theory, and which could satisfy this need, is elaborated in Habermas's *Theorie des kommunikativen Handelns*.[35] In an important and persistently controversial departure from the classical theoretical paradigms, Habermas depicts the structure and dynamics of modern societies not as an antagonism rooted in the sphere of production, but as a collision between the 'sub-systems of purposive-rational action' mediated by money and power, on the one hand, and a 'life-world' that 'stubbornly' resists these systems, on the other hand. For more than two decades, Habermas has elaborated a critique of the 'epistemological dominance of labour' in Marxism;[36] despite all its accompanying controversies and ambiguities, this critique corresponds to a broadly 'anti-productivist' current within the Marxist tradition of sociological theory and research. That the factory is neither the centre of relations of domination nor the site of the most important social conflicts; that the 'meta-social' (e.g. economic) parameters of social development have been replaced by a 'self-programming of society'; and that, for Western societies at least, it has become highly misleading to equate the development of the productive forces and human emancipation – all these assumptions and convictions, to be found especially among French theorists like Foucault, Touraine and Gorz, have pervaded our thinking so thoroughly that Marxist 'orthodoxy' no longer has much social-scientific respectability. Perhaps also symptomatic of this emerging need for new conceptual orientations are the growing references to 'modes of life' (instead of the more orthodox 'modes of production') and 'everyday life' in 'Marxist-Leninist' sociology in the German Democratic Republic.[37]

This evident transformation of the background assumptions and conceptual frameworks of many areas and schools within the social sciences is obviously related to the new types of social and political conflicts, whose emergence Raschke has characterized in terms of a transition from a political paradigm of 'distribution' to one of 'form of life'.[38] Social-scientific research on values has demonstrated, although not explained convincingly, an analogous transformation of the prevailing content of socio-political conflict through the conceptual distinction between 'materialist' and 'post-materialist' values. There is now a broad social-scientific consensus that in many Western societies social and political conflict themes (such as peace and disarmament, protection of the natural environment, the definition and institutionalization of sex roles, human and civil rights) dominate the scene. These themes share at least the negative feature that they cannot be interpreted plausibly as derivative conflicts, whose 'real' point of origin is to be found in the sphere of production. Rather, such conflictual issues are to a certain extent confronted by the sphere of production from the outside, where they frequently encounter the unified resistance of *both* labour and capital. These serve as the surprising and confusing structures of conflict which contemporary social scientists seek to reconstruct through such conceptual dichotomies as materialist vs. post-materialist, mode of production vs. form of life, purposive-rational action vs. communicative action, industrial production vs. household, and industrial vs. post-industrial society.[39]

The use of such dichotomies nevertheless typically suffers from two weaknesses, with whose overcoming theoretical development and research in the social sciences will likely (and rightly) be preoccupied during the coming period. First, there is a marked asymmetry in the degree of elaboration of the respective sides of these conceptual pairs: while the dimension of work and production is well known, the structures, actors and rational principles in the realm of 'form of life', as well as the categories appropriate for their analysis, are much less clear. This weakness perhaps explains the noticeable tendency of the social-scientific literature on this subject to borrow heavily from historiography, literature, journalism, politics or philosophy. The other weakness of these binary conceptual schema is that, with the few exceptions of Habermas and (in part) Bell, they amount only to *ad hoc* classifications which remain unintegrated into a dynamic theory of social change. A dynamic theory of social change must seek to explain why the sphere of work and production, in consequence of the 'implosion' of its power to determine social life, forfeits its structuring and organizing capacity, thereby releasing new fields of action marked by new actors and a new form of rationality.[40]

# 6

# Interest Diversity and Trade Union Unity

In both trade union and social-scientific literature, the concept of the unified trade union refers primarily to the political and ideological 'non-partisanship' or 'non-affiliation' of union organizations and policy with political parties. Underlying the concept of a unified trade union is the assumption that the labour movement can realize its goals most effectively when it is organized in such a way that it cannot be split along political and ideological lines, either from within or from without. This 'tactical advantage of unity' of organization and action in turn rests on a conviction that has been fundamental since the early days of the continental European labour movement: the conviction of the *real unity* and common interests of all those people who, being propertyless, are dependent upon selling their labour power and are materially dependent upon the wages they receive for this labour. The fundamental assumption of the labour movement is that, compared with the common interests which are held to arise from this socio-economic situation, special interests – such as those arising from the occupation, economic sector, gender, or nationality of the individual employee – play only a subordinate role.

It is extremely doubtful whether this assumption can still serve as a reliable basis of union politics today. We wish to pursue this question here, by discussing a series of cultural, economic, organizational and political factors that justify corresponding doubts about this assumption. We agree that a crucial problem for

Translated by Karen Grislis and Raymond Morrow. This essay was written with Rolf G. Heinze, Karl Hinrichs and Thomas Olk, and first published as 'Interessendifferenzierung und Gewerkschaftseinheit', *Gewerkschaftliche Monatshefte*, 6 (1981), 336–54.

union policy is whether and how the unity of interests of all 'employees' (a unity which can no longer readily be taken for granted in developed, capitalist industrial societies) can possibly be *restored*, or at least prevented from further disintegration, by trade union organization. We will conclude that this problem can be overcome, but only under the somewhat paradoxical condition that trade union organization does not limit its political activity to the fact that its members are *employees*, but rather concentrates additionally on those living conditions that are not determined directly by wage labour relations and have, therefore, traditionally been included under the jurisdiction of state rather than union policy.

## Crises of Orientation in Worker Consciousness

Today's youth represent a growing political challenge not only for 'people's parties'. While political parties experience a certain discomfort from the fact that the young are voting in above average numbers for 'alternative parties' – or not at all – the specific problem for trade unions is the clear aloofness of the young from union organizations.[1] It is generally evident that a growing number of young people are not active in parties and large organizations, but in such 'grass-roots' social movements as citizen initiatives against nuclear power/weapons.

This tendency of youth to turn their backs on unions, also judged to be problematic by the executive of the Federation of German Trade Unions (*Deutscher Gewerkschaftsbund*), is apparent less in the quantitative change in the degree of organization of young workers, as in the qualitatively decreasing activity of youth on the job and in unions. For a growing number of young workers, the union is no longer perceived as the primary representative of their interests – a development which is only reinforced by signs of a bureaucratic paralysis of labour union work with youth.[2]

This scepticism toward union organizations can be plausibly interpreted as symptomatic of an orientation crisis in worker consciousness that is expressed most strongly among the young. There is little reason to believe that this crisis will be resolved by itself with the passing of the phase of youth; we must at least expect that the attitudes and modes of conduct observable among youth could be the precursors of orientations that will become characteristic of a large part of the work-force. Experiences in the rest of Europe, above all in Italy, show that the collective, union-led fight against poor working conditions is today no longer a mobilizing theme for many young workers. As soon as significant portions of the young cease to understand the factory, 'the job', and the conflict of interests they are collectively exposed to as the 'centre of their life', they withdraw (in thought and deed) from the regular working world, seeking their future on the periphery or even outside the production system. In these circumstances, trade unions and their policies become caught in the predicament of no longer being able to offer these young people any perspective at all.

To be sure, this process of distantiation may still be in its early stages. Yet there are developments in the structure of union membership and the conduct of members that indicate that the capacity of unions for action could be critically impaired in the long run. Work in small commercial enterprises, shops, and agricultural cooperatives,[3] that until now has been sought as an 'alternative' to regular wage labour, is not very well developed in the Federal Republic of Germany. Nevertheless, we are faced with a crisis of orientation or, at least, a reorientation of the consciousness of many wage-dependent workers that will gain in importance in the coming years, as the young 'move up' in the age-structure of the work-force.

That the young show symptoms of such crisis to a greater degree is, of course, also conditioned by their position in the labour market, which has worsened with the economic crisis of recent years. For them the two chief problems are the strict regimentation and lack of autonomy in the work-place, on the one hand, and the growing shortage of jobs on the other. As far as the first point is concerned, it is well known from empirical studies that younger workers place 'new' demands on work – demands, for instance, for more 'self-realization' and for substantially expanded possibilities for self- and cooperative determination.[4] But precisely these demands are not satisfied because of the widespread intensification and regimentation of work, as well as because of the dramatically heightened risks of youth unemployment. One result is that it is especially young workers who flee the working world, whether in the form of absenteeism, 'job hopping', or of 'deviant behaviour' such as drug-use and violence. Confronted with the expectation and perception of less than attractive, and often dismal and insecure futures in the labour market, those young people still concerned with defining their role in society often develop attitudes that differ sharply from the traditional mode of continuous occupational employment as the 'normal' (at least for men) and central determinant of their fate in life.

Empirical studies of changes in work orientation undertaken in the Federal Republic of Germany show that 'traditional' values and work-oriented attitudes (such as income, security, diligence, subordination, discipline) generally have less importance for younger workers (those under thirty-five). 'New' values such as personal self-realization, creativity, and freedom to make decisions have partially taken their place. Corresponding to this 'value transformation' is a certain inevitable change in the spheres of life where these values are to be found or can be realized; with this transformation of values the subjective importance of the work sphere declines, and the domain of leisure increases in importance. There are also signs that this shift in orientation is in no way limited to younger employees. Indications of disintegration or a decreasing valuation of what can be termed the 'traditional work ethic' have been repeatedly demonstrated.[5] These findings suggest that we are faced with neither a 'conjunctural' problem, nor one characteristic only of certain phases of life, but rather with a structural change that will not leave untouched the social structure and organization of the industrial 'work society', including trade unions.

It would of course be mistaken, or at least premature, to diagnose or predict a general 'transformation of values' affecting all strata and age-groups of the working class. Such uniformity on the basis of 'new' cultural values is, we suggest, not at all to be expected. Arising out of conditions of economic crisis and tendencies of cultural change, the problem consists rather in an accentuation of the economic and 'moral' divisions within the working class. The result, in other words, is a growing heterogeneity in the objective situation of different groups of employees, as well as in their subjective perceptions and interpretations. These lines of division emerge more clearly as a consequence of the worsening labour market situation. Even though until the middle of the 1970s unemployment was a largely insignificant, marginal problem in the Federal Republic (with certain regional and conjunctural exceptions), the number of registered unemployed has been on average about one million since 1974–5. The 'problem groups' in the labour market, that is, the young, women, elderly, and handicapped, are those primarily affected by persistently inadequate employment policy. This unequal distribution (or 'structuring') of unemployment has sharpened further in recent years. Many of those affected have been forced into 'alternative roles': 'immigrants' have been sent back to their home countries, the elderly have been retired early, youth have sought later entry into the work-force through prolonging their schooling or delaying it by 'helping out' at home, and women have been urged to take on the role of full-time housewife and mother. In this way it has been possible to partially defuse the political problem of unemployment. The burdens of crisis have been largely shifted on to those 'problem groups' least capable of resistance, and hidden away in various positions within the 'silent reserves' of the labour market. Accordingly, the psychological and social consequences of persisting mass unemployment (in contrast to the various economic ones) have dropped out of the focus of public attention.

According to the findings of Schumann,[6] the risk of becoming unemployed is experienced by a majority of workers as an individual threat and source of uncertainty for which they have no counteracting perspective of solidarity or collective action. This attitude of disoriented powerlessness, which makes unemployment seem more an individual failure or an individual risk than a result of the 'faulty construction' of our economic system, is also likely to be connected with the failure of trade unions and political parties to provide a collective interpretation of the crisis – one that applies to workers as a whole. To make matters worse, a workers' culture that could sustain such a collective, solidaristic interpretation of the situation hardly exists in the Federal Republic any more. The subjective reactions to unemployment and employment risks among the different groups of employees are correspondingly mixed, and even contradictory. Among many the willingness to engage in union activity increases; for others, conservative and liberal ('free market') interpretations gain ground and motivate strongly individualistic competitive behaviour (as if they were following the maxim, 'Everyone for themselves'). The trade unions have not searched adequately for a unified interpretation of the crisis because, in close cooperation with the social-liberal government, and particularly the Social Democratic Party, their hopes have long been placed in the success of state economic and employment policies. Since this success has failed to materialize and also cannot be realistically expected for the medium term, there looms an 'orientation vacuum' (for which trade unions are themselves partially responsible) in which contrary interpretations of the causes and consequences of the crisis, as well as the conditions for overcoming it, multiply. We will, therefore, be able to speak less and less of *the* consciousness of the worker, as if it were a unified and organizationally supported and mediated complex of experiences and orientations. This fact, in turn, has a negative effect on the future capacity of trade union organizations to unify and mobilize support.

These developments thus speak unanimously for the proposition that many wage-dependent workers no longer subjectively see the work sphere as the central fact of life, as the dominant reality from which the social interests, conflicts and communicative relations of the individual are derived. As much as society may 'objectively' remain a 'work society', it nonetheless nourishes and provokes subjective orientations that do not correspond to it. This may also be related, finally, to the fact that the family, welfare state, and the middle class market for goods and services offer a variety of niches in which people can accommodate themselves at least temporarily, even if with considerable material deprivation, without putting their labour power at the disposal of the labour market.

If wage labour is no longer the self-evident centre from which the subjective perspectives on life of the propertyless segments of the population emerge, problems arise for the organization and policy of those associations – the trade unions – that traditionally presupposed precisely this. The global aim of the labour movement – 'emancipating labour' – becomes unclear and even contradictory to the degree that it is interpreted by some as 'liberation *through* work', and by others as 'liberation *from* work'. This conflict was already found in Marx's conception of the emancipation of the working class, and today again dominates many writings on the future of the labour movement.[7]

## The Employment Crisis and the Division of the Labour Market

Today there are many indications that tendencies of polarization and division within the labour market lead to a relative antagonism between the interests of different groups of employees, and that these antagonisms extend into trade union organization.[8] Manifest differences among the interests of particular groups of workers should not be overlooked. Since the members of these different groups or segments of the labour market are organized to varying degrees and, most importantly, contribute to policy formation within the trade union, crises and labour market divisions increasingly put unions in a highly problematic situation. They can only successfully defend the interests of the 'well-organized' groups who 'set the agenda' of discussion by simultaneously accepting impairment of the interests of other groups and segments. All signs indicate that this highly explosive organizational and political constellation will intensify in coming years.

According to prognoses presently at hand regarding the further development of the labour market in the Federal Republic of Germany, unemployment will rise sharply until the middle of the 1980s, if only because of the increasing numbers of potential employees in coming years. Even the current level of unemployment could only be stabilized if the gross national product were to grow by a yearly average of 3.5 per cent. Rates of growth of this order hardly seem realistic. For example, the German Institute for Economic Research (*Deutsches Institut für Wirtschaftsforschung*) expects a middle-range yearly rate of growth of 2.5 per cent,[9] which does not take into account the probable real 1 per cent decline in GNP expected for 1981 due to the conjunctural downswing. The situation is intensified because the rate of growth of productivity will not diminish substantially, since over the next few years the massive repercussions of labour-saving technological change, due primarily to the development of 'micro-electronics', will have to be borne. A doubling of registered unemployment to over two million by 1985 is probable; in trade union circles an increase to four million unemployed by the end of the decade is considered possible.[10]

Since global Keynesian demand policies have in recent years shown themselves to be of only limited effectiveness in dealing with unemployment, their continuation increasingly meets with resistance because of government deficits (among other reasons). In these circumstances a trade union policy oriented towards increasing employment by shortening working hours and increasing flexibility (which has been referred to as 'the' contribution of unions to diminishing employment problems)[11] acquires increased importance, even if this is not generally understood.

The global increase in unemployment in the Federal Republic anticipated by all experts will, however, affect individual sectors and regions in very different degrees. Whereas 'obsolete' regions, those exposed to particularly strong international competition, and those that are structurally weak must anticipate unemployment rates of over 20 per cent,[12] prospects are substantially more favourable in other regions. Consequently, here as well, trade union policy is confronted with intensified problems of unification. The same holds true in another way given the massive consequences of rationalization, such as those already becoming evident in the printing and paper industry (IG Druck und Papier). In this situation, unions are forced to give priority to qualitative questions (such as job security and prevention of loss of membership) that touch on very restricted groups of workers, in addition to 'quantitative' questions such as wage and labour contracts. Moreover, the introduction of new technology offers enterprises substantially extended leeway for the control and supervision of employees through personal information systems,[13] by means of which it is possible for them to categorize employees on the basis of individualized data, and to play them off against each other. New challenges to trade union and business policy result from all of these tendencies.

These considerations and possible developments point to an increase in various types of conflicts of interest and relations of competition between individual employees and groups of employees. An important future line of division along which these conflicts could crystallize is that between male, native, highly qualified employees of middle age, on the one hand, and poorly qualified employees burdened with greater labour market risks (women, immigrants, youth, the elderly and handicapped) on the other. This division has of course traditionally dominated the politics of interest representation in business and trade unions. Under conditions of higher and sharply structured unemployment, nearly every union demand and bargaining position necessarily has clearly recognizable beneficial effects for one side and disadvantages for the other; this has already been demonstrated in business and labour regulations and also in socio-political protective measures such as early retirement.[14] In negotiating social priorities, individual company councils have fallen back on these same discriminatory categories (age, absenteeism, health, etc.) in the case of dismissals, on criteria that were traditionally used by management as the basis for selection. This example provides graphic evidence that the crisis is not only shifting the balance *between* labour and capital, but additionally *within* the working class, opening up a gap between 'winners' and 'losers' such that the unity of the countervailing power of trade unions is in turn being impaired.[15]

The 1981 programme of the Federation of German Trade Unions (as previously in the 1963 programme) says: 'As a collective organization of workers, salaried employees and civil servants, trade unions look after the economic, social and cultural interests of all employees and their families, and serve the needs of the common good.' Obviously the strong 'universalistic' claim of trade unions to represent 'all' interests of 'all' employees is put to an exceptionally difficult test in view of the developmental tendencies and threats discussed above. In the event that this test cannot be passed by means of new political demands and new types of organization, the Federation of German Trade Unions and its affiliates would have much more to lose than the credibility of their programmatic normative claims. If opposing organizations and political forces succeed in pointing to a systematic 'bias' and 'distortion' of interest in the policies and organizations of the Federation's unions, and thus reveal them as not of 'the' worker, but rather as a privileged part of this totality, the political importance of the Federation, its legitimacy and effectiveness would be damaged. At the very least, impetus would be given to proposals for an association law, on the one hand, and the foundations of competing organizations, on the other. The lines of division and tendencies towards polarization within the working class that would appear more evident under these conditions would of course not be the fault of the trade unions. Yet this outcome would open up new possibilities for attack by their political opponents, not to mention the organizational and political weakening of the trade unions that would always be associated with such polarizing tendencies. The capacity for action of the Federation and its individual members could, therefore, be decisively determined in the future by their answer to the question of how far the marginalized groups of employees can successfully be reintegrated, or at least prevented from being objectively and subjectively more distant from the 'core groups' of employees. Until now, the dimensions and risks associated with these 'problems of unification' of the unified trade union do not seem to have been adequately understood.

## Trade Union Policy under Changed Structural Conditions

Generally speaking, there are three different levels of action available to trade unions for articulating and implementing their demands, and they have sharply varied in importance depending on economic and political conditions. These levels of action are (i) the wage-contract; (ii) policy in the firm and company agreements; and (iii) attempts to influence political actors (parties, parliaments, governments). Since 1969, the Federation of German Trade Unions and its members have relied heavily on their chances of influencing state policy, without completely neglecting the other two levels (those of wages and the enterprise). This is strongly connected with their traditional close cooperation with the Social Democratic Party (SPD), which in that year became the governing party. The prevailing trust in the effectiveness of the cooperative 'trade union-state' axis has, of course, noticeably disintegrated because of (among other things) the obvious failure of the SPD in implementing a satisfactory codetermination policy. Since then, there has been a noticeable tendency of workers to instead rely on 'their own forces', that is, on the effectiveness of the wage-negotiation level of action.

Wage-contract regulations must, of course, be implemented and changed on the first level (as is the case with state labour and social policy) before they become an actual element of working life. Direct and formal control by trade unions over this process of implementation is, to a considerable degree prevented, however, by the Federal Republic's 'dual' system of interest representation, which distinguishes sharply between the works council and the trade union. The works council is an extremely legalistic body that takes on a 'buffer position' in the highly charged field of opposing interests between personnel and management, on the one hand and trade unions, on the other. In particular, the works council – controlled in detail by the norms of respecting the 'good of the company' and a 'duty to keep the peace' – does not have at its disposal the means of struggle and sanction necessary for carrying through its own demands or altering wage and state decisions. Still, social and political improvements for individual groups of employees have been realized now and again by way of company agreements that became models for 'cover-all' regulations in wage contracts or laws.

Nevertheless, in view of the economic developments expected throughout the 1980s, as well as the foreseeable aggravating technological and organizational changes (such as micro-electronics), the work-force within firms is going to come under increasing pressure, not only in terms of employment security but also with regard to the quality of work (qualifications and working conditions). The danger in this situation is that the representation of workers' interests within the firm will be compelled to give priority to implementing firm-specific regula-tions which seek to preserve the relatively favoured position of the regular work-force, that is, to reach agreements that indeed do *not* improve the positions of already disadvantaged groups in the firm and, consequently, to expose them even more to the market-power strategies of capital.[16] These 'advantageous regulations' for the members of the regular work-force would no longer be 'forerun-ners' of a trade union policy aimed at evening out labour market situations, but would widen even further the gaps within the labour market and the living situations of the working class.

There has been a series of successful and promising attempts to 'link' policy within the firm (for instance by way of union negotiators) to trade union policy and thus to unify them on a trans-firm basis. Today, on the other hand, there are already tendencies that point to an independence of the representation of interests within the firm *vis-à-vis* trade union policy. In particular, the importance of the level of the firm has grown considerably in the course of the development and solidification of the partial labour markets to be found in large industries. Wage contract regulations are supplemented by firm-specific agreements to an increasing extent. But, since the autonomous power opportunities of works councils are not sufficient to control the personnel strategies of management, the politics of interest representation in the firm is often limited in scope to accepting management decisions at the outset, and then negotiating the execution and distribution of the negative consequences for the employed. Works councils therefore see themselves forced, in the case of dismissals, to accept and actively defend 'second-best' solutions by, for instance, urging the older and less efficient to consent to early retirement, even though such a 'solution' goes against the more comprehensive demands of trade union policies for humane working conditions. In order to avert social hardships among other groups of employees, especially 'core groups', and in the absence of a countervailing power position, the councils are often forced to agree to such selection processes. In any case, the problem for trade unions of unifying interests seems to be further complicated by the growing importance of the level of the firm (and the correspondingly growing weight of 'egoistic' demands within it). The works council, both because of its relative weakness and the fact that it quite naturally deals primarily with particular problems and interests within the firm, is a body whose noticeable strengthening *vis-à-vis* the wage-contract level must lead to 'centrifugal' tendencies in trade union policy, and this means an intensification of the problem of unification.

The works councils have gained in organizational and political influence over the past few years within trade unions. Conflicts within the firm have also increased relative to wage-contract conflicts. Some authors interpret these local and often militant labour disputes – which of course have been almost exclusively of a defensive character – as signs of a general sharpening of class conflict.[17] To us, however, there is considerable doubt whether the recently observed tendency of trade union policy to relinquish trust in the effectiveness of the state, and to turn to the level of the firm, can be understood as the expression of active and solidaristic 'class politics'. Any hasty optimistic evaluation of this development is rebutted by the fact that trade union political dominance of works councils amounts to a stronger orientation to the (relatively privileged) 'core groups' of employees and it has, accordingly, a largely reactive and defensive character.[18]

While previous hopes for a division of labour and cooperative effort between trade unions and the policies of a social democratic government have given way to a recognizable disillusionment, forms of cooperative social partnership on the 'political' level (often referred to as 'neo-corporatism') can in no way be completely written off. Now, as before, there are strong reasons why both state policy makers and the trade union leadership have an interest in the cooperative regulation of conflict and crisis, as Streeck in particular has demonstrated.[19] Streeck merely intimates, however, that this cooperation also comes at the price of a further dissolution of the capacity for integration or unification within associations. And this is particularly the case for 'unified trade unions' such as the members of the Federation of German Trade Unions who are, of course, committed to at least nominal party-political neutrality. Moreover, not all employees profit equally from this cooperative strategy which is increasingly pursued to avert local and regional crises: those who are favoured and still employed, and are anyway primarily from the privileged 'core groups'. As bureaucratically structured, complex organizations, unions are drawn into a precarious situation to the degree that they allow themselves to be held responsible for fulfilling general economic functions and stabilization requirements. If this happens, they must extensively weaken their ideologies, symbols and mobilizing perspectives in order to be able to effectively play their role as 'trustworthy', 'responsible' and 'committed' discussion partners in the formation of public policy. They thereby abandon the inner-organizational means of negotiating agreement and unification which alone could help to bridge the centrifugal and fragmenting tendencies that characterize the situation and consciousness of employees as a group.

The dangers addressed here are by no means presented simply from the biased political viewpoint of a 'leftist' conception of trade unions. The lines of division (as well as the cultural, economic, and organizational factors that will probably cause them to deepen further) are, rather, phenomena whose effects will undermine the prospects for success of even a trade union policy that is consciously 'modern', 'reformist' and cognizant of the realities of a capitalist social and economic structure. What is crucial for trade unions (more than for any other type of association) is that they are only capable of action *as organizations* to the extent that their membership base is prepared to act in solidarity in the service of interests that are recognized as common interests. Under the influence of growing heterogeneity, or even antagonism between the interests of particular, increasingly differentiated groups of employees (resulting from cultural, economic and organizational processes of differentiation), the chances of realizing employee interests will lessen to the degree that the level of effective solidarity among the membership base shrinks, that is, in so far as these tendencies toward differentiation and division cannot be successfully counteracted. The risks for *any* conception of trade union policy that arise here result from a creeping erosion of the trade union potential for opposition and bargaining, a potential which could be mobilized in case of conflict through the effective willingness of the membership base to struggle. In addition, these risks result from the foreseeable 'counter-attack' by opposing political and social forces, which would be anxious to either legally restrict trade union domains (to 'all' interests of 'all' employees, as in the Federal Republic of Germany's plans for an 'association law') and/or to occupy these domains *de facto* through the establishment of competing organizations.

## Towards a Strategy of Solidarity

If one begins with the reality and weight of these threats to the inner continuity of the 'unified trade union', and accepts the need for a policy to counteract these diverse fragmentation tendencies, the main features of such a policy are not difficult to specify. In the first instance, it is a question of whether and how the means of trade union policy can overcome or unify the differences and antagonisms between the interests, labour market position, and consciousness of the different categories of employees.

Apart from a 'solidaristic' wages policy aimed at levelling the wage differentials between groups with different levels of training and types of activity, we see a primary point of departure in the increased receptiveness to the 'qualitative' demands that correspond to the needs of those groups of employees affected by particularly high work and employment risks. By concentrating on such demands, it might be possible to thwart those strategies on the part of capital aimed at intensifying the segmentation of the. labour market and, thereby, the chances of playing off different groups of employees against each other. Further points of departure for a compensatory unification of trade union interests have recently been raised in discussions in the Federal Republic and internationally,[20] and are evident in efforts to influence state, and specifically municipal, politics through proposals for effective 'equalization of life' situations which depend crucially upon the reproductive sector (regional structural policy, as well as transportation, educational and cultural policy). To counteract the divergence of interests between core groups in the labour market (i.e. between essentially spec lized, skilled labour, on the one hand, and the 'marginal group ' of employees who are poorly qualified and burdened with high unemployment risks on the other), the 'professionalizing' strategy outlined by Crusius and Wilke would also have to be considered.[21] This strategy would place certain obstacles in the way of the present tendencies toward the 'deskilling' of work, and qualitatively expand the demand for the 'right to work' in the sense of a 'right to *career-oriented* work'.

It is obvious that the success of such a strategy of solidarity, one that re-establishes and defends the common interests of all employees, could not be envisaged without very vigorous efforts to also anchor and secure this unity on the level of trade union and political consciousness. This would have to take place through education, enlightenment and mobilization grounded in a distinct awareness of the hazards that would result from the creeping splintering of the interests of employees into 'sectionalized', conflicting special interests.

As immense as these proposed wage, organizational and educational efforts seem, it is also clear that the division between privileged and underprivileged categories of employees is only *one* of the points at which the trade union claim to universally represent employee interests is becoming increasingly precarious. Another division is that between the totality of those employed and the growing number of those who have temporarily or permanently 'dropped out' of a labour market that is increasingly less capable of integrating them, and who are no longer oriented subjectively to life-long wage-dependent employment (as has been discussed above in the example of youth). The development of the labour market not only permits vertical barriers to emerge between privileged and disadvantaged categories of employees, that is, between the 'above' and the 'below'; it also allows lines of division to emerge between the employed and the (more or less permanently) unemployed, that is, between the 'inside' and the 'outside'.

The more *this* split within the totality of those who are 'wage-dependent' becomes clear, the more trade unions will lose their political and organizational footing because even more people will have 'dropped out' of the labour market, hence out of the (traditionally understood) domain of trade union organization and responsibility. The seriousness of this problem cannot be overcome by means of trust in the state's capacity to 'restore full employment', to say nothing of trust in the 'self-healing powers of the market economy'. Rather, the view seems to be gaining ground (although it may only be voiced behind closed doors and in hushed tones) that strategies promising the successful creation of 'full employment' are not on the cards for the foreseeable future of capitalist industrial society, and that the concept of 'full employment' itself has, therefore, become unrealistic and utopian in the worst sense. This is true at least if one understands full employment to be not merely an arbitrarily manipulable social statistic, but rather a condition in which all those individuals who are not, or do *not* wish to be, supported through the family system, public security or support payments, or capital income, have a real chance of earning a labour-market income. There is a growing tendency, for the sake of nominally improving labour market statistics, to transfer an increasing number of workers into the 'silent reserve', where they are certainly provided for, but also patronized and put 'out of action'. Since the organizational and policy self-interest of trade unions will no longer be served by thoughtless passivity, concepts and strategies will be necessary for dealing with the foreseeable acute 'employment gap'. Thus far the guides for 'an orderly retreat from a work society' (Scharpf) have only involved hesitant and unsuccessful proposals for shortening working time and increasing its flexibility. These visions suffer from a lack of powerful trade union support for their realization, the great uncertainty of their efficacy in dealing with the employment problem, and the fact that the demand for more 'leisure time' itself would have to be concretized with regard to the type of useful and satisfying activity that would then take place in the framework of this leisure time.

Given this situation, only a 'forced withdrawal' of increasing portions of the population from the labour market can be envisioned as an alternative to an 'orderly retreat'. This is, of course, completely unacceptable for any trade union policy worthy of the name, because of the accompanying discriminatory effects and the disastrous political and wage policy consequences it could easily lead to. What could then be more obvious than to have the trade unions themselves give priority to consciously assuming responsibility for representing those groups of wage-dependent individuals who have dropped out of the labour market, whether for objective or subjective reasons, whether temporarily or permanently? This could happen, among other ways, through a revival of such organized forms of human activity outside the labour market as self-help groups, cooperatives and voluntary associations, for which there are still models to be rediscovered in the tradition of the socialist labour movement.[22]

A third division becomes evident when one considers long-term shifts in the composition of the life interests of the mass of the population. It is the fundamental. assumption of the labour movement, both in its political and, especially, its trade union wings, that the most important life interests of the entire population can be satisfied to the degree that *work and earning* interests of *the employed* are also satisfied. The above quotation from the programme of the Federation of German Trade Unions also begins from this premise – what else can it mean when it speaks of 'the economic, *social* and *cultural* interests' of employees '*and their families*', as well as of the 'needs of the common good'? Today, there is some doubt whether this equation of income interests and the collective interest still holds, and under what conditions. It is undeniable that only strong trade unions can defend and improve the material living conditions of those who are dependently employed, and that only strong trade unions can ward off attacks on basic rights and political democracy. But, on the other hand, it is also obvious that a growing number of people see their central life interests in domains that do not automatically form part of (and are sometimes even damaged by) the trade union struggle for improving the purchasing power of employees.

We will give only two examples of this. The more social relations and the conditions of reproduction are maintained 'collectively' in complex industrial societies, the more the individual's earned income becomes *insignificant* for the quantity and quality of this maintenance. For many inhabitants of over-crowded urban centres, it is already the case that they could not 'purchase' satisfying living conditions, to say nothing of other, less 'purchasable' aspects of the quality of life, even if their income was suddenly doubled. Stated in a somewhat exaggerated and paradoxical fashion: there seems to be a 'law' which states that the higher our income, the smaller the portion of our needs that can be satisfied with it. The second example is related to the social and economic costs of industrial growth: the more the income interests of the employed can be successfully advanced, the more severely other interests, namely those of consumers and 'affected' third parties, are harmed by the consequences of the resulting industrial growth, and the more questionable becomes the trade union claim to be the 'universal' representative of interests.

This vicious circle could remain concealed only as long as there was a functioning division of labour and cooperation between the trade union and political wings of the labour movement. The trade unions concerned themselves, so to speak, with the advancement of the income interests of employees; and the associated, but not identical political labour movement – above all in the form of social democracy – concerned itself with social security, the construction of housing, and environmental and consumer protection. The reasons why this cooperation no longer seems to function as smoothly today, following the end of reform politics and the now-manifest hopelessness of state policies of full employment, are quite well known and otherwise not of interest in this connection. Here it is only important to note that as a consequence of this no longer functioning division of labour, trade unions find themselves in a situation in which they are confronted with a third division within the category of those who are wage-dependent: the line of division between income interests and the consequent interest in economic growth on the part of consumers and 'affected' third parties on the other. This division, which often cuts across individuals, manifests itself organizationally in the Federal Republic of Germany (as in most other comparable countries) in the opposition between the established political formations of the labour movement and 'green', 'multi-coloured' and alternative social and political movements or groups within and outside those formations.

As with divisions in which the interests of privileged and underprivileged workers become strongly opposed, the obvious strategic reaction of trade unions to the tension between 'income' and 'life' interests would consist of withdrawing into their own, increasingly narrow domains and accepting developments as apparently unavoidable. Our interpretation is that such a retreat and the associated reduction of demands would place trade unions in a losing position (in part because they would then be weakened organizationally, and also because they would be made vulnerable externally in their claim to representation). The retreat would sooner or later initiate a spiral of continuous restriction of trade union claims to responsibility. The alternative would be to capture back the (by no means irrevocably) lost terrain by means of a 'leap forward'. The precondition for this would be not only the attempt to unify the interests of the privileged and underprivileged politically and through a wages policy; nor would it involve only the further attempt to establish a common trade union represent-ation of employed and unemployed wage-dependent workers. In view of the mentioned split between 'income' and qualitative 'life' interests, there would also have to be an attempt to develop a unifying trade union conception of a 'tolerable' production system and of the use-value of its products, that is, an attempt to reconcile the interests of affected third parties and consumers with the perspective of producers. This would not only be a matter of defending the 'right to work' as well as the 'right to career-oriented work' (or a right to meaningful and secure activity outside the labour market). It would also involve defending the right to 'useful' work.

# 7

# Two Logics of Collective Action

## Introduction

Two plus two *equals* four; person X and person Y have *equal* access to higher education. It is not just playing on words if we start with the observation that the relationship of 'equality' is both a logical and a sociological one. Moreover, the two dimensions of the term *equality* are connected in an interesting way. Sociological measurements of social equality/inequality of income, wealth, power, prestige, etc. provide us with information only to the extent that they indicate the distance or approximation of a given social reality to a normative ideal of equality. Knowing something about actual patterns of distribution is of interest only because we make at least implicit reference to a logical equation, which is stated in a normative form, the cognitive substance of which is something like the belief that 'all men are equal', that is, their rights or claims or legitimate aspirations *are* equal in a logical sense. To those who are unaware of this logical equation, and to those who are neither supporters nor opponents of the norm based upon it, the sociological information about actual equality/inequality is quite useless. What matters is not information about degrees of equality as such, but the conclusions we can draw from it regarding the degree of conformity between sociological and logical equality. In this sense, it is its critical function that makes sociology interesting.

There was no need for sociology in feudal societies or during the transition from the feudal to liberal-capitalist social formations.

This essay, co-authored with Helmut Wiesenthal, first appeared in M. Zeitlin (ed.), *Political Power and Social Theory*, (1980), 67–115.

What was needed was *normative* political theory, which leads, in the works of the eighteenth-century philosophers, to the establishment of the normative equation: each member of civil society is entitled to the same rights and freedoms as every other member of the community; citizen equals citizen. What was needed in order to establish equations of this kind was not sociological research, but normative-deductive reasoning and sophisticated speculation about the conditions under which such equality might materialize. Why was no sociology needed? Because in order to discover the contrast between the normative equation and actual inequality, one had not to conduct empirical research, but only to look into the legal codes and statutes that regulated the privileges and hierarchies of feudal society. The conflict was one of norm vs. norm, not norm vs. fact, for inequality was itself *institutionalized* by explicit privilege. All the early liberal philosophers had to do was to argue that the realization of an alternative set of norms would lead to the greater happiness of the community. They did so by attacking the *institutionalized* and *explicitly normative* order of the old society and confronting it with the new liberal equation – an equation, of course, that was victorious only because it became the programme and ideology of the ascending class of merchants and industrial capitalists. The basic schema of their social philosophy was to demonstrate that what deserves to be treated as equal was actually institutionalized as unequal. On the philosophical plane, the two sets of normative statements opposed each other.

Quite different from this model of critique is the way in which the radical critique of bourgeois society proceeds. Its *modus operandi* is the demonstration that, although the liberal equation has been institutionalized, granting free and equal access to the market and even free and equal access to the political process, the institutionalization of bourgeois freedom and equality has not, in fact, led to anything approaching *actual* equality; it has, rather, produced and continually reproduces factual inequality on the largest scale. The difference between the two modes of critique is this: while the power of the aristocracy over peasants was institutionalized and sanctioned as part of the political order in feudal society, the power of the capitalist class over the working class is not only not institutionalized in bourgeois society but is even apparently neutralized by the institutional pattern of equal citizenship. How then can inequality emerge under the auspices of the institutionalized liberal equation? Any answer to this question must be sociological. It must leave the plane of a normative discourse, which challenged the legitimacy of the feudal order, and engage in the 'sub-institutional' analysis of the facts and causal links among facts which lead, on the basis of institutionalized equality, to the inequality of classes and groups. The confrontation is no longer between one set of norms and another, but between norms and systematic causal theories of social life. The critical objection is no longer that what properly deserves (according to a normative theory) to be treated equally is treated unequally, but that what *is* strictly equal by institutionalized norms still turns out (according to causal processes established by sociological research) to be vastly unequal, in actual fact. The objects of the two models of critique are reciprocal. The philosophical tradition criticizes doctrines that help to institutionalize and defend inequality where equality *should* prevail. The sociological model of critique demonstrates that, due to systemic causes, inequality prevails even though economic and political equality *are* institutionalized. The one puts into question and challenges the false '*hierarchization*' of the equal; the other, the ideological *equalization* of those who in fact remain unequal. What the philosophers attacked were doctrines that treated equals as non-equal. The radical sociologists and political economists attack ideologies (such as liberal pluralism) that created the mere appearance of equality, where, in fact, vast inequalities persist. Social philosophy aims at the normative critique of institutionalized *inequality;* its historical place is the ascending bourgeois-capitalist social formation. Sociology aims at the empirical critique of institutionalized *equality* (of universal citizenship and market participation) and at a theoretical understanding of how such equality is perverted into actual inequality; its historical place is industrial capitalism.[1]

What this crude schematization of the history and political implications of social thought should be able to demonstrate is this: there are two categories of errors or mistakes that we can fall victims to as social scientists. One is to conceive of the equal as hierarchical – the mistake of the reactionary defenders of the old order. The other one is to conceptually equate the elements of what, in fact, remains a hierarchical structure – the business of the liberal ideologists. In both of these cases it is true that mistaken logic, i.e. the muddling of identicalness and difference, not only turns into bad sociology but also has political implications.

Although the first mistake has a longer history, it is hardly to be found less frequently than the second one. A familiar example is the conceptual distinction between blue-collar and white-collar workers[2] The problem here is not that sociologists take into account the many and well-documented differences in character of work, lifestyle, political behaviour, and attitudes that exist between the two groups. It is rather, that in doing so, many sociologists fail to take into account the possibility (a) that such differentiations within the working class as a whole may well be different responses to the identical situation of wage labour, and (b) that the underlying sameness of this situation becomes increasingly clear under the impact of mechanization, deskilling, and the increasing job insecurity that affects white- as well as blue-collar workers. The criticism of such eliptical conceptualizations is that they are wholly concerned with the subjective awareness of differences, while ignoring the equality of the objective conditions to which all wage workers are subject.

In our present context, the reverse mistake is of greater interest, namely, that of conceptually equating the unequal. An example is the juridical treatment of strikes and lock-outs as 'equivalent' and therefore equally legitimate measures of the supply and demand sides of the 'labour market'. Another example is the economic concept of the labour market itself, to the extent that it suggests (a) the principal sameness of markets (i.e. markets for goods and services and markets for labour) and (b) the equality of freedom of choice that 'partners' in markets (i.e. agents on the supply and demand sides) enjoy in making contracts with one another. Such conceptual equations tend to de-emphasize, to say the very least, structural differences between labour power and any commodity,[3] as well as the resulting asymmetry of power and freedom that emerges between the supply and demand sides as soon as labour power is allocated through markets, i.e. as soon as it is institutionally treated as if it were a commodity, while in fact it is not, because it cannot be physically separated from its 'owner', it does not come into being due to the expectation of its saleability, it is of no use-value for its (propertyless) 'owner', and because its owner is, therefore, forced to enter into a wage contract. Such intellectual

categorizations of the world correspond quite neatly to the real
categorizations according to which social and economic life is
organized, and they tend to neglect differences which are not
recognized by the practice of capitalist social arrangements.
Liberal social science does not perform its ideological (and thus
political) function by normatively advocating certain policies,
supporting established elites, or giving advice to the ruling class.
Though it does all these things, too, they are contingent upon
*individuals* acting within the system of science and do not
constitute part of its intellectual structure. This intellectual
structure itself performs an ideological and political function by
committing either the 'feudal' error of 'false differentiation' and/or
the 'liberal' error of 'false identity'. Consequently, the intellectual
practice of coding reality by the dramatic use of non-equations
and equations is (and has always been) the object of criticism, not
only of the Marxist tradition in social science, but also of all social
scientists who do not want truth to be perverted by the positivistic
standard of conformity to existing social arrangements.

It is in this spirit and on the basis of these epistemological
premises that we want to examine the hidden difference that is
ignored by the prevailing practice of 'coding' social reality by
employing the concept of 'interest group' (or 'organized interest').
Our argument will try to provide theoretical evidence for the
proposition that, just as much as economic concepts (of market,
commodity, freedom of contract, supply and demand, as they are
applied to both capital and labour) tend to deny (and even to
block the cognitive access to) the reality of class, the political
science concept of interest group (as the outgrowth of some
class-unspecific 'logic of collective action' and a neutral form that
can be filled equally by heterogeneous 'interests')[4] performs the
same function of obscuring the category of social class by the
intellectual practice of equating the unequal. Again, the link
between logical and sociological uses of 'equality' is obvious: if, as
interest-group theory suggests, the pure organizational form of
organized-interest representation is equally accessible (and in this
sense logically equivalent) to the 'groups' of capital, labour, and
others, then there is no reason to assume that the use of this
perfectly neutral instrumentality will result in anything like
systemic asymmetry of wealth and power (i.e. social inequality).
Charles Lindblom has remarked: 'One of the conventional

insensitivities of contemporary social science is revealed in scholarly works on interest groups. By some unthinking habit, many such works treat all interest groups as though on the same plane, and, in particular, they treat labour, business and farm groups as though operating at some parity with each other.'[5] Let us see what can be done about this 'unthinking habit'.

## Beyond the 'Interest Group' Stereotype: the Associational Practices of Labour and Capital

If one compares associations of business firms with labour unions solely with respect to these properties of formal organization, there seem, at first glance, to be a number of similarities; these are normally used to define the concept of 'interest groups', of which both types of organizations are then said to be sub-cases. For instance, in these kinds of organizations we find voluntary membership, a more or less bureaucratic structure of decision making, dependence upon material and motivational resources, efforts to change the respective environments into more favourable ones, and so forth.

What we want to do in this section is to go beyond these formal analogies in order to analyse the different functions that the common practice of formal association performs for labour and capital and, more specifically, to find out in which way each of the two succeeds in gaining power through organization. Such an analysis requires more than merely looking into the process of organization itself. What is needed in addition is to look into the specific characteristics of what, in terms of organizational analysis, may be called the *input* factors (i.e. what is to be organized) and the nature of *outputs* (i.e. the conditions of strategic success that are to be found in the organizations' environments). These contextual factors are seen here as major determinants of those structures and practices that make up the internal process of the two types of organization.

In dealing with class-specific differences of the respective types of input factors, internal processes, and relative organizational advantages (outputs) of the two types of organizations, we will focus on the principal relations that unions, on the one hand, and business and employers associations, on the other, entertain in their environments. Our aim is to demonstrate that, in each of the three aspects, labour and capital show substantial differences with respect to the functioning and performance of their associations. These differences, we will argue, are consequences and manifestations of antagonistic class relations.

## 1   *Input factors*

What do unions organize? This simple question cannot be answered in quite such simple terms. Do they organize labour, or workers, or the interests of workers; or is it what Marx thinks of as the only value-producing potency, namely labour power? For a better understanding of exactly what the 'input' of unions is, we must, first of all, keep in mind that unions are associations of members who, before they can become members of unions, are already members of other organizations, namely employees of capitalist enterprises. Thus, unions are 'secondary' organizers, and capital itself functions as a primary organizer.

In what sense does capital organize workers? Its function is to combine labour and capital goods in such a way that surplus value is produced. Both of these elements that capital combines consist, however, of social labour; they differ only in that the one is the result of labour power that has been applied in the past (past labour congealed into capital goods which are, therefore, sometimes referred to by Marx as 'dead' labour) and the other is labour power as a present potency ('living' labour).

Before capitalists can start to combine these two categories of elements, they first have to acquire them. The form in which this is done is, in both cases, that of a contract. Such contracts do not involve any problems in the case of 'dead' labour, or capital goods; the capitalist simply transforms money capital into particular machinery and raw materials. Contracting with the bearers of labour power, i.e. employing 'living labour', is, however, by no means as simple as buying and installing 'dead' labour. Obviously, capitalists cannot buy labour itself – a certain quantity of activity, as it were. Instead, they have to apply incentives, force, etc. to the *bearers* of labour power – that is, to workers – in order to get them to work and to keep them working. This very special condition leads to the peculiarities of the exchange relationship between capital and labour, which are unlike those of any other markets (and which make it, incidentally, quite inaccurate to speak of labour power as a 'commodity', even though it is treated as if it were a commodity). The fundamental problem with which the capitalist has to deal is the fact that the labour that he or she wants to combine with the other 'factors of production' is not physically separable from the bearer of labour power. It always remains under the physical control of the workers, whose aspirations, experiences, interests, and subjective willingness to work will always influence the concrete labour process. The work can only be done *by* the workers although their labour legally 'belongs' to the capitalists. If the capitalists want to get the work done, they have, for better or worse, to rely on the willingness of the workers to 'give away' their physical and intellectual capacities by applying them to concrete labour tasks. In this way, the quantity and the quality of actual work performance remains subject to a permanent conflict that is not to be resolved by formal contractual relations in which both sides have engaged. Both 'partners' of exchange, therefore, try to improve their respective positions by resorting to a wide variety of positive and negative sanctions. This is the only way in which the 'equivalence' of a certain amount of labour and a certain wage is established, challenged, and re-established.

Looking upon this situation from the point of view of the workers, one wonders how they can deal with this condition of indeterminacy and conflict. First of all, there is very little scope of choice for them to act as individual workers. But how can they possibly act otherwise? After all, labour power is, physically and legally, controlled and 'owned' by discrete individuals. The important point here is the following: while you can add one unit of (money) capital to another unit of money capital so that you get an integrated total in which the constituent parts are as entirely unrecognizable and indistinguishable as if you had poured two glasses of water into the same pot, you can do this only with 'dead' labour, not with living labour. One simply cannot add one unit of labour power to another so as to obtain what would be a 'double-worker', who could then legally contract for and physically control twice the amount of labour power; two rocks put into the same pot remain two discrete rocks. Living labour power is both indivisible and 'non-liquid', and it is this *insuperable individuality* that we will show to be of the greatest consequences for labour's specific 'logic of collective action'.

But, first of all, this individuality of living labour is (among other things that also have to do with the fact that it is 'living') the cause for the emergence of a power relationship between labour and capital. The latter normally comprises many units of 'dead' labour under a unified command, whereas each individual worker controls only one unit of labour power and, moreover, has to sell this under competitive conditions with other workers who, in turn, have to do the same. In other words, the *atomized* form of living labour that stands in conflict with the *integrated*, or liquid, form of 'dead' labour causes a power relationship; the capital ('dead' labour) of each firm is always united from the beginning, whereas living labour is atomized and divided by competition. Workers cannot *'merge'*; at best, they can *associate* in order to partly compensate for the power advantage that capital derives from the liquidity of 'dead' labour.

In the absence of associational efforts on the part of workers, the conflict that is built into the capital/wage labour relationship is bound to remain very limited. The workers would simply have no bargaining power that they could use to improve their conditions of work or wages, because each individual worker who started to make such demands would risk being replaced either by another worker or by machinery. The formation of unions and other forms of workers' associations is not only theoretically, but also historically, a response to the 'association' that has already taken place on the part of capital, namely, in the form of the fusion of numerous units of 'dead' labour under the command of one capitalist employer. In all capitalist countries, the historical sequence is this: the first step is the 'liquidation' of the means of production of small commodity producers and the merging of these into capitalist industrial firms; the second step is the defensive association of workers; and the third is associational efforts that are now made on the part of capitalist firms who, in addition to their continued merging of capital, enter into formal organizations in order to promote some of their collective interests.[6] What follows from this sequence is that, contrary to the 'unthinking habit': (a) the two types of organization that we are trying to compare emerge at distinctly different points in the history of class struggle, which can be analysed as a sequence of strategic steps taken by the two sides; and (b) that capital has at its command three different forms of collective action to define and defend its interests – the firm itself, informal cooperation, and the employers or business association, whereas labour has only one.

But what are the interests that unions organize? We have seen before that, whereas the capitalist is physically and legally separate from the capital he/she controls, labour power is inseparably tied to the worker who 'sells' it. Since the worker is at the same time the subject and the object of the exchange of labour power, a vastly broader range of interests is involved in this case than in that of capitalists, who can satisfy a large part of their interests somewhat apart from their functioning as capitalists. In the case of workers, those interests that have directly to do with, and are directly affected by, the exchange of labour power that they are subject to, include not only material rewards but also such things as job satisfaction, health, leisure time, and continuity of employment. Unions are, therefore, confronted with the task of organizing the entire spectrum of needs that people have when they are employed as wage workers. The multitude of needs of 'living' labour is not only comparatively more difficult to organize for quantitative reasons, but also for the reason that there is no common denominator to which all these heterogeneous and often conflicting needs can be reduced so as to 'optimize' demands and tactics. How much in wages, for instance, can 'rationally' be given up in exchange for which amount of increase in job satisfaction? The answer to this question cannot be found by any calculus that could be objectively applied; it can only be found as the result of the collective deliberation of the members of the organization. In contrast, capitalist firms as well as business associations do not have to take into consideration a comparative multitude of incommensurable needs. All the relevant questions can be reduced to the unequivocal standards of expected costs and returns, i.e. to the measuring rod of money. The optimization problem in respect to demands and techniques is thus much easier to resolve collectively. More precisely, it does not have to be resolved *collectively* at all but often can be analysed and decided upon by a staff of experts.

A further dissimilarity that results directly from the capitalist structure of the 'input-environment' of the two types of organizations is this: capitalists, being in control of the process of production in which they combine rationally 'dead' and 'living' labour, are in a position to constantly evaluate and improve the efficiency and effectiveness of this combination. Whereas capitalists can (and, under the competitive pressure that they put upon each other, must) improve the efficiency of production, workers do not have the opportunity to increase the efficiency of the process of reproduction of their own labour power. In other words, by introducing (labour-saving) technical change, capital can release itself partially from its dependence upon the supply of labour, thereby depressing the wage rate. On the other hand, labour cannot release itself from its dependency upon capital's willingness to employ it, because there are next to no possibilities of reproducing itself more efficiently, namely, on the basis of low wages or even outside the labour market. This is particularly true in view of two conditions which are typically present under industrial capitalism: (i) the legal prohibition and strict regulation of forms of life outside the labour market; and (ii) the concentration of the working class in large urban agglomerations in which living conditions are designed to make it virtually impossible for propertyless workers to subsist in ways other than those offered by the labour market. Because of this asymmetrical dependency relationship, the collectivity of all workers must be, paradoxically, more concerned with the well-being and the prosperity of capitalists than the capitalists are with the well-being of the working class. This increases the lack of homogeneity of those interests that working class associations have to accommodate and the concomitant difficulties of the intra-organizational decision-making process, which we will discuss presently.

Our main argument throughout this essay is that differences in the position of a group in the class structure (we consider here only the classes of labour and capital), not only lead to differences in power that the organizations can acquire, but also lead to differences in the associational practices, or logics of collective action, by which organizations of capital and labour try to improve their respective position *vis-à-vis* each other. These differences tend to be obscured by the 'interest group' paradigm and the underlying notion of a unitary and utilitarian logic of collective action that covers all associations.

We now want to illustrate our proposition that differences in power lead to differences in the type of collective action by which this power differential is to be balanced. We do this on the basis of a formal and extremely simplified diagram.[7] Figure 7.1 represents two corresponding options of individual capitalists and individual workers: (i) that, on the part of the capitalist, to employ labour power or not; and (ii) on the part of workers, to be employed or not. For both sides, the respective first option is the preferred one, while they try to avoid the second one. However, the *extent* to which the first option is preferred over the second differs between the two classes; some of the reasons for this have been explored above. This difference is represented in the respective preference curves *A* and *B*. The steeper preference curve *B* means simply that

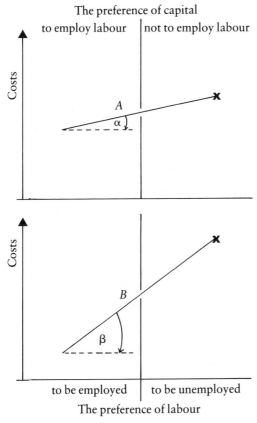

*Figure 7.1*

the individual owner of (only) labour power is less likely to be able to afford to be unemployed than the individual capitalist is likely to be able to refrain from employing him/her. Of course, both want to avoid the second alternative but the worker does so more strongly than the capitalist. Generally speaking, the essence of every relationship of social power is a difference between angles $\alpha$ and $\beta$ and the magnitude of power can be expressed by the magnitude of this difference.

Let us suppose now that this power differential results in social conflict. What are the strategies by which the two sides will conduct this conflict? Generally speaking, the more powerful side will try to minimize $\alpha$ and maximize $\beta$, and the less powerful side will try to accomplish the opposite. However, the power position that the two find themselves exposed to in the first place does not allow them to pursue these strategies with the same chance of success. The reason is that the potential to *change* power relations is itself determined by (i.e. proportional to) those power relations that are to be changed. To illustrate, the individual worker has hardly any chance of making his/her avoidance-alternative (unemployment) personally more acceptable (e.g. by moving to a rural commune and thus reducing reproduction costs), nor does he/she have much leverage for making the employer's preference curve steeper (e.g. by working harder and thus making him/herself relatively more indispensable to the employer). Compared with these highly limited options of conflict strategy, the effectiveness of power-maintaining strategies of the already powerful tends to remain superior. What we get is a more or less unchanged replica of the initial power relationship.

More interesting is the case where both the more powerful and the less powerful join with others of their respective social categories in order to conduct the conflict in an organized and *collective* way. As we know from Olson's analysis of the logic of collective action, however, the situation is not more likely to be changed dramatically by this collectivization of conflict. The reason is, briefly, that superior power also means superior ability to defend and reproduce power. The powerful are fewer in number, are likely to be divided among themselves, have a clearer view of what they want to defend, and have larger resources for organized action, all of which imply that they are likely to succeed in recreating the initial situation.

How, then, is it all possible to explain that there are cases of changes in the power relationship that actually occur? This question leads us to a third possibility: to employ a form of collective strategy of conflict which not only aggregates the individual resources of the members of the association in order to meet the common interests of these individuals, but which also overcomes the individuality of those resources and interests as well as the obstacles to effective organization, by defining a collective identity on the basis of which the chance to change existing power relations is no longer exclusively determined by these power relations themselves. That is to say that those in the inferior power position can increase their potential for change only by overcoming the comparatively higher costs of collective action by changing the standards according to which these costs are subjectively estimated within their own collectivity.[8] Only to the extent that associations of the relatively powerless succeed in the formation of a collective identity, according to the standards of which the costs of organization are subjectively deflated, can they hope to change the original power relation. Conversely, it is only the relatively powerless who will have reason to act non-individualistically on the basis of a notion of collective identity that is both generated and presupposed by their association. The very fact that the more powerful will find the individualistic and purely instrumental form of collective action sufficiently promising for the preservation of their power position prevents them from transcending their basically utilitarian mode of collective action. In contrast, workers' organizations in capitalist systems always find themselves forced to rely upon non-utilitarian forms of collective action, which are based on the redefinition of collective identities, *even if* the organization does not have any intention of serving anything but the members' individual utilitarian interests, for example, higher wages. No union can function for a day in the absence of some rudimentary notions held by the members that being a member is of value in itself, that the individual organization costs must not be calculated in a utilitarian manner but have to be accepted as necessary sacrifices, and that each member is legitimately required to practise solidarity and discipline, and other norms of a non-utilitarian kind. The logic of collective action of the relatively powerless differs from that of the relatively powerful in that the former implies a paradox that is absent from the latter – the paradox that interests can only be met to the extent they are partly redefined.[9] Therefore, the organizations in which the collective action of the relatively powerless takes place, must always be (and, in fact, always are) construed in such a way that they simultaneously express and define the interests of the members. In sharp contrast, capital associations are confined to the function of aggregating and specifying those interests of members which, from the point of view of the organization, have to be defined as given and fixed, the formation of which lies beyond the legitimate range of functions of the organization. This leads us directly to a more detailed discussion of the internal structures and functions of both types of organization.

## 2   Internal processes

In order to succeed in accomplishing stated interests, an organization must be able to mobilize sanctions. The strike is the ultimate sanction that unions can mobilize. Although the term 'capital strike' is sometimes used metaphorically to describe the type of sanctions available to capitalists, this analogy is somewhat misleading in that it obscures the differences that exist between the two types of organizations in regard to the way in which the respective sanctions are mobilized. Such organizational measures as strike assemblies, strike votes, picket lines, etc. are, of course, absent from the strategic repertoire of business associations. We must clearly distinguish between those sanctions that can be mobilized by the organization in the strict sense and those that can be mobilized by the constituent members outside the organization of which they are members. Once we take this distinction seriously, we see immediately that the potential to sanction, as well as to make concrete decisions to bring this potential to bear on a particular situation, reside outside the organization, namely, with the individual capitalist in the case of business organizations, whereas this potential has to be built up in a communicative process *within* the association of workers, whose *individual* potential to sanction is minimal because of their atomization. Business organizations have a comparatively low potential for sanctioning. What they can do is to threaten to withdraw those functions that they perform as an organization in their environment, for instance, by withdrawing the functions of information and advice that they may give to government bureaucracies. At most, they can (at least in some countries) refuse to recognize other organizations as legitimate partners in bargaining. That is to say, what there *is* in terms of sanctioning potential of the organization can be put into effect by the leadership of the organization alone.

In contrast, even in the most bureaucratic unions, the leadership is much less able to use sanctions at its own discretion. Whatever sanctioning potential there is in workers associations becomes effective only through the organized members and their explicitly coordinated action. Somewhat paradoxically, the rank and file members thus seem to be the top executives of unions as far as sanctions are concerned; while some sanctioning potential of business and employers associations resides with the organizations' executive group alone, the overwhelming sanctioning potential remains on the plane of the behavioural options of the constituent members who remain outside the range of organized activity. In order to mobilize power *vis-à-vis* the outside world, business organizations need part of the resources (such as membership fees and information) from their members, resources which then will be used in an instrumental-purposive fashion by the expert leadership of the association. What unions need in addition, is the conscious and coordinated *active participation* of their members, namely, as a final resort, the willingness to go on strike. In the simplest terms, a difference between the two types of organizations lies in the fact that the one depends upon its ability to generate the members' 'willingness to pay', whereas the other depends, in addition, on its ability to generate its members 'willingness to act'. These two different organizational requirements assign different tasks to the respective leadership group.

For instance, it might appear reasonable for organizations of both types to maximize membership, that is, the ratio of actual to potential membership. This appears 'rational' because it maximizes the resources that are available to the organization and it supposedly minimizes internal competition among those who are members. However, this standard of rationality does not apply equally to business associations and to unions. Whereas it would be rational for the former to follow this rule, maximization of membership involves a specific dilemma for the latter, the consequence being that they are forced to 'optimize' rather than to maximize. This is so for at least two reasons. First, if the success of unions depends upon their sanctioning potential, and if the sanctioning potential of the union depends upon its ability to generate a 'willingness to act' on the part of its members, and if an increase in membership leads to a *bureaucratic* relationship between the leadership and the rank and file members, and if bureaucratization undermines the organization's ability to mobil- ize the particular source of sanctioning power that we have called 'capacity to generate willingness to act', then we would expect union 'strength' to be related to union size by an inverse U-curve. In other words, unions are confronted with the dilemma that there is an optimum size beyond which union power decreases (see figure 7.2). As an illustration of this structural dilemma of unions which results from the fact that they simultaneously depend on their members' 'willingness to pay' *and* 'willingness to act', consider the two extreme cases of (a) an extremely militant union that is, however, too small to actually conduct a strike because it

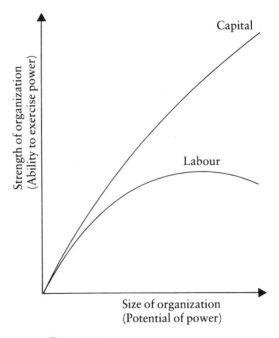

*Figure 7.2*

lacks the necessary strike funds, and (b) a large and highly bureaucratized union that has accumulated enormous strike funds but is unable to use them because, for lack of internal communication and mobilization, members are likely to have become extremely apathetic. Second, as union size increases, the *heterogeneity* of members' positions, occupations, and immediate interests tends to increase, too, which makes it more difficult to formulate generally agreed-upon demands and to mobilize a common willingness to act that flows from a notion of shared collective identities and mutual obligations of solidarity.

Both aspects of the unions' specific dilemma of size and power, can, of course, easily be traced back to the standard problematic of democracy vs. bureaucracy. These relationships are illustrated, together with the names of social theorists who have explored some of these relations, in figure 7.3. For the sake of their power, unions are forced to maintain a precarious balance between mobilization of resources and mobilization of activity, between size and collective identity, and between bureaucracy (which allows them to *accumulate* power) and internal democracy (which allows them to *exercise* power). None of these dilemmas applies with comparable seriousness to business and employers organizations for the reason that they do not depend on internal

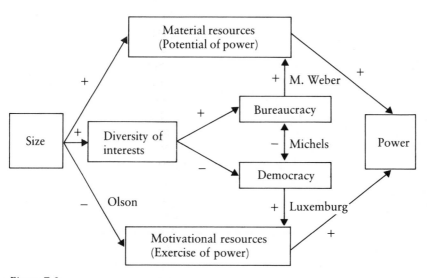

*Figure 7.3*

democracy, collective identity, or the willingness to engage in solidary action, because of the very fact that they are *already* in a structural power position which renders complications such as these avoidable.

Let us explore the dilemma of heterogeneity versus collective identity a step further. The problem entails not only the diversity of position and interest that exists between workers, but also the diversity that exists, as it were, among the workers themselves. The three major interests that arise directly from the conditions of working-class life can be categorized as wages, the continuing receipt of wages (employment security), and working conditions. Moreover, workers are, at the same time, not only subject and object of the exchange of labour power, but also consumers of the product of labour power as well as inhabitants of the social and natural environment that is affected by the impact of capitalist industrialization. The larger the unions, the more necessary it becomes for them to find some way of reconciling all or at least some of these heterogeneous concepts of interest.[10]

The notorious difficulty of doing this in the absence of some unequivocal standard (such as the monetary one) that makes all these diverse interests commensurable, leads to a tendency for unions to 'delegate' issue areas that they find too hard to deal with internally (this is the basis of the European pattern of a division of labour between unions and socialist parties). Or they may restrict the agenda of demands by refusing to deal with certain sets of demands which, although clearly related to the life interests of their rank and file, are too difficult to reconcile with other, equally essential demands and interests (this corresponds to the American patterns of recent decades). Thus, union leadership is constantly caught between attempting to provide comprehensive representation for all the interests of its working-class constituency and being limited in its ability to find a formula that reconciles these partly contradictory interests without endangering their internal acceptability and/or external negotiability. In respect to the unions' agenda of demands, we thus have another optimal size dilemma which, again, is absent from business associations.

In what sense, now, are the problems that business associations have to deal with in their internal processes of organization, communication, and decision making different? What has already become clear from our previous discussion is (i) that formal business associations are only one of three forms of collective action of capital; (ii) that business associations carry only a very limited sanctioning potential, whereas the decisive source of power remains with the individual firm and its strategic choices; and (iii) that the establishment of formal organization tends to be, as a defensive response to the formation of unions (as well as to incipient state-interventionism), a relatively late development in the history of capitalism. As a consequence, the problem of creating and maintaining unity among members and of mobilizing members' resources is considerably less serious for business associations than for unions, despite the divergence of hetero-geneous and conflicting interests among the former's members. Nevertheless, maintaining unity remains a problem because one would hardly be justified in assuming that such divergences (for example, between large and small firms, firms oriented toward a domestic market and those exporting goods, firms competing with each other on the demand side of labour and capital markets, as well as on the supply side of goods markets) would be absent from the internal dynamics of business associations. What we rather wish to suggest as an answer to the previously posed question is that there are two mechanisms that facilitate a comparatively easy and non-contradictory reconciliation of internal divergences. One has to do with the greater potential of 'by-products' to maintain internal integration, and the second has to do with the greater specificity and calculability of the association's objectives.[11]

In order to provide an incentive for numerous small firms to become members of a business association despite differences of interest that separate them from large firms, the business organization can provide various services (or 'private goods') on which small firms are considerably more dependent than large ones (which probably find it worthwhile to provide such services for themselves). Such services (for example, highly specific advice and information) are more valuable for small firms because the expense of producing them individually is high. To become (and to remain) a member of a business association that provides access to such services becomes almost imperative in those (frequent) cases where no alternative access to such services exists.

In contrast, those services that unions can (and do) provide in order to stimulate and stabilize the motivation to join (such as, in the case of the Federal Republic of Germany, the services of insurance, book clubs, travel agencies, legal advice, automobile clubs) provide only relatively minor advantages over those services that can be obtained *outside* the union on the free market, which provides basically the same services. In contrast to unions, too, business associations do not have to be concerned that the 'privatistic' type of membership motivation, which is stimulated by such individualistic incentives as the demand for 'private goods', will interfere with the general ability of the association to achieve its objectives; for the achievement of these objectives does not depend, in their situation, on a sense of solidarity and the resulting 'willingness to act' on the part of members. This is because the executive leadership, composed of a staff of experts and analysts, can 'speak for' members without previously having had to 'speak to' them in order to form a broad consensus.

The latter point has to do with a second advantage which business associations enjoy as regards the problem of internal integration. That part of the totality of interests of individual members which arises as an issue for the association (as opposed to an issue that the member has to deal with privately) and which must, therefore, be processed through the organization, can certainly be said to be much smaller in the case of business associations than for unions. There are hardly any of what have been called the 'central life interests' of workers that do not, at least potentially, appear on the agenda of unions, whereas most of the 'central life interests' of capital are either resolved *beneath* the level of association (within the individual firm) or *above* the level of association (within the state apparatus). Consequently, the range of issues and interests that the association has to deal with is much more limited and specific; this means there is the dual advantage of greater commensurability and calculability of what the 'right' demands and tactics are, and of a comparatively smaller probability of internal conflict. Since the organization does not interfere with, or in any way attempt to regulate, what remains within the range of decision making of the individual firm,[12] the obligations and commitments that the individual member firm takes upon itself are quite marginal and thus less likely to involve any disincentive to join. Taken together with the first point – the comparatively greater attractiveness of the specific by-products which the business association has to offer – this point contributes to an explanation of the empirical fact that the proportion of actual members to eligible members is regularly much higher in business associations than in unions.[13] The limited range of members' interests that are processed by the association rather than individually, plus the fact that these interests can relatively easily be decided upon on the basis of quantitative criteria of costs and returns, also helps to save the costs of internal communication within business associations. Furthermore, business associations do not have to bother with the problem of formulating an explicit ideology, which, in the case of unions, serves to attract some members while antagonizing others. And even if the need to rely on some explicit common understanding of interests should come up, the task is an easier one to solve because one can assume a presupposed consensus of social, cultural, and political values, to which one can always refer. Thus, the problem of creating and maintaining the integration of members within the association can be described as being solvable in a one-dimensional and 'monological' way, which does not require the simultaneous and partly contradictory processes of expressing *and* forming common interests.

### 3   Organizational outputs

Lindblom has argued forcefully that capital, be it on the level of the individual firm or of business associations, is in a privileged power position which results from the fact that, in a capitalist society, the state depends on the flourishing of the accumulation process. Even before it begins to put explicit political pressure and demands upon the government, capital enjoys a position of indirect control over public affairs: 'Businessmen thus become a kind of public official and exercise what, on a broad view of their role, are public functions.'[14] This situation makes it advisable for governments to pay special attention to what businessmen have to communicate either individually or through their associations. 'In countless ways governments . . . recognize that businessmen need to be encouraged to perform . . . Although governments can forbid certain kinds of activity, they cannot command business to perform. They must induce rather than command.'[15] Because businessmen 'appeal as functionaries performing functions that government officials regard as indispensable . . . businessmen cannot be left knocking at the doors of the political system, they must be invited in.'[16] The very attentive attitude toward business interests that every government of the capitalist state is structurally forced to assume substantially reduces the efforts of 'knocking at the doors'. The entire relationship between capital and the state is built not upon what capital can do *politically* through its associations, as the critical theory of elitism maintains, but upon what capital can *refuse* to do in terms of investments decided upon by the individual firm. This asymmetrical relationship of control makes comparatively inconspicuous forms of communication and interaction between business associations and the state apparatus sufficient to accomplish the political objectives of capital.[17]

Compared to the communications between unions and the state, the communications of business associations with the state differ in that they are less visible publicly (because there is less need to mobilize the support of external allies), more technical (because the insight into the political 'desirability', that is, factual indispensability, can be presupposed as already agreed upon), more universal (because business associations can speak in the name of all those interests that require for their fulfilment a healthy and continuous rate of accumulation which, from the point of view of capital *and* the state, is true of virtually everybody), and negative (because, given the fact that the government has to consider as desirable what is in fact desirable for capital, the only thing that remains to be done is to warn governments against imprudent, 'unrealistic', and otherwise inopportune decisions and measures).

The dependency of the state apparatus upon the performance of capital (which includes the indirect dependence upon capital of all those interests which, in their turn, depend upon the state and the goods and services delivered by it) is unparalleled by any reciprocal dependency relationship of the capitalist class upon the state. This structural asymmetry is exploited and fine-tuned by the operation of business associations, but it is by no means constituted or created by them. Their success is not accomplished by or because of the organization itself; rather, it derives from a power relationship that is logically and historically prior to the fact of any collective action of businessmen.

So far, we have analysed some general characteristics of business associations in terms of a network of communication that exists between members and their association, the association and the state, and capitalist firms – whether associated with 'interest groups' or not – and the state. Let us now summarize the differences we see between the ways business associations and unions communicate with their environments. We do this in a rather schematic fashion, that is, by listing a set of dichotomies in which the first alternative always designates the characteristics of business associations and the second those of unions.

(1)  Operation on the level of *system integration* vs. operation on the level of *social integration*. Disintegration on the first level is equivalent to *'malfunctioning'*, the absence of basic require-ments of the material process of societal reproduction; disinte-gration on the second level means *conflict*, the absence of consensus and compliance.

(2)  *Instrumental-monological* patterns of collective action vs. *dialogical* patterns. In the former, the association, almost exclusively, aggregates and transmits interests, and debates about the proper objectives of the organization occur only at the *leadership* level, if at all. In the second pattern, the organization plays an active role in defining and transforming members' interests; communication about objectives is, therefore, at least occasionally, extended to the rank-and-file level. (This dicho-tomy describes structural differences between capital and labour organizations, in that the first can afford to follow the first alternative *exclusively,* whereas the latter must reconcile both patterns within the organization.)

(3)  *Power potential outside the organization* vs. *power poten-tial created by* the organization.

(4)  Exercise of power through the *leadership* of the organiz-ation vs. exercise of power through the *activity of the members.*

(5)  *Defensive* use of power vs. *offensive* use of power.

(6)  *Hidden and dispersed* use of power vs. *open and concen-trated* use of power. (To illustrate, no one thinks of the nature of communication between business associations and their environment as consisting of 'profit demands', because such 'demands' are made outside the organization by individual firms; in contrast, unions, in the public eye, are most readily associated with the making of 'wage demands'.)

(7)  Communication in terms of *technical imperatives* vs.

communication in terms of demands and explicit *normative claims*.

(8)   Legitimation of organized activity in terms of the '*interests of the whole*' vs. the *particularistic advocacy* of specific interests of the prospective beneficiaries of demands.

## Interests and Political Form

There is no one who knows what is for your interest so well as yourself.                                                                 (Jeremy Bentham)

The sole evidence it is possible to produce that anything is desirable is that people do actually desire it.      (John Stuart Mill)

The interest is first, last and all the time strictly empirical. There is no way to find it except by observation.                             (A. Bentley)

It is apparently one of the basic assumptions of classical liberal, as well as modern democratic, theory that all empirical interest articulations are equally 'true', that is, equally representative of the *genuine* interests of the actors. On the basis of this assumption, the very concept of 'true' or 'objective' interests (as distinct from 'false' or 'erroneous' ones) can be safely dropped from the theoretical discourse, for it is both methodologically impossible, as well as undesirable for its allegedly 'totalitarian' implications, to attribute differing degrees of validity to empirical interest articulations. Schumpeter, whose book *Capitalism, Socialism and Democracy* made him the forerunner of much of today's liberal democratic theory, went so far as to consider any imputation of counter-factual interests as inspired by anti-democratic intentions (even if there were indications that the actors in question would be willing to accept them as their manifest interests once they were brought to their attention). The dogma is what we could call practical positivism – the belief that 'an individual's interest . . . is simply what he says it is.'[18]

The weakness of the naive version of this 'liberal equation' is too obvious to require much elaboration. A moment's reflection (if not, indeed, elementary prescientific experience) tells us that there are two possible deviations from this equation – deviations which premature acceptance of the above dogma prevents us from taking seriously. The first is if a person expresses something that does not coincide with his or her interest (for instance, due to the impact of deception, self-deception, or force). The second occurs if (due to the lack of opportunity to do so) a person does not articulate what he or she actually perceives as the real interest. Confronted with the existence of these two possibilities, the liberal political theorist can respond in either of two ways: he/she can remain faithful to his/her original equation, thus methodically ignoring the distorting effects of force, manipulation, intimidation, etc. which would place him/her in the immediate theoretical vicinity of such advocates of the fascist state as the German law professor Carl Schmitt, who proclaimed that 'in particular, a dictatorship cannot come into being by other than democratic means.'[19] In doing this, any distinction between democratic and non-democratic forms of political organization vanishes. Or he/she can respond by stipulating that the logical and methodological equivalence of empirical and 'true' interests be in fact contingent upon the presence of institutional arrangements which make such deviations negligible or unlikely.

Clearly, most of today's liberal theorists would opt for the second alternative. They would assume the operation of some mechanism that reliably eliminated either of the two distortions and hence guaranteed the actual equivalence of the two sides of the equation. Supposedly, such a mechanism would be the institution of citizenship, civil liberties, and the competitive political process. Together, they are supposed to guarantee that no expression of interest deviates from actually perceived interests (due to the impact of force, etc.) and that no major interest remains unexpressed in the open and competitive political process. Thus, the 'principal function of constitutional and democratic institutions is to ensure a reasonably close convergence between expressed and actual interests'.[20]

To this hypothetical assertion, which has already reduced the original conceptual equation to an empirical one, the validity of which is contingent upon certain institutional arrangements and their effectiveness, we can again respond with two arguments. It could be argued that the dynamics of state interventionism and bureaucratization; the mode of operation of the mass media; the extent to which modern state apparatuses make use of repression, intimidation and 'symbolic politics'; as well as other structural features of the modern state, have rendered those democratic 'equating mechanisms' ineffective. This is the line of argument that has been developed by such critics of the 'elitist' and 'realist' schools of democratic theory as Bachrach and Baratz, Crenson, Edelman, Connolly, and Schattschneider. Or one could argue that, even though we might be prepared to accept the functioning and validity of the democratic 'equating mechanism' and, consequently, to work with a fairly generous definition of what constitutes 'reasonably close convergence', the argument is at best only partially valid because it is restricted to the sphere of institutionalized democratic politics, whereas interests are formed to a large extent beyond the boundaries of this sphere. Clearly, the two arguments can be used cumulatively. Confining ourselves to an exploration of the implications of this second argument, we find that the spheres of 'civil society' (for example, the interactions between consumer and producer, workers and management, among family members, church members) are simply not constituted according to *any* principle that could be expected to bring empirical and 'true' interests into close proximity.[21]

In other words, there is no mechanism which could conceivably neutralize distortions that lead to an incongruity between the two. Moreover, since the spheres of democratic politics and civil society are not separate, but are interconnected by the sameness of the individuals who play roles in both spheres, we can expect that unchecked distortions are transmitted from the life of civil society into the political process; 'false' perceptions of need and interest, as generated and conditioned by social life, are likely to have substantial repercussions on the political plane.

However, even if every citizen were equally likely to err as to his/her 'true' interest, and even if deviations from accurate insight were equally likely to occur in all conceivable directions, a somewhat more cautious version of the basic liberal equation might still remain defensible. For the proponents of such a theory could argue that, due to some kind of randomization effect, the individual distortions would amount to zero, leaving the democratic process itself undistorted.

But is it really reasonable to assume that the likelihood of a misconception of interest is equally distributed among classes? We shall argue here that it is not, and that, on the contrary, the probability of distortion of interest is greater on the part of the working class than on the part of the capitalist class under capitalist relations of production. According to our argument, the members of one class experience greater difficulties in finding out what their 'true' interest is; that is, they have more difficulty in bridging the gap between their empirical and 'true' interest. This asymmetry has to do with class domination itself. Ambiguity, alienation, mystification, and fetishism directly affect working class *consciousness* as much as exploitation and the commodity form imposed upon human labour power affect its *material* and social conditions of life. If such asymmetry existed on the level of interest awareness, then we would expect to find different types and degrees of organizational and communicative efforts to 'rationalize' the respective interest, that is, to overcome the specific distortions and deviations which are a result of the specific class position. Such class-specific organizational and cognitive require-ments, which are needed in order to find one's 'true' interest, could then help to clarify the differences between the two logics of collective action that we have described and contrasted in the second part of this article. Finally, if we succeed in making a convincing argument concerning the structural reasons for the differential distribution of interest distortions among classes, we should also be able to draw a critical conclusion regarding the dogma of liberal political and social theory, which claims that empirical and 'true' interests are congruent. Thus, the plan for the following paragraphs is (i) to establish some theoretical arguments in support of our proposition that the interests of the working class and those of the capitalist class are subject to differing degrees of distortion under capitalism, and that different organiza-tional forms are required within each class in order to overcome these specific distortions; and (ii) to evaluate the liberal dogma and its intellectual, as well as political, impact.[22]

## 1   The differential fallibility argument

Karl Deutsch has defined power as 'the ability to afford not to learn'.[23] In a sense, this is an accurate characterization of the capitalist class's relation to its own class interest. Although this class, under the competitive pressure that its individual members put upon each other, has to seek constantly to find the *means,* or the most rational purposive behaviour, by which its interest is to be met, the interest itself (the end) can safely remain remote from any conscious reflection or effort to learn on the part of the class members. Compared to that of any individual member of the working class, the interest of a capitalist is far less likely to be ambiguous, controversial, or wrongly perceived. To be sure, there may be numerous uncertainties as to the most effective or efficient means of meeting this interest, that is, of achieving what is valuable and desirable. But, in a capitalist society, the interest itself is firmly established and hard to overlook. This is because, first, the pursuit of this interest is legitimate and generally accepted within this society – this is obviously not the case with everything that workers might conceive of as in their interest. Second, because it is externally supported by those institutional sectors of capitalist society (most notably the state apparatus), that depend for their ability to perform *their* particular functions upon capital's successful pursuit of *its* interest in accumulation. Such an external 'guarantor' and supporter of interest is clearly absent in the case of the working class. Third, in order for his/her interest to be a 'true' one, the individual capitalist does not have to consult with other capitalists in order to reach a common understanding and agreement with them as to what their interests are. In this sense, the interest is 'monological'.

In contrast, any interest that is thought of by the individual worker as a 'true' one, but about which he/she does not find any consensus among fellow workers, is most likely to be experienced as having been an 'erroneous' concept of their interest. Therefore, a 'dialogical' process of definition of interest is required on the part of those who find themselves in an inferior power position and who do, therefore, depend upon a common and collective concept of their interest. Fourth, in case a false notion of what is desirable and valuable occurs, the situation is likely to be corrected much faster and more easily in the case of a member of the capitalist class than in the case of the worker. This is because errors on the part of the capitalist are fed back to him from his market environment in unequivocal quantitative-monetary terms and within a relatively short time, whereas erroneous concepts of interest are not easily and rapidly detectable in the case of the worker. Fifth, there is a strongly asymmetrical relationship between the chances of the two classes mutually to shape their respective conceptions of what is in their interest. Here we refer to the mechanisms of bourgeois hegemony (or the 'preceptorial' function of capital, in Lindblom's terminology), which allows the capitalist class to partly control the symbols and values that play a role in the identities and aspirations of the members of the subordinate class. Consequently, much greater communicative and organizational efforts are required on the part of the working class if such hegemonic impact of cultural domination is to be neutralized.

To summarize, in order to achieve an *equal* amount of accuracy in awareness of the respective interests, vastly *different* efforts are required on both sides of the major dividing line of social class. This view is directly opposed to those versions of a Marxist theory of class consciousness which hold that there is a spontaneous and almost automatic development, propelled by what is sometimes called a 'class instinct', toward the 'true' interest of the working class as a whole. Such a view is clearly unsupported by both theoretical arguments and contemporary experience.[24] Moreover, it is hardly to be derived from the basic categories and conceptualizations that underlie the Marxist sociology of wage labour, which rather leads us to expect a number of objective and subjective ambiguities in the social situation of wage workers. On the one hand, wage workers are defined by their position of being forced to sell their labour power (because they have nothing else to sell and their labour power is perfectly useless unless it is sold to a capitalist for a wage; this is because they do not own any means of production with which they could combine their labour power). On the other hand, however, labour power cannot suitably be treated like any other commodity, because it is the only 'commodity' that cannot be physically separated from its 'owner'. Consequently, wage workers are forced to 'sell' something that remains part of their own living activity; in the labour contract, they legally surrender control over something that physically remains under their own control. Thus, they are separated from the control over their labour power while at the same time being the subject of it – a subject that is inseparably tied to everything that happens to its object of 'sale' even after it is 'sold'. As a consequence of this paradoxical position, wage workers are permanently exposed to 'cross-pressures' of the most dramatic sort; they are at the same time the objects of what is sold in the labour market transaction and partners in the labour contract, object and subject of the exchange relation. The ambiguity in interest derives from the concept of market participants of themselves as each having a particular unit of labour power, as well as skills, experience, and so forth (i.e. a concept of *what* they have to sell) and a concept of themselves as *being* wage-labour – thus, being implicated with all their human potential in the process of utilization of that mysterious 'commodity' (i.e. a concept of themselves in terms of the fact that they *have* to sell). All the other ambiguities in consciousness and defining interest follow from this basic one, namely, the ambiguity between individualistic vs. collective improvement of one's condition, between economic vs. political concepts of one's interest, between the identities as consumer and producer, between the priorities of higher wages vs. better working conditions and more secure employment, and between the behavioural alternatives of individual competitiveness and class solidarity.

The points developed so far should suffice to support the conclusions (i) that there are different degrees of interest distortion in a capitalist society; (ii) that these differences are not randomly distributed but are, to a significant degree, determined by structural differences of class position (rather than by such factors as quantitative group size, which is emphasized as the determining factor by Olson); and (iii) that differences in the organizational practice and problems, strategies and structures, that we find between workers' and capitalists' 'interest groups' are either a reflection of this underlying structural difference (e.g. the fact that capitalists can organize either in cartels *or* in associations, whereas labour has only the second of these options because it is tied to discrete, non-summable, individual units) or it is a specific response to a condition we have called asymmetrical interest distortion (e.g. labour, in contrast to capital, uses dialogical patterns of intra-organizational communication in order to overcome the diversity and non-calculability of those interests which are represented by unions).

## 2   A critique of the 'liberal equation'

We have argued before that the non-randomness of the distortions of interest-awareness, together with the limited range (and effectiveness) of the neutralizing mechanisms of constitutional democratic institutions, causes a serious problem for liberal democratic theory. Once the possibility of error in one's perception of interest is at all conceded, once differential and class-specific distortions appear to play more than a negligible role, and once we acknowledge the limitations of democratic procedure, the hidden cynicism of the liberal equation becomes apparent. If every articulation of interest is to be taken at face value, then those interests which are least likely to be affected by distortion and error (which, according to the arguments in the preceding paragraphs, would be the interests of the bourgeoisie) are clearly favoured. Although this conclusion may be considered fatal to the *truth* of the liberal equation and the theory upon which it is based, it is not immediately, and of itself, fatal to the political forms and the institutional *practice* of liberal democracy derived from and legitimized by this theory. The practical question that emerges from the theoretical critique of the liberal equation is this: To what extent do the political forms of liberal democracy provide asymmetrical chances to the members of different classes to be able to articulate enlightened interests? To what extent do they leave room for those mechanisms to become effective that are required to overcome the specific obstacles to non-distorted interest-awareness that we find in the ranks of the working class? Or, conversely, to what extent are liberal democratic forms of political conflict, which favour the accurate articulation of bourgeois interests and impede the organizational practices that facilitate the articulation of undistorted working-class interests, imposed upon the working class? If it is true that political forms are not neutral, but are rather schemes for the preferential recognition of certain class interests (as we believe the above arguments strongly suggest), then they must themselves be considered as part of, and as objects of, the class conflict which they appear to merely regulate and to channel.

What needs to be explored here is the difficult relationship between class power, class conflict, and political form. The liberal equation inspires and legitimates political forms which in turn favour those interests that, for structural reasons, are likely already to be 'enlightened', i.e. accurately perceived. At the same time, it opposes, usually in the name of 'individual freedom', those political forms able to increase the accuracy of interest articulation on the part of the subordinate class, that is, it opposes those forms which could methodically help to resolve the structural ambiguity that characterizes the consciousness of the working class. Those interests that can be assumed to be already clarified and 'identical with themselves', can be fed into the political process in an individualistic form (e.g. by voting) and over long chains of representation without being damaged or distorted by the form through which they are articulated. In contrast, those interests that are exposed to structural ambiguities, and which require a collective discourse for their articulation and an on-going dialog- ical pattern of communication between leaders and those whom they represent in order to become 'true', are less likely to be articulated with equal accuracy within the framework of these political forms. In view of such class-specific effects of differential penetrability, or selectivity, of political forms, we can think of a class conflict that goes on simultaneously on two levels: class conflict *within* political forms and class conflict *about* political forms.

The first, class conflict *within* political forms, is manifested in, and occurs between, those interests that are able to crystallize within given organizational and procedural 'rules of the game'. The second, class conflict *about* political forms, is latent, hidden by a pretence of 'neutrality' concerning those very political forms that are to be attacked or defended on this level of conflict. This second conflict has to do with the question of which political forms are most conducive to the articulation of the undistorted interest of various classes; supposedly each class tries to generalize and institutionalize those political forms most conducive to the self-enlightenment of its members about its 'true' interest and that, at the same time, minimize the adversary class's chance of articulating its interests.

While this second level of class conflict is theoretically denied (and sometimes prohibited in practice) by liberals, it has also received little attention by Marxists, whose economic theory (which corresponds to the first level) is generally, and probably rightly, considered to be much more advanced than their political theory. It is this relative blind-spot in Marxist social theory that Esping-Andersen and others have in mind when they write:

> The capitalist class attempts to create state structures which channel working class political activity in ways that do not threaten capitalist political dominance and objective interests . . . It is necessary to understand the ways in which class struggle . . . is shaped by those very structures . . . The internal structure of the state is simultaneously a product, an object and a determinant of class conflict. State structure is itself a source of power. The organization of political authority differentially affects the access, political consciousness, strategy and cohesion of various interests and classes. State structure is not neutral with respect to its effects on class conflict.[25]

By 'state structure' or 'organization of political authority', the authors obviously mean a specific set of political forms which are institutionalized in a state and which generally define to what extent and through which channels citizens as members of classes and groups are allowed to participate in the formation of public authority. The notion that these forms are themselves the object of class conflict coincides with our proposition concerning the duality and inter-connectedness of the two levels of conflict. On the first level, the conflict is about distributional issues, i.e. the 'who gets what?' of normal politics. On this level, the question of what is valuable, and hence desirable to get, is presupposed as a question that has already been answered through the existing political forms and the preferences that are revealed within them. The question of politics is thus reduced to, How much does each group get of what it has already defined as desirable to get? Parallel to this conflict, there is always the second-level one which focuses on the question, In which way do we most reliably find out what it is that we want to get? And, What notion of collective identity embraces the totality of those who want to get it? This is the conflict over political form.

In order to conduct the conflict on the first level, where the definition of 'cost' and 'benefit' is a fixed parameter of the game, the Olsonian logic of collective action describes and predicts the rational mode of behaviour of all parties involved, and even contributes to an understanding of why some groups are more likely to win than others. It is easy, however, to see now why this logic of collective action is incomplete and why it provides only a limited understanding – it is unable to include and to describe the second level of conflict, where parameters become variable, and collective action is concerned with a redefinition of what we mean by 'costs' and 'benefits'. In the absence of such predetermined parameters, the mode of action and struggle cannot be informed by any purposive-rational calculation, but rather by a notion of the *intrinsic* value and preferability of a particular mode of collective action. The purpose of this second type of conflict is, not to 'get something', but to put ourselves in a position from which we can see better what it really is that we want to get, and where it becomes possible to rid ourselves of illusory and distorted notions of our own interest.

Liberal political theory maintains that, since everyone knows at every point in time with incontrovertible certainty what his/her interest is, there is no need to shift from the first to the second level of political conflict, from one logic of collective action to the other; nor is there a need to challenge those established political forms which are nothing but forms for registering whatever preferences are revealed. From this liberal point of view, the possibility of level-two conflicts and the corresponding logic of collective action are simply denied. Class theory demonstrates what is wrong with this position. It can do so (and often does) by claiming, on the basis of Hegelian metaphysics of history or by reference to some even more controversial intellectual standard, to have insight into a positive definition of the 'objective interest'. Contrary to such varieties of class theory, we have argued here, at least by implication, that such an argument claims more than is necessary for (and, in fact, is less than successful as) a criticism of the liberal dogma.[26] Instead, we have argued that the transition from level-one ('distributive') to level-two conflict (over the appropriate political and associational form of collective action) is necessary because of class-specific differences in the probability of interest distortion, i.e. there is a greater likelihood of members of the working class coming to recognize their own prior individual perception of interest as erroneous and distorted than is the case with the members of the capitalist class. Due to the specific ambiguities that are inherent in the economic and social conditions of the working class (and which are absent from those of the bourgeoisie) the former is, so to speak, in constant search of modes of collective action that allow for a more 'reliable', less distorted conception of interest. The ruling class, however, not only has no reason to look for such alternatives, but also has good reason to comply with the existing ones because of the disorganizing effects that these are likely to have upon working-class consciousness.

What we have called before 'economic' class conflict differs from 'political' class conflict in two respects. One is the fairly obvious distinction that, on the former plane, the institutionalized modes of collective action are respected and taken for granted by both sides while, on the latter, these institutionalized forms themselves become the object of struggle. But there is also a second difference, which is deeper and more complicated. In economic class struggles, the working class as a whole or particular segments of it, as represented by unions and other working-class associations, is confronted with smaller or larger segments of the bourgeoisie. In contrast, struggles over the political form involve both a confrontation between working class and bourgeoisie and political struggles *within* the working class. This is because the two types of organization – business associations and unions – which we have compared and contrasted in this essay, are by no means strictly parallel to the two logics of collective action that we have distinguished. The incongruity of the two dividing lines can be represented by the scheme shown in figure 7.4.

| Type of organization | Capital | Labour |
|---|---|---|
| Pattern of collective action | monological $A_1$ $A_2$ | dialogical $B$ |

*Figure 7.4*

While business organizations represent a political form of individualistic rationality and thus come close to a pure example of what we have called the 'monological' form of collective action, labour organizations are always a 'mixed case' that contains elements of both logics, a condition which leads to an on-going contradiction between bureaucracy and internal democracy, aggregation of individual interests and formation of a collective identity, and all the other antinomies we have discussed. In other words, the second difference between the economic and political planes of class conflict lies in the fact that on the level of political conflict there is not only the external division that coincides with the dividing line between the two classes but, in addition, the internal division resulting from the unions' dilemma of being simultaneously based on both of the logics of collective action.

Underlying the political class struggle is a dual cleavage. Accordingly, we can conceive of three alternative courses and outcomes of the struggle. As a first possibility, we can think of an expansion of the 'dialogical' logic of collective action, which would eventually displace both the bureaucratic elements of collective action that we find within working-class organizations and the 'monological' mode of collective action that underlies capitalists' forms of collective action. This alternative could, within figure 7.4, be described as an expansion of cell $B$ and a gradual elimination of cells $A_1$ and $A_2$. Any elaboration of such an outcome, and of the process of which it is the outcome, would clearly take us far beyond the limits of the present paper, as it would require nothing less than a model of socialist transformation. It is for this reason, and due to the absence of any concrete historical process by which such a transformation could be illustrated, that we drop this alternative from further consideration in the present essay.

As a second alternative, we could think of the opposite case, namely, the expansion of the 'monological' pattern of representation of pre-established and largely fixed interests over the entire range of diverse class interests and organizations. This would mean the expansion of $A_1$ and $A_2$ to the right and the gradual elimination of cell $B$. This alternative, of course, has nothing to do with socialism (but rather with the corporatist transformation of the political form of capitalism), nor are concrete instances and tendencies in which the 'monological' form of collective action is *imposed* upon working-class organizations absent from contemporary experience. Some of the characteristics of this process will, therefore, be discussed in the following section of this essay.

There is, however, a third and intermediary case which we would have to imagine as an expansion of cell $A_2$ toward the right.

If it is true that the class struggle on the political plane occurs simultaneously between classes and as an antagonism within the working class, then we could think of it as a dynamic process that leads to the assimilation of working-class patterns of organization with those found within capitalist associations. In this case, however, the process could by no means be reduced to, or explained by, ruling-class initiatives leading to the *imposition* of individualistic political forms upon the associational forms of the working class (which is what happens in the second case); but it is rather a process in the course of which the precarious balance and coexistence of $A_2$ and $B$, that is, of monological and dialogical patterns of association, are dissolved in favour of the former and at the expense of the latter as a result of some *internal* dynamic of the working-class organization itself. More concretely, this would mean the growth of the bureaucratic and individualistic elements within unions and the virtual disappearance of dialogical patterns of collective action and collective identity. It is the dynamics of this third alternative that we want to return to and explore in the final section of this essay.

## The Imposition of Liberal Political Forms on Working-Class Organizations

Let us first consider the conflict over political form as an *inter*-class conflict. Unions have been accepted, in all advanced capitalist states, as an indispensable element of interest representation and of order and predictability, in the absence of which labour conflict and the disruption of social peace would be much harder to control than is otherwise the case. On the basis of this general assumption, which is shared even by the most conservative political forces, there is, however, considerable controversy over the legal and institutional framework in which unions should be allowed to operate. The coincidence of stagnation and inflation, the political alliances between unions and social democratic, socialist, and communist parties that shape the political life of all Western European countries, the extension of the range of issues and conflicts on which unions take an active position, and other recent developments, have given prominence to the political issue of the *appropriate institutional framework of union action*. These concerns have resulted in numerous plans and programmes for a new 'institutional design' and 'union reform' which, if implemented, would result in a substantial alteration in the power of unions. The 1974 electoral campaign in Britain that was conducted under the slogan, 'Who Governs Britain?' (meaning, of course, 'the unions' or 'the government') is a case in point, as are the various experiments with the introduction of income policies, voluntary wage restraint, 'concerted action', and 'social contracts'. What these plans, programmes and experiments amount to is an imposition of political forms upon workers' associations and a limitation of either the types and objects of demands they are legitimately allowed to make and/or the tactics that they are permitted to employ in struggles for these demands.

Depending on national traditions, conjunctural circumstances, political alliances, and the divergent union systems that exist in the Western European countries, these attempts to impose restrictive political forms upon workers' organizations and their mode of operation take a broad variety of forms, which we obviously cannot describe and compare empirically within the limits of the present article. Neither can we analyse, on any level of specificity, the complicated problem concerning the extent to which the 'imposition' of certain forms of action and/or of certain exclusive categories of demands and issues is fused with 'voluntary' tactics of self-restraint and the acceptance of restrictive regulations (a problem to which we return in the last section of this essay). All we can do here is to suggest a classification of mechanisms that are presently being discussed, proposed, and have in part already been adopted in order to curb the freedom of action of unions. The common denominator of these measures is the attempt to push back the dialogical pattern of collective action and to impose the monological pattern as the dominant one. This common denominator, in other words, is the *forced assimilation* of the working-class pattern of collective action to the pattern of collective action that dominates any other 'interest group'.

Within this general strategy of transforming the organizational and legal parameters of working-class collective action, there are a number of distinct approaches. Most notably, there is a major tactical difference between conservative and social-democratic proponents of the common strategy of imposing tighter formal discipline upon working-class organizations. This difference is based on contrasting assumptions about why unions tend to behave 'irresponsibly' unless such discipline is made operative. Conservatives generally believe that unions behave irresponsibly in their demands and tactics because *union leaders,* whom they often characterize as arrogant autocrats gifted with demagogic talents and striving for personal power, mislead the rank and file into making demands and waging struggles that will seriously hurt the members' interests as well as the health of the economy. In contrast, social-democratic analysts are much more inclined to see the dangerous dynamics of unionism in the autonomous, non-compliant behaviour of the *members* in their opposition to a leadership which, in spite of its better insights and laudable intentions, is forced, again and again, to advocate militant demands and tactics.

Irrespective of such differences of attitude and assumption, which are easily explained if we look at the respective loyalties that these parties want to maintain and the electoral constituencies they want to draw upon, their common conclusion is that the formal parameters of unionism must be redesigned so as to minimize risks of 'irresponsible' union behaviour. The principal varieties and mechanisms of these institutional disciplines which are imposed upon (and, as we will see later) are sometimes accepted by unions for quite 'rational' reasons, can be categorized in the following way.


## 1   Limitations of the substantive areas of interest representation by unions

Under this title, of course, we refer to an old and continuing tactic, which is aimed at a restrictive definition of the range and type of demands that unions are legally allowed to make and on which they can employ their specific sources of power. It dates back, in the case of Germany, to the 1880s when, under Bismarck's ban on the political activity of the Socialists, unions had to strictly limit their activity to 'non-political', economic issues. The division of labour between the political wing (party) and the social and economic wing (unions) of the labour movement, institutionalized both from within and from outside the unions in the first decade of the century, has contributed to the deepening of such thematic limitations. The prohibition of 'political' strikes, and of political agitation within factories, has been a further step in the same direction. Today, in the Federal Republic of Germany, unions are forced by law and by court decisions to remain formally 'neutral' *vis-à-vis* political parties. Even more far-reaching regulations are presently in the stage of preparation. The German Employers Association (BDA) has in recent years launched a vigorous campaign against what it considers the disproportionate political power of unions. In the course of this campaign, the federation of trade unions was accused of illegitimately taking positions on such issues as abortion legislation, foreign policy, and developmental aid to Third World countries, which is considered to transcend the trade unions' legitimate range of interest representation and to interfere with the prerogatives of party politics.[27] A recent proposal for an 'association act', authored by a group within the liberal party (FDP) makes it mandatory for all interest groups (including unions) to set up for themselves an exclusive list of specific areas in which they intend to represent the interests of their members, with the implication that any activity in areas other than those listed becomes automatically illegal.

## 2  Institutionalization of alternative, non-associational modes of working-class interest representation

Instructive illustrations of these tactics can again be found in the case of the Federal Republic, which seems to be the most advanced instance of a development that can also be observed in other Western European countries. Since the early years of the Weimar Republic, there has been a three-level system of interest represent-ation of the working class, namely (a) socialist and communist parties, (b) unions and (c) works councils (*Betriebsräte*). In the early fifties and the mid-seventies, 'codetermination legislation' (*Mitbestimmungsgesetze*) was added to complement a system of class and industrial conflict in which the conflict based on *organization* was gradually transformed into a conflict based on *legal entitlement* to participation – a process to which German literature refers with the term 'juridification' (*Verrechtlichung*) of industrial and class relations. Advantageous as many of these legal statutes and procedural rules have been for the defence of workers' interests, the reverse side of the coin of 'juridification' is clearly the uncoupling of *representation* and *activation* of interests. The more the relative share of interests decreases – interests represented by unions in their capacity as parties in collective bargaining – the more limited becomes, too, that part of interest that can be defended by strikes and other forms of collective action and mobilization. The more interest representation is assigned to either state agencies and/or works councils (which are not allowed to initiate strikes), the less room there remains for struggles that involve the activity of those whose interests are represented. As a consequence, the dialogical pattern of collective action is made 'unnecessary' and is discouraged in the course of the long-term transformation of industrial relations from associated into legally constituted forms of interest intermediation. Within the framework of such legal procedures, it is almost entirely left up to the respective functionary to decide what the interests are of those whom he represents and from whose immediate control his decisions are largely exempt.

'Juridification' seemingly provides an alternative, more convenient road to those objectives for which it is no longer deemed necessary to engage in associational activity. Legal statutes replace organized activity. But they simultaneously undermine the structural preconditions for such activity, even in the absence of explicit legal prohibitions concerning certain tactics and categories of demands, such as those that have been experimented with in recent British industrial relations legislation.[28] The basic mechanism by which monological and bureaucratic patterns of collective action are favoured and dialogical ones displaced is the *dissociation of representation and struggle*. The same mechanism underlies various schemes to grant corporatist rights of participation to unions in 'concerted action' and other tripartite public-policy bodies. Similar ideas of routinized, legalized, and hence conflict-free interest accommodation are what inspire advocates of 'social contracts' and wage indexation (i.e. automatic escalators compensating for inflationary losses in real wages).

### 3   Statutory increases of diversity and conflict within unions

This third category of tactics facilitates the emergence of disunity within unions by strengthening the statutory position of those who wish to criticize the ways in which leaders conduct union affairs. This can be done, for instance, by making the postal ballot mandatory in all elections and votes within the organization. The underlying intention (although not necessarily the result) of this proposal for procedural reform is to mobilize the 'silent majority' which stands outside those communicative networks and informal channels of social control that remain operative in the membership. The demand for the introduction of the postal ballot has been a favourite of conservative union 'reformers' both in Britain and the Federal Republic in recent years.[29] Another way to accomplish the objective of accentuating disunity is the imposition of regulations that make it more difficult for unions to deny access and/or to expel dissident members and thus to narrow the spectrum of positions within the membership.[30] Such regulations, commonly advocated in the name of 'intra-organizational democracy' or 'pluralism', appear, in the light of the argument that we have developed about class-specific distortions of interest perception, as measures to paralyse those associational practices which could help to overcome interest distortions or 'fetishism'. They also appear to perform the function of tying union members closer to that which is interpreted as their interest by the media and encountered in other expressions of the dominant liberal political and economic paradigm, and of making it proportionately more difficult for unions to partially suspend the individualistic orientations of members in a dialogical process of collective interest articulation.[31]

It is this point on which the numerous designs for the 'reform' and modernization of unionism that we find in various stages of institutionalization in many advanced capitalist countries converge. They subvert the dialogical process of collective interest articulation on which unions' power fundamentally depends, either by declaring some of its potential results illegal, or by making its efforts apparently superfluous, or by making the already burdensome process of internal unification more difficult.

It is only to the extent that these three tactics of imposing bourgeois political forms upon unions become eventually successful that the conceptual equation (of unions and any other interest group), which liberal social scientists start by presupposing, becomes justified.

### Towards a Sociological Theory of Opportunism

We have argued earlier in this essay that the empirical interests of workers and of capitalists are, to a differing extent, subject to the risk of distortion. Once the institutionalized practice of capitalism is firmly established, there is no longer any functional need for capitalists to clarify for themselves what type of society and particular social institutions they want to have. In other words, collective theorizing about the desirability and the functioning of capitalism – an activity which would involve particularly high risks of error – becomes unnecessary and obsolete. From then on, they learn their lesson about 'rational' modes of individual behaviour, not from a shared doctrine about the nature of society, but from the market. Conversely, as long as social life is dominated by the mechanisms of the market and private accumulation, the risk is minimal that, as a capitalist, one would experience the insight that obeying the imperatives of the market was against one's interest.

In this respect, the experience of the working class is quite different. Chances are that after you have learned the lessons of the labour market, you will also learn that you have learned the wrong lessons. Both the individual and organizational problem is to find out, in the course of a process that is bound to be full of errors, misconceptions, and distortions, which are the right lessons to learn, i.e. how ambiguities in orientation can be overcome so as to lead to a definition of interest that is 'enlightened' and consistent with itself. The problem is that workers can neither fully submit to the logic of the market, nor can they escape from the market. Caught in this trap, workers and workers' organizations are involved constantly in the immensely complicated process of finding out what their interests are and how they can be pursued in a way that does not turn out to be self-contradictory and self-defeating.

In the final section of this essay, we want to explore an alternative that has already been hinted at, namely that, even in the absence of politically imposed modes of collective action such as corporatism and 'juridification', workers' organizations adopt 'opportunism' as a solution. In addition to its obvious pejorative connotation, the term opportunism has a clear analytical meaning. As it was first introduced into the political and theoretical debates within the European socialist movement in the first two decades of the twentieth century, it refers to a tendency 'of seizing tactical opportunities without any regard for principles', as Peter Nettl has most concisely described.[32] More specifically, the term 'opportunism', as frequently used in the pamphlet on the 'Mass Strike' and other writings of Rosa Luxemburg, refers to what she perceived and criticized as a rising tendency within German social democracy of her time. According to her, opportunism includes the tendency towards an exclusive orientation of the working-class movement along established and recognized channels of political action; towards an exclusive reliance upon parliamentary and electoral forms of struggle within the working-class movement; the acceptance of the 'division of labour' between economic and political struggles as it became manifest in the proclamation of the 'independence' of unions from the socialist party; a strategic self-limitation of the means and forms of struggle; and, thus, to put it most abstractly, an interruption of the dialectic of means and ends and the resulting reification of means which are, henceforth, considered to be ends in themselves.[33]

Even today, the theoretical understanding of opportunism, and specifically of the 'voluntary' submission and assimilation of the working-class movement to liberal-bourgeois political forms before and during the First World War, is still one of the most serious desiderata of social history and social theory. Beyond the equally trivial levels of either moralistic rejection of opportunism or its 'pragmatic' acceptance, an explanation is needed of the contextual conditions and the causal mechanisms that give rise to opportunist organizational practices. These practices can be characterized sociologically by three elements.

(1)   The inversion of the means–end relationship, leading to

the elevation of institutionalized or otherwise immediately available means, and their working as a selective filter mechanism over organizational objectives and principles (the '*substantive*' dimension).

(2) The interruption of links between the short- and long-term perspective; priority is given to immediate and short-term accomplishments, whereas future chances and consequences are ignored or discounted (the *temporal* dimension).

(3) Emphasis upon quantitative criteria of the recruitment and mobilization of members rather than on qualitative criteria such as the formation and expression of collective identities. Such emphasis on quantitative criteria can either take the form of *maximization* ('as many as possible', in terms of electoral success and/or membership dues), or of *tactical exclusion* ('only those specifically affected' by some particular issue or conflict). Both of these quantitative orientations render the question of who 'we' are (and who, for that matter, 'they' are with whom 'we' are in conflict) secondary and obsolete (the *social* dimension).

Opportunism, then, is a type of organizational practice that resolves the problems connected with the precarious coexistence of the two logics of collective action that we find as a class-specific element in working-class organizations, by preferring the monological pattern of collective action. If the opportunist resolution of this tension is not to be fully explained (either by the forced imposition of liberal-bourgeois political forms upon working-class organizations, nor by 'corrupt' working-class leaders or 'aristocratic' elements of the working class, nor by any unsociological mystifications such as the 'iron law of oligarchy', what other explanation could account for the overwhelming evidence of opportunism in modern working-class organizations?

As an answer to this question, we want to suggest a model according to which the shift to opportunist practices of collective action appears to be both a rational *and* unstable solution to the dilemma of working-class organizations. The model itself is a sequential one and consists of five stages. Stage I represents the early period of a working-class organization, during which the formation of collective identity, cultivation of the members' 'willingness to act', relatively small-scale, militant conflict, and low degree of bureaucratization characterize the life of the organization. In this stage, the dialogical pattern of collective action is clearly dominant. The dilemma between dialogical and monological patterns emerges at stage II. The organization has then become strong enough to derive some power (i.e. control over its environment) from its recognized *potential* of power. In other words, concessions are likely to be made not because members have struck, but in order to avoid a strike. The recognized potential of power functions as if it were actually exercised, so that the exercise of power can remain virtualized at the bargaining table. In order to exploit the advantages of this situation, the organization comes under partially contradictory imperatives. On the one hand, it must see to it that the image of its being able to exercise power remains a plausible one to the adversary, which means that the organization has to recruit, to mobilize, and to activate members. On the other hand, it has to see to it that the members do not prematurely and imprudently actualize their 'willingness to act', because that would lower the price that is paid by the adversary for the reliable avoidance of strikes and other forms of militant action. If the organization fails to satisfy the first condition, its *survival* is threatened; if it fails to meet the second imperative, its strategic chances of *success* are undermined.

Since there is no safe and permanent solution to this dilemma within the parameters of stage II, there will be strong pressure towards a structural transformation of the organization itself. This transformation can result in a return to stage I, which, however, is likely only under contextual conditions of a high level of politicization of class struggle. In this case, existing chances for success by bargaining procedures could easily be given up because alternative sources of power, for example, those provided by a broad socialist movement and a strong socialist or communist party, could be utilized. In the absence of such favourable conditions, which allow for a regression of organizational practices from stage II to stage I, the only transformation *that neither threatens the survival of the organization nor interferes with its chances for success is the opportunist resolution of the organization's dilemma.* This is reached at stage III. The strategy leading to stage III, or the strategy of transformation, is one that attempts to make the organization's survival as independent as possible of the motivation, the solidarity, and the 'willingness to act' of the members. How can an organization accomplish such independence? The only way of doing so is to substitute external guarantees of survival for those internal ones for which the union organization depends upon its members. Consequently, the union will try to gain as much external support and institutional recognition as possible. This substitution helps the organization to escape the dilemma of size vs. power that we have represented in figures 7.3 and 7.4, and thus enables it to grow bureaucratically without risking its existence and survival, which are guaranteed from the outside. Such guarantees provided by the state can win, under these circumstances, a considerable attractiveness to the union leadership.[34] It will try to become, with the help of its external supporters, incorporated into the formal decision-making process on economic and other policies. It will try to have as many as possible of its bargaining positions, which it had held formerly only because of the 'willingness to act' of the members, institutionalized and sanctioned by legal statutes. Simultaneously, the internal structure of the organization will be transformed into one that maximizes the independence of the organization's functionaries from the collective expression of will and activity of its members. This can be accomplished by the bureaucratization and professionalization of internal decision making, on the one hand, and by the individualization of members (emphasis on individualistic incentives to join, provision of stable career patterns for functionaries, and the restrictive exercise of control over the means of collective communication), on the other.

In order to substitute external for internal guarantees of survival, the organization has to adopt all those practices that we have described as the elements of opportunism. For instance, external support can only be won if the organization does not put into question the established political forms, if it does not raise suspicions about its long-term goals. And it will achieve relative internal independence from members only by emphasizing quantitative and individualistic, instead of qualitative, criteria in its interaction with members. Seen in this way, opportunism no longer appears to be an organizational pathology that results from treason or external manipulation; it rather appears to be a perfectly rational strategy of transformation which, in response to the above dilemma, in fact *secures the chances for success* while *escaping the threat to survival*. Empirically, it seems particularly likely that stage III – the establishment of external guarantees of survival – is reached when and where social democratic parties are strong political forces, because they are most likely to be willing to generously provide such institutional support and sanctions.

This rational solution to the dilemma, however, turns out to contain a dilemma in itself. The problem that emerges at stage IV of our model is this: once relative independence of the organization from its members' 'willingness to act' is achieved and internal guarantees are substituted by external ones, the organization no longer has any capacity to resist attempts to withdraw external support and the externally provided legal and institutional status. In other words, the organization itself becomes incapable of guaranteeing the guarantees.[35] Since it would be naive to assume that such externalized supports would become eternal and irreversible once they were established, the problem arises as to how their continuity could be enforced, since now the organization is immediately exposed to a political 'business cycle' that affects its status and thereby its chances of survival. This problem could be treated as negligible only if all forces which could possibly be interested in reverting to what we have called external supports had been neutralized in the process through which such supports had been built up. This would have meant, of course, nothing less than a substantial reduction of the economic and political powers of private capital which must be constantly interested in exploiting conjunctural possibilities to subvert the legitimacy and legal recognition of the unions' status. Failing such neutralization of the structural power position of private capital, the organization is most likely to experience a *reversal* of the process of institutionalization that has taken place at stage three as soon as political and/or economic conditions are favourable enough to attempt an attack on those supportive institutional arrangements. This can result either in the outright withdrawal of institutional supports or, more likely, in a course of events in which the maintenance of the institutional supports becomes conditional upon the cooperative, responsible, etc. behaviour of the organization. Once again, the contradiction between 'survival' and 'success' asserts itself; survival continues to be guaranteed only if success (i.e. certain categories of demands) is sacrificed. At this point the long-term costs of opportunism become manifest, in response to which a new phase of mobilization and activation of members becomes necessary in order to defend both the survival and the chances of success of the organization. Stage V is now reached. This return to a type of collective action in which the members' 'willingness to act' is of predominant importance is generally equivalent to stage I of our cyclical model, but differs in two respects: first, because it is likely to be based upon a faction or division within an already existing organization, and second because it tends to focus on a much broader range of political, legal, and institutional arrangements, which have played such an important and deceptive role in the prior stages.[36]

Although we believe that the usefulness of this model could be demonstrated by interpreting the history of various European unions as a cyclical sequence of these five stages, we cannot extensively delve into the history of labour movements here. We rather want to return to the more limited question of a sociological theory of opportunism.

The view of opportunism that is implicit in the above model differs from the way in which opportunism has traditionally been used, and continues to be used in the labour movement, in three respects. First, whereas in the political discourse on working-class organizations the term 'opportunism' is regularly used in the pejorative and descriptive sense, we have used it in the analytical sense and have distinguished between three of its empirically connected dimensions. Second, while opportunism is normally exclusively used by its proclaimed opponents, we have argued that it can well be defended as the only rational and realistic solution to those tensions, dilemmas, and internal contradictions that become manifest as a consequence of stage II. If an organization wants to protect both its existence and its potential accomplishments, then there simply seems to be no other way than the partial sacrifice of an autonomy that has become a burden rather than an asset. We thus conceive of opportunism, not as an attitude or a structure, but as a rational *strategy* to which there is no alternative given the internal and contextual conditions we have indicated. Third, although it is perfectly legitimate from the point of view of the organization and the interest it tries to serve to adopt opportunist strategies in response to the otherwise insoluble dilemmas, it is also a self-defeating solution and thus limited in its rationality – rather than a self-regenerating structure that is as much abhorred by the leftist critics of opportunism as it is hoped for by

H

neo-corporatist ideologues. For as the sequence of our model goes on, opportunist practices cease to be justifiable by standards of either survival or goal attainment. The organizational security provided by the achievement of corporatist status and the corresponding independence *vis-à-vis* members turns out to be a contradictory accomplishment as soon as it is fully established. At this point, survival and power of the organization are threatened by the very arrangements that opportunist practices had relied upon *in order to save* the organization's survival and power.

If this is so, both the leftist criticism of, and the liberal euphoria about, trade union opportunism are mistaken. The former, because it refuses to appreciate the seriousness of those problems that result from the precarious coexistence of the two logics of collective action within working-class organizations and therefore fails to understand the *transitory rationality of opportunism*. The latter, because it ignores the built-in reversal of the unions' opportunist practice of corporatist cooperation, and because it prematurely believes, under the impression of growing opportunist practices, in the unions' eternal approximation to the liberal model of 'the interest group'.

# 8

# The Attribution of Public Status
# to Interest Groups

Like all social phenomena, interest groups can be analysed from three theoretical perspectives. We can start with the individual social actor and explore his/her intentions, values, and expectations in joining the organization and his/her actual chances of influencing its policies and utilizing the resources and achievements of the organization. Or we start with the organization itself, the generation of its resources, its growth, internal bureaucratization and differentiation, and its relations to other organizations. Finally, we can focus on the social system in general, and start by asking what role it assigns to interest organizations, what legal or other constraints it imposes on the pursuit of certain interests, and what links it establishes between particular interest organizations and other elements of the social structure. Speaking loosely and metaphorically, one could say that these three perspectives look on interest organizations from 'below', 'within', and 'above'.

### Three Dimensions of the Analysis of Interest
### Organizations

It is only when we combine these three dimensions of organized forms of interest representation that we can arrive at a sufficiently complex explanation of their operation. We ask such questions as:

This essay focuses on the Federal Republic of Germany. It was written during the latter months of 1977. It is here reprinted, with minor alterations, from the version published in S. D. Berger (ed.), *Organizing interests in Western Europe: pluralism, corporatism, and the transformation of politics* (Cambridge, 1981), pp. 123–58.

What factors lead to the formation of an interest group? What determines its relative influence and power in the political process? How can the specific articulation and definition of those demands be understood that an interest organization puts forward as being in 'the interest' of those represented by the organization? Then we immediately encounter the need to proceed on three levels of analysis simultaneously. These are (i) the level of will, consciousness, sense of collective identity, and values of the *constituent* members of the interest group; (ii) the level of the socio-economic 'opportunity structure' of the society within which an interest group emerges and acts; and (iii) the institutional forms and practices that are provided to the interest group by the political system and that confer a particular status upon its basis of operation.

One of the biases of pluralist political theory results directly from its failure to take into account the relevance of the second and third elements of interest organizations. Pluralist theory tends to explain the existence, strength, and particular articulation of interest organizations by reference to properties of the constituent elements of the organization: the values, their willingness to sacrifice resources for the pursuit of their interest, their numbers, and so on. That this type of explanation leads at best to a very limited understanding of the dynamics of interest representation becomes evident as soon as we realize that an identical number of interested individuals with identical degrees of determination to defend and promote their interest may produce vastly different organizational manifestations and practices, depending on the strategic location of the groups' members within the social structure and depending on the political-institutional status their organization does or does not enjoy. The concrete shape and content of organized interest representation is always a result of interest *plus* opportunity *plus* institutional status. To employ structuralist language, we can also say that interest representation is determined by ideological, economic, and political parameters.

Such categorization of 'factors' and 'dimensions' should not, however, prevent us from expecting (and exploring) the empirical connections among these three types of parameters. All three of the elements that together determine the shape and content of the system of interest representation do not operate with the same relative weight and importance. Historical changes in the system of interest representation (which would become manifest in a differentiation of organized interests, changes in the nature of conflict and cooperation, in the level of militancy, etc.) can be explained by changes on the level of values and ideologies in one period, of strategic positions and social power of groups in a second, and on the level of political institutionalization of interest groups in still another period. In other words, there exists some historical variability of the relative importance of ideological, economic, and political parameters as they jointly determine the shape and content of interest organizations such as unions, trade and employers' associations, and professional associations. Policies that provide status to interest groups, assign certain semipublic or public functions to them, and regulate the type and scope of their activities are, under conditions of advanced capitalist social and economic structures, far more important factors affecting on-going change in the system of interest representation than factors that have to do with changes of either *ideological* orientations or *socio-economic* opportunity structures. Interest representation, for a number of reasons to be explored, tends to become predominantly a matter of 'political design' and thus, in part, a dependent rather than independent variable of public-policy making.

## Two Types of Political Rationality

In a highly schematic fashion, the changing relationship between the system of interest representation and public-policy making can be represented as the shift from one type of political rationality to another. Under conditions where the formation and activity of organized interest groups is not regulated by specifically attributed collective status given to the organization and its members, policy makers do not have much control over the intensity and content of specific demands that are being made in the political process, nor over the number and identity of organized collectivities by which such demands are being made. At best, political parties are able to perform a reconciling function, thus overarching the specific conflicts of interest between organized groups and providing some programmatic directives and priorities to policy makers. Under such conditions of low institutionalization of interest groups – conditions that come closest to the liberal-pluralist model of the political process – articulations of interest and demand have to be accepted as given from the point of view of the policy maker. His/her objective – and standard of political rationality – would be to serve as many of the specific demand inputs as possible, given the limitations of fiscal and other resources, so as to satisfy a maximum of special interests. This requires, in turn, increasing the efficiency and effectiveness of the governmental use of resources, maximizing predictive capacities, measuring cost–benefit ratios, employing sophisticated methods of policy and budgetary planning, using social indicators, and so forth. Because demand inputs have to be treated as given, the only thing that can and must be rationalized by a 'good' policy maker is the efficiency and effectiveness of outputs. The working of civil society itself is considered as given, both in the sense that it can be taken for granted and that it is neither feasible nor legitimate to attempt to interfere with its internal dynamic. The political problem is one of compensating for market failures, resolving conflict, supervising rules, and fine tuning. To be sure, there is a considerable range of conflict over the extent and nature of such policies and which may be more or less 'interventionist'; but the policies converge on the notion of the separation between the political and the socio-economic spheres of social life – the underlying notion without which the very term 'intervention' does not make any sense.

This type of political rationality, which we would associate with 'active' interventionist policies aiming at optimal and comprehensive satisfaction of manifest (as well as some anticipated) interest is, however, not the only conceivable type of political rationality. If political parties fail to aggregate and reconcile, on the basis of their respective programmatic orientations, major segments of the electorate, and/or if policy makers find it difficult or impossible to accommodate significant interests due to the lack of sufficient fiscal and institutional resources at their disposal, the inverse type of political rationality is likely to take over. This one follows the imperative of keeping output constant, that is, at levels that are considered reasonable or affordable, while channelling demand inputs in a way that appears compatible with available resources. The variable to be manipulated and balanced, in this case, is not policy outputs, but the system of interest representation and the modes of resolution of conflict. It is this standard of political rationality that inspires 'the search for the stable ordered society, for a system where competition, class conflict and political disunity [are] structurally rendered impossible.'[1] The standard of a 'good' policy here, to put it in the simplest terms, is not to satisfy demands but to shape and channel them so as to make them satisfiable.

A parallel alternative of standards of political rationality can be found in the field of economic policy making. Just as the policy-making doctrine of 'active interventionism' considers 'interest' as the variable that is to be taken for granted, and attempts to respond through effective policies, so, for Keynesian economic policy, the strategic point of intervention is the *demand* side of markets. Again, the standard of rationality is to make 'adequate' responses to problems that are accepted as they emerge. The configuration of macro-economic conditions that raises serious doubts about the validity of this standard of political rationality includes such phenomena as stagflation and the 'dualization' of the economic structure. Stagflation renders demand management unpractical as an instrument of economic steering, for it exposes the Keynesian policy makers to contradictory imperatives: expand demand and state indebtedness in order to fight stagnation, and reduce it in order to achieve monetary stability. They necessitate the shift to an alternative type of rational economic policy making, the shift to the *supply side* of the economy. Here the effort is to structure problems so as to make them manageable. Quantity and skill level of the work-force, energy and raw materials, the price level at which labour power and natural resources are available, and the level and rate of technical change are the foci of economic policies that no longer merely respond to problems but that try to change their nature so as to make future responses possible.

Both in the case of political rationality and economic policy, the common characteristic of the respective second alternative is to establish institutional parameters and/or physical and economic parameters that guarantee that the problems that have to be dealt with do not exceed the scope of the available resources and strategies of problem solving.

The distinction between the two modes of political rationality can be conveniently made in terms of 'conjunctural' vs. 'structural' policies. Conjunctural policies would seek to maximize the adequacy of policy responses to problems as they emerge and appear on the agenda; the concomitant expectation is that such problems and demands will remain within a range of manageability defined by existing capacities of state action and their continuing improvement. Structural policies, in contrast, become the predominant mode of intervention as soon as this expectation is no longer supported by experience. They are adopted in response to conditions of economic and institutional crisis. In response to such crises, the physical and economic parameters of production and the institutional parameters of interest representation, which together constitute the nature of the problem, become subject to redesign. The shift is from policy output and economic demand management to the shaping of political input and economic supply – from 'state intervention' to 'politicization'.

This essay argues that the transition from 'conjunctural' to 'structural' modes of political strategy has been a dominant trend in advanced capitalist nations since the late sixties. It concentrates on strategies of institutional change concerning political inputs and explores the strategic significance and consequences of such changes. Using materials from the Federal Republic of Germany, we consider (i) whether changes in the structure of interest representation can actually be explained by the intention to influence the volume and nature of political problems that appear on the political agenda and (ii) whether the strategy of elimination of 'problem overload' by institutionalizing filter mechanisms designed to reduce the magnitude of problems to manageable proportions, is actually a workable and successful strategy, or whether it generates its own specific failures and contradictions. We should be careful, however, not to mistake a conceptual distinction for an evolutionary sequence. It would be far too simplistic and quite inaccurate to work with an historical periodization of this kind, arguing, in effect, that there was a time when instrumental rationality was the dominant mode and that, at the end of this period, there was an unequivocal shift toward the rationalization of inputs and the supply side of markets. Although it may turn out to be justified to describe a particular historical period or configuration of political forces as being dominated by either of the two types of political rationality, it may well be more fruitful to study the simultaneity and interaction of the two. At what point and for what reasons does the orientation of policy makers toward problem solving and the achievement of stated goals turn into an orientation towards regulating the institutional setting that leads to the emergence of goals and problems? To what extent does the achievement of goals presuppose the creation of a new balance of supportive forces and the construction of new channels through which demands and political opposition are channelled? Our theme, then, is to explore the mechanisms by which new issues, new items on the agenda of the state apparatus, and new imperatives of intervention lead to changes in the system of interest representation, or how functional changes of public policy affect the institutional framework of politics. Growing state interventionism and increasing political institutionalization through corporatist forms of 'functional representation', although conceptually distinct and even opposite modes of political rationalization are, nevertheless, empirically connected developments.[2]

## Reordering the System of Interest Representation – A New Political Issue

Although a harmonious and often euphoric view of a social and political order characterized by group processes prevailed throughout the fifties, a much more disenchanted attitude has become prominent since the mid-sixties. What was discovered then, and has become part of the academic as well as non-academic political discourse, was the propensity of a political order based on the uninhibited interplay or organized interest group forces to reproduce and even to exacerbate exactly those 'anarchic' and disruptive tendencies that seemingly had been overcome in the transition from 'competitive' to 'organized' capitalism. More specifically, it came to be suspected that the bargaining power and political influence of organized interests undermined responsible parliamentary government based on political parties, caused an intolerably high rate of inflation and/or fiscal strain, and interfered with attempts at long-term and comprehensive social and economic planning. In addition, it appeared that conflict among the most powerful interest groups was settled, quite frequently, at the expense of social categories that are poorly organized (e.g. consumers, independent middle classes) and hence economically and/or politically vulnerable. These and similar concerns underlie various attempts to reorganize the relationship among interest groups and the relationship between interest groups and the state. In all cases, the rationale has been to impose a certain measure of self-restraint, discipline, and responsibility on interest groups and to make the interaction between organized interests, on the one hand, and the legislative and executive branches of government, on the other, more predictable and cooperative. In short, the dynamics of 'organized capitalism' were themselves seen to be in need of reorganization.

There can be little doubt that this wave of post-pluralist realism, concerning the urgency of institutional changes in the framework of interest representation and the conduct of politics, reflects new policy problems confronting the capitalist state. In spite of vast differences in kind and degree between the problems of the first German republic in the mid-twenties and those of the second in the mid-sixties, in both cases the question arose of the compatibility of serious economic policy problems, on the one side, and the dynamics of uncoordinated interest-group pluralism, on the other. The conflict was not one of contradictory demands but of political and economic demands, and systemic requirements. Certain 'excessive' demands generated by interest-group pluralism appeared to transcend the limits of tolerance of the economic order.

To be sure, in the history of the Federal Republic there has always been a tradition of political commentary and analysis that is highly critical of the role played by organized interests.[3] In sharp distinction to current contributions, however, the critical argument of this literature was not functionalist but normative, appealing to such values as the bureaucratic ethos, the rule of law, the preservation of constitutional authority, and the separation of powers. What these authors were calling for was not institutional *innovation* in the system of interest representation but, rather, stricter adherence to *existing* constitutional norms that would protect the political system against illegitimate forms of influence and control that subverted state authority. Although this normative argument has never been fully abandoned in the academic and political literature, it figures only as an ideological façade for models and recommendations derived from functionalist

The Attribution of Public Status to Interest Groups 229

arguments.[4] That is, the focus of concern, the notion of what is threatened, has shifted from constitutional *norms* to the requirements of socio-political *stability* and the effective performance of public policy which, by more recent authors, is held to make institutional changes of the system of interest representation an urgent imperative.

The broad literature on planning and public-policy making that has been produced in the Federal Republic since the late sixties started by exploring the organizational, informational, and budgetary requirements for effective and efficient policy making, thus trying to provide the necessary knowledge for the conduct of 'active reform policies', which were the programmatic base of the early years of the Social Democratic administration after 1969. Their belief in the desirability of innovative (rather than merely responsive), highly coordinated (rather than fragmented), and long-term policy strategies led their proponents to realize that such rationalizations *within* the state apparatus were insufficient to improve the reform capacity of the state. They realized that under conditions of party competition and interest-group pluralism, such reformist activism would face insurmountable political difficulties: lack of consensus, short-term mobilizations, and increased levels of conflict.[5] Strategies that would facilitate the creation of consensus and the absorption of conflict, including institutional devices to secure coordination not only among the various agencies of the state apparatus but also among state and *private* actors and organizations were increasingly held to be the most crucial prerequisites of active reformism.[6]

The need to achieve a 'new social order' by 'reforming democracy' had already been the substance of a political programme by which Chancellor Ludwig Erhard, the leader of the last post-war administration without Social Democratic participation, tried to inaugurate a new form of politics for the Federal Republic in May 1965 – one and a half years before he had to quit office as a direct consequence of the first major recession that affected the German political economy since the Second World War. This programme which, more precisely because of its lack of precision, should be called a vision of political order advertised under the title of a 'societal formation' (*Formierte Gesellschaft*), was directly deduced from normative social theories of authors such as Eric Voegelin and Goetz Briefs. Basically, the theory consists of a grandiose developmental scheme specifying three stages in the development of non-totalitarian industrial societies. The first of these is 'capitalism', characterized by extreme inequalities of wealth and power and the resulting high level of class conflict. The second, generally reached by European nations after the First World War, is liberal-pluralist democracy, which is basically a transitory stage: it solves the structural problems of the old 'capitalist' order by allowing for the development of powerful mass organizations (such as unions and recognized social demo-cratic parties) and by providing a mechanism for equalizing power differentials based on economic power. At the same time, however, liberal-pluralist democracy introduces centrifugal ten-dencies that reach dangerous proportions the more the on-going process of industrialization transforms the political economy into a highly complex and interdependent whole. The pluralist dissolution of values, disciplines and traditions – the 'end of ideology' – renders this precarious sytem even more vulnerable. Hence the need for a transition to a third stage: its rationale is the adaptation of politics to the requirements of the advanced industrial 'technostructure' and the overcoming of the disruptive impact of liberal-pluralist democracy. Shortsighted, narrow-minded, irresponsible, and illegitimate mass organizations must be curbed. Most important, distributional and social-policy demands must be reconciled with the imperatives of economic moderniz-ation growth, and competitiveness.[7]

This diagnosis leads to the following dilemma: in an advanced industrial economy, interest organizations have the power to interfere with public-policy making in highly dysfunctional ways; hence, the need to 'keep them out'. At the same time, however, such representative organizations are absolutely indispensable for public policy, because they have a monopoly of information relevant for public policy and, most important, a substantial measure of control over their respective constituencies. Therefore they must be made *integral components* of the mechanisms through which public policy is formulated. Their potential positive function is as significant as their potential for obstruction. The trick, from this perspective, is to utilize the first while avoiding exposing public policy to the second. Any conceivable solution to this problem would imply more than what is required to solve the problem of neutrality and the enforcement of rule-of-law norms.

In the latter case, the solution would consist in strengthening the demarcation line between private powers and public policy, although leaving the nature of organized interest representation itself unaffected. In the first case, any solution would be insufficient that does not change the internal structure and composition of the system of interest representation so that their indispensable potential for cooperation is maximized, and their potential for the 'selfish' and 'irresponsible' pursuit of particularistic interests is eliminated.

The new political problematic that has occupied the centre of the stage since the mid-sixties is characterized by the growing sense of the failure of the purposive-instrumental type of rationality and the increasingly perceived need to 'rationalize' the polity in terms of what Anderson calls a new 'design'.[8] Because the claims and interests articulated within the framework of liberal-democratic institutions can no longer be reconciled with the basic prerequisites of capitalist stability and growth, these institutions themselves are at issue. The pervasive shift is from conflict over group interest to conflict over ground rules, from the definition of claims to the definition of legitimate claimants, from politics to metapolitics. This shift takes place in the conservative as well as the social democratic camp, even though in different variants. The conservatives propose the restoration of 'order' and call for the abolition of state interventionism; the social democrats understand that reformist interventionism presupposes for its success and continuity new arrangements over orderly cooperation and relatively conflict-free modes of interest representation. Both variants imply changes in the mode of interest representation, new regulations for the conduct of group and class conflict. Both are forced to design these regulations not according to some normative conception of a good and just political order but by pragmatic reference to functional requirements, limits of tolerance, and economic mechanisms. Modern conservatives find themselves forced to acknowledge the irrevocable reality of mass democracy, the welfare state, and collective representation of the working class in wage and other negotiations, although their ideologies of an organicist order or a world of free competition may leave no place for such phenomena. Social democrats, however, find themselves forced realistically to recognize the non-transformability of essential premises of the capitalist political economy, in spite of the socialist visions of their individual or collective past.

For both conservatives and social democrats, the question is thus raised concerning not so much the desirable goals and the most effective/efficient purposive rational courses of action to accomplish them, but the ground rules, structural arrangements, and institutional designs that would be the most appropriate environment of public policy. The policy area of monetary stability is a good case in point: the controversial debate that goes on among policy makers on the left and on the right is no longer about the undesirability of inflation (on which they agree) or about the best state policies to control it (on which the options seem to be exhausted), but on how the relative power position of actors *outside* the public-policy making system (e.g. unions and highly concentrated industries) can be altered in a way that appears to be more conducive to a lasting success.

## Instances of Institutional Design

In the case of the Federal Republic, a partial list of institutional changes and proposals for such changes would include the following items, in chronological order.

1    In the early sixties, the programmatic notion of a *Formierte Gesellschaft* was launched by conservative politicians and intellectuals. The term, as described above, carries the connotation of growth, predictability, and unity. It was used to describe the projected social and economic order to follow the 'end of the post-war period' of reconstruction.

2    In 1964, a Council of Economic Advisers (*Sachverstaendigenrat*) was instituted which has since reported annually on the course and further prospects of the economy.

3    In 1967, a coalition government of Christian Democrats and Social Democrats passed legislation creating the *Konzertierte Aktion,* a highly informal mode of discussion and negotiation that provides an opportunity for state bureaucrats, employers,

unions, and some other interest organizations to exchange views on current economic issues on the basis of policy goals suggested by the government.

4    In the course of the period 1965–9, an explosive growth took place in the frequency with which committees of the Bundestag resorted to parliamentary hearings (*Anhoerungen*). In the same period, consultations between government officials and interest-group representatives became established as a routine practice during the preparatory stage of legislation.

5    In 1972, a 'code of honour' (*Verhaltensregeln*) for Members of Parliament was adopted, regulating the extent and manner in which deputies were supposed to disclose their relations to interest groups.

6    At the same time, all interest groups were required to register with the chairman of the Bundestag and to indicate their substantive area of interest and the number of members they represented.

7    In 1971, the Federation of German Unions (DGB) proposed legislation introducing an Economic and Social Council (BWSR) into the constitutional order. This new institution was intended to have far-reaching powers in the legislative process. Its proponents recommended the legislation because it would have the potential of concentrating all major government interest-group interaction in one institution, thus making such inter-action more visible and transparent.

8    In 1969, after the Social Democratic/Liberal coalition government came into office, various pieces of reform legis-lation, most notably the Urban Renewal Act (*Staedtebaufoer-derungsgesetz*), assigned a legal status to certain interest groups and prescribed the involvement of such groups in the planning and implementation of policies. Similarly, various Social Demo-cratic proposals for an 'active industrial policy' (*Strukturpolitik*) and 'investment steering' (*Investitionslenkung*) would create joint decision-making bodies (e.g. '*Branchenausschuesse*') com-posed of delegates of industry, unions, and state agencies and

authorized to consider and recommend investment decisions. A similar model of 'tripartite' decision making was recently adopted and institutionalized in the area of health policy, in which the problem of the 'explosion' of health services costs is now being attacked by state-supervised and state-initiated inter-group negotiations.

9   In 1975, the Christian Democratic Party (CDU) proclaimed in its electoral platform that 'the democratic state is called upon to establish a framework regulating both the internal organization and the external activities of social groups'. The promise to introduce such a framework was accompanied by complaints over the 'irresponsible' behaviour of such organizations in the past. The control of their allegedly enormous power and the need for its more balanced use in favour of hitherto unrepresented groups amounts to, according to the CDU platform, a solution of the *Neue soziale Frage* ('new social question' – *soziale Frage* being the traditional Catholic and liberal term for class conflict). Although this notion of uncontrolled interest-group power was clearly aimed at the 'irresponsible', 'inflation-causing' behaviour of unions, the general thrust of the argument is not too different from a declaration in a Social Democratic policy document (OR 85) adopted in 1975, which promised 'to resist vigorously any attempt at group-egotistic blackmail', an appeal that, among other things, reflected the experience of a paralysing air-traffic control assistants' strike and several incidents in which employer organizations boycotted vocational training programmes. The issue of illegitimate and uncontrolled interest-group power was raised by both major parties during the 1976 campaign, in the course of which highly emotional terms such as *Unternehmerstaat, Gewerkschaftsstaat, Filzokratie*, all of them suggesting particularistic practices of corruption and patronage and illegitimate uses of power, became part of the common political vocabulary.

10   This issue has turned out to be neither superficial nor ephemeral, as can be seen from the continuing (and highly technical) political and academic debate on the desirability and the specific terms of a *Verbaendegesetz* (Association Act), which was proposed by the Christian Democrats with the aim of

imposing constraints of 'common interest orientation' (*Gemein-wohlbindung*) on interest organizations. It is of some interest to observe that the legal term *Gemeinwohlbindung* has so far been exclusively used to refer to the use of private property; the extension of this criterion to organizations implies the view that organization today is as much a source of social power as private property has long been recognized to be; hence it needs to be subjected to analogous limitations.

The relations between interest organizations and the state, and the restructuring of these relations through political means, have been issues in all these institutional changes and legislative proposals. Diverse as they are in significance and political context, a few generalizations emerge. First, all political parties represented in the Bundestag have recognized and accepted the problem of state/interest group relations. Minor indications of reluctance on the part of the SPD notwithstanding,[9] the issue can today be considered a non-partisan one. Second, such institutionalization, or assignment of political status to interest groups, is always two-sided in its effects.[10] Any attribution of status means that, on the one hand, groups gain advantages and privileges although, on the other, they have to accept certain constraints and restrictive obligations. In a typical case, access to government decision-making positions is facilitated through the political recognition of an interest group, but the organization in question becomes subject to more or less formalized obligations, for example, to behave responsibly and predictably and to refrain from any non-negotiable demands or unacceptable tactics.

Third, *none* of the changes or suggested plans for the political reorganization of state/interest group relations were inspired by motives foreign to the liberal-pluralist doctrine of representative democracy that today constitutes the creed of political elites of advanced capitalist societies. They are neither proposed by reference to Catholic doctrines or authoritarian images of society as an organically ordered whole, nor inspired by socialist aims of overcoming exploitation and oppression by the introduction of new mechanisms of popular control of political and social power.[11] The underlying motives are, rather, of a pragmatic and 'functionalist' nature: to facilitate the resolution of distributive conflict, to obtain more reliable and predictive knowledge needed by policy makers, to relieve the state bureaucracy from the veto power of shortsighted interest groups, to combat inflation, recession, and fiscal crisis more effectively, and so forth. Such 'nonideological', highly pragmatic reasoning, on which programmes for interest-group institutionalization are based, is both the strength and weakness of the programmes. It is a source of strength because no principled political opposition is likely to be raised against proposals for more interest-group institutionalization. At the same time, however, it is a source of weakness because no one is able to justify and legitimate (other than on an *ad hoc* basis) which groups are entitled to what kind of status, and for what reasons. As Anderson observes: 'It is extremely hard in democratic theory to find grounds for investing the interests of capital and labour [or, for that matter, any other group] with the authority to make what are in effect public decisions. This is the flaw in any corporate theory of representation'.[12]

Fourth, regardless of whether institutionalization operates primarily through the attribution of privilege or the imposition of constraints (the two being, in effect, two sides of the same coin), we can conveniently categorize instances of institutionalization as belonging to one of three political approaches: (i) the mode of interest representation *vis-à-vis* legislation (sometimes including participation in the administration and interpretation of legal norms in the court system); (ii) the role of interest groups in policy implementation; and (iii) the process of interest group organization itself (i.e. the relation between the organization and its members) is regulated.

## Neo-Corporatism – The Dependent Variable

In recent contributions by Anderson, Ionescu, Lehmbruch, Panitch, Ruin, Schmitter, Winkler, and others, the term 'corporatism' sometimes used in conjunction with qualifiers such as 'neo', 'liberal', or 'societal' has been used as an analytical concept to describe global changes in the political structure of advanced capitalist societies. Corporatism is a concept that does not describe a situation, but rather an 'axis' of development. In other words, political systems can be more or less corporatist, more or less advanced in the process of corporatization, depending on the extent to which public status is attributed to organized interest groups. This process is relatively advanced when many interest groups have a publicly attributed status in all or most of the relevant dimensions of institutionalization, and it is relatively undeveloped where none or only few groups are institutionally defined in only a few of the dimensions. Empirically, approximation to the 'ideal type' of corporatism thus depends on the number of groups affected and the number of dimensions in which they are affected. To begin with the latter, corporatization increases with the following.

(1)   The extent to which the resources of an interest organization are supplied by the state. This can take the form of direct subsidies or tax exemptions, compulsory membership, privileged access to state-controlled mass communication, and so forth.

(2)   The extent to which the range of representation is defined through political decision. Examples include a public definition of the range of substantive areas in which an interest organization may operate and/or of the potential membership (e.g. by number, region, individual position and status, etc.).

(3)   The extent to which internal relations between rank-and-file members and executive members of the organization are regulated.

(4)   The extent to which interest organizations are licensed, recognized, and invited to assume, together with a specified set of other participants, a role in legislation, the judicial system, policy planning, and implementation, or even are granted the right of *Selbstverwaltung* (self-administration).

We can label these four dimensions of the concept of corporatism *resource status, representation status, organization status,* and *procedural status.* In all cases, by status we mean the specifically attributed formal status of a group, as opposed to relations of informal cooperation between political and other segments of the elite, clientelistic relations, and status resulting from *ad hoc* tactical considerations of various groups or branches of the state apparatus. Formal status is based on legal statute and formally adopted procedural rules that give the interest group some claim on a specific status. In other words, a group that has status in any of the four dimensions ceases to be exclusively determined in its actions and accomplishments by the interests, ideologies, need perceptions, and so forth of its members, as well as by the relative strength it enjoys in relation to other groups with whom it is engaged in competition or alliance. In pluralist political theory, only these two factors determine behavioural outputs. Consequently, pluralist theory is rendered obsolete by the emergence in the real world of the third of those three factors that we have distinguished in the first section of this essay, namely, specific political status. The attribution of positive political status to, for example, an organization of political refugees, a sports association, or an association of automobilists directly results in an incomplete determination of the organization's behaviour by constituent members (because now the organization has resources to spend that do *not* flow from the willingness of members to contribute to a common objective; it has commitments to honour that are the price for political subsidy and hence are irreducible to the membership level); nor can the manifest behaviour be explained by reference to the relative strength of conflicting groups or allies.

Positive political status allows an organization to enjoy partial immunity from its members as well as from other organizations. Not all instances of corporatization imply, however, the attribution of *positive* status. Equally common is the attribution of *negative* status as part of the dynamics that occur along the corporatism axis. For instance, subsidies may be taken away from an interest group; its representational status may be reduced by a restrictive redefinition of the substantive areas in which organizational activities are allowed to take place; and organization rules may be altered so as to make the achievement of internal consensus more complicated and time consuming. Also, corporatist institutionalization does not mean that, in reference to one particular interest organization, *all* status definitions must either be in the negative or the positive direction. We frequently find 'mixed cases' in which, as a consequence of its institutionalization, an organization gains in procedural status but loses in resource status, or gains in resource status but loses in representation status, and so forth.

The second major component of the corporatism concept refers to *groups* that are affected by status attribution.

1 *'Market participants'*. This category includes all organized collectivities representing the supply or demand sides of either labour markets or goods and services markets. Here we find unions and employer organizations, investors, and consumers (as organized by branch of industry, region, size of firm, etc.). The chief reason they associate is to influence state policies that bear on the relative market position of their members. These organized collectivities are able to influence the state by directly making demands on policy makers, and their actions may have destabilizing effects on the social and political order. Although their influence varies greatly according to their class position, they are able to significantly affect state policy making – either by demands, negative sanctions, or side-effects of their operation that are more or less unintended (such as inflation) but that nonetheless have direct implications for the stability of the social and political order.

2 *'Policy takers'*. This is another category of interest groups in addition to organized collectivities of market participants, whose members are affected directly by state policies. They are participants in a political 'market' in which taxation, subsidies, transfer payments, group privileges, and so forth are exchanged for political support and opposition. Coalitions of urban and regional governments are the most obvious and probably the most significant example of this category *vis-à-vis* the central state. Other examples are associations of taxpayers, welfare recipients, students, public hospitals, and automobile associations. The common denominator of all these groups is that they are affected by policy decisions made on the level of the central state.

This distinction between organized interest groups that are in fact class organizations (at least to the extent that they comprise either the supply or the demand side of the labour market) or organizations of class fractions, on the one side, and organized interest groups representing collectivities that are specifically affected by state policies, on the other, raises a serious problem, which is brought up again and again in the corporatism literature.[13] The dilemma is this: either to transcend the limitations of the pluralism paradigm and base the analysis on categories of class and class conflict or to maintain the basic idea of pluralism, namely, the notion of structural differentiation of industrial society and the mechanism of collective action that leads to a multiplicity of interest organizations, which increasing state intervention stimulates. The first interpretation of corporatism has the advantage of taking into account the aspect of repressive discipline imposed by corporatist arrangements specifically on the unions, suggesting that such arrangements can primarily be understood as the outcome of a ruling class strategy to co-opt, integrate, and discipline working-class organizations and to create conditions that typically lead to a high degree of internal bureaucratization and hence to the containment of economic and political struggles. The shortcoming of this interpretation lies in its failure to come to grips with the phenomenon of corporatization of non-class organizations (e.g. taxpayers, students, city governments, doctors, etc.), to which we have referred as 'policy takers'.

The alternative conceptual framework, however, is no less deficient. Although recognizing that corporatism affects groups far beyond the limits of class organizations, it fails to account for the impact of corporatist arrangements on the terms and institutional channels of class conflict and for the fact that such arrangements are typically advocated and promoted where the economic and political power of working-class organizations has grown beyond what the ruling class is willing to accept in the interest of continued and balanced capitalist accumulation.

The phenomenon of corporatist developments thus seems, in view of this theoretical dilemma, to require a *dual* or *combined* explanation that exclusively relies neither on the social class nor on the pluralist group paradigm. In such an explanation, the state would pursue quite different objectives when granting the right to functional representation to unions, on the one hand, and to any 'pluralist' interest group (e.g. doctors) on the other. We hypothesize that, despite apparent similarity in the two cases, the underlying function that corporatization serves in the two cases is quite different. For working-class organizations, what is to be achieved is restraint, discipline, responsibility, and the greater predictability of conflict behaviour that results from bureaucratization. In the case of ordinary pluralist interest groups, which are granted a public law status and the right to 'self-administration', the dominant motive is the delegation, devolution, and transfer of political issues and demands into an arena in which they do not directly affect the stability of (central) government and the cohesion of its supporting party or party coalition but, on the contrary, help to reduce overloaded agenda. To be sure, *every* instance of the institutionalization of functional representation involves an exchange: the organized group gives something up and gains something in return. The political reason for instituting such arrangements, however, may well be to reduce power in one case (i.e. loss of power in the case of working-class organizations) and, in the next, to grant autonomy (i.e. the right to 'self-government' or privileged access to the institutions of government granted to pluralist groups for the sake of devolution). We would expect, then, that corporatization entails quite different 'terms of trade' for the different collectivities affected by it and that the trade-off of losses and gains differs depending on whether 'restraint' or 'delegation' is the prime motive. This two-sidedness of corporatism is essential: it implies restrictions imposed on the power base of groups as well as a gain in autonomy. It means 'étatization' of group politics in one case and 'contracting out' of state power to private groups in another case. The question is what the balance of losses and gains, or discipline and autonomy, looks like in the case of particular groups and class organizations. Before we turn to this question, we have to look into the thorny problem of a functional explanation of the rise of corporatist arrangements.

Only after we understand the functions performed and the specific benefits achieved by interest group institutionalization can we explain why it is precisely corporatism (and not, say, the socialization of the means of production, the restoration of market forces uninhibited by monopolization and state intervention, or other solutions) that seems to be so attractive as a solution to the problems just mentioned in advanced capitalist economic and political systems.

In the next section I shall try to give two tentative answers to why it is precisely corporatism that becomes broadly considered and accepted as an effective and efficient solution to problems that we typically find in these systems. One answer deals with political institutions of the liberal democratic state, and the other with class forces and their relative social power. In the final section, I shall explore the possibility that corporatism, in spite of its apparent virtues as a solution to some systematic problems of the political economy, turns out to be a mixed blessing, which may not only heal major institutional defects but also generates new patterns of political conflict.

In a developed corporatist system, a second circuit is added to the machinery of the democratic representative polity. The institutional order of which periodic elections, political parties, and parliamentary government are the main elements is supplemented by a political arrangement consisting of major organized interest groups, their relative procedural status, and bodies of consultation and reconciliation. The characteristic feature of modern corporatism, in contrast to authoritarian models,[14] is the *coexistence* of the two circuits with only a limited substitution of functional for territorial representation. The advantage of corporatist modes of interest representation over democratic representative ones resides in the potential of the former for *depoliticizing conflict*, that is, in restricting both the scope of the participants in conflict and the scope of strategies and tactics that are permitted in the pursuit of conflicting interests. The explanation of such a shift would be that more traditional arrangements generate more conflict than can be processed. Traditional channels of the democratic policy lead to 'over-participation' or an 'overload' of unresolved issues. The major reason for the attractiveness of corporatist rearrangements of political decision making is its presumably greater capacity to deal with conflict.

In order to support this argument, it is essential to demonstrate that the hypothesized 'need' for depoliticization has actually become manifest in the political institutions of the democratic representative 'circuit'. The following sketchy observations on the political system in the Federal Republic of Germany may serve to make it plausible that such a need exists. These concentrate (i) on the functions performed by political parties and (ii) on dilemmas of bureaucratic policy making and policy implementation.

## *Political parties*

Political parties, according to representative democratic theory, are to perform the dual function of aggregating votes, thereby providing the major channel for political participation to citizens, and designing comprehensive programmatic policy alternatives to be executed once the party has achieved sufficient electoral success to occupy government positions. There is considerable agreement among political scientists that parties today are much more successful in performing the first function – attracting voter support – than the second function – designing coherent policy alternatives. This is certainly true in the German case. Whereas voters vote for political parties, or even the government personnel that represent political parties, the parties themselves seem no longer to be the main authors of programmatic policy decisions. Such policy decisions (e.g. on tax reform, nuclear energy, economic policies, education reform, etc.) tend to result not from *intra*-party deliberations and consensus building but, rather, from *inter*-party negotiations involving the parties in coalition.[15] Or else the proposals emerge from and are advocated by clearly identifiable segments, wings, and factions *within* the party and fail to get approval of the party as a whole. In fact, there is presently not one major issue of domestic-policy making on which one party opposes another party more strongly than factions oppose each other within one and the same party. It is hardly an exaggeration to argue that the party as a political institution has ceased to perform the function of formulating and securing agreement on programmatic policy guidelines. More often than not, such decisions emerge from levels either superior (coalition government) or inferior (faction) to the party level.[16] This condition might well be explained as the paradoxical effect of the secular transformation of 'class parties' into 'mass integration parties' (*Volksparteien*). The more diffuse and heterogeneous the electoral basis of a party, and the more it attenuates its theoretical and ideological identity in order to become acceptable to as many groups and strata within the electorate as possible, the less it can decide on clear-cut policy options and alternatives. The erosion of the identity of political parties is also reflected in the changes in the organizational structure of the Christian Democrats that result from an increase in the strength of interest group wings and fractions *within* parties. Both the Social Committees (*Sozialausschuesse*) and the Economic Council (*Wirtschaftsrat*) of the CDU, as well as the Committee for Labour Questions (*Arbeitsgemeinschaft für Arbeitnehmerfragen*) and the Young Socialists (*Jungsozialisten*) within the SPD, have become major centres of intra-party conflict (as well as channels for intra-party political careers). The dissolution of party identities, orginally hailed as a healthy sign of the 'end of ideology' and the victory of the 'catch-all-party' model, seems to have resulted in the growing inability of political parties to perform any major function. The burden of building a programmatic consensus on policies is shifted to the level of coalition governments.

This condition of often unresolvable intra-party conflict, plus the concomitant instability of governing party coalitions, generates demands for simpler, more reliable and predictable ways of reaching policy agreements. Governments depend on more direct supportive relations to major organized interests and, thus, supplementary corporatist relations (as well as more plebiscitarian parties of government conduct) are the solution to a problem emerging from the disorganization of political parties. Somewhat contrary to Lehmbruch's notion of an alternative mode of consensus building being 'increasingly required for economic steering', I would argue that it is not any specific characteristic of the policy area in question (i.e. economic steering) that gives rise to corporatist structures but the failure of political parties to perform as agents of the 'formation of political will of the people' (a task that the Constitution of the Federal Republic assigns to political parties) and the 'functional gap in consensus-building' that results.

### Bureaucratic policy making and implementation

There is still another gap that corporatist modes of interest representation are more likely to close than any other political arrangement. This becomes visible when we look at the policy 'techniques' through which a government can control certain critical variables in its environment, that is, national and international society. To summarize what I have elaborated elsewhere,[17] there are three basic alternatives, or policy methods, that can be applied to attain such control, and that appear to be used in a certain sequence and cumulatively, due to inherent limitations. The first of these methods of political control is the application of positive and/or negative incentives that are intended to affect courses of action citizens choose to follow. Hypothetical consequences (monetary rewards, punishment, etc.) are attached to specified kinds of action or inaction, to induce individual actors to produce the desired aggregate outcome. The limitation of this method of political control becomes manifest whenever actors do *not* respond to such incentives, especially if there are actors who are strategically placed to ignore them; an example of the latter occurs when a business firm does not react positively to tax exemptions and other benefits because of the expectation that a higher dose of incentives will, as a consequence, be offered by government. Sooner or later the exclusive use of this method becomes too costly in fiscal terms (or otherwise impractical as far as detailed surveillance of behaviour and administration of sanctions are concerned).

The additional method of political control that is then likely to be put into practice is transformation of the production and distribution of certain goods and services into 'public goods', increasing state spending on investment and consumption infra-structure, nationalization of certain vital industries, and so forth. The underlying theory in this second method of political control is that a framework of conditions is created that individual actors *cannot* escape even if they want to. Reliance on this method of political control, however, eventually stirs up significant political opposition to the regulations involved in producing and distribut-ing these goods and services publicly and to the taxes required to finance them, which are interferences with individual freedom of choice and action. The objection is raised that such politically supplied goods and services cannot meet standards of efficiency and effectiveness. Active reformist policies of capitalist states have always encountered such resistance – in the area of welfare policies, socialized medicine, nationalized industries, education policies, and so forth.

The impasse of political techniques that are politically feasible but economically ineffective (namely, control by parametric incentives) and political techniques that might achieve the desired ends but are uncertain in their effectiveness and impractical because of political resistance (namely, the state production and distribution of 'public goods'), constitutes a favourable condition for corporatist rearrangements of the political structure. This third political technique rests on the premise (i) that the return to purely parametrical types of control is not tolerable, and (ii) that the government cannot possibly acquire sufficient directive capacity to enable it to design and implement policies over the political resistance that interventionist programmes are especially likely to provoke. What remains is the political method of absorbing potentially obstructive political resistance by granting 'voice' options to those who are, due to the use of the second method, deprived of some of their 'exit' options in order to prevent them from exerting their veto power on policies. The price for cooperation is to delegate parts of the policy-making power to those who might object to more 'étatist' approaches to the solution of social and economic problems. Procedural status is, therefore, attributed to groups whose resistance could become critical to the implementation of policies.

In the areas of economic, labour-market, education, and social policies, the establishment of tripartite bodies (consisting of labour, capital, and state representatives) has become a widely used instrument of policy making. It leaves an often considerable range of discretion about public policy to inter-group negotiations. Resort to the method of tripartism suggests itself, as many observers have noted, because of its anticipated conflict-reducing effects. This effect can be the combined outcome of three separable mechanisms. First, the formal admission of corporate groups to the process of public policy formation favours the production of decisions that minimize the probability that social power will be used in order to obstruct or resist public policy, because the actual power of labour and capital, respectively, are already 'registered' and taken into account in the process of its formation. Second, to the extent that interest organizations do control the attitudes and behaviour of their members (which is, as we shall see, more likely in the case of labour than in that of business organizations), this organizational discipline can be used to prevent opposition from groups within the organization's membership. In this way the authority of the group's leadership is, so to speak, added to that of the state. Thus it functions as a mechanism of extended governmental control. Third, in case a policy meets or creates conflict and opposition, in spite of these safety mechanisms, the government alone is not to blame: all the actors that have participated in the process of making the decision in question would be held responsible. This makes such opposition less likely than otherwise, for any 'relevant' opposing group would have to attack not only the government but also its own leadership. Combined, these three mechanisms can be expected to reduce the likelihood and intensity of conflict over public policy, and thus to depoliticize public life.

The fact that such corporatist policy-making bodies often provide equal rights and equal numbers of representatives to labour and capital does not contradict the conclusion that a partial privatization of political power takes place. For in these bodies, the use of political power becomes a group privilege (i) in so far as common interests of all participating groups are concerned, which may well differ from a politically defined 'common interest' and (ii) in so far as equal votes of labour and capital by no means balance differences of market power that prevail, due to structural as well as conjunctural reasons, between the demand and supply sides of the labour market. As soon as we have left the realm of those political institutions for which representative democratic political theory can provide legitimation (as we certainly have if we consider, say, the tripartite managing board of the Federal Republic's labour market agency – *Verwaltungsrat der Bundesanstalt für Arbeit*), a 50:50 proportion of votes for labour and capital is by no means more justifiable than is either 10:90 or 90:10. The only virtue of the 50:50 formula is that of creating the appearance that things are open and not decided in advance on the level of procedural rules, thereby relieving the state that has instituted such 'balance' from the objections of either of the two sides.

To summarize the argument, corporatist structures are the solution to situations in which parametrical methods of political control have become insufficient for economic reasons and interventionist methods have become impractical for political ones. In such situations, parademocratic political structures serve to contain and depoliticize conflict in a fragile reconciliation of the functionally required and the politically feasible.

## Differential Impact of Corporatization on the Organizations of Labour and Capital

Thus far, the analysis has led us to the identification of two 'gaps', or instances of malfunctioning of the institutions of democratic representative government, which are serious enough to explain the resort to corporatist political structures: one is the erosion of party identities, the other is the typical impasse in bureaucratic design and implementation of policies. Explaining corporatist tendencies from institutional defects, however, is at best an intermediary step toward a theory of corporatism. It raises the question: (i) Why do political parties, at least in the German case, seem increasingly unable to catalyse the 'political will of the people'? and (ii) Why, in turn, has bureaucratic policy-making capacity declined?

Instead of speculating about causes of political decay, I prefer, rather, to explore some of the consequences of corporatist changes in the political structure. Here my argument will be that corporatist transformation not only compensates for the functional deficiencies of democratic institutions by depoliticizing conflict in terms of groups, issues, and tactics but also that it does so in an *asymmetrical* way. First, I want to demonstrate that organizations of labour and capital, although affected by exactly the *same* forms of institutionalization (i.e. attribution of political status, which provides them with the licence to participate directly and jointly in the process of policy formation), are inhibited to a greatly *differing* extent in their freedom to pursue their respective interests. Second, I argue that current proposals for interest-group institutionalization are specifically *designed* so as to impose much more far-reaching restrictions on labour than on capital.

The social power of both capital and labour rests on ultimate sanctions of economic obstruction or withdrawal. Capital can threaten to discontinue its purchases of capital goods and labour power; and labour, to withhold labour power. The power of economic obstruction distinguishes labour and capital from traditional middle-class interests and interest groups, such as farmers and shopkeepers. Because very often there are too many of them in the first place, withdrawal of their contributions to the economic process would not help to improve their economic situation but would simply accelerate an economic process against which members of the traditional middle class are indeed trying to defend themselves. It is for this *economic* reason that if the traditional middle class is to win at all, it must withdraw *political* resources (votes) or become politically active (as in demonstrations, etc.), which is why the old middle class defies definition and analysis in economic terms.[18]

Although the social power of both labour and capital rests on the possibility of withdrawing something, their organizations play a different role in mobilizing these sanctions. Whereas capital can bring its obstructive power to bear even if it is *not* organized as an interest group, the withdrawal of labour power can function as an instrument of power only if it is practised *collectively*, that is, if it is organized in at least a rudimentary way. If a firm decides not to invest and/or not to employ workers, its decision is made autonomously on the level of the individual accumulating unit and in accordance with calculations of individual profitability. If workers decide to strike, they need some mechanism of aggregation and coordination; individual attempts to exercise their 'negative' market power would be, in all but the most exceptional cases, negligible in effect and therefore counterproductive from the viewpoint of the individual actor.

Moreover, workers' interests are normally divided not only between different strata and segments of the working class but, as it were, within the individual worker. In contrast to business firms, workers do not have an unequivocal standard of 'rationality' by which they can 'optimize' among conflicting ends. Workers are always simultaneously interested in wages, continuity of employment, and working conditions. As long as they live in capitalist market societies according to the rules of which labour is treated *as if it were* a commodity, those three ends or interests remain to some extent mutually exclusive. The 'optimal' mix of those conflicting ends cannot be calculated by individuals but only collectively by an organization. *Organization* thus provides both the quantitative aggregation of the *means* of power and the qualitative definition of the *ends* to which power is to be applied. This dual role is reflected in the importance working-class organizations have always attributed to such non-individualistic principles as 'solidarity' and 'discipline'. In other words, workers' organizations – in contrast to business organizations – are effective only to the extent that they manage to partially suspend the ties of their members to the environment of individualistic monetary incentives.

Neither of these principles is of major significance in the internal operation of employers' and investors' associations. Such organizations do not generate power that does not already exist, nor do they formulate ends that do not derive directly from the ends that are already defined and consciously pursued at the level of the individual member firms. What the organization does is provide services to member firms (which in this way may achieve a substantial cost reduction relative to a situation in which they would have to provide such services themselves) and to formulate and defend in the political arena those *individual* interests (relating to taxes, tariffs, regulation of industrial relations, etc.) that are *common* to all or most member firms. In contrast to unions, employers' and investors' associations do not create power and definitions of interest as the result of an organized process of mobilization and internal discourse among members; they merely state power positions that are already established and interest definitions that are already decided on.[19] Interest *organization* is thus much more essential to the defence and promotion of labour interests than to capital interests, because capital, mergers, monopolies, cartels, and so forth are the decisive instruments of enhancing social power. Conversely, restrictive political regulation of the forms of association and organizational activities must have a stronger impact on labour organizations than on employers'/ investors' organizations.

Given that the power of labour and capital resides in their potential for obstruction, and given the unfeasibility of *eliminating* the power of either by political means, interest organizations must be subjected to constitutional forms and responsibility, or so the argument runs.[20] To the extent that such institutionalization is inspired by principles of democratic representation and aims at democratizing relations between the organization and its individual members, the group's participation in public-policy making will gain in legitimacy.

It is obvious, however, that internal democratization cannot provide the same measure of legitimacy to interest organizations as it is able to provide, according to representative democratic theory, to governments, because it is not the entire people but functionally defined organization members who 'legitimize' organization policies. Moreover, as becomes evident from a recent legislative proposal written by a committee of the German Liberal party (FDP), the principle of internal 'democratization' has very different meanings for labour and capital. (Although this legislative proposal failed when it was first introduced, a new initiative along the same lines was taken in 1984 by the Free Democratic Party – FDP.) Its (latent) function is not to confer greater legitimacy on corporatist elements within the political structure but to make it more difficult for labour in particular to mobilize power through organization. Although the proposal never specifically mentions unions but is rather intended to apply to 'all politically significant associations', the organizational rules it imposes on such organizations would have quite selective impacts for organizations defending and promoting *workers'* interests as a result of the differences between labour and capital previously discussed. For instance, section 6 of the proposed law requires all interest organizations to 'limit clearly' in their statutes those interests on which the organization wishes to represent its members. Because capital organizations are generally not instrumental in *articulating* those interests but simply in stating and transmitting them, it is much easier for them to comply with this specific requirement than it is for labour organizations, whose first task is to formulate a unified interest, the specifics of which cannot be stated in advance. If a union were forced to do so, this would limit its range of legitimate issues and activities, including those that might well be considered to bear on the defence of workers' interests. Similarly, the absence of a 'calculus of optimization' in the case of unions that could be used to reconcile conflicting goals makes intra- or inter-organization competition, disunity, and rivalry much more likely in labour unions than in business organizations. Here the question is, To what extent do unions achieve, in spite of such divisions, some measure of unity? Such unity is less likely to be achieved if the law prescribes the extensive protection of minorities (section 14), if it guarantees to non-members a legal claim to membership, taking partially away from the organization the right to deny admission (section 10), if it punishes acts of an interest organization designed 'to discriminate against competing interest organizations' (section 22), if it requires state agencies to 'give equal treatment to competing organizations with parallel goals' and to 'maintain pluralism' among them (sections 4 and 23) and, finally, if it entitles members to sue organizations in court for 'partisan one-sidedness in represent-ation or information of members' (section 25). Although these rules are meant to apply equally to labour and capital organiza-tions, their impact will be highly asymmetrical, causing increased divisions and fragmentation only within the fomer.[21] Other proposals for interest group institutionalization are equally quite explicit about the aim of taming 'radical' and 'irresponsible' inclinations within organizations to which political status is attributed, especially unions.

Yet another reason for the class bias of corporatist interest group institutionalization must be discussed. I have argued above that organization and leadership are of particular importance to the defence and promotion of working-class interests because they provide the only means of uniting and reconciling the social power of labour that otherwise would remain atomized in means and fragmented in ends. If this is true, any constraints imposed on the leadership and the forms in which organizational activities are conducted will have direct consequences for the type of demands that are being made, as well as the intensity and unity by which they can be supported. Control of institutional form means at least partial control of political content and demands – in the case of labour, but not in the case of capital. Contrary to labour unions, capital organizations do not have any substantial control over the actions that their *members* choose to pursue. The attribution of political status to employers'/investors' groups does not, therefore, justify any expectation that the behaviour of member units of such organizations will thereafter be under any greater political control than before such status was attributed. The traffic runs in one direction, because the viewpoint of organized capital can be transmitted to the political system but the spokesmen of these groups can make no binding commitments,[22] and seem to have no more than a highly informal and unreliable influence on the behaviour of their member units. In contrast, institutionalization in the case of unions means an exchange transaction in which cooperation is traded for formal participation in policy decisions or moderation is achieved as a consequence of imposed 'democra-tic' organizational rules. No such 'return' can be safely expected from government interaction with investor interest groups. Para-doxically, the political power of investors depends to some extent on the condition of powerlessness of their interest organizations, which have, neither *de lege* nor *de facto,* more than marginal control over members' investment decisions. What the govern-ment can do, then, in order to secure the willingness of investors to cooperate, is to design policies that are most conducive to profits – which remain the only channel by which investors are to be 'controlled' – and win the support of organized labour for such policies.[23] Only with this important qualification can we speak of corporatism as implying a 'shift from a supportive to a directive role for the state in the economy'.[24]

## Alternative Patterns of Political Conflict

In what direction and within which limits will corporatist changes in political structure affect the intensity of social and political conflict and its content? In order to explore these interconnec-tions, I shall sketch three alternative cases, one stable and two unstable.

### Stable corporatism

Stable corporatism is a condition in which corporatist political structures succeed in providing an interest-group consensus unchallenged by radical or 'immoderate' demands or tactics of conflict. The viability of this solution depends on how the political system manages to deal with the basic theoretical (as well as highly practical) deficiency of corporatist arrangements, namely, that no legitimizing principle can be provided for this particular fusion of private power and political authority. Why should *these* interest groups, in particular, be admitted to policy-making positions (instead of other groups)? Why should they be licensed to decide on *these* issues (as opposed to any wider or narrower agenda)? Or why should they follow *these* (rather than any other) procedural rules? Answers to such questions are, if given at all, at best pragmatic and hence debatable. Even if questions of justification of a particular institutional arrangement are usually of concern mainly to intellectuals, and of little concern to most people most of the time, will this indifference continue when significant material advantages are at issue? The on-going debate on industrial co-determination as well as on macro- and sectoral co-determination in the Federal Republic of Germany demonstrates that there are hardly any generally agreed-on principles about which group deserves what political status. Consequently, neither a 'solution' nor the programmatic acceptance of given routines is in sight; but continued conflict is more probable. At the very least, corporatism, in order to be stable, must not only continually *generate* consensus; it must first of all *presuppose* consensus, that is, a solid and undisputed acceptance of a certain mode of interest representation and accommodation.

This requires, first, a certain tradition and organization of labour unions, which results in their willingness to accept the rules of 'social partnership' (*Sozialpartnerschaft*); 'countries with a conflict-oriented labour movement are not so well suited for liberal corporatism.'[25] Apart from political traditions of the national working class, the attitude of 'social partnership' seems to be reinforced by the organizational doctrine of a 'unitary' union (*Einheitsgewerkschaft*), as opposed to organization by partisan affiliation or organization by trade; this type of organization is favourable to the maintenance of a highly 'cooperative' attitude, because German 'unitary' unions are quite fragmented internally but lack the centralized political mechanisms to resolve their internal factional disputes.[26] Second, this condition of undisputed acceptance can be maintained if those oppositional forces that are unwilling to comply with the rules of corporatist political structures are deprived of some of their political and civil rights. Finally, corporatist arrangements could win *de facto* acceptance if the goals of prosperity and growth are accomplished to an extent that makes the quest for – and the conflict over – principles legitimizing such arrangements irrelevant. Although economic crisis, as Winkler maintains, is a precipitating factor in corporatist arrangements, it seems unlikely that prosperity will resolve or even obscure the issue of legitimacy.

Without engaging in social prophecy, all we can say is that if corporatist political structures develop and stabilize, this will most probably be due to specific national traditions and forms of organization of the labour movement and/or to a high level of political repression and/or to a condition of uninterrupted economic prosperity.

## Increase in non-institutional political conflict

The standard liberal warning against corporatist arrangements (or at least their extension) is that subjecting interest groups to overly rigid status obligations might reduce their 'integrating capacity' and hence undermine their ability to influence and discipline rank-and-file members who would rather engage in conventional and unpredictable modes of conflict.[27] This argument clearly focuses primarily on the unions because, as we have seen, other interest organizations do not have any significant measure of control or influence over their constituencies. A wave of unexpected unofficial strikes that broke out in the Federal Republic in September 1969 is often cited in evidence to support this claim. These strikes were disapproved of by unions and partly directed against union leadership. Another recent phenomenon that is often interpreted as indicative of serious deficiencies in the 'integrating power' of interest groups (and political parties) is a dramatic increase of militant citizen groups and single-issue movements focusing on urban, environmental, educational, and other issues (*Buergerinitiativen*) and occasionally using violent tactics. Thus, the second scenario would be one of polarization between highly institutionalized modes of representation of 'core' interests and highly amorphous social movements of 'marginal' segments of the social structure. This pattern of conflict appears most likely to emerge where core interests are not only highly institutionalized but also have interacted in a way that suggests the disappearance of conflict and outright class collaboration.

In such situations, the archetypal image of the 'traitor' tends to be projected on unions, social democratic and communist parties, or parliamentary government as such. This image in turn provides justification for focusing on particularistic identities and causes as being the only thing left that is worth struggling for. For instance, there has hardly ever been a more sudden increase in non-institutional political conflict in the Federal Republic than in December 1966, when the Christian Democrats and the Social Democrats formed a 'grand coalition' government. The current large anti-nuclear energy movement received broad support when cases of collaboration between union officials and the nuclear-energy industry that bordered on corruption, became public.

Two important consequences follow from the polarization between institutional and non-institutional conflict. The first is that such movements may well be able to undermine the feeble legitimacy of political institutions, to disseminate feelings of suspicion and cynicism, and sometimes even to interfere with the functioning of political institutions. The second is that such 'marginal' militancy, without any tradition, theoretical foundations, or organizations might, under unfavourable circumstances, remain unable to establish the coherence and continuity that would be needed in order to create a serious alternative to what it perceives as the solid alliance in power of the corruptor and the corrupted. Taken together, these two aspects suggest the scenario of a stand-off confrontation, unproductive of major social changes except for an escalation of repression and violence.

### Balancing the class bias of corporatism

This third scenario includes developments that result from the two unresolved tensions inherent in any corporatist system. One, as we have seen, is the class bias of corporatist arrangements, the depoliticizing effect of which favours capital organizations and discriminates against labour ones. The other inherent tension is the polarizing effect that leads to a joint increase in both the institutionalization of conflict *and* non-institutional conflict.

These tensions could precipitate a process in which, in order to maintain the loyalty and allegiance of their rank-and-file members, union leaders would insist on demands and strive for accomplishments that are impossible to achieve *unless* the inherent bias of corporatism is overcome. This would require equalizing the participatory status of labour and capital within the framework of economic policy-making institutions so as to make agreements binding on investors to the same extent as they have already been accepted as binding by unions in the past. More specifically, it would mean that economic programmes on which agreement has been achieved in tripartite policy-making bodies can be put into effect irrespective of whether or not investors, who are represented at the bargaining table by their respective interest organization, find it individually profitable to comply with such programmes. This, of course, would imply doing away with a key element of the property right of investors, namely, the right *not* to invest, which is the source of the social power of private capital. Because unions, by accepting the status obligations assigned to them and by participating in tripartite policy making, *do* in fact give up some of the right to struggle more militantly for more far-reaching demands, an analogous 'sacrifice' of employers'/investors' interest groups could hardly be considered disproportionate. It would, however, shake the economic system at its foundations.

The idea of developing and using forms of functional representation to expand working-class power has a long tradition in the European labour movement. For instance, the concept of 'functional democracy', according to which factory councils and workers' cooperatives were to play a strategic role in securing socialist power and overcoming bourgeois hegemony in the Parliament and administration, was central to the programmatic thinking of Austro-Marxism,[28] and has been taken up by some Eurocommunists. Even if not thought of as an instrument of socialist transformation, the possibility has been raised that, contrary to the intentions of its inventors, the political status attributed to unions within the policy-making apparatus of the state might become usable not as a means of containing the working class but to enhance its power. Esping-Andersen and others have argued this thesis:

> Corporatism is an internally contradictory mode of incorporating the working class. The premise of a corporatist strategy is that the inclusion of . . . working class organization . . . in formal state planning processes will reduce working class opposition to state policies without requiring massive concessions to popular demands . . . If [however, the working class] leadership maintains close ties to the working class and remains a legitimate instrument of real working class organizations . . . [this will] undermine the planning function of corporatism and bring class struggle into the administrative heart of the state apparatus itself.[29]

As is the case with the two other scenarios, it is not difficult to find indications in Germany that lend some plausibility to the expectation that things will develop along these lines. For instance, union models of 'co-determination beyond plant level' (*ueberbet-riebliche Mitbestimmung*) have, since 1971, been a demand in the trade-union (DGB) programme that was given highest priority by union leadership. Union leaders and intellectuals close to the unions argue that wage restraints must be compensated for by institutional gains, because otherwise the legitimacy of unions would suffer in the eyes of rank-and-file members. After the Federation of German Employers' Associations (BDA) had filed legal complaints over a recent co-determination act with the Supreme Court, the unions for the first time used their option of strategic non-participation and refused to continue to cooperate in the 'concerted action'. One conservative opposition leader warned in Parliament that concerted action was in danger of being inadvertently transformed into an instrument of macro-codetermination. The issue may no longer be participation as such but, rather, the equalization of the extent to which parties will be constrained by decisions reached within corporatist policy-making bodies.

How likely an outcome this is may well be questioned, especially in view of the present condition of high unemployment, which generally tends to force unions to adopt defensive and cooperative strategies. One also must question the prospects for either of the two alternative scenarios. Which of them, if any, will be realized is certainly beyond the responsibility of the social scientist to predict.

# 9

# Legitimation Through Majority Rule?

Collectively binding decisions cannot be reached if a logically prior decision has not already been made. This concerns the procedures according to which decisions shall be made. The principle of majority rule is a decision-making procedure according to which state power, in a democracy, 'derives from the people'. Normally, actors involved in a political decision-making process are spared the problematization of, or even the encounter with, such prior decisions regarding procedures. For procedural decisions are already established in constitutions, statutes, routine orders, etc. which are familiar to actors and removed from their control, such that they enter into their actions as established premises. This pre-established nature of procedure in everyday decision-making processes does not, however, withdraw the procedure completely from contingency. The possibility of modifying the procedures is always 'in principle' foreseen and reflected upon. The *pouvoir constitué* would, in extreme cases, be revised by the *pouvoir constituante*.

But procedural decisions also become necessary, and are provided for, in constitutionally institutionalized procedures. An example is the procedurally appropriate decision about procedures according to which matters concerning immigrant workers should be decided in the local political system: should the

Translated by Jean Cohen. This essay was first presented as a discussion paper to the conference 'Democracy and the Majority Principle', İstituto Filosofico Aloisianum, Gallarate, Italy, in September 1980. It was first published as 'Politische Legitimation durch Mehrheitsentscheidung?' in B. Guggenberger and C. Offe (eds), *An den Grenzen der Mehrheitsdemokratie* (Opladen, 1984), pp. 150–83.

immigrant resident population be represented by special advisory councils, or should they be put on a par with the native population concerning local voting rights? This example shows that for newly emerging political fields and for new material requiring decision, very often not only the new decisions (about laws, measures, programmes) but also decisions about new decision-making procedures, become necessary. Such 'political designs' lead to the construction of political 'arenas' which are specialized to deal with specified themes and interest complexes, and to designate who should take part in the necessary production of decisions (and in which way).[1]

Procedural decisions, however, are not only required in such cases of innovation. The odd binding power of even the highest of them, such as those laid down in a state constitution, does not consist in their irrevocability as inviolable facts established once and for all. Rather, the binding power of such decisions derives from their ability to continuously pass the test of their own rationality and stability. This presupposes that the *pouvoir constituante* is by no means only a short-lived phenomenon absorbed by or perishing in the *pouvoir constitué*. Instead, the *pouvoir constituante* preserves a power of continuous control whose criteria have to be complied with. In that case, the 'stability' of the highest procedural rules would amount to a remainder against which no claims or demands can be made, but which most certainly concedes the possibility of dissent. Such an interpretation of the ground of the obligatory character of (the 'highest') procedural norms can be expressed through the formula, 'Stability through reversability'. It conforms, moreover, with the liberal interpretation of J.S. Mill, who presupposes that 'true' norms can be established as such only and solely through their stability, which is tested in the context of constant rivalry with 'false norms'.

For the contemporary dogmatists of public law, this is an absurd and, moreover, politically risky idea.[2] Nevertheless, it is at least negatively confirmed by numerous social-scientific and political works in so far as: (a) they articulate doubts as to whether those procedural rules which the constitution designates for the acquisition and use of power could be recognized by the mass of citizens as 'correct', and thus granted legitimacy; and (b) as a result of this discrepancy, they foresee risks for the maintenance of the constitutional order itself. This idea, variously expressed today through the catchwords of hostility to parties, to democracy and to the state, attests to nothing less than the fact that procedural rules for political decisions, in order to exist at all, have to be really 'sociologically' compatible with and supported by the cultural and economic structures of a society. That means that such rules, despite massive juridical-intellectual and other efforts, are not in the position to guarantee or confirm themselves as procedural decisions established once and for all. Rather, in addition, they must continuously stand the test of their real recognition. Even if it is not, as Varain thinks, the 'absence of contradiction' that brings to an end the debate over such a fundamental procedural rule as the majority principle,[3] but rather the absence of an alternative, the embarassment which arises as a result of the question 'What else?' can scarcely replace this recognition for long.

The fundamental procedural rules of collective decision-making acquire a curious double status. On the one hand, they must be presupposed as unquestionably valid whenever decisions have to be made. On the other hand, their validity can be presupposed only if its claims can *withstand questioning*. Indeed, where else could procedural rules attain their institutional stability if not from the empirical confirmation of justification claims that appear trifling and dismissible in principle only from the narrow standpoint of the discipline of juridical constitutional theory? Accordingly, I shall end this preliminary reflection with the conclusion that the permanent problem of confronting and grounding procedural decisions (that is, decisions of the type, 'to choose how to choose')[4] stands in the background not only of decision-making in the context of political innovation of the type mentioned above, but also of routine decisions.[5] Such procedural decisions follow their own normative criteria and empirical argumentation. This is also the case for the apparently self-evident and traditionally secured 'democratic' rules of decision of the majority principle, for which it is well to consider the advice that 'questions of principle ought to be punctually and regularly ventillated "in advance", in order to avoid being taken unawares by political developments.'[6]

## In Support of Majority Rule

If one chooses between defined action alternatives (or between persons who represent a bundle of future action alternatives), according to the principle of majority rule, one also chooses one among many conceivable and possible decision-making procedures. To vote or elect, instead of either commanding or debating until complete agreement is reached, is a procedural decision which must be firmly grounded. We can introduce three basic reasons in favour of deciding for the principle of majority rule:[7]

1   From the standpoint of the costs of producing decisions (above all time costs), the procedure of simple command is better than majority rule (which is superior to the procedure of debating until unanimity is reached). However, the problem with the procedural alternative of 'command' consists in the fact that we cannot always be certain who has the right to command. It is also possible that, even given clarity regarding who has the right to command, he/she/they will refuse to make a decision, thereby delaying the decision-making process. In light of such eventualities, majority rule has the clear advantage of being able to produce decisions promptly and reliably. Accordingly, one can say that majority rule presents a decision-making procedure that is technically optimal in so far as it offers a maximum of certainty that decisions will, in fact, be made and with relatively small costs.

2   Yet normally what interests us is not only the *fact* that decisions will be made, but also their *quality*. As regards the quality of decisions (their justice or 'rationality'), one can argue that majority rule provides a second advantage, especially under societal conditions in which the distinction between the *pars major* and the *pars sanior* has lost its basis and where no societal group can make the claim, with any expectation of acceptance, that it has, *a priori*, a higher insight or superior judgement than any other group. (The only exception to this rule is the 'head start in reason' that is attributed to adults over minors.) Under such egalitarian conditions and premises, one could maintain, in favour of majority rule, that it brings into play a maximum of

heterogeneous but not hierarchically ordered criteria that are represented in the empirical body of voters. It is, thus, better able than any other decision procedure to guarantee the 'justice' of the resultant decision. This can be accepted, especially given the additional condition that majority rule is preceded by a debate or an electoral campaign during which those participating in the decision mutually reveal their respective preferences that they apply in deciding. Naturally, one can grant the superior rationality of majority decisions only for those situations in which the criteria for the justice of the decision apply approximately, that is, where there is no absolute measure of the rightness of a decision. It is interesting that the majority rule will be applied accordingly, in contexts where otherwise the (scientific) criterion of truth is decisive (e.g. faculties, courts, the college of cardinals), exactly at the point in the decision-making process when scientific truth no longer works as a criterion of rightness – for example, in personnel decisions.

3    Finally, there is the standpoint that speaks for the application of majority rule. It derives from the fact that decisions must not only save time and be as substantively adequate as possible, but also that they must be *recognized* as just. That means that decisions are 'good' if the probability is maximized that they will be recognized as binding premises for the future action of others. If this is the case, we can describe a decision as worthy of recognition or 'legitimate'. The principle of majority rule acquires a double advantage in relation to this problem of legitimacy, first, presupposing *equal* and *secret* voting rights, the indirect effects of dependency and influence are neutralized by majority rule; and second, presupposing *universal* and *direct* voting rights, the totality of those affected by decisions become, in an unfalsified manner, the participants in the decision. Finally, an argument for the legitimating power of majority decisions follows from their *periodicity*: elections and votes produce decisions that are never 'final' but are, rather, tied to a specific vote and period of office. This means that the obedience of the minority *vis-à-vis* the majority decision is made easier because the minority is certain to have 'another chance' to re-pose the question and the decision. This 'consolation effect' is strengthened, moreover, by the fact that the public announce-

ment of the results and figures of elections respects not only the decision but also the *disavowed alternative* (not only the victor but also the losers and their voting strength) through formal mention.

In what follows I am exclusively concerned with the third argument for the majority principle, that is, with its alleged superior legitimating function, and I formulate some conditions under which one could grant that majority decisions really are legitimate, in the sense that they are empirically followed and theoretically obligatory and groundable. We shall see that the legitimating function of the principle of majority rule in modern capitalist democracies is thoroughly problematic and disputable. This demonstration can, however, by no means provide an answer to the question that follows, namely, Which alternative decision-making procedures could offer a higher degree of legitimating capacity? There is also a further question which I shall attempt to discuss from a political/social scientific perspective rather than from a standpoint of legal or constitutional theory: Under which conditions and on what grounds can the compliance of the minority with the decision of the majority be 'expected' – in the sense of a factual statement as well as in the sense of a normatively grounded demand?

## The Institutionalization of Majority Power

In nearly all countries of the Western world, the end of the First World War concluded a period of constitutional development which could be described as political modernization or democratization. The three most imporant results of this modernization process were: (i) the achievement of universal and equal *suffrage,* that is, the lifting of limits, above all of property (and also partly of education, sex, age) qualifications which until then had stood in the way of the universalization of the right to political participation; (ii) the recognition of the *freedom of organization* and the legitimacy of action for political parties and especially unions; (iii) in many countries, the *parliamentarization of the government,* that is, the expansion of the constitutional rights of elected parliamentary bodies not only to decisively dispose of budget votes and other laws but, in addition, to elect and change the government.

The dominant interpretation of these constitutional/political achievements doubtless amounts to the thesis that the universaliz- ation of political participation and organization rights has changed the inner structure of class society. A new balance of class forces is supposed to have been created, since the proletariat's deficit in *societal* power is compensated for by an *advantage in political power*. According to this interpretation, market and state, economy and politics no longer form a monolithic unity stamped by the class dominance of capital (a thesis that was further developed especially by Hilferding and other Austro-Marxists, as well as by the later entire social-democratic movement). Rather, it has become possible through the newly institutionalized power of the majority of wage workers to correct the economic power of capital.

There is another thesis that stands in sharp contrast to this well-known interpretation, namely, that the institutionalization of class struggle on the political level and the granting of the right of political participation and freedom of organization to the working class has in no way increased its real societal power. Instead, it has broken the revolutionary potential of the workers' movement and integrated it so as to maintain the domination of capital. In the tradition of the workers' movement, this critical interpretation of the democratic republic and its constitutional order can be found in Lenin (above all in *State and Revolution*) and among the anarchists. But Max Weber's theoretical writings on parties and organizations ('Parliament and Government in a Reconstructed Germany', 1917) and Robert Michels' work (*Political Parties*, 1911) also offer a range of reference points for this sceptical thesis. By drawing upon a range of heterogeneous political and analytic arguments and findings, its champions demonstrate that the recognition of the 'political rules of the game' of party competition, on the one hand, and union organization, on the other, must affect the goal of the workers' movement rather strongly.

Even today, the controversy between these two interpretations is not settled, although a consideration of the dominant literature in political science and democratic theory, especially the followers of Schumpeter, could easily give the impression that the first thesis is generally accepted. The *theoretical* opposition between the two positions can be characterized with the concepts 'domination through exclusion' vs. 'domination through inclusion'. The predominantly social-democratic champions of the introduction of universal suffrage wanted to break a relation of domination that rested, in their opinion, on exclusion, that is to say, on the fact that the majority of the population was denied political-institutional and lawful possibilities of participation. For them, accordingly, the legal equalization of the organizations of the proletariat and of single members of the working class had to appear as real progress. As opposed to this, the second position mentioned above operates with a concept of domination based on 'inclusion': precisely the taming of the revolutionary struggle, and the bureaucratic-opportunistic destruction of the emancipatory impulse (as through the 'iron law of obligarchy') are suspected to be the objective meaning and unavoidable result of this 'achievement'. This problematic, which since Rosa Luxemburg has seldom been as deeply thought out, lies at the heart of the modern struggles around the dispute between 'parliamentary' and 'autonomous' strategies in the realms of both production and reproduction.

I shall not pursue or decide this controversy here. But it is obvious that the position one takes and is able to ground in this rather comprehensive controversy would decidedly affect the assessment of the legitimating power of majority rule, which does concern us here. In any case, it would be sociologically naive to assume without further ado that a *social* generalization of individual or collective participatory rights must somehow necessarily lead to an increased diversity of substantive 'inputs' (and thus to additional conflict) derived from the new channels of participation. On the contrary, through studying many institutions of mass democracy – parties, parliaments, groups, media, elections – one can see how the opening of access both carries and conditions, in an only apparently paradoxical manner, precisely a narrowing of the choice of substantive results and issues of political communication.

The problem of 'choosing how to choose' was of immediate political relevance in, for example, the controversy over statutes in the British Labour Party, which contributed heavily to the splitting off of the new Social Democratic Party in 1981. Here the question was how much weight should be given to the parliamentary faction, the unions, and the members at large in decisions regarding fundamental programmes and questions concerning the leadership of the party. The urgency of this question was obviously the result, in the British case, of the unresolved problem of whether the party should understand itself as a 'class party' or as a 'people's party'. The Labour Party explicitly does both; it 'defined itself as the party of the working class, though in an essentially populist way'.[8] The decision in favour of the 'people's party' solution taken by the 'Right' (later to become the Social Democratic Party split-off faction) derived from this double nature of the party. This meant, concerning the internal majority decision-making procedures of the party .that protected the autonomy of the party elite and of the parliamentary faction *vis-à-vis* the base, that, 'decisions about the leadership, and by extension about candidates and policies, should be taken by the whole membership of the party, by secret ballot'.[9] What displeased the party Left arguing for 'class politics' about this solution was that it entailed an evasion of collective discussion of decisions and attributed excessive weight to 'individualist vote aggregation'. In order to avoid the anticipated corresponding distortions of the decision-making process, the unions were granted a quasi-estate-like procedural privilege in internal party decision-making processes. It was felt, moreover, that it was only in this way that the influence of the bourgeois media and other agents of political socialization could to some degree be neutralized; otherwise the individualist-majoritarian procedure would take over completely:

> By enfranchising the least committed and the least knowledgeable, it is felt largely to enfranchise the hostile media . . . Ballots would carry the risk of merely plebiscitary appeals to a membership influenced far more by mass media than by face-to-face discussion. It would reduce the automatic weight given to political activists merely by virtue of their commitment and participation.[10]

On the other hand, a double objection could be made against the above plea for a federal and corporative procedure of will-formation internal to the Labour Party. The burden of proof remains on its advocates to show that:

(1)   unions and other collective actors inside the party really do bring the results of a lively discussion supported by collective identity into the politics of the party, and not merely the preferences of 'oligarchical' functionary bodies; and

(2)   those 'different interests and social constituencies that can share socialist goals'[11] must be really capable of consensus regarding the meaning of these 'socialist goals', in order to maintain a federal structure of the socialist party and not merely a tactically motivated party alliance.

Regardless of how this question might be answered in the context of the British Labour Party or elsewhere,[12] the example of this internal organizational constitutional conflict illustrates how little self-evident, how contestable, and how much in need of grounding is the egalitarian universalistic majority rule as a procedural principle for collective decision, for the political left, even today.

Nevertheless, in modern Western industrial societies, majority rule is the most important decision-making principle both on the level of electoral decisions and on the level of parliamentary elections or votes, in the sense that it can claim to be the ultimate source of democratic legitimation.[13] Both election campaigns and parliamentary strategies exist, however, in an organizational context that sheds doubt on the legitimating power of the applied majority rule. This doubt arises out of the internal organizational dynamic of party apparatuses, on the one hand, and of government bureaucracies, on the other. One would be able to dispute the empirical decisions of voters as well as the parliamentary majority's political authority from a variety of standpoints, of which the following are examples.

(1)   If it is correct, as Max Weber and Robert Michels maintain in very similar formulations, that the organizational dynamic of mass parties individualizes the single voter reducing him/her to the status of a passive consumer and inevitably limiting his/her political judgement, while a small and totally unrepresentative ruling stratum (unrepresentative as measured by its social-structural composition) within the party exercises unlimited control over both the personnel put up for election and the substantive alternatives.

(2)   If it is also true that the dynamic of party competition in the 'political market place' leads to an emphasis on the 'political centre', to the short-term nature of strategic orientation, and to the inability of the 'party apparatus' to innovate.

(3)   If it is also the case that the members of parliamentary bodies are really in no serious sense 'autonomous' either *vis-à-vis* the party apparatus which dominates them, or *vis-à-vis* the government bureaucrats who inform (or disinform) them.

At least it becomes clear that majority rule cannot be judged by collective actors as such, but only in the context of organizational structures which condition the effects of majority rule.

We must carefully distinguish between a social-scientific analysis of the *conditions* of validity of majority rule and a principled political-philosophical *rejection* of it. The conservative variety of such political-philosophical objections to the majority principle makes use of the traditional antithesis between freedom and equality. This is evident, first, in claims to the effect that the use of majority rule could be turned into a dictatorship of the majority over the private sphere as well (Tocqueville) or that it could lead to the repression of 'structural minorities' of a national or religious sort (Jellinek). It is also evident in attacks on the principle of equality underlying majority rule ('One person, One vote') on the basis of the argument that one cannot presume that the capacity for 'reasonable' political decision is equally distributed, and thus majority decisions must always be qualitatively inferior to 'aristocratic' procedures. The tradition of political philosophy founded by Rousseau provides a 'radical' equivalent to these objections, especially in the differentiation between *volonté générale* and *volonté de tous*, which contains the idea of a cognitively graspable 'true' common good that is not equally accessible to all citizens. Doubtless, political-philosophical objections of this kind can no longer be raised today against the validity of majority rule, although they too provide important reference points for the social-scientific analysis of the conditions of validity of the majority principle.

## Conditions of Validity

### *The public realm*

All modern commentators are agreed that the majority principle is a valid decision-making rule for the 'public' or 'political' realm of human affairs but not, however, for a 'private' sphere to be distinguished from the former. Usually it is from the liberal standpoint of the protection of freedom and property that the demand is made to restrict the majority principle to 'public affairs'. But, interestingly, this demand is also made partially in terms of the reciprocal standpoint of the protection of the majority principle itself: if one were to apply that principle to decisions regarding the distribution of private goods, then it could be continuously subjected to an unendurable test, since the concerned interests would be so intense and unmediated that no (expropriated) minority could be expected to follow a majority enriched at its expense.[14] Scheuner speaks of a 'limit to the application of the majority principle', namely, its 'inapplicability to questions that stand outside the zone of political decisions'.[15] At the same time, however, he adds: 'To be sure, where the boundaries lie in areas such as the economy or education (regarding the political space) remains a difficult question which cannot be treated more closely'.[16] However understandable a renunciation of treating this question might be in the context considered by Scheuner it would, nevertheless, be frivolous to assume that constitutional guarantees of civil rights (above all, the protection of property, profession, the spheres of family and education, opinion and religion) suffice to preclude the misuse or illegitimate application of the majority principle, that is, 'majority' encroachments in the 'truly' private sphere of the citizen.[17] Instead, we in the modern interventionist welfare state have to reckon with a large degree of overlap between the sphere the citizen claims for the development of private autonomy and that which belongs to 'public affairs'. The difficulties involved in precisely defining the concrete areas in which majority decisions are valid are implied by the fact that there is such overlap, or that in many areas (for example, housing policy) public regulation is a presupposition for one to be able to speak at all of a freedom of private discretion that is not simply nominal. Naturally, there are always areas of decision for which majority rule is in this respect unproblematic (for example the appointment of a government) as well as areas of a 'private' nature for which majority rule would, without doubt, appear as absurd (for example the possibility of a majority decision regarding the choice of clothing colour).

Between these obviously extreme cases, however, lie a range of concerns requiring decision where the protection of freedom and the majority principle came into conflict. In such cases, it is not easy to find grounds for the expectation that the minority will acquiesce to formal majority decisions. Examples of conflicts emerging in such areas of overlap are: resolutions regarding the planning and renovation of residential areas in cities, decisions regarding the location of polluting industries, the question of the freedom or regulation of abortion, the problem of the defence of constitutional freedoms in the context of social and health services, problems of police surveillance and punishment, and questions of the protection of data and similar issues.

Here, the typical conflict is not that between the minority and the majority but, rather, over the *prior* question of whether the issue up for decision is one which *may* in general be handled by majority rule. As long as this question is controversial, minorities will see themselves as justified in opposing majority decisions. Problems in dividing spheres between 'public' and 'private', upon the solution of which the majority principle depends, become sharper in the context of the political and economic strategy of capitalist industrial societies with a high degree of satisfaction of consumer needs and a distinctive tendency toward stagnation. In such political-economic systems, the only growth strategies that are considered are those that have as their common denominator the *political* nature of decisions regarding investment, the *political* financing of investment, and the distribution of products through the *political* disposition over collective 'forced consumption', regardless of the alternative between 'Keynesian' or 'supply-side' strategies. Investments in armaments, energy, transportation and communication media are examples of strategies of growth of large industry for which this is true. While the corresponding decisions regarding need, location, and quality are derived out of majority decisions (votes and parliamentary legislation), they affect areas of life (such as health) through direct and indirect consequences for users and those affected, for whom the application of 'majority decisions' cannot be legitimated. It becomes increasingly difficult to draw boundaries between 'public' and 'private' spheres. This reveals the simple but pregnant truth that 'the lack of consensus on . . . the scope of the government's tasks means that there is no rational argument to accept majority rule if this leads to decisions in areas which one considers ought to remain free from government interference.'[18]

## Legal constitution

Contemporary studies of the majority principle agree that it can be applied only in areas of legally constituted organs.[19] This means concretely that wherever a majority decision ought to take place, a structure of legal positions must be presupposed that is *not* at the disposal of the majority (at least not of the 'simple' majority). Correspondingly, it would appear to everyday consciousness as a crass perversion of the majority principle if the majority could decide that the members of the minority, simply because their vote remains in the minority, could lose their right to participate in future elections. Hence, the principle that majorities can legitimately make decisions only in the framework of a lawfully and factually secured structure over which (the same) majority *cannot* decide.

However obvious and trivial this principle may appear, it is easy to doubt whether the institutional mechanisms of party states and mass democracies really are appropriate to ensure its unlimited validity. Are there not, on the contrary, tendencies through which the majority principle exhausts its own presuppositions of validity? This would be the case, for example, if a majority were able to increase its future chances of becoming a majority simply because it already is one; here the majority would be in a position to diminish the procedural status of the subordinate minority factually and even legally, relatively or absolutely, and in this way obtain the permanent status of a 'majority'. This need not occur through the physical liquidation of the members of the minority by the majority, or in the somewhat more subtle manner of destroying the minority's opportunities for publicity through the power which the majority has *qua* majority, over the control of newspapers, radio stations, etc. Today, a certain capacity of majorities to make themselves *permanent* (and to make minorities *structural* minorities) rests on mechanisms like the electoral 'incumbency-bonus' or the voting laws of the Federal Republic of Germany that specify the 5 per cent exclusion procedure.[20] Moreover, competition to attain a majority is mediated through party apparatuses that have a near-monopoly position that renders the entry of new 'suppliers' on the political 'market' extraordinarily difficult while (as is well known from the theory of oligopolistic competition) they also tend towards 'product' or programme assimilation.

It would be a speculative, but not entirely irrelevant consideration, to imagine that a more open party system based on different political fundamental positions regarding parties could create entirely different 'majorities'. In any case, this reflection illustrates the claim that majority decisions can be capable of legitimating power only in so far as the relevant majority can immunize itself against the suspicion that it rests on the strategic self-perpetuation and self-consolidation of the power position of political elites. Yet, the structure and dynamic of the political public sphere of representative party democracies offers many reference points for strengthening this suspicion, several of which have already been investigated by Kirchheimer.[21] Both the modern welfare interventionist state and the mass communication media offer a multitude of means for such self-consolidation of majorities and the repression of actual and potential competitors on the political market. The strategic introduction of material resources ('clientelism', 'campaign donations'), as well as the access to media that lends a permanent plebiscitary-charismatic presence to the political elite in the minds of the citizens, allow us at least to ask whether we ought to interpret the empirical will of the majority as an independent or, rather, a dependent variable in the political process (in a way analogous to the imperative establishment of the delegate's will through the directives of internal party leadership groups).

The more evidence there is for the will of the majority being a *dependent* variable, the less difference it would make if, instead of the totality of the voting public, only the members of the editorial staffs of large media concerns were permitted to vote. The difference would come down only to the renunciation of that 'calming effect' consisting of the fact that the people themselves, acting according to the majority rule, demonstrate how hopeless – in the context of these rules – a change in the redistribution of political power actually is. Empirical majorities would, in such cases, only play the role of a numerical indicator (for these purposes, if need be, also falsifiable) of how tightly the political elite controls its following by virtue of the symbolic force it exercises over them or, conversely, how narrow the chances really are for rival elites. Coming from the critique of 'elections' in totalitarian states, this point of view clarifies to what extent the legitimating effects of majority decisions stand and fall with the effective protection of rights to freedom and participation, which neither the political elite itself nor their majority can dispose of. The majority principle is grounded in the institutionally secured and factually inviolable autonomy of those who announce their will as their own in the act of elections and of voting.

The formal elegance of classical liberal-democratic theory (Mill and Tocqueville) rests on the fact that they saw individual autonomy not only as the *presupposition* but also as the inevitable *result* of democratic participation.[22] The participation by citizens in public decisions served not only to increase their quality but also, and above all, it served the intellectual and moral perfection ('development') of citizens themselves. Today we lack any sociological equivalent of this clever theory that we could take seriously (i.e. one that is not intended to be only pedagogic). At best, we might still find such thinking in the twentieth-century ideas of democratic reform for the factory and the economy that have recently resurfaced.[23] What is also lacking, if I am correct, is a theoretical concept of democracy which can with good reason assume that a citizen is a subject endowed with voting rights (or even the parliamentary delegate) whose *competence* to decide keeps pace with the *results* of his/her decisions aggregated through the majority principle. To be sure, we should not conceive idealistically of the criteria for 'the competence to decide', that is, autonomy, responsibility, and independent ability to judge. But simply in so far as the information aspect of the competence to decide is concerned, we would not want to dispense with criteria for the 'capability of synthesizing vast amounts of information that more or less clearly bears on the problem at hand, in such a way that no element is given undue importance.'[24]

It is also a commonplace that if measured by this criterion, most citizens would come to grief regarding most 'problems at hand'. The same holds true for the normative principles of the citizens' competence to judge. Here, gaps could not be compensated for through the self-evidence of an embedded political culture nor through the 'ideological' global concepts of political parties. We might add that however much we wish to weaken the demand for an 'autonomous' decision-making competence on the part of voting citizens (and delegates) in individual cases, we would have a hard time generating the willingness to sacrifice the *egalitarian* premise of the majority principle which is expressed in the maxim: 'One person, One vote', that is, that no vote shall have more weight than another. One cannot, however, empirically demonstrate that it is a question only of an average deficit *vis-à-vis* self-chosen criteria for competence, for there is, above all, a strong class- and strata-based *inequality* in the distribution of decision-making competences. Accordingly, the majority principle, against its original egalitarian pathos, privileges the members of those strata who 'know what they want'.

The findings sketched here concerning the average quality and social-structural distribution of autonomous decision-making competence make it superfluous, for my purposes, to investigate further the institutional-legal limits which underlie the autonomy of individual decision-making in welfare-state mass democracies. Even without such an investigation, it should be clear to what degree the presupposition of majority rule (at any rate of its democratic legitimating power) that there is an equal distribution of competences to decide adequate to the problems posed on the part of active citizens, is a fiction. The more this is the case, the more likely it is that the majority elections will become a sounding board for elites or for strategies to assure their power, with the result that the empirical will of the majority will itself be seen as politically irrelevant and discredited as a mere artifact that can conceivably be abandoned in favour of other strategies for acquiring power.

Questions regarding the 'genuineness' or 'authenticity' of empirical majority relations are also posed in connection with the so-called 'Ostrogorski Paradox'.[25] This paradox appears if one combines simple and not unrealistic assumptions about the conditions under which elections in mass democracies take place. Included among these assumptions are:

(1)   that there are fewer parties than political issues (let us take an example of two – party X and party Y); the parties are 'platform parties' which take positions in their campaign statements on several *issues* (e.g. three issues such as foreign affairs, economic and social questions);

(2)   voters are 'issue-oriented' and, thus, are not faithful to a specific party but rather vote for the one that offers the preferred alternative on most of the issues.

Figure 9.1 indicates what can happen.

| Groups within the constituency | Percentage | Issue-related preference | | | Election results according to constituency groups | Final election results |
|---|---|---|---|---|---|---|
| | | Issue 1 | Issue 2 | Issue 3 | | |
| A | 20 | X | Y | Y | Y | Party Y |
| B | 20 | Y | X | Y | Y | wins |
| C | 20 | Y | Y | X | Y | with |
| D | 40 | X | X | X | X | 60% of the votes |
| Majority for party X regarding issues (per cent) | | 60 | 60 | 60 | | |

*Figure 9.1*

The paradox consists in the fact that party Y wins, although the political alternatives offered by party X are preferred by a majority of voters. The majority of party Y can thus be discredited as 'not genuine'. It is obvious which structural presuppositions increase the probability of the paradox's occurrence. First, there is the question of the degree of differentiation of social positions and political preferences within the electorate (structural 'pluralization'). Second, is the expansion of the list of themes and issues that have to be decided politically. Third, is the 'political oligopolist' tendency in the party system, which leads to the factual and/or legal limitation of entry into the political market place. And, fourth, there is the qualitative transformation of political parties into platforms and 'people's parties' which neither seek nor are in the position to relate the issue-specific alternatives they offer to a stable 'red thread' of a (liberal, Christian, socialist, etc.) political theory (and thus ultimately polarize 'mixed'-preference structures of type A, B, C, in one or another direction). Nor are they capable of establishing a 'hegemonic' or 'binding' political-cultural role regarding their respective electorates (and thus preserving 'consistent' voter bases of type D). The other side of this substantive, temporal, and social liquidity of the political content of parties and their ideological conjunctural 'quick-silver quality' is the apparent growth of 'issue-oriented' decisions of voters who respond to the political parties' versatility and 'liquidity preference' with signs of growing cynicism.[26]

### Voter autonomy

A third condition of validity of the majority principle is linked to the principle of voters' autonomy which, thanks to the independent judgement of the voters, offers the given minority at least the formal opportunity to become the majority at some future point. Majority decisions can legitimately be made only regarding questions that are, in principle, revisable, reversible or, in respect of their potentially negative consequences, correctable. The right to create irrevocable facts (whose risks and threats are not reversible) for an indefinite time and thus, by definition, to limit the freedom of future majorities with different preferences, cannot be derived even from the largest majority.[27] Conservative political economists apply interesting versions of this argument in order to fight against increased public indebtedness and the long-term repayment obligations it imposes on the state (obligations which are alleged to jeopardize the 'future of our youth'). The argument, however, is far more topical and aggravating in relation to majority decisions over huge technological installations, especially nuclear plants and, above all, in the case of the creation of a plutonium cycle that cannot simply be switched off (as it can in the case of nuclear plants, at fantastic economic investment costs that then become 'unproductive') but, rather, literally determines the natural life conditions of future generations for thousands of years. A similar problematic arises in connection with military and armament decisions, whose economic and physical effects can become simply irreversible and uncontrollable – which is why the right of no matter how large a majority to the submission and obedience of no matter how tiny a minority is contestable, and is indeed being contested. The securing of the ecological system and of peace are presented as two modern political functions whose urgency and long-term effects limit the legitimating power of the majority principle.

The time-structure of majority decisions entails other problems well worth reflecting upon. As mentioned earlier, whenever it is a question of the quick production of decisions, the majority principle is recommended on the technical ground that one does not have to wait until all the participants agree (nor does one have to wait until all those in command arrive at a decision). With today's conventional technical means, one can ascertain and announce the collective decisions of millions of voters within hours; the decisions of parliamentary bodies can be known in seconds through the pressing of a button. However, this tempo is paid for by the extreme orientation of decisions to the particular instant; the momentary moods, perceptions, impressions, experiences – often of a decisive margin of voters – determine the result. In normal cases, voters may reckon 'in the future' with a narrowly limited risk that extends until the end of the following legislative period (after which they can decide on new and possibly different courses of action); retrospectively, it is the achievements of the last legislative period which the ruling party, at least, will advertise for its re-election. The oft-commented-upon phenomenon of the short-term practice and orientation of governments and legislatures derives from this short-term character of voter orientation. It would be to the advantage of rationally acting politicians dependent on majorities if they were to concern themselves exclusively with matters whose time-span is short enough to permit the display of success before the next election day.

The disadvantage of this structural disregard for the long-term past and long-term future, which spreads from the majority vote to the whole political process, is reflected in the curious and bizarre suggestion of von Hayek: that each citizen should have the right to vote only once in his/her life, around the time of his/her fortieth birthday. What is intended is that the voting act itself acquire the meaning of a once-in-a-lifetime decision, thereby heightening the responsibility with which it would be undertaken. The entire accumulated experiences and value-orientations of the first half of one's life would inform this act of voting and the decisions would be related to expectations and fears which those of the age-group entitled to vote would carry over into the second half of their lives. Regardless of how unrealistic this idea is from the standpoint of the principle of equality, it illuminates clearly the problem of establishing the timing of the voting act. The gravity of this problem increases as long-term, irreversible side effects on life conditions emerge out of electoral and governmental decisions motivated by short-term considerations. Like market transactions, electoral decisions and votes on the basis of the majority principle tend to discount the future, that is, to bracket from the calculus of rulers and ruled foreseeable long-term effects and delayed consequences of decisions. As the majority principle makes the creation of a majority the highest condition of political success for the political elite – and a majority which must be created *today* – the result is the opportunistic 'platform party' oriented to the political market place. On the other hand, the quality of the 'supply' can be controlled by the voters only if they are prepared to free themselves from any traditional loyalty to 'their' party and to behave as 'shifting voters'. If one regards the principled maintenance of established goals and priorities over a long time-period and the consistency and continuity of action over time as a sign of political rationality, then it turns out that the struggle for a majority conditions the action of voters, parties and candidates in such a way that *this* rationality is not *required*.

Another characteristic of the time-structure of majority decisions is their periodicity, which is either established for a given legislative period or, as in Britain, for a time-period that varies within fixed limits. This leads to the strange result that numerous momentary circumstances, such as the weather on election day (which has a strong and strata-related influence), create facts that will last for the entire time-span. Not infrequently, losing candidates will explain their defeat – and thereby discredit the 'mandate' of their victorious rival – by referring (often plausibly) to the fact that the election took place two weeks 'too early' or too late; or by claiming that different news, weekend traffic, or even the forecast of economic development could have shifted the decisive percentage points. (An entirely plausible hypothesis, albeit difficult to test, would be the autonomous 'Sunday effect' on election decisions; in the Federal Republic of Germany, for instance, the timing of elections is on a day when leisure, the family, and church activities are accentuated, while contacts with the sphere of work are relatively remote. This 'Sunday effect' could well affect the result, in the possibly decisive order of magnitude of some tenths of percentage points.)

A completely unresolved problem in the normative political theory of majority elections is how a majority vote that emerges through such contingent and accidental conditions would be in a position to provide a legitimate 'mandate' for the entire parliament and government for several years and for the totality of their decisions. Why should this be possible for a period of four years and not two, or ten?[28] Would it not be technically possible and consistent 'to reduce politics to the execution of daily and hourly ascertained majority preferences of the population and thereby realize democracy?'[29] If one does not wish to stoop to really magical thinking, then there remains only the pragmatic consideration that governmental and parliamentary bodies require a certain conventionally established time-period for their work, and that for this period they must be *freed* from the cares of electoral self-preservation. However convincing this argument may be – and it is certainly not *equally* convincing for all objects or forums of decision – there is the reverse consideration that elections come to be regarded more as a 'disturbing factor' in the decision-making routine than as a process that grounds this routine and legitimates its results.

### Equal intensity of preferences

A commonplace in the conservative critique of the majority principle is that majority rule plays off quantity against quality, the number of the masses against the dignity and insight of the individual. In so far as the use of this argument attempts to revive the distinction between '*pars major*' and '*pars sanior*', it is certainly normatively untenable under egalitarian premises. We could, however, accept the critique of the 'mechanical levelling' implicit in the majority principle in so far as majority decisions in fact rest on the counting of individual preferences, whereas the *intensity* of the preferences of the electorate is not considered. The problem, in the words of Dahl, is, 'What if the minority prefers its alternative much more passionately than the majority prefers a contrary alternative?'[30]

In empirical social-psychological and opinion research, instruments are used that are able to measure both the quantitative distribution and the intensity of opinions, so that a combined indicator of the 'weight' of one or another opinion can be ascertained. It has even been suggested that we should bring the degree of intensity into the political process of building majorities. The naivety of this suggestion is, however, immediately obvious: out of interest in the victory of their own preferences, voters would tend to inflate the intensity with which they represented them, while the truth or untruth of their feelings would not be verifiable. Whether every voter had five votes instead of one vote, the effect would probably be the same. Nevertheless, these reflections are instructive in so far as they point to a *fourth* limit to the legitimating power of majority rule: majority decisions are unproblematic only if it can be presumed that the intensities of preferences of the majority and minority are not drastically different.[31] The legitimacy of majority rule would be contestable, however, if a minority with very strong preferences is outvoted by a majority whose preferences are of no great concern to it. One could argue against this objection (and demonstrate empirically) that such differences in intensity cancel each other out though the variation of group-specific electoral participation. The practice of referendums in Switzerland, for example, reveals the tendency of a large proportion of citizens unaffected by a specific issue to refrain from exercising their right to participate. But then the question immediately arises regarding the legitimating power of elections in which no more than 11 per cent of the electorate participate, as is often the case in Switzerland (or as in the American presidential election in 1980, when only 52 per cent of the electorate participated). This demonstrates that the apparently trivial question as to what precisely is a majority and how it can be ascertained, especially in indirect electoral systems and in respect of the majority vote vs. proportional representation question, is hardly superfluous.[32]

Instead of discussing in detail the design problems of electoral systems and their substantial procedural difficulties, I would like to state my thesis that *the policies of modern welfare and interventionist states are typically concentrated on those issues for which it is not safe to assume that there is an equal distribution of intensity of interest between the members of a 'majority' and a 'minority'*. Rather, the growing 'disaggregation', together with the increased 'depth of intervention' of these policies leads to legislative decisions that affect and/or favour ever-smaller groups or social categories (defined by profession, income level, age, residence, family status, line of business, etc.), while simultaneously an ever-larger majority of the slightly involved or totally disinterested (or only informed) develops. As the proportion of such highly 'specialized' policies that are especially important to those affected increases, and as the capacities of political organizations to maintain or rebuild global theoretical constructions or 'ideologies' (which serve as rules for the determination of preferences even for those not immediately affected) decreases for structural reasons, the willingness of the 'minority' to behave in a 'secessionist' manner and to break with the formal majority by referring to the special urgency and intensity of their preferences, will increase. Rousseau's construction of the social contract, in which citizens are equally absolute subjects and absolute sovereigns, already rested on the untenable assumption that, because of this identity, the collective sovereign would not burden the collective subject with any 'unreasonable' duty of obedience that could lead to the dissolution of the contract. Rousseau presupposed a practically undifferentiated society and/or a narrow degree of legislative intervention. Nevertheless, this construction is, today, even less convincing than in the past.

> As soon as a law regulates concrete relations, it necessarily affects some categories of the population more than others . . . The duty to obey a law is oppressive only for those citizens who contest the draft of the law and who then, on the grounds of the results of a democratic vote, are forced to submit to the will of the majority. How is one supposed to convince the subordinate minority that they thereby 'only obey themselves'?[33]

The same misleading fiction underlies the economic concept of 'purely public goods', in so far as it is applied to any real form of appearance or expression of the modern state. For this concept presupposes – like Rousseau's identification of the collective sovereign and the collective subject – an identity between collective beneficiaries and collective taxpayers. It has been convincingly argued, against the actual content of this concept,[34] that in the modern state there are no 'public' but only 'collective' goods, that is, ones whose use and costs are limited to non-congruent sections of the citizenry: a new railroad line serves many and burdens few (those living next to the tracks); a social-welfare programme works in the opposite way, and so on.[35]

## The nation state

There is a parallel problem for the legitimating power of majority rule in any extension of the spatial and social area for which majority decisions are valid. A questioner in the 1960s ironically asked why the Vietnamese National Liberation Front should not participate in a vote over the ending of the American war in Vietnam. Similarly, one could ask whether the interests of aeroplane passengers of the whole world should be represented and not only local or national decision-making bodies, in the conflicts over the construction of airports which are presently occurring in regions of Europe and the USA. It will be clear from the embarrassment created by such questions that majority rule is closely connected with the *nation state*. This is the political space in which the subjects and objects of political domination are, in their totality, congruent. Below the level of the nation state there are rights to regional self-administration (sanctioned by the state), in whose framework municipal or regional bodies can regulate 'their own affairs'. Presuppositions for the application of majority rule are, however, lacking for the supra-national level as well as for cases where persons other than the citizens of a nation state are affected by decisions. Here one finds the problematic mix of corporate and majority-rule decision-making procedures, as in the United Nations assembly: 'One nation, One vote', which means in practice that all decisions that are *not* merely declamatory, such as those taken by the UN Security Council, must be unanimous.

K

Obviously today, as stated above, it is unrealistic to assume that decisions of the nation state touch *all* citizens (and with equal intensity) as implied in the link of majority rule and the nation state. Yet the reciprocal assumption that decisions of the nation state affect *only* its citizens is also unrealistic. Hence the untenability of the not-yet-democratic formula already familiar to legal thinkers of the Middle Ages: *quod omnes similiter tangit, ab omnibus comprobetur.* The practice of limiting the application of majority rule to the nation state led to the appearance of *both* logically conceivable deviations from this rule that are on the agenda today: either the scope of those affected is *smaller* than those participating, or it is *larger.* Even if we leave aside the somewhat differently situated problem of representation, it would not be easy to find areas of decision for which one could compellingly demonstrate, in the case of conflict, that both ranges are congruent. Illustrative of this problematic is the issue of national, as compared to European, agrarian policies within the EEC, or the irritating fact that nuclear power plants and similar projects tend to be placed near the borders of neighbouring countries. It is thus clear that the fiction of a 'national community of fate' is presupposed for the legitimating power of majority rule, and that this fiction is undermined increasingly by the nature of the themes which must be confronted by the modern state.

## Shared traditions

The classical justification of majority rule that we find, for example, in Locke, assumed not only that the 'national community of fate' existed objectively and functionally, but also that it was experienced and consummated by citizens on the basis of shared cultural traditions. In order to be willing to submit to a majority vote, citizens had to be convinced that for the sake of the higher values of a collective identity it was worth accepting an electoral defeat without reacting through resistance or separatism. This conviction had to be supported by the trust that the majority would not disturb the fundamental tenets of this cultural commonality, but would rather practise a materially-just rule that respects and spares the minority. The fact that the problematic of the nation emerges and is discussed not only in conservative or reactionary camps, but also on the left,[36] where for a long time this concept was used primarily with reference to the people of the Third World, demonstrates how precarious and presently contested is the image of such a national collective identity to which the majority has to refer if it is to justify the minority's duty to obey. Only the connection with an historically and culturally grounded national identity can provide the necessary basis for the subordinate minority not to choose secession (or its 'anarchist' equivalent) in relation to important questions. This connection was affirmed by Abraham Lincoln in his first inaugural address:

> Plainly, the central idea of secession is the essence of anarchy. A majority held in restraint by constitutional checks and limitations, and always changing easily with deliberate changes of popular opinions and sentiments, is the only true sovereign of a free people. Whoever rejects it does, of necessity, fly to anarchy or despotism.

But a positive moral fact corresponded to this reprehensible principle of secession:

> We are not enemies, but friends . . . The mystic chords of memory, stretching from every battlefield and patriot grave to every living heart . . . all over this broad land, will yet swell the chorus of the Union, when again touched . . . by the better angels of our nature.

This citation makes it clear that there is little serious equivalent today for the positive side of Lincoln's argument, which alone justifies compliance with majority rule. Not only are there more occasions for but also fewer inhibitions about casting doubt on the obligatory power of majority decisions. This is what Guggenberger maintains – with good reason – for the Federal Republic of Germany (and one could find traces of this in other countries): 'What is emerging here is a fundametnal polarisation of the entire population which little by little is putting the pacifying, conflict-channelling model of parliamentary-representative democracy out of commission.'[37] Above all, Guggenberger has in mind the question of the recognition of majority decisions.

*Prohibition of private influence*

Probably the most important and most problematic presupposition of the validity of majority decisions complements the first condition mentioned above. There I postulated that majority decisions have legitimating power and are obligatory only if they are strictly limited to 'public' affairs and leave the sphere of private discretion untouched. However, the limits between 'public' and 'private' spheres have to be *mutually* ensured regardless of how difficult it is to define them in interventionist welfare states. This point of view leads to the formulation of a further condition of validity for majority rule: majority decisions have rationally binding power if they are applied *exclusively* to public affairs but simultaneously to *all* public affairs in their full range and *without exception*. In other words, just as majority decisions may not interfere in the private sphere, so the private prejudicing of public decisions through societal power positions cannot be tolerated. Majority decisions can only command obedience if those decisions are applied to the entire realm of 'public affairs' and if private power positions are effectively prevented from influencing public decisions in any way other than through the egalitarian struggle for majorities.

Everyone would find a chess game totally absurd if the following rules were introduced: (a) black wins if the white king is checkmated; (b) white wins if the black king is checkmated; (c) black also wins if it unilaterally ends the game or if it threatens to do so. Rule (c), which appears so absurd for a chess game has, nevertheless, a fairly exact analogue in the dynamic of the acquisition and maintenance of power in capitalist societies. In these societies, majorities do not exclusively programme the action and decisions of governmental and parliamentary bodies.[38] As contemporary parties, governments, and parliaments regularly take on a certain degree of political responsibility for economic growth and full employment, they make themselves dependent on the action and omissions of owners and functionaries of capital who decide, in the last instance, whether and how much growth and employment will be realized. We could hardly deny that these strategies of investment, which are obviously not subject to determination by majority principle, affect, through their breadth and intensity, the common good either positively or negatively, no matter how it is defined. Today this interconnection is recognized nearly everywhere as the central problem of liberal-democratic theory: 'The economy, the prime concern of modern governments, cannot prosper without business activities. But business cannot be forced to be active. It cannot be punished, given the ruling ideology and legal system, for scaling down its activities. So business is free to use the threat of doing less.'[39]

Even so, there is widespread agreement that welfare-state methods that are designed to restrict the transformation of private resources into political power (and to thereby prevent the subversion of the egalitarian premises of universal suffrage and the majority principle) by establishing minimums (universal duty to attend school, social insurance) or maximums (party financing) are useless *vis-à-vis* 'omission phenomena' such as the 'investment strike'. It is equally indisputable, finally, that the investment strategies of banks and large investors influence, even if only indirectly, the decisions regarding 'public' affairs not through the majority principle, but through threats, pressure and compulsion, from the side of the possessor of private power. Areas where majority rule is, by definition, valid are intermingled in capitalist industrial societies, with domains in which societal resources and social power can be converted into determining factors of state policy which bypass universal and equal suffrage. Moreover, there are strong grounds for the suspicion that democratization processes (i.e. party competition, voting rights and majority principle) are as a rule permitted only where strong societal power and veto positions offer guarantees that the democratization will not touch the social/economic *status quo ante*. I am relying here on an unpublished comparative study by Przeworski on democratization processes in Latin America and Southern Europe in the 1970s. He summarizes his results in the following way: 'Social and economic conservatism may be the necessary price for democracy . . . Political democracy is possible only at the cost of limiting social and economic transformations.' One can draw on the binding power of majority rule only as long as the operative interconnectedness of the majority principle and societal structures of privilege remain opaque, and as long as voters are unaware of the fact that by no means *all* 'public' matters are exclusively determined by majorities in capitalist society.

Another category of pressures that escapes regulation by the majority principle is the possession of positive or negative sanctions for specific governmental decisions that depend on governments of *other* states, or on supranational organizations such as the European Common market, NATO or the World Bank. In all of these cases, the majority principle loses binding power for minorities in so far as it is only applied partially and not to *every* decision that touches on the public good. The legitimating power of majority rule is especially weak if there are well-founded and plausible reasons for suspecting that not only the decisions of parties, governments, and parliaments, but also the majority decisions of voters come under the influence of pressures which become effective through the private exercise of the means of power. For example, this is the case if electoral decisions come under the influence of a widespread fear of inflation and/or unemployment, or if voters are deceived, disinformed, or moved to unrealistic hopes by the publicity powers of private media of information. Naturally, what is at issue here are questions that cannot be decided completely 'objectively' but, rather, rest on the plausibility and convincing power of *ad hoc* arguments. It is to be expected, however, that in so far as such plausibilities *can* be created (and the characteristic effects of the private disposition by possessors of capital over public concerns in capitalist societies offer a structurally great opportunity to do exactly this) the binding power of majority decisions can and will be questioned.

A somewhat different problem for majority rule arises when additional political decision procedures are applied which do not make use of *private* resources and means of power. In most of the political systems of Western industrial societies we find corporatist or federal decision procedures coexisting with majority votes and elections. Indeed, recent work in political science on the development of *corporatist structures* propounds the thesis that majority decisions are lagging behind and declining in importance in comparison with corporatist decision-making procedures, deals and compromises between interest organizations and territorial bodies. Wherever the principles of territorial representation (through party competition, elections and parliaments) and functional representation (through 'incorporated' groups or federal bodies) coexist on the constitutional level, the question is posed as to what real value 'majorities' have for the results of decisions, and whether non-majoritarian-rule democratic strategies for acquiring power would not be more promising. Rokkan has answered this question with a sobering reply: 'Votes count, but organizational resources decide.' Even if votes were given to pluralistically constructed group councils or to commissions of single groups, the absurdity would not be resolved: 'the principle of voting equality is necessarily violated whenever units . . . are granted equal votes.'[40] Since, however, modern governments cannot dispense with the formal introduction of mechanisms of functional representation and, indeed, are obviously making increasing use of such procedures of decision-making – in the interest, among others, of unburdening the state – the result is a gradual discrediting of the majority principle and of the theory of legitimation on which it is based.

One can support the observation that the majority principle is not the only principle of decision-making and, moreover, that it is losing ground in the political reality of Western industrial states, with reference to the fact that governmental and party decision-making practice is increasingly programmed by techniques of survey research that ascertain the 'popular will'. In parties, 'the methods of social survey become the principal means of predicting and synthesizing putative majorities, aggregating the attitudes of masses of individuals. Parties do this rather than creating and responding to collective, deliberative expressions of political goals'.[41] Here one might object that poll-taking is actually only a varied (and cost-saving) procedure for ascertaining the majority will. Scheuner has brought enlightening arguments against this position, however, referring to 'the qualitative difference between legally meaningful votes by the electorate and opinion polls'.[42] This difference consists in the formality of the majority vote and in the formlessness of opinion polls. Key institutional elements belong to the majority principle, such as the periodicity of elections and votes (and at least the defined rights of the minority to call elections and votes); the frequent requirement of a quorum (and not merely a random sample); and a time-span which provides room for debates and electoral campaigns as well as the obligation of specified agents to make known the results of elections promptly, publicly, and completely (and not, as is possible with opinion polls, at one's pleasure, at an arbitrarily chosen time, and selectively). Moreover, in the institutional arrangement of the majority principle we find the principle of guaranteed secrecy of the vote (at least upon request or regarding specific categories of decision), while in poll-taking such secrecy is not a legal claim of the electorate but rather a pragmatic research consideration of the opinion researchers.

One can interpret all these formal rules with which the application of the majority procedure to political decisions is institutionally endowed as serving to maximize the independence and autonomy of the decision-making process of the electorate. The widespread use of polling techniques by governments as well as by parties – like the advances of 'corporatist' decision-making procedures – lead to the undermining and discrediting of the limited rationality of the majority procedure by the political practice of the state apparatus itself. Recent analyses of the functioning of federalism in the Federal Republic of Germany confirm the findings of a *de facto* repression of the procedural principles of party competition and of the underlying majority rule:

> Precisely the imposition of a 'party structure' on the upper house entails a result . . . that cannot be reconciled with the principle of parliamentary party government: namely, the dissolution of the mechanisms of conflict-regulation through dualistic party competition, through processes of negotiating deals; the dissolution of the rule of the will of the parliamentary majority through an *ad hoc* consensus established among all parties.[43]

The objections raised so far to the claims to validity of the legitimation theory that itself underlies the majority principle have in no way challenged the basic *normative* idea of that principle: that of the equal right of citizens to participate. The argument developed here has nothing in common with elitist or particularistic justifications for the rejection of the majority principle. On the contrary, it has been demonstrated that majority rule in capitalist democracies is diluted and by-passed by a series of mechanisms that empty it of its egalitarian claims. There is, however, a need to be more specific about these claims.

In his study of the majority principle, Berg distinguished between three variants of the concept of political equality.[44] The first and most modest is called 'equality of participation' and refers to the equality of *participation in procedure.* This is guaranteed through universal and equal suffrage (for adult citizens), but from the standpoint of the legitimation of the *results* of the procedure, it remains weak in so far as citizens have no basis for recognizing its results as binding simply because they have an equal right to participate in the proceedings. This is the case because, and in as much as, the second form of equality – the *equality of influence over the outcome* – does not follow from the equality of procedural status. For the outcome can be determined by influencing factors that are effective outside the equality of procedural rights, and the control over them is unequally distributed. Everyone has his/her vote, but some, in addition, have what Rokkan calls 'organizational resources'. But even the effective equalization not only of the right to participate but also of control over the factors that can influence the results of the procedure does not eliminate all objections. For such an arrangement ignores the fact that different themes and results of decision affect and interest citizens in very different degrees. It thus fosters those violations of the principle of equality that consist in the equal treatment of the unequal: every citizen has equal influence on a result that actually touches some far more than others. We have seen that matters of decision with this characteristic are, in interventionist welfare states, the rule rather than the exception. One could find a solution for this problem only through a further radicalization of the principle of equality which Berg calls '*weighted* equality of influence' and which he defines in the following way: 'that individuals are given a greater share in the control of decisions in which they are more interested than in the control of decisions in which they are less interested'.[45]

The difficulty which is encountered if we try to apply this third (and most demanding) interpretation of the equality principle to modalities of institutional arrangements, consists above all in the definition of a non-subjectivist criterion for 'those concerned'. How can one *know* (and that means, how can one clarify in case of conflict), to what degree a claim of 'being concerned' should be recognized or rejected? We cannot pursue these questions here. The purpose of this discussion of the three versions of the concept of equality was to show that a critique of the majority principle and of the legitimacy of majority decisions need not imply or derive from anti-egalitarian positions. Rather, this critique flows precisely from the evidence that the majority principle satisfies only the weakest version of the norm of equality – the equality of participation. The equality of influence on the results of decisions (or influence among those concerned with the results) is in no way assured. Only if this were the case, could one disqualify resistance to majority decisions as illegitimate.

## The Future of Majority Rule

The enumeration and illustration of the internal fictions and aporias of the majority principle suggest conclusions of various sorts. One possibility is to leave the theme alone and to mobilize all the available moral and political resources against those who bring it up.[46] Another reaction consists in the 'realistic' recognition of all the gaps and bottlenecks in every attempt to claim that the presuppositions made by democratic theory concerning the majority-rule principle are fulfilled, and a corresponding withdrawal of the normative claim that universal suffrage according to the majority principle even approximately satisfies political values such as equality, rationality, or legitimacy of collective decisions. Riker provides an example of this approach with a sharp résumé of his position:

> the products of majority rule are probably seldom defensible as consistent or as the true choice of the voting body . . . what comes out of majority rule is a function not only of the tastes of persons, but also of the political institutions surrounding the process of voting, of the skill with which individuals manipulate the selection of alternatives and the statement of issues, and indeed even of the intelligence and character of the voters . . . there is simply no possible way to interject meaning into majority rule decisions.[47]

The only meaning that Riker is willing to grant to majority rule is its defensive potential regarding (negative) majority decisions over persons: 'the protection of rights by means of popular vetoes over officials'. This thoroughly realist view of the problem, totally unembarrassed by democratic ideology does, however, invite two questions: First, why should the manipulative skill of political elites and/or the silent force of institutional arrangements also not succeed in weakening the potentially threatening *veto* power of majorities? Second, even if this does not happen, why should there not be other and more effective (perhaps even less risky) forms for defending individual rights against the intervention of the authorities than the majority principle? Riker's position evidently entails a renaissance of an (in principle) pre-democratic proprietor-liberalism which half-heartedly holds on to the democratic-majority-rule form of participation as a defence weapon against sovereign infringement of the sphere of individual freedom.

Luhmann strips the majority principle of its legitimating function with other social-theoretical and rather sophisticated arguments. In modern complex societies, according to Luhmann, it is totally naive to cling to the liberal idea that 'just' procedures and 'correct' results can constitute a unity. Elections and majority decisions are an expedient route to the construction of correct political decisions only to the limited extent that in a courtroom 'procedural fairness' can be interpreted as the (most appropriate) means for the production of a correct judgement. Today, the 'convergence of instrumental and expressive procedural functions' is just as *passé* as the correspondence of motives and functions generally is in complex social systems.[48] Because this is so, the 'left-over' procedures take on new functions: the participants do not control or programme decisions but instead console themselves, as it were, by acting out their emotions over the fact that the actual decisions would occur even without their participation. Precisely because citizens are drawn into certain *procedures* (as the public into court actions, and voters into politics), it is all the more possible to keep them out of the real decision itself. Politics is, thereby, able to construct and defend its required space for discretionary action and autonomy. Luhmann discusses this salutary unburdening effect – mutually so for both citizens and elites – which explicit reference to elections,[49] and to the majority principle.[50] Neither transmit to state decisions anything like the interests, demands, or directives of the voting population, nor do they lead to the formulation of a 'voter mandate'. Such 'ideological corollaries' of the function of democratic institutions are nowadays totally obsolete: 'The majority principle is . . . not a means of legitimation but rather a solution to an embarrassment.'[51] The function of elections consists in granting the voter the opportunity of goal-free expressive behaviour in order to attain satisfying 'release' of the motives of protest or support. If, then, it is not 'the voter' who determines the content of future collectively binding decisions, the institution of the election and the majority principle nourish the confidence that at any rate no one *other than* the voter makes the ultimate decision over the personnel of parliaments and the government. This, to be sure, is an effect that can just as well be achieved by a few throws of the dice.

Accordingly, elections and majority decisions are mechanisms through which the political system accomplishes its 'self-legitimation' and which lead citizens to acquiesce in those decisions which are anyway not directed by them, in an attitude of 'practically motive-free acceptance'. However enlightening and 'realistic' this analysis appears in its specific arguments and claims, it remains unrealistic in so far as it clashes both with the official interpretation of the institutions of voting and the majority principle as the means of setting in motion the 'sovereignty of the people' and, above all, with the pre-scientific self-interpretation of the action of voters and majorities. The convincing power of Luhmann's analysis is consequently self-destructive: were voters to be 'enlightened' by sociologists over the real function of their actions, they could no longer carry them out – as little as one can intentionally commit an error or acquire self-consciousness.

A third possible reaction to the analysis of the conditions of context and applicability of the majority principle would be to take seriously both the empirical violation of its normative claims as well as the social reality of these claims and to investigate the possibilities of redeeming them to a higher degree than is today the case, through appropriate institutional modifications or supplementation of the majority principle and its societal conditions of applicability.

There are two alternative ways of resolving this 'constructive' problem: first, through the restriction of the realm of applicability of the majority principle and, second, through its expansion. As far as the first alternative is concerned, there are numerous means at our disposal which can be (and in part are) combined in various ways to restrict the reach of the majority principle and to weaken its perverting effects. We could mention the following means:

1   *Federal decision-procedures,* which would take into consideration the protection of the minority, as well as relieve the decision-making process from the pressures of electoral opportunism. In relation to the first function, however, there is the difficulty that 'in the rarest cases the minority is regionally concentrated',[52] and that, moreover, there are 'minorities within minorities'.[53] In relation to the second function, I refer the reader to the examples in the Federal Republic of Germany in the relevant findings of Lembruch.[54]

2   *Decentralization/centralization* could be introduced to come to grips with the problem of the nation state discussed earlier, or the spatial and social incongruities between those affected and those participating. The limits to this solution would undoubtedly lie in the quickly increasing external effects such as coordination costs on the one hand, and the narrow performance capacity of *supra*national problem-centralization, on the other.

3   Strengthening of the *proportional component* in the suffrage and in parliamentary legislation, although the dangers here lie in the formation of 'latent grand coalitions' that might no longer operate through majority decision but, rather, through trade-offs and compromises, thereby carrying the alternative danger of a decision-blockage or immobilization.

4   Procedurally adequate strengthening of the *protection of minorities* (or even majorities) through greater usage of *quorums* and *specification* about where (beyond 50 per cent) a 'majority' begins; here too, however, one quickly comes up against the problem of decision blockages.

5   A completion of the *civil rights* and institutional *guarantees* of the constitution, as well as legal 'negative catalogues' which (like a series of questions in German Federal law concerning universities) would make certain specified issues 'majority-immune'.

6   Measures to secure the autonomy and *decision-making competence* of the voters and the delegates through political

education, new forms of communication between science and the public, material and institutionally secured freedom of the media and of science, institutional, material, and pedagogical guarantees of the formation of 'rational' political will with restrictions against its control by political parties.

7 'Concise' *mechanisms of legitimation and conflict regulation* in the relationship between the affected citizen-clients and the administration, in order to homogenize the 'degree of intensity' through strengthening forms of self-help, self-management, and autonomy of clients; a corresponding thinning out of detailed legal rules and the expansion of space for administrative discretion regarding the implementation of programmes; a general testing of forms of citizen participation directly linked to administrative agencies and, finally, of new forms of 'voter specialization' or 'specialized electorates'[55].

8 Expansion of welfare-state participation rights and thus control of private economic mechanisms of 'blackmail' and 'coercion' through the extensive use of instruments of public control over banks and industries; corresponding 'protectionist' efforts to lessen the impact of foreign-trade dependency and supranational military/political pressures.

The purpose of this enumeration is simply illustrative; it is neither complete, systematic, fully consistent, nor in any way meant to be a programme for constitutional reform. It should simply indicate to what extent, what limits, and with what side-effects the majority principle can be combined with other procedural rules so as to reduce its problematic effects.

The other route toward the solution of the 'constructive' problem, the *extension* of the majority principle, is only apparently opposed to the above solutions. This extension could take the form of placing the objects, modalities, and limits of the application of the majority principle itself *at the discretion of the majority* – that is, the majority principle would be applied reflexively to itself. Such a 'reflexive loop' is absent from the usual forms of applying majority decisions through elections and votes. Here the complete parameters of the decision-making process are established through prior actions, legal normatization, or hierarchical arrangements, and the only decision that remains to be taken is that between yes/no/abstention for the options *a*, *b*, *c* . . . *n*. Other alternatives are only those of non-participation (not foreseen in the procedure) and the 'misuse' of the procedure for communications that are not offered as an option; both possibilities are treated as 'invalid' (even as illegal where voting is mandatory) and are rendered inconsequential by the procedural process. The following parameters are thus withdrawn from the discretion of the electorate/voters (at least at the time of election or vote):

(1)   whether a question in general is to be decided through an election or a vote;

(2)   the personnel or material alternatives to be voted on (limited exception: primaries);

(3)   the time of the election, duration of the previous campaigns and debates, as well as the time of the next election;

(4)   the delimitation of who is entitled to vote, and the quantitative spefication of quorums and effective majorities beyond 51 per cent;

(5)   the modalities of converting electoral decisions into the parliamentary distribution of seats (majority or proportional representation); the conversion of the distribution of seats into the formation of the government (coalition building);

(6)   the degree of spatial and social 'disaggregation' or aggregation of themes of decision, that is, the question whether this global mandate of action provided through majorities is valid for communal, state and federal levels, and potentially for other categories of those affected and participating.

The exceptional rigidity of the procedural framework under which majority decisions are raised would be loosened in the interest of an increase in its legitimation potential, but this, for reasons discussed above, is highly dubious. Naturally, we cannot decide everything all at once, and thus the application of the majority principle to itself can occur only within certain limits. A further limit derives from the fact that majority decisions about (some of) the procedural *modalities* of collective decision making could be inspired by the substantive outcomes that are expected to emerge from one or the other of the procedural alternatives to be decided upon; this would lead to the introduction of a procedure by the existing majority that stabilizes its own position. However, what speaks against this is the fact that the subtantive consequences of procedural choices cannot always be known and calculated and, therefore, the debate about the 'correct' procedure must at least be conducted in terms of adequacy, justice and fairness. Moreover, historical examples show that a problematization of procedures occurs also where the initiators *can* expect to suffer a loss (at least in the short run) in their position due to the alteration of procedure (for example, labour parties have intervened for women's suffrage), while initiatives are sometimes not undertaken even when there are tempting prospects for electoral advantage. (An example of this was the defeat in the 1970s of the Social Democrats in municipal elections in cities in the Federal Republic of Germany, in part because of the high proportion of immigrants in the resident population. In this situation, part of the classical reservoir of voters for the SPD – the workers – suffered a *de facto* loss of voting rights; despite this, only isolated Social Democratic drives for the local voting rights of immigrants have so far been forthcoming.)

Such 'reflexive' arrangements are not entirely alien to the exising form of suffrage. Thus, for example, in Bavaria, Baden-Würtemberg, and recently Niedersachsen, through the techniques of accumulating offices or alternate voting (*panaschieren*), the local election laws place at the discretion of the voter not only the choice between given personnel alternatives (lists) but also, within narrow limits, the *choice between the alternatives themselves*. Finally, the instrument of the initiative, provided for in different state constitutions within the Federal Republic, offers a procedurally adequate possibility (assuredly difficult and limited) of deciding which questions at which time should be taken out of routine parliamentary procedure and be placed under a different one.

Were we to continue to think along these lines, then we would have to consider procedure-related majority votes taken for *specific* decisions in areas such as ecology, energy, urban renewal, construction, traffic, and women's and family politics. All of these political areas are distinguished by the fact that decisions are taken (indirectly) 'by all', while the costs and side-effects affect more-or-less sharply delineated categories of the population. Accordingly, the obvious choice is to democratize the decision-making procedures (around the decision of the criterion for 'those concerned') instead of schematically and dogmatically insisting on the democratic content of the majority principle. It is not at all certain (and it would even be highly surprising if it did) that the majority always would make the decision that the majority should decide. Rather, it would be plausible and conceivable, even in the case of strong interest-bound constituencies, and according to the specific distribution of costs and benefits implied in a specific issue to be decided, that one could more or less deviate from the schematic rule through the establishment of moratoriums, prerogatives, quorums, repetitions of votes, issue-related redefinitions of constituencies and districts, the delegation of decisions to specified councils, new definitions of the suffrage according to age, sex and income categories, and so on.

Through the continuous, yet not inappropriately burdensome introduction of such procedural decisions before substantive decisions are taken, a part of the highly ambivalent 'advantages' of the majority principle would no doubt be lost, especially the speed with which it allows decisions to be produced. This loss would, however, be more than compensated for by the intensification of public insight into the fact that the majority principle in no way guarantees 'by itself' the justice or correctness of political decisions, and that it, rather, offers such guarantees at best only after a procedure in which citizens have been given a chance to decide whether this is the case in view of the concrete issues at hand.

# 10

# The Divergent Rationalities of Administrative Action

## Two Criteria of Rationality

When Max Weber described 'pure bureaucratic administration' as 'capable of attaining the highest degree of efficiency from a purely technical point of view' and, thus, 'the most formally rational means of exercising domination known,'[1] he envisioned a situation in which formal rationality was equivalent to the continuous and inexorable application of legal norms. The advantages of such an administration ('precision, stability, stringency of discipline and reliability', as well as 'a high degree of calculability of results for the heads of the organization and for clients') rest on a structure which, with the help of modern political-systems theory, can be described as follows: at all times, premises of action exist which are not at the disposal of the actors themselves; action is tied to 'inputs' which cannot be expanded, modified, or avoided. The principle of 'orientation to the files' (one of the distinguishing marks of bureaucratic rule) is an example of this. What has significance for the action of officials is not what they know from hearsay, trusted reports, suppositions or an independent inquiry, but only what is present in written form and thereby accessible to everyone (at least to every superior). Hierarchy and the division of labour are additional aspects of the same basic structure: it is clear in every instance who gives orders to whom, and with respect to

Translated by Jean Cohen and John Keane. This essay was first presented as an inaugural lecture (*Habilitationsvortrag*) at the University of Konstanz, in June 1973. It is here translated (and slightly expanded) from the version later published as 'Rationalitätskriterien und Funktionsprobleme politisch-administrativen Handelns', *Leviathan*, 3 (1974), 333–45.

what, so that the possibility of negotiation, interpretation, or consultation is eliminated. A further aspect of bureaucratic administration is that it emerges only given the presence of a state based on taxation, and only when rights for civil servants (including comprehensive pension rights) and life-time employment (linked to the prohibition of strikes and other forms of workers' struggles) are guaranteed. The economic subsistence of officials needs thereby no longer to be subject to their interested action, and thus they become incorruptible.

The same holds for training certificates as the (only) personal precondition for recruitment. Officials are not required to continuously prove their professional competence or even to defend themselves against doubt, but rather act under assumptions of generalized competence over time. Most important, however, is the irrevocability of the internal premises of action, of obedience to general rules of positive law. 'Legality is the functional mode of bureaucracy' (Carl Schmitt).

In all these (and other) respects, we can say that bureaucratic administration is that improbable and conditional form of organization of social action that precludes the thematization of its own premises. The strict separation between administration and politics in the ideal-typical form of bureaucracy rests above all on this fact.

Today, we are used to associating the phenomena which Weber understood as a (formally) rational system of action with such negative attributes as inflexibility, conservatism, and rigidity.[2] Let us, therefore, summarize in what sense Weber could speak of the (formal) 'rationality' of this kind of bureaucratic arrangement. For him, the greatest chances of exercising state authority (and thus of 'efficiency') exist only if its implementation is organized so as to exclude the risk of contamination by deviant or supplementary motives. This type of rationality – the unadulterated realization of norms – comes into existence through the perfect disjunction between action premises, on the one hand, and the apparatus which realizes them on the other. Quite apart from this criterion of rationality is the question whether the Weberian ideal-type of bureaucratic domination and the corresponding organization of state domination is also rational in the *other* sense of satisfying the *functional requirements* and needs of a highly developed, industrial, capitalist society to the extent to which the latter have to be

302   *The Divergent Rationalities of Administrative Action*

fulfilled by state administration. This question concerns the rationality (or functional adequacy) of a type of action which, from the (narrower) standpoint of the carrying out of abstract rules, cannot be contested. Thus the differentiation of these two (equally formal) criteria of rationality permits us to ask how 'rational' (in the sense of functionally adequate) the rationality of the Weberian model of bureaucracy actually is.

Weber's failure to distinguish between these levels of the problem, indeed his establishment of a conceptual continuum between the rationality of bureaucratic action and a world-historical process of rationalization, gave rise to a series of philological and theoretical debates.[3] As a consequence of these debates, it can be stated that the two concepts of rationality – one of them, the organizational, referring to the subsumption of bureaucratic action under general rules and the other, the systemic, referring to the bureaucratic fulfilment of the functional requirements of their societal environment – cannot without further argument be assumed to be congruent with each other. Under conditions of developed, welfare-state capitalism, the rationality of bureaucratic action does not guarantee, but rather perhaps conflicts with, the functional rationality of the political system. Bureaucratic domination is not, as Weber supposed, the irrevocable structural feature of all future societies. Rather, it turns out to be tied to a specific historical phase and contingent from the standpoint of functional rationality. The two criteria of rationality are congruent only under societal conditions in which the highest degree of unrestricted application of abstract rules suffices to fulfil, at the same time, the functions of the sub-system of state administration for the larger society.

My argument here, and in what follows, is not 'empirical' in the sense that I do not seek to trace the actual determinants of action that rule over the specific bureaucracies, past and present. Instead, these reflections are concerned with the modes of strategic rationality which are referred to by administrative organizations as models or normative schema (*Sollschemata*) of their own structures and processes. Such strategic models of criteria of rationality play a role in every social situation, independently of whether and to what degree they are actually *realized* in action. At the same time, the choice of such models of administrative organization is not determined by chance or by the arbitrary will of its members. Rather, they must conform to the imperatives of their socio-economic environment. If such conformity does not occur, one would conclude that 'irrational' criteria of rationality have been adopted by state institutions. In such cases, in which an organization approximates the strategic model that has been raised to the level of a normative schema, but in so doing endangers its relation to its environment, one speaks of bureaucratic pathologies. These cases indicate an incongruity between internal structure and relation to the environment or, more simply, a discrepancy between structure and function.

Such situations are often studied by the sociology of organizations from both the theoretical and prescriptive points of view of how to re-establish an equilibrium either through learning processes inside the organization or through enforced learning processes, such as reform of the organization. In such studies, it is always the *organization* that is presented as obsolete, in need of change, and deficient. One can rely on this position only on the understanding that adequate criteria of rationality for administrative action are 'in principle' not only thinkable but also practicable. Everything then depends on the discovery and introduction of these 'adequate' criteria. The following reflections will hypothetically abandon precisely this premise of 'perfectibility'. For it could easily be the case that the incongruity between the internal modes of operation and external functional demands on the state administration have their basis in the quality of the *socio-economic environment*, rather than in 'deficient' bureaucracies. This environment binds the state administration to specific modes of operation, yet simultaneously makes claims on its performance which cannot be satisfied by these same modes of operation. It is obvious that this incongruity between the normative schema of the administration and these external functional demands could not be solved by a reform of the administration, but only through a 'reform' of the environmental structure that caused the contradiction between the structure and performance capacity of the state administration.

## The Dilemma of Welfare-State Policies

I cannot summarize here the historical, theoretical and empirical evidence and arguments which refer to a historically increasing discrepancy between the two criteria of rationality. It was especially the literature on constitutional theory, administrative and political sociology which referred at quite an early stage to the emerging unresolved tension between bureaucratic and system rationality in state action. The fact that today authors with the most varied political and scientific-theoretical views find difficulties with the traditional disjunction between politics and administration entitles us, without further proof, to proceed on the basis of the reality and relevance of a mixed type of welfare-state administrative policy, which partly supersedes the legal-bureaucratic type of domination. This functional model is to be distinguished from legal-bureaucratic administration not on the level of empirical description, but on the level of institutionalized normative schema that reinforce a *reversal of the direction of the conversion process,* that is, the process that links the inputs and outputs of the political system.

The meaning of the concept of the 'reversal of the direction of the conversion process' should be understood in the following way. In a legal-bureaucratic administration, as we have seen, efficiency means the reliable subsumption of action under premises: the *inputs* of administrative action determine and guide the output, and the clearer and more exclusively these premises are carried out in decisions, the more rational is the administration. Its outputs are, in the ideal case, and for all those involved, calculable reflexes of legal norms, organizational programmes, codified procedural rules, and routines.

Exactly the opposite is the case in the structural model of welfare-state administrative policy. Here, administrative action is rationalized with respect to specific premises of action and *concrete results.* Often these premises are understood in terms of notions of some general 'adequacy' but they must, nonetheless, be given a very concrete meaning according to the specific, situation-dependent circumstances. For instance, the meaning, and actual requirement, in a given situation, of providing a certain category of people with 'adequate housing' must be 'operationalized'. In such a situation, the task of the administration often turns from implementing given rules in compliance with established routines towards an active search for the *acquisition* of inputs which are adequate to the fulfilment of these concrete tasks and quasi-autonomously interpreted goals. Thus, while for the first (bureaucratic) model, inputs function as the sole authoritative 'motor' of conceivable outcomes, in welfare-state administrative policy, by contrast, the projected results of administrative action (the fulfilment of concrete tasks) serves as the primary criterion for judging actions and decisions internal to the administration; the inputs which are sought after and used depend upon these projected administrative outcomes. Efficiency is no longer defined as 'following the rules', but as the 'causing of effects'. From the standpoint of the concrete tasks and the purposive action required by them, the administration must consider its own inputs and premises as contingently dependent upon criteria of instrumental suitability. It is efficient to the extent that it succeeds in doing precisely this. The premises of administrative action are no longer rules to be imperatively complied with, but are instead treated as *resources* which are to be weighed from the standpoint of their adequacy for specific tasks.

This holds true also for legal norms. Authorities in the Federal Republic of Germany such as the Federal Criminal Investigation Department (*Bundeskriminalamt*), the communal administration of large cities, and the Federal Labour Market Agency (*Bundesanstalt für Arbeit*) clearly force upon federal parliamentary bodies an interpretation of their own problems according to which the fulfilment of their tasks requires the expansion and reform of their jurisdiction and legal authorities to act. By implication, legal norms are transformed from 'commands' into 'resources'. An analogous reversal of the direction of action is visible in the process of formulating state budgets, wherein the required expenditures rather than the expected income become the criterion for defined tasks. Parallel developments are evident at the level of the personnel structure and recruitment policies of the administration. The suitability of persons with a specific education, the adequacy of specific determinations of service and maintenance rights, even the appropriateness of specific training paths for the preparation for service in public administration, become variables to be manipulated instrumentally from within the administration. In other words, the basic staffing arrangements of the administration are also placed at the disposal of functional considerations.

The same holds for the organizational structure of the administration, as is indicated by current efforts at organizational and regional administrative reform. Finally, the administration cannot rely on the assumption that the prior information and professional knowledge in the heads of its members is adequate for solving existing tasks. It is, therefore, forced to introduce or create *ad hoc* outside experts, research staff, and information systems. In short, what public administrators, who are charged with performing those regulative and compensatory functions on which industrial capitalist societies depend, do in fact do, can by no means be exclusively by the notion of 'following rules' that are politically predetermined; rather, they extract and acquire resources that are required for the purposive accomplishment of their concrete tasks.

Indeed, the switch from a 'conditional' to a 'goal-oriented' programme results in a dilemma that we can paradoxically describe as follows:[4] the environment does not fully permit the administrative system to pursue the very same rational schema of goal-oriented action which it at the same time demands from the administrative system. On the one hand, the steering of administrative action through fixed and situation-independent rules fails wherever non-standardized matters are involved that are not capable of subsumption under general routines. Welfare-state steering tasks are distinctive above all in that they have to be resolved in a (temporal, substantive, and socially) *ad hoc* manner and, thereby, escape generalized jurisdictional rules, schematized competences and instructions. These must, instead, be discovered with respect to consideration of the particularities of the case and on the basis of expert knowledge. On the other hand, however, the administration's latitude for concentrating on 'tasks' and discovering adequate rules with which to carry them out, is limited by institutional and fiscal constraints.

These premises are carried out in such a way that, in spite of the increasing claims upon it by goal-oriented programmes, the administration is not entirely free from its 'conditional' connection to legal-bureaucratic premises. This results in the interference or in the interaction and mutual penetration of two criteria of correctness of administrative action. The administrative system must, in a certain sense, be adequate both in terms of compliance to norms *and* achievement of goals. It is consequently dependent for its self-legitimation upon a double strategy which, not infrequently, leads to emergency solutions that are adequate to neither criterion. At the level of personnel recruitment, this dilemma leads to an oscillation between a 'monopoly of lawyers' and their replacement by 'generalists', from whom 'effective administrative management' is expected.[5] In budgetary planning, the same problematic is precipitated in the division between revenue-orientation and expenditure-orientation.[6]

A further example of the same structural conflict is the debate between 'centralists' and 'decentralizers' in the administrative organization.[7] There is a common basis for this pair of alternatives in a contradictory relationship which, in the meantime, has become a prominent theme within the scientific discussion of administrative problems. In a capitalist social formation, the state, on the one hand, leads a distinct and limited existence in relation to its possibilities for manoeuvring and acting (and this identity is watched over by jurists, held together at the centre and, according to given criteria of fiscal revenues, is financially nourished); this aspect of the state is normatively described by the principle of the 'rule of law'. On the other hand, the state itself must increasingly organize and regulate the socio-economic functional coherence of the whole order (which requires experts, appropriate means of investment, and decentralization adjusted to particular contexts); this aspect presupposes flexibility and an instrumental relation to rules. In respect of this structural problem, it seems that the search for new, adequate problem-solving strategies inside the administration can succeed only in oscillating between the two sides of this dilemma, but not in resolving the dilemma itself.[8]

In this context, I should like to briefly address the significance of the partial reversal of the direction of administrative action (from input-determined decisions to a function-determined concern with resources) for the principle of rule of law and thus for the *legal* legitimation of administrative action. If laws are contingently established from the standpoint of their adequacy for specific tasks, and if, furthermore, their abstract universality has to be virtualized and loosened through reference to criteria of opportunity and interpretation, they naturally become unfit for the legitimation of administrative action that has attained this degree of reflexivity towards legal rules. In other words, as soon as legal norms become disposable from the standpoint of their suitability for concrete tasks, they lose their capacity to legitimate the choice and fulfilment of these tasks on the basis of any substantive *validity*. For example, in the well-known situation where educational, tax, or pension laws are continuously revised, it is not only the Weberian predictability and calculability of bureaucratic action for all members that is lost. In addition, the administration robs itself of legal legitimacy for the content of the revision it itself initiates. The legal-constitutional problem that emerges with respect to the constitutional state does not interest us so much here. What is of concern is the specific constraint on the administration that follows from the bracketing of the legal securing and binding of legal norms: at the very least, the administration is forced to complement its legally established mandate and its legitimacy based thereupon with a criterion – successful and acceptable political implementation – which evades the legal form as such. To the extent that the administration suspends the input-orientation of legal norms and makes them disposable from the standpoint of their suitability, welfare-state administrative policy becomes dependent on extra-legal legitimations, that is, upon the substantive realization of some values (rather than compliance to rules), and upon the resulting processes of empirical consensus formation.

## The 'Politicization' of Administration

In addition to legal norm-conformity and adequacy to goals (both of which, as I have demonstrated, conflict with each other), there is a third possible criterion for the 'correctness' of administrative action: its effectiveness in building political consensus. Recourse to this third mode of rationalization is suggested by a variety of circumstances. Where the above-mentioned dilemma leads to friction between legal and goal-oriented methods of settling business by the administration, the temptation arises to replace legal norms with a substantive establishment of values as the court of appeal for executive action.[9] Apart from recourse to this 'escape' route, the administration can fulfil its concrete goal-oriented functions, by which it responds to the need for authoritative solutions to specific societal problems, only to the extent that it can rely on the readiness of its societal target groups to cooperate voluntarily in the attainment of administrative goals.

In such cases, where the administration becomes dependent upon the acceptance and willingness to cooperate of its social 'partners', the following two consequences can be observed. First, even the combination of conditional and goal-oriented programmes comes to nothing unless the administration is ready to sacrifice a part of its sovereign claim upon authority in negotiations with strategic societal actors, thereby bringing their premises into administrative action. In this way, the administration 'buys' compliance in a mode that is often described as 'political exchange'. Second, conceptual distinctions (for instance, those proposed by Luhmann) are quite doubtful when they suppose that a division of labour is built into the political-administrative system, such that 'politics' are responsible for focusing on the generalized creation of consensus while the task of 'administration' is programme development and implementation, each system thus mutually unburdening the other.[10] The more specific and concrete the administrative intervention, the less the division of labour appears to function in this way. The result is that the administration must concern itself with assuring that its programmes meet with understanding and a willingness to cooperate; it becomes dependent upon consensus and support that must be generated by itself among its respective clientele.

The task of actively generating an accommodation of interests and of building consensus is posed for the administration not only when, as in the above example, the resistance of specific 'veto-groups', equipped with the power to obstruct, has to be processed through bargaining. This task is also posed in relation to the administration's clients (see below) as well as in relation, finally, to the 'inner environment' of its members and their professional, economic, and political values and interests.[11]

Looked at in this way, the 'politicization of administration' results not so much from new ambitions and initiatives it has adopted, as from the fact that the old constitutional, strictly conditional programme of action has become unreliable and insufficient. To the extent that public administration must dispense with these action premises, it is left with no other alternative than to create *other* (extra-legal) legitimations for action. Administrators must rely on the short-cut of direct interest intermediation with their clientele where the reference to specific legal authorization of administrative action does not suffice. The moment legal norms lose their capacity to programme administrative action because the legislative process is itself perceived as being controlled in accordance with the administration's need for legal and administrative resources, alternative legitimations can be created in either of two ways. There must be recourse to the *supra*-legal level of concrete evaluative notions which are designed to stabilize the social order (as, for instance, in the use of the 'free and democratic order' as the ultimate source of legitimacy for virtually all kinds of administrative action), or recourse must be had to the *sub*-legal level of *ad hoc* consensus formation among the strategically relevant segments of social actors.

In what follows, I shall address only the second of these two possibilities, since the reference to supra-legal values normally only has a prohibitive aim. Concepts such as the 'free and democratic order', 'free and social market economy' and 'freedom of scientific inquiry' become activated empirically only for the purpose of denouncing and administratively repressing some boundary violations.[12] An administration that is only in part legally *programmed* and which depends, in addition, on exercising broad discretion in mobilizing the legal and other resources that it *needs,* will hardly find such value-laden mystifications of the social order an instructive guide for its positive actions. It is, therefore, referred to the 'sub-legal' level of bargaining and consensus building as a source of legitimation. This is especially true in respect of its clients. My thesis is that, today, public administration is faced with a situation, in many of its areas of operation, in which the completion of state planning and functions can no longer be accomplished by the administration itself, but must involve individual citizens and their societal organizations as sources of assistance in the 'authoritative' performance of executive functions. In other words, the outcomes of administrative action are in many areas not the outcomes of the authoritative implementation of pre-established rules, but rather the result of a 'co-production' of the administration and its clients.

A feature of many state-organized services is that in the course of their production the distinction between 'consumption' and 'production' is blurred. The 'production' carried out by schools, hospitals, prisons but also welfare systems and transportation systems, is in principle completed through the *collaboration* of agents with users. Consequently, their 'productivity' depends on the characteristics of each side and on the corresponding interaction between them. The 'object' which is worked on – the clientele – cannot be objectified in the same way as in material production. Rather, the 'object' (e.g. pupils) completes the 'production' (the acquisition of knowledge and capacities) *by itself* under administratively established conditions which, in contrast to the production of goods, do not suffice to guarantee the formation of the product. Services additionally presuppose that clients are ready to engage in 'productive interactions'.

Citizens become the final and decisive executive-organ of state policy wherever the existing tasks of politics and administration are such that they cannot be solved with the classical means of the threat of punishment or the distribution of goods, that is, through positive and negative sanctions. Instead, state policies require a task-specific mobilization of the 'base' and its willingness to cooperate. The action variable of the 'base' becomes the decisive criterion for whether, and at what fiscal and administrative costs, administrative policy can carry out its declared goals. Examples which reveal this dependency-relationship of the administration include such problems as: the improvement of traffic safety; the expansion of a preventive system of health care; the increase of the responsiveness and standardization of the educational process; the transformation of local city traffic into mass transit; the enhancement of environmental protection; the preservation of monetary stability, and so on. In all of these areas of public administration, a 'politically supportive' role-definition of vehicle drivers, patients, the elderly, pupils, students, transportation users, income-recipients and consumers decides the success, costs, and timing of administrative policy, the individual measures and decisions of which must be 'sold' to the respective segments of the public.

This dependence of welfare-state administrative policy upon the willingness to cooperate of actors outside the political system extends not only to individual citizens, but also to collective societal actors. Unions and federations, professional associations as well as the media, become indispensable executive organs or auxiliaries of administrative policy.

One could well argue that the construction of complementary action among the negotiation partners of the administration is neither a new nor a particularly difficult problem. This is because the administration need only establish the parameters or the boundary conditions within which the calculable particular interests of societal partners can be processed along the desired lines of action. Examples include tax exemptions or shut-down premiums, for they are doubtless intended to bring the investment behaviour of (for example) specific branches of industry into agreement with state planning within a short period. Here, too, citizens are the instance that completes the implementation process. But the administration can be confident that the citizens, due to their capacity of rational action and their awareness of the relevant positive and negative incentives, will in fact fulfil the policy objectives in question. The limit of such a model of cooperation between the administration and citizenry lies above all in the fact that it only works in modes of interaction that assume the form of purposive-rational and calculative strategies on the part of the citizen. A different problem emerges if the strategic interests and motives of action of citizens are not yet established (and can thus not be steered through the state's allocation of appropriate incentives) but where, instead, the motives of action must themselves be constituted or changed and preferences formed. This process of constitution is especially difficult, time-consuming, and costly if formerly recognized priorities or the dimensions of utility calculations (individual income or individual transportation, for example) must be downgraded.

The difference between the two cases referred to here concerns the fact that the task of administrative steering is much easier in policy areas where the client or policy-target is a strategic actor engaged in some calculating, optimizing behaviour. Whereas such an actor must only be provided with appropriate positive and negative incentives, the much more demanding (as well as unpredictable) situation is one in which clients have either no (or 'false') notions of what is in their interest, or where they do not act within a cognitive framework of constantly calculated 'costs' and 'benefits'. What is required here is, therefore, a quasi-educational effort on the part of the administration, aimed at creating 'awareness' and changing prevailing attitudes and evaluations.

## The Risks of Consensual Policies

To the extent that welfare-state administrative policy is forced, in order to fulfil its concrete tasks, to at least partially emancipate itself from the directives of *legal* programmes of action and, thereby, to become directly dependent upon processes of consensus that are no longer mediated through 'rational-legal' forms of legitimation, two analytically distinguishable risks emerge. Each equally threatens the efficiency of the administration's action. First, the heterogeneity of affected interests and motives, and the structures of power and opportunity for blackmail built into the capitalist economy, can block the implementation of policy objectives, such that the corresponding administrative programme is paralysed from the outset. It is not then possible to find a formula, on the basis of which the administration could proceed and all the relevant action partners and reference groups could be satisfied: the material, social, or (above all) temporal scope of the consensus is too narrow to be able to support the implementation of policies which would be adequate in terms of certain functional requirements of the social system. Accordingly, administrative policy is faced with the alternative of having either to 'buy off' opposing groups and interests (thereby quickly reaching the threshold of fiscal overload) or to carry out policy objectives at the open expense of the dissenting groups (a course of action which would predictably lead to serious costs in terms of political conflict).

The second main risk for an administrative policy that breaks with legalistic intermediations and in this sense reduces its 'distance' from the citizenry, is the possible autonomization of the consensus-building process, whose results can place the administration under premises that clearly overburden it. This danger has been indicated by neo-conservative authors who, with a certain degree of plausibility, discuss the modern state in terms of its problems of 'demand overload' and the consequent danger of 'ungovernability' due to the expansion of demands for democratization and participation.

These two categories of risk are relevant to welfare-state administrative policy that has become dependent on consensus. They can neither be secured against the danger of a too-limited and particular consensus, nor against the opposite danger of a consensus that goes too far and is too demanding in terms of the institutional and fiscal constraints that the administration must respect. In this sense, I must also agree with Scharpf's thesis that the major difficulties of state regulation lie directly in the competitive democratic and pluralistically mediated surplus of demands on the state's capacity to perform and distribute, or in the fragility and limitedness of the basic political consensus about social policy that results from this political structure.[13] I think, however, that this diagnosis must be evaluated as a symptom of the inability of welfare-state administrative policy to bring its indispensable ordering and intervention functions into harmony with its equally indispensable need for consensus.

In any case, two control mechanisms must play a central role wherever and as long as this harmony is secured. I am thinking, first, of the sciences, especially the social sciences, in their political advisory function. What is widely accepted as scientific is not a statement that reinforces and *generalizes* the problematization of societal relations and contexts, but rather one which could *substitute* for a consensus, because it does not tolerate contradiction and can disqualify the dissension of the average citizen on the grounds of his/her incompetence. In this role, and as long as they are utilized, the social sciences substitute for the guiding function of strictly legal programmes and are, thereby, able to some extent to protect administrative action against the incalculable risks of dependency on direct consensus and politicization. Due to the dynamics of their own progress in knowledge and method, however, the advisory sciences that take on this protective function constantly end up *producing* more action alternatives than they are able to vertically order as preferences and priorities with their own corresponding means. In this situation, science imposes additional burdens of decision-making upon the administration, which must now decide when, and from whom, it will accept advice, and how binding it will treat the results of such advice.

The other control mechanism, which is to a limited extent capable of removing the risks facing an administration tied to unmediated processes of consensus, consists of the creation of a *crisis-ridden image of reality,* be it through real or fictive crisis processes. In view of their potential for simplifying decisions, crisis-rhetoric and the actual interpretation of situations in terms of 'crisis' offer a double advantage: they provide clear criteria for what needs to be given highest priority, and they permit those claims which can*not* be formulated in relation to the crisis to be pushed into the background or, at any rate, to appear as postponable.

This simplification of decision making, however, succeeds only to the extent that a 'functional' interpretation of the crisis ('a crisis is a situation in which $X$ must be done') prevails over a 'causal' interpretation ('the situation was caused by specific interests, actions, omissions, and power relations'). In other words, the above-mentioned simplification strategy works only for crises in which there are no culpable actors and which, in this sense, are *anonymous.* It certainly is no accident that, in the Federal Republic of Germany and elsewhere, major policy innovations and breakthroughs (in such areas as economic policy, education, or environmental protection) have become possible only after the respective problems were successfully dramatized as a 'crisis', the urgency of which reduced opposing interests to irrelevance. The use of these simplifying schema nevertheless always carries the danger that their attempt to render the crisis anonymous will fail, and that causal accounts of the crisis will emerge, thereby resulting in a polarization rather than a consensus.

If, in conclusion, the key points of my arguments are summarized, there emerges a three-tiered and contradictory concept of rationality which is decisive for administrative action under the conditions of the advanced capitalist welfare state. On the first level, the administrative process is tied to legal rules as its standard of 'correctness'; all that administrators are supposed to do is to act in conformity with politically pre-established formal-legal rules. This model of action may be rational in the Weberian sense, but it is hardly rational in the functional sense, according to which the administration must respond to concrete needs and requirements of the larger society (and not just to the will of its political 'master'). On the *second* level, therefore, the test of *functional effectiveness* underlies administrative action. The direction of the conversion process is reversed, and the problem for the administration henceforth becomes that of choosing and extracting *adequate* legal, organizational, and personnel resources and action premises. The dividing line between 'administration' and 'politics' disintegrates, since parliamentary bodies as well as the political heads of ministries have themselves become dependent on the administration and respond to its needs rather than guiding, directing and controlling it. By partly reversing the authoritative relationship between 'politics' and 'administration', however, the administration also subverts its authority relation with social actors and clients; this relation is often transformed from a relationship of 'vertical' authority into one of bargaining and cooperation. Thus, a further, *third* standard of administrative action emerges: the generation of consensus, support and cooperative relations between the administration and its specific clientele.

These levels do not follow one another in an historical sequence, although it may be plausible to speak of a shift of emphasis towards the second and third levels. The problem of administrative action is that it is at the same time suspended between these contradictory criteria and standards of rationality: it must simultaneously conform to its basic legal principles, its functions, and the declared interests of its clients and reference groups. In this situation, there is no available over-arching criterion of rationality that would permit the respective premises of the three levels to be brought into an hierarchical relationship.

# Notes

## Introduction

1. The term 'disorganized capitalism' has also been used by Scott Lash and I am grateful to him for agreeing to my use of it.
2. C. Offe, *Contradictions of the Welfare State*, J. Keane (ed.), (London, 1984).
3. Cf. R. Hilferding, *Das Finanzkapital* (Frankfurt, 1968; 1st edn 1910), and *Zwischen den Stühlen*, C. Stephan (ed.), (Berlin, 1982); H. A. Winkler (ed.), *Organisierter Kapitalismus: Voraussetzungen und Anfänge* (Göttingen, 1974).
4. In relation to the so-called new social movements, I have discussed these problems in my 'New Social Movements: Challenging the Boundaries of Institutional Politics', forthcoming in C.S. Maier (ed.), *Changing Boundaries of the Political*.

## 1 The Political Economy of the Labour Market

1. Cf. among others, K. Rothschild, 'Unterschiedliche Dimensionen der Lohntheorie', in H. Arndt (ed.), *Lohnpolitik und Einkommensverteilung, Schriften des Vereins für Sozialpolitik* (Berlin, 1978), N.F., vol. 51, pp. 53–81.
2. Cf. Bundesanstalt für Arbeit, *Überlegungen zu einer vorausschauenden Arbeitsmarktpolitik* (Nürnberg, 1974).
3. Cf. A. Sen, *Employment, Technology and Development* (Oxford, 1975).
4. E. Lederer and J. Marschak, 'Die Klassen auf dem Arbeitsmarkt und ihre Organisation', in *Grundriß der Sozialokonomik* (Tübingen), 9 (1927), p. 112.
5. K. Polanyi, *The Great Transformation* (Boston, 1944), p. 94ff.

6.  E. Preiser, 'Besitz und Macht in der Distributionstheorie', in E. Salin (ed.), *Synopsis. Festgabe für Alfred Weber* (Heidelberg, 1948), p. 346; cf. also C.B. Macpherson, 'Elegant Tombstones: A Note on Friedman's Freedom', in his *Democratic Theory. Essays in Retrieval* (Oxford, 1973), pp. 143–56.

7.  W.G.F. Roscher, *Grundlagen der Nationalökonomie* (Stuttgart, 1892), vol. 1, p. 428.

8.  Cf. R. Edwards, *Contested Terrain : The Transformation of the Workplace in the Twentieth Century* (New York, 1979).

9.  K. Marx, 'Das Kapital', vol. 1, in *Marx-Engels-Werke* (East Berlin; 1964), vol. 23, p. 249.

10. N. Altmann and G. Bechtle, *Betriebliche Herrschaftsstruktur und industrielle Gesellschaft. Ein Ansatz zur Analyse* (Munich, 1971), p. 54.

11. Cf. F. Böhle and N. Altmann, *Industrielle Arbeit und soziale Sicherheit. Eine Studie über Risiken im Arbeitsprozeß und auf dem Arbeitsmarkt* (Frankfurt am Main, 1972), p. 192ff.; B. Lutz and W. Sengenberger, *Arbeitsmarktstrukturen und öffentliche Arbeitsmarktpolitik. Eine kritische Analyse von Zielen und Instrumenten* (Göttingen, 1974), p. 64ff.

12. Cf. B. Lutz, 'Vorläufige Notizen zur gesellschaftlichen und politischen Funktion von Beruf', in R. Crusius, W. Lempert and M. Wilke (eds), *Berufsausbildung – Reformpolitik in der Sackgasse?* (Reinbek 1974), p. 34ff.

13. See M. Weber, *Wirtschaft und Gesellschaft,* 5th edn (Tubingen, 1972), p. 201ff.; R. G. Heinze, K. Hinrichs, C. Offe and T. Olk, 'Einheitsprobleme der Einheitsgewerkschaft. Arbeitsmarktmacht und organisationspolitische Vertretungschancen verschiedener Kategorien von Arbeitnehmern', *Soziale Welt,* 32 (1981), 19–38; F. Parkin, 'Strategies of Social Closure in Class Formation', in F. Parkin (ed.), *The Social Analysis of Class Structure* (London, 1974); and R. Kreckel, 'Soziale Ungleichheit und Arbeitsmarktsegmentierung', in R. Kreckel (ed.), *Soziale Ungleichheiten* (Göttingen, 1983), pp. 137–62.

14. R. Herding and C. Sabel, '"Business Unions" in den USA. Eine Verteidigung gegen ihre falschen Feinde', in J. Bergmann (ed.), *Beiträge zur Soziologie der Gewerkschaften* (Frankfurt am Main, 1979); cf. also J. Rubery, 'Structured Labour Markets, Worker Organization and Low Pay', *Cambridge Journal of Economics,* 2 (1978), 17–36.

15. R.G. Heinze, K. Hinrichs, H-W. Hohn and T. Olk, 'Armut und Arbeitsmarkt. Zum Zusammenhang von Klassenlage und Verarmungsrisiken im Sozialstaat', *Zeitschrift für Soziologie,* 10 (1981), 219–43.

16. Cf. E. Lederer and J. Marschak, 'Die Klassen auf dem Arbeitsmarkt und ihre Organisation', p. 116.
17. On these particular groups, see the essays in Projektgruppe Arbeitsmarktpolitik and C. Offe (eds), *Opfer des Arbeitsmarkts – Zur Theorie der strukturierten Arbeitslosigkeit* (Neuwied, 1977).
18. Cf. B. Lutz and W. Sengenberger, *Arbeitsmarkstrukturen und öffentliche Arbeitsmarktpolitik*.
19. Cf. R. Dombois, 'Massenentlassungen bei VW: Individualisierung der Krise', *Leviathan*, 4 (1976), 432–64.
20. Cf. W. Sengenberger, *Die gegenwartige Arbeitslosigkeit – auch ein Strukturproblem des Arbeitsmarktes* (Frankfurt am Main 1978); R. Schultz-Wild, *Betriebliche Beschaftigungspolitik in der Krise* (Frankfurt am Main, 1978); B. Lutz, 'Wirtschaftliche Entwicklung, betriebliche Interessen und Arbeitsmarktsegmentation', unpublished manuscript, (Munich, 1978); B. Lutz and W. Sengenberger, 'Segmentationsanalyse und Beschaftigungspolitik'.
21. Cf. R. G. Heinze et al., 'Armut und Arbeitsmarkt'.

## 2 The Future of the Labour Market

1. K. Marx, 'Das Kapital', *Marx–Engels–Werke* (Berlin, 1968), vol. 23, p. 183.
2. M. Weber, *Wirtschaft und Gesellschaft,* 5th revised edn (Tübingen, 1972), pp. 23, 70ff.
3. K. Polanyi, *The Great Transformation. The Political and Economic Origins of our Time* (Boston, 1957), p. 73. Originally 1944.
4. G. Muller, U. Rödel, et al., *Ökonomische Krisentendenzen im gegenwärtigen Kapitalismus* (Frankfurt, 1978), p. 14ff.
5. Polanyi, *The Great Transformation,* Ch. 6.
6. Ibid., p. 73.
7. Cf. W. Bandes, P. Weise et al., *Arbeitsmarkt und Arbeitslosigkeit* (Wurzburg, 1981), p. 20.
8. Cf. C. Offe and K. Hinrichs, 'The Political Economy of the Labour Market' in this volume.
9. J. Schumpeter, *History of Economic Analysis,* E. B. Schumpeter (ed.), (New York, 1954), pp. 972–3.
10. Assessments of social policy interventions in the market place differ according to whether they are seen as effective or ineffective, as compatible with, or contrary to, the system. Without being able to pursue further here the question of the function of social policy in a capitalist society, we simply mention it to complete the picture of the

possible reactions of society to the principle of free competition in the labour market. On this problem, see G. Lenhardt and C. Offe, 'Social policy and the theory of the state', in *Contradictions of the Welfare State*, J. Keane (ed.), (London, 1984), pp. 88–118.

11. 'Work, Workers and the Age of Uncertainty. An Interview with Stuart Holland', *Social Alternatives*, 1, 4 (1979), 53.

12. Cf. V. Hauff and F. W. Scharpf, *Modernisierung der Volkswirtschaft. Technologiepolitik als Strukturpolitik* (Cologne, 1975).

13. Cf. E. Lederer, *Technischer Fortschritt und Arbeitslosigkeit. Eine Untersuchung der Hindernisse ökonomischen Wachstums*, revised edn, (Frankfurt, 1981).

14. With respect to the Federal Republic of Germany on this question, see H. P. Spahn, *Die Stabilitätspolitik des Sachverständigenrates* (Frankfurt, 1979).

15. P. Lafargue, *Das Recht auf Faulheit* (Frankfurt, 1966), p. 19.

16. K. Hinrichs and H. Wiesenthal, 'Arbeitswerte und Arbeitszeit. Zur Pluralisierung von Wertmustern und Zeitverwendungswünschen in der modernen Industriegesellschaft', in C. Offe, K. Hinrichs H. Wiesenthal (eds), *Arbeitszeitpolitik, Formen und Folgen einer Neuverteilung der Arbeitszeit* (Frankfurt, 1982), pp. 116–36.

17. If such entrance and exit options *vis-à-vis* the labour market were instituted successfully, a contribution to the pacification of social conflict would also be made, as is recognized for good reasons in several new articles originating from the Frankfurt Institute for Social Research: 'Not labour conflicts generated by "real subsumption" but rather a general lack of work, the impossibility of basing social security on work, appears to be developing as the dominant social problem of the future.' (C. Deutschmann, 'Das Theorem der reellen Subsumption der Arbeit unter das Kapital und die gegenwärtigen Tendenzen der Automation', unpublished manuscript, (Frankfurt am Main, 1981), p. 10.)

18. Cf. the similar programmatic conception of 'social diversity' defended by P. Rosanvallon, 'Für eine Wirtschaft der Autonomie', in J. Huber (ed.), *Anders arbeiten – anders wirtschaften* (Frankfurt am Main, 1979), p. 219ff, and (in the same volume) the concept of a plurality of allocative principles for labour formulated by A. Gorz, 'Abschied vom Proletariat'.

19. For a convincing formulation of this critique of the liberal renewal strategy, see J. H. Goldthorpe, 'The Current Inflation: Towards a Sociological Account', in F. Hirsch and J. H. Goldthorpe (eds), *The Political Economy of Inflation* (London, 1978), pp. 186–214.

20. The first-mentioned objection – that the increased pressure upon labour power to conform is not likely to lead to an increased

investment propensity of entrepreneurs and, hence, the eventual re-establishment of 'full employment' – depends on a critique of the assumption that there could ever be an equilibrium wage that would clear *both* the labour market and the commodity market. Expressed in Marxist terms: the dilemma (ignored by neo-liberals) consists precisely in the fact that investors, as soon as they are freed from the 'exploitation problem' consequent upon high wage costs, encounter the 'realization problem' of insufficient demand and so, in anticipation of this problem, refrain from an 'adequate' or full employment-producing investment effort.

21. The concept of juridification – the transformation of informal rules and situations into formal-legal regulations – is well discussed in R. Erd, *Verrechtlichung industrieller Konflikte. Normative Rahmenbedingungen des dualen Systems der Interessenvertretung* (Frankfurt, 1978), as well as in the articles in R. Voigt (ed.), *Verrechtlichung. Analysen zu Funktion und Wirkung von Parlamentarisierung, Bürokratisierung und Justitialisierung sozialer, politischer und ökonomischer Prozesse* (Königstein/Ts., 1980).

22. Of the vast amount of social-scientific and legal literature on the problem of a 'right to work', see especially M. Rath, *Probleme einer Garantie des Rechts auf Arbeit* (Lubeck, 1974); U. Achten et al., *Recht auf Arbeit, eine politische Herausforderung* (Neuwied, 1978); H. Hummel-Liljegren, *Zumutbare Arbeit* (Berlin, 1981), especially pp. 172–93; M. Kittner (ed.), *Arbeitsmarkt-ökonomische, soziale und rechtliche Grundlagen* (Heidelberg, 1982), especially pp. 52–123.

23. For the case of Britain, see the impressive argument by R. Bacon and W. Eltis, *Britain's Economic Problem. Too Few Producers* (London, 1976).

24. Data according to EEC, Eurostat, Brussels, 1977.

25. Cf. Gerd Vonderach, 'Die "neuen Selbständigen", 10 Thesen zur Soziologie eines unvermuteten Phänomens', *Mitt AB*, 13, 2 (1980), 153–69.

26. Here it should certainly not be overlooked that this type of negative and denunciatory assessment is in recent political debate also mixed up with traces of a more positive judgement, one which recognizes the innovative character and quasi-entrepreneurial, self-organizing and self-helping impulse of other forms of the 'new self-employment'. Even if combined with critical amendments and inconsistencies, this appreciation is mostly evident in the Federal Republic of Germany among some representatives of the Christian Democratic Party (CDU).

27. C. Leipert, 'Theoretische und wirtschaftspolitische Konsequenzen

322 *Notes*

aus der Kritik der Wachstumgesellschaft', *Aus Politik und Zeitgeschichte*, 25 (1981), 31–52. Important contributions to the new theoretical and empirical social science literature on the forms and functions of a 'self-organized', 'deprofessionalized' and 'debureaucratized' provision of health and socialization services to households include: C. Badelt, *Sozioökonomie der Selbstversorgung* (Frankfurt, 1980), especially pp. 225–83; B. Badura and C. von Ferber (eds), *Selbsthilfe und Selbstorganisation im Gesundheitswesen* (Munich, 1981); and I. Kickbusch and A. Trojan (eds), *Gemeinsam sind wir stärker! Selbsthilfegruppen und Gesundheit* (Frankfurt, 1981). For the parallel discussion in the USA, see A. Gartner and F. Riesman, *Self-Help in the Human Services* (San Francisco, 1977).

28. Cf. Badelt, *Sozioökonomie der Selbstversorgung*, p. 33., as well as P. Starr's sceptical reflections on the theme 'the personal is the political', in 'The Phantom Community', J. Case and R. Taylor (eds), *Co-ops, Communes and Collectives, Experiments in Social Change in the 1960s and 1970s* (New York, 1979), pp. 245–73.

29. Cf. Badelt, *Sozioökonomie der Selbstversorgung*, pp. 266–72.

30. On the financing of self-organized activity, see Badelt, *Sozioökonomie der Selbstversorgung*, pp. 135ff, 262ff., 277ff.

## 4 The Growth of the Service Sector

1. E. Lederer, *Die Privatangestellten in der modernen Wirtschaftsentwicklung* (Tübingen, 1912); K. Marx, *Grundrisse der politischen Ökonomie* (East Berlin, 1953), p. 592ff.

2. See R. Bacon and W. Eltis, *Britain's Economic Problem: Too Few Producers* (London, 1976).

3. R.R. Grauhan and W. Linder, *Politik der Verstädterung* (Frankfurt am Main, 1974).

4. P. Herder-Dorneich and W. Kötz, *Zur Dienstleistungsökonomik* (Berlin, 1972).

5. Cf. J. Berger and C. Offe, 'Die Entwicklungsdynamik des Dienstleistungssektors', *Leviathan*, 8 (1980), 41–75; and U. Berger and U. Engfer, 'Strukturwandel der gesellschaftlichen Arbeit', in W. Littek et al. (eds), *Einführung in die Arbeits- und Industriesoziologie* (Frankfurt, 1982), pp. 302–8.

6. J. Gershuny, 'Post Industrial Society? The Myth of the Service Economy', *Futures*, 9 (1977), 103–14, and *After Industrial Society? The Emerging Self-Service Economy* (London, 1978).

7. Cf. B. Badura and C. von Ferber (eds), *Selbsthilfe und Selbstorganisation in Gesundheitswesen* (Munich, 1981).
8. David Lockwood, 'Social Integration and System Integration', in G. K. Zollschan and W. Hirsch (eds), *Explorations in Social Change* (London, 1964), pp. 244–57.
9. R. M. Hartwell, 'The Service Revolution: The Growth of Services in Modern Economy', in C. M. Cipolla (ed.), *The Economic History of Europe* (London, 1973), pp. 360, 362ff. 366, 368; cf. also the summary of Sidney Pollard's argument: 'This explanation concentrates on the growing complexity of industry and the growing specialization within the modern economy, requiring functions that at one time were part of the manufacturer's job, like design, marketing or advertising, to be transferred to specialized agencies, thus merely transforming hidden services into open ones, or needing many more services than before.' ('The Rise of Service Industries and White Collar Employment', in B. Gustafson (ed.), *Post-Industrial Society* (London, 1979), p.26.)
10. G. Bäcker, 'Entprofessionalisierung und Laisierung sozialer Dienste richtungsweisende Perspektive oder konservativer Rückzug?', in *WSI-Mitteilungen*, 10 (1979), 532. A similar point is made by G. Stevensen, 'Die gesellschaftlichen Verhältnisse der Produktion und Konsumption im Bereich der immateriellen Dienstleistungen', *Monthly Review* (German edition), 3 (1976), 79.
11. See G. J. Stigler, *Trends in Employment in the Service Industries* (Princeton, 1956), p. 159ff.
12. R. M. Hartwell, 'The Services Revolution', p. 365.
13. Cf. H-J. Pohl, 'Kritik der Drei-Sektoren-Theorie', *Mitteilungen aus der Arbeitsmarkt-und Berufsforschung*, 3 (1970), 324, and R. M. Hartwell, 'The Service Revolution', p. 360.
14. L. Hirschhorn, 'The Theory of Social Services in Disaccumulationist Capitalism', *International Journal of Health Services*, 9 (1979), 295ff.
15. M. Nicolaus, 'Proletariat and Middle Class in Marx', in J. Weinstein and D.W. Eakins (eds), *For a New America* (New York, 1970), p. 273.
16. Ibid., p. 273ff.
17. A. Hansen, *Keynes' ökonomische Lehren: ein Führer durch sein Hauptwerk* (Villingen, 1959), p. 72ff.
18. E. Hönekopp and H. Ullmann, 'Auf dem Weg zur Dienstleistungsökonomie? Wirtschafts- und Beschäftigungsstrukturen ausgewählter Industriestaated im Vergleich', *Mitteilungen aus der Arbeitsmarkt- und Berufsforschung*, 13 (1980), 259. A slightly different argument is defended by H-J. Pohl, 'Kritik der Drei-Sektoren-Theorie', p. 321.

324 *Notes*

19. E. Hönekopp and H. Ullmann, 'Auf dem Weg zur Dienstleistungs-ökonomie?', p. 259.
20. K-D. Schmidt, 'Der Dienstleistungsbereich als dynamischer Faktor im Prozess des wirtschaftlichen Wachstums,' *Gespräche der List – Gesellschaft e. V* (Baden-Baden, 1980), vol. 2, *Wachstum und Konjunktur unter veränderten Bedingungen,* p. 136ff.
21. H. L. Browning and J. Singelmann, 'The Transformation of the U.S. Labor Force: The Intervention of Industry and Occupations', *Politics and Society,* 8 (1978), 486.
22. G. Voss, *Trend zur Dienstleistungsgesellschaft?* (Köln, 1976).
23. R. Bacon and W. Eltis, *Britain's Economic Problem: Too Few Producers.*
24. G. Voss, *Trend zur Dienstleistungsgesellschaft?,* pp. 24, 45ff.
25. F. Decker, *Einführung in die Dienstleistungsökonomie* (Paderborn, 1975), p. 32ff.
26. A. G. B. Fischer, 'Production, Primary, Secondary, and Tertiary', *The Economic Record,* 15 (1939), 24–38; C. Clark, *The Conditions of Economic Progress,* 3rd edn (London, 1960); J. Fourastié, *Die grosse Hoffnung des 20. Jahrhunderts* (Cologne, 1954).
27. H-J. Pohl, 'Kritik der Drei-Sektoren-Theorie', pp. 316–17; H. G. Graf, *Der Einfluss des Einkommens auf die Struktur des Dienstleistungssektors* (Zürich, 1968).
28. H-J. Pohl, 'Kritik der Drei-Sektoren-Theorie', p. 316 (and the additional references mentioned there).
29. A. Maslow, *Motivation and Personality* (New York, 1954).
30. E. Hönekopp and H. Ullmann, 'Auf dem Weg zur Dienstleistung-sökonomi?', p. 267.
31. J. Gershuny, 'Post Industrial Society? The Myth of the Service Economy', and *After Industrial Society? The Emerging Self-Service Economy.*
32. Cf. J. Heinze, 'Strukturwandel in der Bundesrepublik, eine Auseinandersetzung mit der Drei-Sektoren-Hypothese', *IFO – Schnelldienst,* 33 (1979), 9, and H-J. Pohl, 'Kritik der Drei-Sektoren-Theorie', p. 323.
33. In the Federal Republic of Germany, state-directed service labour accounted for almost three-quarters of the overall volume during the period 1960–76: see J. Heinze, 'Strukturwandel in der Bundesre-publik', p. 12.
34. J. Heinze, 'Strukturwandel in der Bundesrepublik', p. 15ff.
35. Ibid.
36. K-D. Schmidt, 'Der Dienstleistungsbereich als dynamischer Faktor im Prozess des wirtschaftlichen Wachstums', p. 127ff.
37. G. Voss, *Trend zur Dienstleistungsgesellschaft?,* and E. Dähne, *Die*

*Bedeutung der Dienstleistungswirtschaft für die Arbeitsmarktent-*
*wicklung in der BRD* (Munich, 1974).
38. E. Hönekopp and H. Ullmann, 'Auf dem Weg zur Dienstleistungs-
    ökonomie?', p. 267.
39. J. Heinze, 'Strukturwandel in der Bundesrepublik', p. 19.
40. S. Pollard, 'The Rise of Service Industries and White Collar
    Employment', pp. 40, 30.
41. Ibid., p. 34. For the American case, see H. L. Browning and
    J. Singelmann, 'The Transformation of the U.S. Labor Force', p.
    504ff.
42. Prognos Aktiengesellschaft, 'Entwicklungstendenzen des Dienstleis-
    tungsbereichs der Bundersrepublik Deutschland', (Friedrichshafen,
    1976), p.d.
43. K. Kumar, *Prophecy and Progress : The Sociology of Industrial and
    Post-Industrial Society* (London, 1978).
44. S. Pollard, 'The Rise of Service Industries and White Collar
    Employment', p. 29.
45. H. Schelsky, *Der selbständige und der betreute Mensch* (Stuttgart,
    1976); I. Illich, *Disabling Professions* (London, 1977); M. Jänicke,
    *Wie das Industriesystem von seinen Mißständen profitiert* (Opladen,
    1973). It is of some interest to note that the same empirical
    observations of these and other authors are used to support widely
    diverging socio-political recommendations and conclusions. These
    range from polemical diagnoses concerning the rise of a 'new class'
    to arguments in defence of industrial democracy and alternative
    forms of economic organization.

## 5   Work: The Key Sociological Category?

1. See R. Dahrendorf, 'Im Entschwinden der Arbeitsgesellschaft:
   Wandlungen der sozialen Konstruktion des menschlichen Lebens',
   *Merkur,* 34 (1980), 749–60, as well as B. Guggenberger, 'Am Ende
   der Arbeitsgesellschaft', in F. Benseler et al. (eds), *Zukunft der
   Arbeit* (Hamburg, 1982), pp. 63–84 and F. R. Volz, *Die Arbeitsgesellschaft* (Frankfurt, 1982).
2. 'The industrial revolution methodically undermined the older system
   whereby work, family and leisure life were all of a piece, performed
   as an undifferentiated whole.' (K. Kumar, 'The Social Culture of
   Work', *New University Quarterly,* 34 (1979), 14.)
3. On the history of these concepts, see W. Conze, 'Arbeit', in
   W. Conze and R. Koselleck (eds), *Geschtliche Grundbegriffe: His-*

*torisches Lexikon zur politisch-sozialen Sprache in Deutschland* (Stuttgart, 1972), vol. 1; and H. Arendt, *The Human Condition* (New York, 1958).

4. See E. Durkheim, *The Division of Labour in Society* (New York, 1960), pp. 62, 400: 'Through the division of labour, the individual becomes cognisant of his dependence upon society . . . The division of labour becomes the chief source of social solidarity.'

5. This change of perspective, as well as the thesis of a 'specifically political determination' of industrial processes, which necessitate an 'overcoming of the scientific and practical separation of *industry* and *policy*' is illustrated in G. Dörr and F. Naschold, 'Arbeitspolitische Entwicklungen in der Industriearbeit', in G. Schmidt et al. (eds), *Materialien zur Industriesoziologie,* special issue of *Kölner Zeitschrift für Soziologie und Sozialpsychologie,* (1982), 433–56; and U. Jürgens and F. Naschold, 'Arbeitspolitik, Entwicklungstendenzen und Politikformen', in J. Hesse (ed.), *Verwaltungswissenschaft und Politikwissenschaft,* special issue of *Politische Vierteljahresschrift,* (1982).

6. See, for example, the symptomatic (and equally programmatic) contribution of B. Mahnkopf, 'Das kulturtheoretische Defizit industriesoziologischer Forschung', *Prokla,* 12 (1982), 41–60; cf. C. F. Sabel, *Work and Politics: The Division of Labour in Industry* (Cambridge, 1982).

7. Cf. U. Beck, 'Auf dem Weg in die individualisierte Klassengesellschaft?', unpublished manuscript (Bamberg, 1981): 'The whole paradigm of stratification and class theories must, given their immanent contradictions, be debated on the strength of their realism' (p. 5). Beck speaks of a 'pluralization of forms of life . . . which bursts the limits of the firmly established schema of stratification and class differentiation' (p. 52), and of 'an "income stratum" which no longer corresponds to any one kind of adopted form of life' (p. 53). S. Hradil writes in a similar vein ('Die Ungleichheit der "Sozialen Lage": eine Alternative zum schichtungssoziologischen Modell sozialer Ungleichheit', unpublished manuscript, Munich, 1982, pp. 1ff, 19, 21):

> The sociological approach to stratification does not disclose the entire phenomenal realm of social inequality . . . The inequality model utilized by the sociology of stratification evidently 'worked' better in the past than today . . . In general, it is precisely the forms of social inequality evident especially in recent times which do not support the basic tenets of stratification sociology. It was assumed [falsely] that specific

structural factors (e.g. income and status) are to a great extent, indeed, equally relevant for the life of all members of society.

Also consistent with this trend is the development and application of the concept of a 'welfare class' by R. M. Lepsius, 'Soziale Ungleichheit und Klassenstruktur in der Bundesrepublik Deutschland', in H. U. Wehler (ed.), *Klassen in der Europäischen Sozialgeschichte* (Göttingen, 1979).

8. In this connection, see R. G. Heinze et al., 'Sind die Gewerkschaften für "alle" da?', in O. Jacobi, E. Schmidt and W. Möller-Jentsch (eds), *Moderne Zeiten – alte Rezepte. Kritisches Gewerkschaftsjahrbuch 1980/81* (Berlin, 1980), pp. 62–77, and the essay later in this volume, 'Interest Diversity and Trade Union Unity'.

9. Cf. J. Berger and C. Offe, 'Die Entwicklungsdynamik des Dienstleistungssektors', *Leviathan*, 8, 1, (1980), 41–75; U. Berger and C. Offe, 'Das Rationalisierungsdilemma der Angestelltenarbeit', in J. Kocka (ed.), *Angestellte im Europäischen Vergleich* (Göttingen, 1981), pp. 39–58; and C. Offe, 'The Growth of the Service Sector', in this volume. The quantitative significance of the splitting of 'workers in general' into productive and service-producing forms of work only becomes clear if one does not (as is usually done) disaggregate according to 'sectors', but according to jobs. The 1980 mini-census in the Federal Republic of Germany indicated that approximately 27 per cent of wage earners are involved in activities that deal mainly with the manufacturing and production of material products, while an overwhelming 73 per cent produce services.

10. Cf. B. Bruce-Briggs (ed.), *The New Class* (New York, 1979); and H. Schelsky, *Die Arbeit tun die anderen* (Opladen, 1975).

11. Cf. Daniel Bell, *The Cultural Contradictions of Capitalism* (New York, 1976).

12. R. Dahrendorf, 'Im Entschwinden der Arbeitsgesellschaft', p. 756.

13. Since these two cases (and their empirical variants) concern only the motivational 'bonding' of workers to their work, they do not highlight the possibility that 'pure' work (i.e. in its modern form of a sharply differentiated, special sphere of social action) could be relativized and enriched with elements drawn from the sphere of the household and consumption, on the one hand, and from the public-political spheres, on the other. This possibility of de-differentiating work and other spheres of life (through programmes of work humanization or the expansion of self-help and personal activities within the household) dominates most of the contemporary political and social science discussion of 'the future of work'. See the contributions in F. Benseler et al. (eds), *Die Zunkunft der Arbeit*

(Hamburg, 1982); A. *Gorz*, Farewell to the Working Class (London, 1982); J. Strasser and K. Traube, *Die Zunkunft des Fortschritts* (Bonn, 1981); and C. Offe, 'The Future of the Labour Market', in this volume.

14. This hedonism is strongly evident in the tourism and leisure industry, whose prospectuses read occasionally like a manifesto against work. Consider, for example, the following advertisement for a leisure exhibit in the *Neue Westfälische Zeitung*, 17 March, 1982: 'Take your leisure seriously. It is the most important part of your life!'

15. Cf. H. Braverman, *Labour and Monopoly Capital: The Degradation of Work in the 20th Century* (New York, 1974). Numerous studies in industrial sociology confirm the drift towards 'the expropriation of skills, experience and knowledge' (E. Hildebrandt, 'Arbeit im Wandel: Subjektive Einstellungen und gesellschaftliche Wertung', *Stimme der Arbeit*, 22, 3, (1980), 75ff.):

> Self-initiative, creative thinking, the capacity for making decisions and social responsibility become not only superfluous as primary human attributes, but suppressed as dysfunctional. Little by little, the production process forces the dependent wage-earners to surrender their occupational and social competence, their shaping of their own work, as well as their own ideas about concrete labour.

16. K. Kumar, 'The Social Culture of Work', p. 15.

17. Cf. R. Crusius and M. Wilke, *Einheitsgewerkschaft und Berufspolitik* (Frankfurt, 1982), especially pp. 174–230.

18. M. Weber, *The Protestant Ethic and the Spirit of Capitalism* (New York, 1958), p. 181. Today, the well-known feelings and remarks about 'inwardly dropping out' stand in contrast to the 'idea of a calling': 'Many persons, including those who are hardworking, have detached their life conduct and their self-image . . . from their work experience . . . without developing a new form of identity beyond work.' (F. R. Volz, *Die Arbeitsgesellschaft*, p. 46ff.)

19. M. Schumann, 'Entwicklungen des Arbeiterbewusstseins', *Gewerkschaftliche Monatshefte*, 30 (1979), 157. In a research report of the SOFI, one of the workers who was interviewed reduced this point to a concise formula: 'Today no one is properly raised to be a worker any more.'

20. Cf. R. Dahrendorf, 'Im Entschwinden der Arbeitsgesellschaft', p. 753: 'The time released by the contraction of work is free in the

sense of lacking structure.' Of course, this thesis is relativized by the empirical findings on the attitudes towards leisure, which identify the *restrictive* effect of the job on the leisure sphere. The external limits established by work consist, *subjectively,* in the physical, nervous and social exhaustion or deactivation of labour power it produces, and *objectively* in the fact that most institutionalized forms of leisure (e.g. tourism) depend to a large extent on disposable income. In spite of this, one should not speak of a 'structuration' of leisure by work but, rather, of a 'limitation' or 'conditioning' of it.

21. D. Anthony explains the sanctitude of work in Western culture, the 'ideology of work', by the mechanism of dissonance-reduction, as a normative exaltation of reality (*International Social Science Journal,* 32, 3 (1980), 419ff.):

> As work has been the lot of man from time immemorial, man has invested work with something of the significance which he believes inheres in life.

The sub-stratum of these cultural norms is, however, in the process of being dissolved:

> The traditional view now requires serious modifications ... These changes have several consequences. They threaten the continuation of the 'ideology of work' in that they make it no longer necessary or useful for society to stress the dominating importance of work and the zealous adherence to its disciplines. They also mean that the coincidental unity of life space and work no longer exists; man's life seems likely to become, in more ways than one, independent of work.

See also D. Anthony, *The Ideology of Work* (London, 1977); and C. Jenkins and B. Sherman, *The Collapse of Work* (London, 1979).

22. All indications suggest that what Kumar concludes for Britain is also true for the West European continent: 'We are faced with a future in which unemployment will be a normal, not aberrant, experience of the population.' (K. Kumar, 'The Social Culture of Work', p. 25.)

23. In the Federal Republic of Germany, for example, every second worker and every third white-collar employee is retired from gainful employment before reaching the age limit, and every sixth worker and every tenth white-collar employee becomes chronically incapable of gainful employment before reaching the age of 50. These transformations of the temporal and social structure of

'post-industrial' existence are often reinforced by different expectations: 'The more time people spend outside of the paid labour force, before, after and during a work career, the more they find that work is no longer a sufficient focus for organizing their lives' (F. Block and L. Hirschhorn, 'New Productive Forces and the Contradictions of Contemporary Capitalism: A Post-Industrial Perspective', *Theory and Society*, 7 (1979), 374.)

24. This point should certainly not be oversimplified, because the moral decentring of work results in a deficit of meaning as such. This deficit, which accompanies the experience of unemployment, can be interpreted as a phenomenon produced by the disorganization of the life-world. The vehement reaction against this (anticipated) experience and in favour of 'meaningful' work which facilitates self-realization is to be found particularly among young people, as the example of the USA, described by B. Berger, indicates. This reaction, Berger shows, is mainly organized in favour of state-organized services, and is in this respect unrealistic and 'structurally inadequate'. She notes the problem of a 'contradiction between occupational aspirations and the existing job market' (B. Berger, 'People Work, the Youth Culture, and the Labour Market', *The Public Interest*, 35 (1974), 61.)

25. Cf. T. Scitovsky, *The Joyless Economy* (New York, 1976) and R. E. Lane, 'Markets and the Satisfaction of Human Wants', *Journal of Economic Issues*, 12 (1978), 799–827, and the well-known argument by F. Hirsch, *Social Limits to Growth* (London, 1977).

26. R. C. Lane, 'Markets and the Satisfaction of Human Wants', p. 803.

27. Ibid., p. 815.

28. Ibid., p. 817.

29. See, for example, U. Mueckenberger, 'Zur Problematik eines Rechts auf Arbeit', in *Arbeitsprozess, Vergesellschaftung, Sozialverfassung* (Bremen, undated).

30. In this connection, see my highly speculative discussion, 'Alternative Strategies in Consumer Policy', in *Contradictions of the Welfare State*, J. Keane, ed., (London, 1984), pp. 220–38.

31. On this point, see W. A. Jöhr, 'Die kollektive Selbstschädigung durch Verfolgung des eigenen Vorteils', in *Wettbewerb, Konzentration und wirtschaftliche Macht*, Festschrift for H. Arndt (Berlin, 1976), as well as the attempted empirical critique of this thesis by P. Windolf, 'Neue Arbeitslosigkeit und die Grenzen der Sozialpolitik', *Soziale Welt*, 33 (1982), 365–99, especially p. 369ff. For a detailed critique of the welfare state, see C. Offe, *Contradictions of the Welfare State*.

32. Cf. the important contribution by S. Bowles and H. Gintis, 'The

Crisis of Liberal Democratic Capitalism: The Case of the United States', *Politics and Society*, 11 (1982), 51–93; as well as J. Berger, 'Wandlungen von Krisenmechanismen im wohlfahrtsstaatlichen Kapitalismus', *Das Argument*, 46, (1981), 81–94.

33. Cf. J. Esser et al., 'Krisenregulierung, Mechanismen und Voraussetzungen', *Leviathan*, 7 (1979), 79–96.

34. G. Brandt, 'Die Zukunft der Arbeit in der "nachindustriellen" Gesellschaft', unpublished manuscript (Frankfurt, 1980), p. 19. More pointed is the observation of C. Deutschmann: 'Not labour conflicts generated by "real subsumption", but rather a general lack of work, the impossibility of basing social security on work, appears to be developing as the dominant social problem of the future'. ('Das Theorem der reellen Subsumption der Arbeit unter das Kapital und die gegenwärtigen Tendenzen der Automation', unpublished manuscript, (Frankfurt, 1981).)

35. J. Habermas, *Theorie des kommunikativen Handelns* (Frankfurt am Main, 1981), two vols; see also J. Berger's critique '*Theorie des kommunikativen Handelns*', *Telos*, 57 (1983), 194–205.

36. A. Giddens, 'Labour and Interaction', in J. B. Thompson and D. Held (eds), *Habermas: Critical Debates* (London, 1982), p. 152.

37. Cf. J. Kuczinsky, *Geschichte des Alltags des deutschen Volkes* (East Berlin, 1983), vol. 5.

38. J. Raschke, 'Politik und Wertwandel in den westlichen Demokratien', *Aus Politik und Zeitgeschichte*, 36 (1980), 23–45.

39. The political and strategic reorientations forced upon the political Left by the objective and subjective decentring of work have become strongly evident since the mid-1970s. Consider the following sample of quotations: 'Workerist forms of socialist ideology are unable to articulate many significant issues of popular concern and, partly for that reason, have a sectional appearance and effect' (B. Hindess, 'Parliamentary Democracy and Socialist Politics' in M. Prior (ed.) *The Popular and the Political*, London, 1981, p. 42). 'The anti-nuclear struggle and reactions mark a considerable change in the political field. It is the first time that the problems of work and production have ceased to hold the central position in political life' (A. Touraine, 'Anti-nuclear Reactions or Anti-nuclear Movement?', unpublished manuscript, Paris, 1981). 'Certainly the anti-capitalist impulses do not disappear, but they come increasingly from other variables (the condition of youth, sexual roles, territorial arrangements, position in the labour market) rather than from the condition of wage workers as such' (A. Melucci, 'New Movements, Terrorism, and the Political System', *Socialist Review*, 56 (1981), 124ff). See also S.M. Lipset, 'Whatever Happened to the Proletariat?', *Encounter*, 5–6 June 1981.

40. On this set of problems, see my essay 'New Social Movements: A Challenge to Politics', in C. S. Maier (ed.), *The Changing Boundaries of the Political* (forthcoming).

## 6   Interest Diversity and Trade Union Unity

1. Cf. P. Glotz, 'Jugend und Gesellschaft – die Herausforderung der 80er Jahre', *Gewerkschaftliche Monatshefte,* 31 (1980), 357–68; M. Wilke, *Die Funktionäre. Apparat und Demokratie im Deutschen Gewerkschaftsbund* (Munich, 1979), p. 237.
2. Cf. R. Crusius, 'Jugend ohne Gewerkschaft? Zu aktuellen Problemen der gewerkschaftlichen Jugendpolitik', *Deutsche Jugend,* 28 (1980), 81–8.
3. Cf. G. Vonderach, 'Die "neuen Selbständigen": 10 Thesen zur Soziologie eines unvermuteten Phänomens', *Mitteilungen aus der Arbeitsmarkt- und Berufsforschung,* 13 (1980), 153–69.
4. Cf. D. Yankelovich, 'The Meaning of Work', in J. M. Rosow (ed.), *The American Assembly; The Worker and the Job: Coping with Chance* (Englewood Cliffs, 1974), pp. 19–47; Institut für Jugendforschung, *Die Einstellung der jungen Generation zur Arbeitswelt und Wirschaftsordnung 1979,* Studie in Auftrag des Jugendwerks der Deutschen Shell (Hamburg, 1980).
5. See B. Strumpel, *Die Krise des Wohlstands,* (Stuttgart, 1977), pp. 55ff, 70ff; P. Kmiectak, *Wertstrukturen und Wertwandel in der Bundesrepublik* (Göttingen, 1976), p. 334ff. On the discussion of the transformation of values and the paradigm of the 'new life style', see J. Raschke, 'Politik und Wertwandel in den westlichen Demokratien', *Aus Politik und Zeitgeschichte,* 30, 36 (1980), 23–45.
6. See M. Schumann, 'Entwicklungen des Arbeiterbewußtseins. Schwierigkeiten, die veränderte soziale Lage zu interpretieren', *Gewerkschaftliche Monatshefte,* 30 (1979), 152–9. See also the summary of findings on the consciousness and activity of workers in J. Esser, *Gewerkschaften in der Krise* (Frankfurt, 1982).
7. Cf. A. Gorz, *Farewell to the Working Class* (London, 1983).
8. Cf. R. G. Heinze, K. Hinrichs, C. Offe and Th. Olk, 'Einheitsprobleme der Einheitsgewerkschaft. Überlegungen zum Zusammenhang von Arbeitsmarktmacht und organisationspolitischen Vertretungschancen verschiedener Kategorien von Arbeitnehmern', *Soziale Welt,* 32, 1 (1981), 19–38.
9. See Arbeitskreis Arbeitsmarktperspektiven, 'Finanzierungsstruktur

und Verteilungswirkungen einer nachfrage-orientierten Strategie zur Wiedergewinnung der Vollbeschäftigung', in *Wochenberichte des DIW*, 46, 13 (1979), 139–47.

10. Cf. K. Marth, 'Technologische Entwicklungen und ihre Auswirkungen auf die Beschäftigung', *WSI-Mitteilungen*, 33 (1980), 434.

11. A claim defended in the central paper delivered by H. O. Vetter to the Conference on Employment of the Federation of German Trade Unions (DGB) on 21 October, 1980, in Dusseldorf.

12. See H. Afheldt, 'Entwicklungsperspektiven der Wirtschaft in der Bundesrepublik – Konsequenzen für die Regionalpolitik', in U. Bruder and T. Ellwein (eds), 'Raumordnung und staatliche Steuerungsfähigkeit', *Politischen Vierteljahresschrift*, 10 (1980), 120.

13. Cf. U. Briefs, 'Aspekte der gesellschaftspolitischen Problematik der Informationstechnologien', *WSI-Mitteilungen*, 32 (1979), 414–26; W. Steinmüller, 'Informationstechnologien und gesellschaftliche Macht', *WSI-Mitteilungen*, 32 (1979), 426–36; D. Marchello, 'Großer Bruder Daimler-Benz. Die Auseinandersetzung um das Personalinformationssystem', in O. Jacobi, E. Schmidt, and W. Müller-Jentsch (eds), *Moderne Zeiten – alte Rezepte. Kritisches Gewerkschaftsjahrbuch 1980/1* (Berlin, 1980), pp. 9–16.

14. Cf. B. Lutz and F. Böhle, *Rationalisierungsschutzabkommen – Wirksamkeit und Probleme* (Göttingen, 1974); K. Dohse et al., 'Probleme einer Beschränkung gewerkschaftlicher Bestandsschutzpolitik auf die Absicherung älterer Arbeitnehmer', *Internationales Institut für Vergleichende Gesellschaftsforschung (IIVG) Papers* (Berlin, 1978).

15. See U. Jürgens et al., 'Die preventive Wendung der staatlichen Sozialpolitik – Formen des Unterlautens und der Verkehrung auf Betriebsebene', in P. Grottian (ed.), 'Folgen reduzierten Wachstums für Politikfelder', *Politischen Vierteljahresschrift*, 11 (1980), 68–87.

16. Cf. B. Lutz, 'Wirtschaftliche Entwicklung, betriebliche Interessen und Arbeitsmarbtsegmentation', unpublished manuscript, (Munich, 1978).

17. On the one hand, see F. Deppe, *Autonomie und Integration. Materialen zur Gewerkschaftsanalyse* (Marburg, 1979), p. 220ff; on the other, see A. S. Markovits and C. S. Allen, 'The human experience of labour in a changing market: the Ambivalence of the West German Trade Unions', paper delivered to the *XI World Congress of the International Political Science Association* (Moscow, 1979).

18. Cf. W. Müller-Jentsch, 'Neue Konfliktpotentiale und institutionelle Stabilität. Die Austauschbeziehungen zwischen Kapital und Arbeit in der Bundesrepublik seit dem Ende der sechziger Jahre', in

J. Matthes (ed.), *Sozialer Wandel in Westeuropa. Verhandlungen des 19. Deutschen Soziologentages Berlin, 1979* (Frankfurt am Main, 1979), pp. 185–205.

19. W. Streeck, 'Gewerkschaftsorganisation und industrielle Beziehungen. Einige Stabilitätsprobleme industrie-gewerk-schaftlicher Interessenvertretung und ihre Lösung im westdeutschen System der industriellen Beziehungen', in J. Matthes (ed.), *Sozialer Wandel in Westeuropa*, pp. 206–26; and *Gewerkschaftliche Organisationsprobleme in der sozialstaatlichen Demokratie* (Königstein, 1981).

20. W. Storz, 'Die Rolle der Gewerkschaften in der Kommunalpolitik', *WSI-Mitteilungen* 33 (1980), pp. 698–704.

21. R. Crusius and M. Wilke, 'Plädoyer für den Beruf', *Aus Politik und Zeitgeschichte* 29 (1979), no. 48, pp. 3–13.

22. For the historical roots of these ideas, see K. Novy, *Strategien der Sozialisierung. Die Diskussion der Wirtschaftsreform in der Weimarer Republik* (Frankfurt am Main, 1978). On the contemporary debate on the 'informal sector', see R. G. Heinze and T. Olk, 'Eigenarbeit, Selbsthilfe, Alternativökonomie, Entwicklungstendenzen', unpublished manuscript, (Paderborn, Bielefeld, 1981); A. Gorz, *Farewell to the Working Class;* G. Vonderach, 'Die "neuen" Selbständigen'; and J. Huber, 'Der Sozialstaat an den Grenzen des Wachstums', *Aus Politik und Zeitgeschichte,* 31 (1981), 3–15.

## 7  Two Logics of Collective Action

1. For a similar argument, see G. Therborn, *Science, Class and Society: On the Formation of Sociology and Historical Materialism* (London, 1976), ch. 3.

2. For a Marxist treatment of this issue, see H. Braverman, *Labour and Monopoly Capital: The Degradation of Work in the Twentieth Century* (New York, 1974); cf. the discussion of the German case in U. Kadritzke, *Angestellte – die geduldigen Arbeiter: Zur Soziologie und sozialen Bewegung der Angestellten* (Frankfurt, 1975); the analysis of the Federal Republic of Germany and the USA, by J. Kocka, *White Collar Workers in America 1890–1940: A Social-Political History in International Perspective* (London, 1979); and the review essay by G. Ross, 'Marxism and the new middle class: French critiques', *Theory and Society*, 5 (1978), 163–90.

3. For a brilliant and influential discussion of this problem, see Stephen Marglin, 'What do bosses do?', *The Review of Radical Political*

*Economics,* 6, 2 (1974), 60–112, and 7, 1 (1975), 20–37. Some of
the structural differences between labour markets and other markets
are expressed in C. Offe, 'The Political Economy of the Labour
Market', earlier in this volume.

4. Here, as well as in the title of this essay, we refer, of course, to the
famous work by M. Olson Jnr, *The Logic of Collective Action –
Public Goods and the Theory of Groups* (New York, 1968). We also
refer, however, to a proposition that we consider a central element
of historical materialism, namely, the proposition that two antagonistic logics underlie the development of capitalism – the 'logic of
profit' and the logic of the increasingly 'social' character of the
forces of production (including human labour power). For recent
elaborations of this historical materialist 'two logics' argument, see
L. Basso, *Gesellschaftsformation und Staatsform – Drei Aufsätze*
(Frankfurt, 1975); H. Gintis, 'Communication and Politics: Marxism and the Problem of Liberal Democracy', *Socialist Review,* 50–1
(1980), 189–232; A. Gorz, *Stratégie ouvrière et néo-capitalisme*
(Paris, 1967); and, above all, the works of Jürgen Habermas. A brief
outline of the organizational patterns of collective action, which
follow from these two logics in which we are particularly interested
in this essay, is to be found in U. Preuss, *Zum staatsrechtlichen
Begriff des Öffentlichen* (Stuttgart, 1969).

5. C. Lindblom, *Politics and Markets* (New York, 1977), p. 193.

6. See, for example, R. Leckebusch, *Entstehung und Wandlungen der
Zielsetzungen, der Struktur und der Wirkungen von Arbeitgeberver-
bänden* (Berlin, 1966). Incidentally, some of these collective interests
can be defined and agreed upon comparatively easily and do not
require much effort of formal organization. In this sense, too, Engels
has argued (*The British Labour Movement – Articles from 'The
Labour Standard'*, London, 1936, pp. 16–17) that

> capitalists are always organized. They need in most cases no
> formal union, no rules, officers, etc. Their small number, as
> compared with that of the workman, the fact of their forming a
> separate class, their constant social and commercial intercourse
> stand them in lieu of that.

Thus, *informal association,* the importance of which tends to be very
much overrated by various 'elitist' approaches as they are applied to
advanced capitalist societies, is a third element of the associational
practices of the capitalist class, in addition to the very nature of
industrial capital to *organize 'dead' labour,* which plays a major role
from the beginning and finds its most powerful expression in the

modern corporation, and the *formal organization* of capitalist business organizations, which comes much later and only after organizing efforts of the working class have occurred. Engels continues:

> on the other hand, the workpeople from the very beginning cannot do without a strong organization, well-defined by rules and delegating its authority to officers and committees . . . The formerly helpless mass, divided against itself, was no longer so. To the strength given by union and common action, soon was added the force of a well-filled exchequer – 'resistance money' as our French brethren expressively call it.

7. The following argument is derived from the discussion in N. Luhmann, *Macht* (Stuttgart, 1975).
8. This argument is developed by A. Pizzorno, 'Identity and Interest', in S. Berger (ed.), *Organizing Interests in Western Europe: pluralism, corporatism, and the transformation of politics* (Cambridge, 1981).
9. This is the essence of an insight that Marx first formulated in his third thesis on Feuerbach – the dialectical relationship between the two components of a revolutionary process. Actors have to change themselves in the process in which they wish to change their objective conditions.
10. See K. von Beyme, 'Der "Gewerkschaftsstaat" – Eine neue Form der "gemischten Verfassung"?', in P. Haungs (ed.), *Res publica Studien zum Verfassungswesen – Dolf Sternberger zum 70. Geburtstag* (Munich, 1977), pp. 22–36; and *Gewerkschaften und Arbeitsbeziehungen in kapitalistischen Ländern* (Munich, 1977).
11. See M. Olson, *The Logic of Collective Action*.
12. When exclusion of members occurs in unions, it is more often for the reason that their sweeping demands and radical politico-ideological positions allegedly endanger internal unity. Ironically, and indicative of the opposite pattern of membership roles, a business firm is not in danger of becoming excluded when taking an intransigent position against labour but, if at all, when it acts in a too conciliatory way.
13. See W. Streeck, 'Das dilemma der Organisation – Tarifverbände zwischen Interessenvertretung und Stabilität', in W. Meissner und L. Unterseher (eds), *Verteilungskampf und Stabilitätspolitik – Bedingungen der Tarifauseinandersetzung* (Stuttgart, 1972), p. 151. In the Federal Republic of Germany only about 30 per cent of the active eligible members are organized in unions, whereas employers' organizations incorporate more than 90 per cent of their eligible constituency.

14. C. Lindblom, *Politics and Markets*, p. 172.
15. Ibid., p. 173
16. Ibid., p. 175
17. Cf. Claus Offe, 'Theses on the Theory of the State', in *Contradictions of the Welfare State*, J. Keane (ed.), (London, 1984), pp. 119–29; and F. Block, 'The ruling class does not rule: Notes on the Marxist theory of the state', *Socialist Revolution*, 7, 3 (1977), 6–28.
18. P. Bachrach, 'Interest, participation and democratic theory', in *Participation and Politics* J. R. Pennock and J. W. Chapman (eds), (New York, 1975); cf. I. Balbus, 'The concept of interest in pluralist and Marxian analysis', *Politics and Society*, 1 (1971), 151–77.
19. C. Schmitt, *Verfassungslehre* (Munich, 1928), p. 237.
20. P. Bachrach, 'Interest, participation and democratic theory', p. 40
21. The distortion of interest awareness that stems from these kinds of sources and that contributes to an 'eclipse of class consciousness', has been at the centre of the theoretical attention and political struggles of the New Left of the 1960s. For a concise statement of the continuing theoretical relevance of the argument, see R. Jacoby, 'Political economy and class unconsciousness', *Theory and Society*, 5 (1978), 11–18.
22. Note that neither so far nor in what follows do we make any claim to be able to provide a method by which a positive definition of 'objective' or 'true' interests could be arrived at. In our view, such a claim is unnecessary for our present argument. It also appears to be generally impossible to sustain methodologically and, incidentally, this claim is nothing that Marxist social theory would pretend to be able to satisfy. The two much more modest and less deterministic assumptions we have been working with are (i) that the only thing that is objective about interests is not their nature and content, but their *fallibility* as perceived by the actor whose interest it is; and (ii) that there are class-specific differences in the probability of interest-distortion, which is the point to be elaborated subsequently.
23. K. W. Deutsch, *The Nerves of Government: Models of Political Communication and Control* (New York, 1966), p. 111.
24. Cf. R. Jacoby, 'Political economy and class unconsciousness'.
25. G. Esping-Andersen, R. Friedland and E. O. Wright, 'Modes of class struggle and the capitalist state', *Kapitalistate*, 4–5 (1976), 190–1.
26. The only notion of 'objective' interest that underlies our line of argument is a purely formal and negative one: the interest not to experience deception or self-deception about what one's interests are.
27. Institut der Deutschen Wirtschaft (ed.), *Auf dem Weg in den Gewerkschaftsstaat?*, 2nd edn, (Cologne, 1974), p. 169.

28. For a sociological analysis of the components and dynamics of this legislation, see J. Goldthorpe, 'Industrial Relations in Great Britain: A critique of reformism', *Politics and Society*, 4 (1974).

29. R. Taylor, 'How democratic are trade unions?', *The Political Quarterly*, 47 (1976), 28 and 38.

30. In order to be fully consistent with the overall objective of strengthening 'cooperative' attitudes and modes of behaviour, and also to bridge the controversy between conservatives and social democrats as to whether the 'irresponsible' elements are likely to be found at the top or at the bottom of union hierarchies, such regulations have to be delicately biased in favour of conservative dissidents and against militant ones. German labour courts managed to perform this trick by developing a legal doctrine which says that conservative dissidents may not be expelled – even if they compete with union candidates on non-union lists for works-council elections – because that would endanger intra-union pluralism, whereas the union has a legitimate right to expel dissidents from the left because their position is inconsistent with the principles of unionism. See R. Erd, *Verrechtlichung industrieller Konflikte. Normative Rahmen- bedingungen des dualen Systems der Interessenvertretung* (Frank- furt, 1978), pp. 243–6.

31. For an analogous argument concerning the modern 'catch-all party', see H. Kaste and J. Raschke, 'Zur Politik der Volkspartei', in W-D. Narr (ed.), *Auf dem Weg zum Einparteienstaat* (Opladen, 1977), pp. 52–5.

32. P. Nettl, *Rosa Luxemburg*, abridged edn, (London, 1969), p. 130.

33. R. Luxemburg, *Gesammelte Werke* (Berlin, 1974), vol. 4.

34. On the basis of a case study of the development of German trade unions, W. Streeck argues convincingly that 'labour unions in developed capitalist societies are as a rule caught in a systemic organizational crisis, which tends to make them dependent for their material subsistence upon assistance from the state' ('Organizational Consequences of Corporatist Cooperation in West German Labour Unions: A Case Study', discussion paper, International Institute of Management, Berlin, 1978, p. 3). This crisis, according to Streeck, is a 'crisis of success' – a problem resulting, as in stage two of our model, from strength and external recognition rather than failure. The willingness of members to 'act' (and even the willingness of potential members to enter the organization) are undermined, which leads to an increasing lack of financial resources (W. Streeck and H-E. Treu, 'Die "Finanzkrise" der Gewerkschaften? Ein Beitrag zur Soziologie der Gewerkschaftsfinanzen', unpublished paper pre- sented to the conference of the German Political Science Association,

Bielefeld, 1976). For the union, there remains no other option than to see to it that the state 'becomes the main underwriter of the unions' material subsistence', that is, to opt for corporatist arrangements which make the organization relatively independent from active membership participation and may even transform such participation into 'a constant threat to the organization's effectiveness' (W. Streeck and H-E. Treu, 'Ursachen und Folgen administrativer Rationalisierung in Gewerkschaftsorganisationen', unpublished paper presented to the conference of the German Sociological Association, Bielefeld, 1976, p. 45). As a consequence, 'members in many ways no longer appear to belong to the organization at all but rather seem to have become part of its environment' (W. Streeck and H-E. Treu, 'Ursachen und Folgen administrativer Rationalisierung in Gewerkschaftsorganisationen', p. 47).

35. As soon as support is 'externalized', i.e. derived from legal and political guarantees provided by the state, it can be *withdrawn* by outside forces. The likelihood that this will happen is greater the more participation of members has been discouraged and thus the potential of resistance has been weakened. The potential of resistance is weakened, among other things, if a union engages in 'non-ideological' forms of communication between members and leadership and thereby reduces the chances of mobilizing members on the basis of some shared conception of collective identity. Piore writes (M. Piore, 'Unions and Politics', unpublished manuscript, 1978, p. 6) that, under these conditions,

> the danger is that if unions appeal too narrowly to the immediate and particularistic interests of their membership . . . they will not provide a justification which is broad enough to attract and maintain the larger political consensus upon which their existence is predicated.

Discussing the problem of unions and politics in the context of the USA, Piore arrives at conclusions that are well applicable beyond the situation of American unionism. In order to preserve the power of unionism, (pp. 18–19),

> What is required is, at once, an ideology, a philosophy, and a kind of scientific understanding – a vision or a paradigm of action that serves at once to define and link together in a unique combination a particular set of means and ends and to express the felt needs of the various groups and individuals involved . . . (Unions' behaviour) is predicated upon a notion of group

action which contradicts and appears to violate the central
tenets of individualism. The basic task of a philosophy of
organized labour is to overcome these contradictions and create
'space' within the individualistic self-conception of Americans
for such a group'. (Offe's brackets.)

36. It is difficult to make any empirical generalizations as to the specific
circumstances under which this repoliticization – stage five – takes
place and the dialogical pattern of collective action reasserts itself
after having been displaced by opportunist strategies. W. Streeck
('Organizational Consequences of Corporatist Cooperation in West
German Labour Unions') leaves open the question whether the
transformation of unions into a liberal-corporatist 'service organization' (that he documents in the German case) will eventually result
in the emergence of 'internal ideological opposition'. Bruno Trentin,
the secretary of the Italian CGIL, has argued in his remarkable book
on workers' democracy (*Da srufatti a produttori*, Bari, 1977), that
this question largely depends upon alliances between unions and
political parties, the overlapping membership between the two, and
the possibility of non-antagonistic internal conflict within unions
that might result in a willingness to forgo economic gains for
increases of political power. But the opposite may also be true in a
different (i.e. North-West European) context, namely, the growing
estrangement between social-democratic political parties, on the one
hand, and unions on the other, leading to the expectation that
unions must compensate for failures and frustrations that workers
have experienced with 'their' traditional political parties.

## 8   The Attribution of Public Status to Interest Groups

1. N. Harris, *Competition and the Corporate Society* (London, 1972),
p. 66.
2. An early example of the relation between new 'output objectives' of
public policy on the one side and new 'input arrangements' on the
other is, in German history, found in the coincidence of Bismarck's
social security legislation and simultaneous legislation outlawing the
activity of the Social Democrats. Less-well known than this
often-analysed parallelism is that Bismarck's social policy innovations coincided with the creation of a corporatist constitutional
body, the Preussischer Volkswirtschaftsrat (1881–7), which formed
one major element of what H. U. Wehler describes as 'authoritarian

interest group syndicalism' (*Das deutsche Kaiserreich 1871 bis 1918*, Göttingen, 1975, p. 90). This 'national economic council' was the earliest corporatist experiment in modern German constitutional history, and it is interesting to note that most of its activity concerned consensus building among industrial, commercial, and agricultural interests on the new social policy (F. J. Dotzenrath, *Wirtschaftsraete und die Versuche zu ihrer Verwirklichung in Preussen-Deutschland*, Cologne, 1932, p. 4). New policy programmes, the adoption and implementation of new state functions, seem to require new participants (or non-participants) in the political process and new institutional forms of interest intermediation.

3. See, for instance, T. Eschenburg, *Herrschaft der Verbaende?* (Stuttgart, 1955), and W. Weber, *Spannungen und Kraefte im westdeutschen Verfassungssystem* (Berlin, 1970).

4. E. W. Boeckenfoerde, 'Die politische Funktion wirtschaftlich-sozialer Verbaende und Interessentraeger in der sozialstaatlichen Demokratie', *Der Staat*, 15 (1976), 457–83; P. Kevenhoerster, 'Kollektive Gueter und organisierte Interessen', in W. Dettling (ed.), *Macht der Verbaende – Ohnmacht der Demokratie?* (Munich, 1976), pp. 189–220.

5. An English summary of this theoretical and empirical literature is provided by R. Mayntz and F. W. Scharpf, *Policy Making in the German Federal Bureaucracy* (Amsterdam, 1976).

6. V. Hauff and F. W. Scharpf, *Modernisierung der Volkswirtschaft: Technologiepolitik als Strukturpolitik* (Frankfurt am Main, 1975).

7. For a critical analysis of the short-lived *Formierte Gesellschaft* campaign of 1965, see R. Opitz, 'Der grosse Plan der CDU: Die "formierte Gesellschaft"', *Blaetter fuer deutsche und internationale Politik*, 9 (1965). Erhard's programmatic statement can be found in his speech 'Programm fuer Deutschland', *Protokolle des 13. Bundesparteitages der CDU* (Bonn, 1965). Although the concept of 'societal formation' has been dropped from the Christian Democratic Party programme, the idea that the major task required of the party is to implement a 'policy of order' (*Ordnungspolitik*) for the transition from the pluralist to the post-pluralist stage of industrial society, including the developmental scheme already mentioned, certainly has not. Among the most recent documents proving this point, see the volumes by W. Dettling (ed.), *Macht der Verbaende* (Frankfurt, 1975) and W. Dettling et al., *Die Neue Soziale Frage und die Zukunft der Demokratie* (Bonn, 1976). For a lucid analysis of parallel American and British ideas developing in the late fifties, see H. Draper, 'Neo-Corporatists and Neo-Reformers', *New Politics*, 7 (1961), 81–106. Draper seems to be one of the first authors to apply

the term 'neo-corporatism'.

8. C. W. Anderson, 'Political Design and the Representation of Interests', *Comparative Political Studies*, 10 (1977), 127–52.

9. The issue of granting (or reducing) political status to organized groups is, of course, a particularly sensitive one for the SPD. Proposals for an alteration of the political design of liberal democracy are most likely to have a negative effect on the power position of the trade unions. But friendly and cooperative relations with the unions are traditionally considered a major political asset by Social Democratic and Labour Parties. The only kind of institutional changes to be seriously and openly considered by a Social Democratic administration are, therefore, those that involve at least apparent status gains for the unions.

10. For an illustration of the two-sided *noblesse oblige* effects of political status attribution, we might consider the extreme cases. Even where a group is attributed the absolute *negative* political status of illegality or prohibition, its (at least temporarily effective) gains resulting therefrom consist in the solidarity and support obtained from other groups and organizations as well as in new tactical opportunities resulting from 'going underground'. This consequence, incidentally, is reflected in the usual second thoughts reactionary regimes are having regarding their own calls for 'outlawing' communist parties. Inversely, even the attribution of the most *privileged* political status to interest groups does regularly force them to at least use more moderate and more broadly acceptable language in stating and pursuing their interests.

11. Many of the recent students of neo-corporatist phenomena and developments seem to agree on the point that the corporatist status of interest organizations is 'new' because of the 'non-ideological' nature of the legitimations offered to justify such transformations. Moreover, as Harris (*Competition and the Corporate Society*) has demonstrated for the British case, the incorporation of interest groups into the state apparatus and the constitutional reliance on the principle of 'functional' (rather than 'territorial') representation has always been among the constitutional aims of both socialist and conservative movements. What is new about *neo*-corporatism is its 'non-ideological' origin and its peaceful coexistence with parliamentary doctrines and practices.

12. C. W. Anderson, 'Political Design and the Representation of Interests', p. 14.

13. For instance, Panitch, arguing from a class-theoretical perspective, insists in his discussion of corporatism that it is a political form that 'is not so general as to encompass ... any interest group-state

relation', but that it is rather specific to the 'associations of business and labour'. (L. Panitch, 'Corporatism in Canada?', unpublished paper, 1978, pp. 2, 3.) He then ends by narrowing the concept of corporatism by describing it as 'a political form designed to integrate the organized working class in the capitalist state' (p. 44). Similarly Bob Jessop argues that 'it is the involvement of organized labour that is distinctive about corporatism'. ('Corporatism, Fascism and Social Democracy', unpublished paper, 1978, p. 15.) In sharp contrast, and not without considerable plausibility, Schmitter develops the concept of corporatism in view 'of highly organized and specialized representatives of class, sectoral, regional, sexual and generational interests', which form 'complexes of specialized associations often bypassing, if not boycotting, more traditional and more general partisan and legislative structures of articulation and aggregation'. (P. C. Schmitter, 'Models of Interest Intermediation and Models of Social Change in Western Europe', *Comparative Political Studies,* 10 (1977), 7–8.)

14. Cf. P. C. Mayer-Tasch, *Korporativismus und Autoritarismus* (Frankfurt am Main, 1971).

15. Sometimes they even appear to be the outcome of what has been called a latent all-party coalition, to which German politicians often appeal by the standard phrase 'solidarity of all democrats' (*Solidaritaet aller Demokraten*).

16. One could even argue that programmatic alternatives and innovations do increasingly originate from sources outside the formally constituted national political system. Such sources include, in the German case, the Protestant church, organized science, and extra-parliamentary single-issue movements; also the imitation of foreign examples often appears to play an important innovative function.

17. C. Offe, *Berufsbildungsreform: Eine Fallstudie über Reformpolitik* (Frankfurt am Main, 1975), ch. 3.

18. Cf. Suzanne D. Berger, 'Regime and interest representation: the French traditional middle classes', in Suzanne D. Berger (ed.), *Organizing Interests in Western Europe: pluralism, corporatism, and the transformation of politics* (Cambridge, 1981), pp. 83–101.

19. For similar arguments emphasizing the different nature of labour and capital interest organizations, see U. K. Preuss, *Zum staatsrechtlichen Begriff des Oeffentlichen* (Stuttgart, 1969), p. 170ff. and S. Ehrlich, *Die Macht der Minderheit* (Vienna, 1966), p. 272.

20. Cf. E. W. Boeckenfoerde, 'Die politische Funktion wirtschaftlich-sozialer Verbaende', p. 475; G. Teubner, 'Verbaendedemokratie durch Recht?', *Aus Politik und Zeitgeschichte,* 8 (1977).

21. For the more limited argument that politically imposed 'democratiz-

ation' may well be considered as being contrary to the interests of group members, see H. Foehr, 'Innere Demokratie in den Verbaenden', *Freiheit in der sozialen Demokratie. Materialen zum 4. rechtspolitischen Kongress der SPD* (Berlin, 1976), p. 50; and E. Mueller, 'Das Unbehagen an den Verbaenden', *Aus Politik und Zeitgeschichte*, 8 (1977), 40. Further proposals for democratizing internal structures of interest groups are summarized in G. Teubner, 'Verbaendedemokratie durch Recht?', pp. 24–5.

22. *Knowing* that they are not binding for their constituencies anyway, employers' and investors' organizations can (and frequently do) make public commitments of the most popular sort. For interesting historical evidence supporting the argument (i) that big industry does not really need interest organizations in order to be politically successful and (ii) that their interest organizations are unable to impose a binding discipline on employers and investors, see H. Abromeit, 'Interessedurchsetzung in der Krise', *Aus Politik und Zeitgeschichte*, 11 (1977), 15–37.

23. E. W. Boeckenfoerde, 'Die politische Funktion wirtschaftlich-sozialer Verbaende', pp. 480, 483.

24. J. T. Winkler, 'Corporatism', *European Journal of Sociology*, 17 (1976), 103.

25. G. Lehmbruch, 'Liberal Corporatism and Party Government', *Comparative Political Studies*, 10 (1977), 115.

26. Cf. J. Bergmann et al., *Gewerkschaften in der Bundesrepublik* (Frankfurt am Main, 1975); E. W. Boeckenfoerde, 'Die politische Funktion wirtschaftlich-sozialer Verbaende', 483.

27. F. W. Scharpf, *Die Funktionsfaehigkeit der Gewerkschaften als Problem einer Verbaendegesetzgebung* (Berlin, 1978), p. 37.

28. Cf. M. Adler, *Politische oder soziale Demokratie* (Berlin, 1926), pp. 151–8.

29. G. Esping-Andersen et al., 'Modes of Class Struggle and the Capitalist State', *Kapitalistate*, 4–5 (1976), 197; cf. Bob Jessop, 'Corporatism, Fascism, and Social Democracy', p. 10.

## 9 Legitimation Through Majority Rule?

1. Cf. C. W. Anderson, 'Political Design and the Representation of Interest', *Comparative Political Studies*, 10 (1977), 127–52; H. Kitschelt, *Kernenergiepolitik: Arena eines gesellschaftlichen Konflikts* (Frankfurt, 1980), pp. 12–34.

2. Cf. M. Kriele, *Einführung in die Staatslehre* (Reinbek, 1975), p. 224ff.

3. J. J. Varain, 'Die Bedeutung des Mehrheitsprinzips im Rahmen

unserer politischen Ordnung', *Zeitschrift für Politik,* 11 (1964), 239–50.

4. J. Elster, 'Risk, Uncertainty and Nuclear Power', *Social Science Information,* 18 (1979), 371–400.
5. C. Offe, 'Überlegungen und Hypothesen sum Problem politischer Legitimation', in R. Ebbighausen (ed.), *Bürgerlicher Staat und politische Legitimation* (Frankfurt, 1976), pp. 80–105.
6. Rudolf Häberle, *Social Movements: An Introduction to Political Sociology* (New York, 1951), p. 241
7. See R. A. Dahl and C. E. Lindblom, *Politics, Economics, and Welfare* (New York, 1953) for a discussion of this distinction of three possible collective decision-making rules.
8. M. Rustin, 'Different Conceptions of Party: Labour's Constitutional Debates', *New Left Review,* 126 (1981), 19.
9. Ibid., p. 24
10. Ibid., pp. 31, 32–3.
11. Ibid., p. 39
12. C. Offe, 'Die Logik des kleineren Übels. Ein Vorschlag an die Sozialdemokraten, sich mit den Grünen zu arrangieren', *Die Zeit 9,* 46 (1979); 'Konkurrenzpartei und kollektive politische Identität', in R. Roth (ed.), *Parlamentarisches Ritual und politische Alternativen* (Frankfurt, 1980).
13. P. Kielmansegg, *Volkssouveränität. Eine Untersuchung der Bedingungen demokratischer Legitimität* (Stuttgart, 1977), p. 244.
14. D. Usher, *The Economic Prerequisite to Democracy* (Oxford, 1981), p. 37ff.
15. U. Scheuner, *Das Mehrheitsprinzip in der Demokratie* (Opladen, 1973).
16. Ibid., pp. 61–2.
17. Häberle, *Social Movements,* p. 243.
18. H. Daudt and D. W. Rae, 'Social Contract and the Limits of Majority Rule', in P. Birnbaum et al. (eds), *Democracy, Consensus, and Social Contract* (London, 1978), p. 336.
19. Cf. Varain, 'Die Bedeutung des Mehrheitsprinzips'; Scheuner, *Das Mehrheitzprinzip in der Demokratie.*
20. Cf. M. Antoni, 'Grundgesetz und Sperrklausel', *Zeitschrift für Parlamentsfragen,* 11 (1980), 93–109.
21. O. Kirchheimer, 'The Waning of Opposition in Parliamentary Regimes', in his *Politics, Law, and Social Change* (New York, 1969).
22. C. Pateman, *Participation and Democratic Theory* (Cambridge, 1970).
23. Cf. K. Novy, *Strategien der Sozialisierung* (Frankfurt, 1978).
24. J. Elster, 'Three Lectures on Constitutional Choice', unpublished

manuscript, (Oslo, June 1981), p. 38

25. Cf. Daudt and Rae, 'Social Contract and the Limits of Majority Rule'; D. W. Rae and H. Daudt, 'The Ostrogorski Paradox: A Peculiarity of Compound Majority Decision', European Journal of Political Research, (1976), 391–8.

26. C. Offe, 'Konkurrenzpartei und kollektive politische Identität'.

27. Cf. the extensive analysis in H. Hofmann, 'Langzeitrisiko und Verfassung: Eine Rechtsfrage der atomaren Entsorgung', Scheidewege, 4 (1980), 449–79.

28. Cf. R. A. Dahl, A Preface to Democratic Theory (Chicago, 1956), p. 57ff.

29. Cf. Kielmansegg, Volkssouveränität, p. 198.

30. Dahl, Preface to Democratic Theory, p. 90; see also E. Krippendorf, 'Legitimität als Problem der Politikwissenschaft', Zeitschrift für Politik, 9 (1962), 1–11.

31. 'Logrolling' has been discussed as another mechanism that mitigates the problem of intensity, at least for the parliamentary level (cf. G. Tullock, 'Problems of Majority Voting', *Journal of Political Economy,* 67 (1959, 571–9). It is possible, however, for the actual voter to express and render effective the intensity of his/her concerns only through *other* means of political action (demonstrations, political strikes, boycotts, etc.) that lend weight to his/her vote – if these forms of expression are not illegal or discredited as plebiscitary pressure of a 'mob' but rather are respected as a necessary addition to the majority vote. Even here, however, there is no clear procedure by which quantity and intensity can be calculated together.

32. Cf. Varain, 'Die Bedeutung des Mehrheitsprinzips', p. 242ff.

33. V. Gitermann, 'Jean Jacques Rousseau und die Problematik der modernen Demokratie', Deutsche Universitätszeitung, 13 (1958), 91–2.

34. R. Benjamin, The Limits of Politics: Collective Goods in Postindustrial Societies (Chicago, 1980).

35. Cf. L. Thurow, The Zero Sum Society (New York, 1980).

36. Cf. T. Nairn, Nationalismus und Marxismus: Anstoß zu einer notwndigen Debatte (Berlin, 1978); M. Walser, 'Händedruck mit Gespenstern', in J. Habermas (ed.), Stichworte zur 'Geistigen Situation der Zeit' (Frankfurt, 1979).

37. B. Guggenberger, Bürgerinitiativen in der Parteiendemokratie: Von der Ökologiebewegung zur Umweltpartei (Stuttgart, 1980), p. 59ff.

38. Cf., for example, M. V. Nadel, 'The Hidden Dimension of Public Policy: Private Governments and the Policy-making Process', Journal of Politics, 37 (1975), 2–34.

39. H. van Gunsteren, 'Public and Private', Social Research, 49 (1979), 268.

40. R. A. Dahl, *Dilemmas of Pluralistic Democracy: Autonomy vs. Control* (New Haven, 1982), p. 92.
41. Rustin, 'Different Conceptions of Party', p. 38.
42. Scheuner, *Das Mehrheitsprinzip in der Demokratie*, p. 56ff.
43. H. Abromeit, 'Die Funktion des Bundesrats und der Streit um seine Politisierung', *Zeitschrift für Parlamentsfragen*, 13 (1982), 462–72; cf. G. Lembruch, *Parteienwettbewerb im Bundesstaat* (Stuttgart, 1976).
44. E. Berg, *Democracy and the Majority Principle: A Study in Twelve Contemporary Political Theories* (Göteborg, 1965).
45. Ibid., p. 125
46. Cf. the exchange of letters between a Bonn ministerial official and the author in L. Mez and U. Wolter (eds), *Die Qual der Wahl* (Berlin, 1980), pp. 135–46.
47. W. H. Riker, 'Implications for the Disequilibrium of Majority Rule for the Study of Institutions', *American Political Science Review*, 74 (1980), 456–7.
48. N. Luhmann, *Legitimation durch Verfahren* (Neuwied, 1969), p. 227.
49. Ibid., p. 115ff.
50. Ibid., pp. 176ff, 196.
51. Ibid., p. 196
52. Abromeit, 'Die Funktion des Bundesrates', p. 78.
53. Dahl, *Preface to Democratic Theory*, p. 115.
54. Lembruch, *Parteienwettbewerb im Bundesstaat*.
55. H. Horn, *Wahlerspezialisierung: Ein Langzeitproblm der Demokratie* (Frankfurt, 1980).

## 10   The Divergent Rationalities of Administrative Action

1. M. Weber, *Wirtschaft und Gesellschaft* (Cologne, 1964), p. 164.
2. I cannot enter here into the difficulties of the Weberian concept of 'rationality' or the misunderstandings that underlie an 'empirical' examination of the rationality of bureaucratic administration. For a treatment of these themes, see R. Mayntz, 'Max Webers Idealtypus der Bürokratie und die Organisationssoziologie', *Kölner Zeitschrift für Soziologie und Sozialpsychologie*, 17 (1965), 493–502; M. Albrow, *Bureaucracy* (London, 1970); and W. Schluchter, *Aspekte bürokratischer Herrschaft* (Munich, 1973).
3. H. Marcuse, 'Industrialisierung und Kapitalismus im Werke Max Webers', in *Kultur und Gesellschaft* (Frankfurt am Main, 1964);

N. Luhmann, 'Zweck, Herrschaft, System; Grundbegriffe und Prämissen Max Webers', *Der Staat,* 3 (1964), 129–58.

4. *Editor's note:* This distinction between 'conditional' and 'goal-oriented' or 'final' modes of state policy draws upon a typology developed by recent German sociologists (for example, N. Luhmann), and is discussed further in C. Offe, *Contradictions of the Welfare State,* J. Keane (ed.) (London, 1984), p., 110. A 'conditional' programme consists of decisions that are implemented automatically if certain *antecedents* (as specified by legal-bureaucratic rules) are present. A 'final' or 'goal-oriented' programme, by contrast, is contingent upon the perceived effectiveness of the intervention in achieving specified outcomes.

5. F. W. Scharpf, *Politische Durchsetzbarkeit innerer Reformen im pluralistisch-demokratischen Gemeinwesen der BRD* (Berlin, 1973), p. 88.

6. F. Naschold et al., *Untersuchung zur mehrjährigen Finanzplanung des Bundes* (Konstanz, 1970–1).

7. R. Mayntz and F. W. Scharpf, *Planungsorganisation* (Munich, 1973); R. A. Levine, *Public Planning, Failure and Redistribution* (New York, 1972).

8. Cf. Preuss's interpretation, which is based on a theory of capitalism, of the *double* mode of functioning of state administration (U. Preuss, *Legalität und Pluralismus,* Frankfurt am Main, 1973). He presents evidence to show that:

> it is structurally specific to the state bureaucracy, which in the Weimar Republic was formulated explicitly in constitutional terms, that it operates under a double mode of functioning, being guided by the rule-governed application of state power as well as by the reliance upon concrete, goal-determined measures . . . State power was and remains continuously applied in accordance with both general rules and the standard of concrete and unregulated situation-determined necessity (pp. 71, 81).

9. U. Preuss, *Legalität und Pluralismus,* p. 22ff.
10. N. Luhmann, *Politische Planung* (Opladen, 1972), pp. 74–5.
11. M. Rein, 'Sozialplanung: auf der Suche nach Legalität', in F. Naschold and W. Väth (eds), *Politische Planungssysteme* (Opladen 1973).
12. U. Preuss, *Legalität und Pluralismus,* pp. 24–5.
13. F. W. Scharpf, *Planung als politischer Prozeß* (Frankfurt am Main, 1973).

# Chronological Bibliography of Claus Offe's Work

### 1965
(a) *Der Begriff der Technik bei A. Gehlen und H. Schelsky*, unpublished thesis, Institute of Sociology, The Free University of Berlin.
(b) With U. Gerhardt, W. Nitsch and U. Preuß, *Hochschule in der Demokratie*, Neuwied.

### 1966
(a) 'Bildungsökonomie und die Motive der Bildungspolitik', *Neue Kritik*, 35.

### 1968
(a) 'Kapitalismus-Analyse als Selbsteinschüchterung', in O. Negt (ed.), *Die Linke antwortet Jürgen Habermas*, Frankfurt, pp. 106–12.
(b) 'Technik und Eindimensionalität – Eine Version der Technokratie/These?', in J. Habermas (ed.), *Antworten auf Herbert Marcuse*, Frankfurt, pp. 78–85.

### 1969
(a) 'Politische Herrschaft und Klassenstrukturen', in C. Koch and D. Senghaas (eds), *Politikwissenschaft*, Frankfurt. English version, see 1972d.
(b) 'Sachzwang und Entscheidungsspielraum', *Stadtbauwelt*, 60 (23), 187–91.
(c) With J. Bergmann, G. Brandt, K. Körber and E. T. Mohl, 'Klasse-Herrschaft-Schichtung', Referat auf dem Deutschen Soziologentage 1968, in *Verhandlungen des Deutschen Soziologentages*, Stuttgart

### 1970
(a) 'Beitrag zur Umfrage der "Stadtbauwelt" über "Plannug als Beruf"', *Stadtbauwelt* (28), pp. 277ff.
(b) 'Das politische Dilemma der Technokratie', in C. Koch ad D. Senghaas (eds), *Texte zur Technokratie-Diskussion*, Frankfurt, pp. 156–71.
(c) *Leistungsprinzip und industrielle Arbeit*, Frankfurt. English edition, see 1976c.

(d) 'Zukunftserwartungen und Strukturpolitik', in Partizipation – Aspekte politischer Kulture, *Offene Welt* (Opladen), 101.

## 1971

(a) 'Bürgerinitiativen und die Reproduktion der Arbeitskraft im Spätkapitalismus', in H. von Grossman (ed.), *Bürgerinitiativen – Schritte zur Veränderung?* Also in 1972a, pp. 153–68.

## 1972

(a) 'Advanced Capitalism and the Welfare State', *Politics and Society*, 2 (4).

(b) 'Bermerkungen zur sozialstrukturellen Position der "Minderheiten"', in *Am Beispiel Angela Davis*, Frankfurt.

(c) 'Bürgerinitiative: eine neue Form politischer Opposition', *Gewaltfreir Aktion*, 4. Jahrgang (12), 12–15.

(d) 'Political Authority and Class Structures – An Analysis of Late Capitalist Societies', *International Journal of Sociology*, 2 (1), 73–108.

(e) Review of S. Melmann, *Pentagon Capitalism* and V. Perlo, *Militarism and Industry*, *Das Argument*, 14 (1/2).

(f) *Strukturprobleme des kapitalistischen Staates, Aufsätze zur politischen Soziologies*, Frankfurt.

## 1973

(a) 'Krisen des Krisenmanagement – Elemente einer politischen Krisentheorie', in M. von Jänicke (ed.), *Herrschaft und Krise*, Opladen, pp. 197–223. English version, see 1976a.

(b) Review of O. Negt and A. Kluge, 'Öffentlichkeit und Erfahrung', *TAZ*, 7 July.

(c) 'The Abolition of Market Control and the Problem of Legitimacy', *Kapitalistate* 1, 109–16 (part I) and 2, 73–5 (part II)

(d) With V. Ronge, 'Fiskalische Krise, Bauindustrie und die Grenzen staatlicher Rationalisierung', *Leviathan*, 2, 189–220.

## 1974

(a) 'Doppelstrategie der planenden Verwaltung', in H. E. Bahr and R. Groehemeyer (eds), *Konfliktorientierte Gemeinwesenarbeit*, Neuwied, pp. 74–82.

(b) 'Rationalitätskriterien und Funktionsprobleme politisch-administrativen Handelns', *Leviathan*, 2, 333–45.

(c) 'Structural Problems of the Capitalist State', in K.V. Beyme (ed.), *German Political Studies*, London, vol. I.

## 1975

(a) *Berufsbildungsreform – Eine Fallstudie über Reformpolitik*, Frankfurt.

(b) 'Bildungssystem, Beschäftigungssystem und Bildungspolitik – Ansätze zu einer gesamtgesellschaftlichen Funktionsbestimmung des

Bildungssystems', in H. Roth and D. Friedrich (eds), *Bildungsfor-schung – Probleme, Perspektiven, Prioritäten*, Deutscher Bildung-srat, Gutachten und Studien der Bildungskommission Bd. 50, Stuttgart, pp. 215–52.

(c) Comments on 'Intensivierung der Arbeit und staatliche Sozialpolitik' von Fritz Böhle and Dieter Sauer, *Leviathan*, 1, 79–83.

(e) 'The Theory of the Capitalist State and the Problem of Policy Formation' and 'Introduction to Part III' in L. N. Lindberg, R. Alford, C. Crouch and C. Offe (eds), *Stress and Contradiction in Modern Capitalism*, (1975f).

(f) With L. N. Lindberg, R. Alford and C. Crouch, *Stress and Contradiction in Modern Capitalism*, Lexington, Mass.

(g) With W-D. Narr (eds), *Wohlfahrtsstaat und Massenloyalität*, Cologne.

(h) With S. Skarpelis-Spark, J. Habermas and P. Kalmbach, 'Ein biedermeierlicher Weg zum Sozialismus?', *Der Spiegel*, 9, (24 February), 44–50.

(i) 'Zur Frage der Identität der kommunalen Ebene', in R. R. Grauhan (ed.), *Lokale Politikforschung*, Frankfurt, vol. 2, pp. 303–9.

### 1976

(a) 'Crisis of Crisis Management: Elements of a Political Crisis Theory', *International Journal of Politics*, 6 (3), 29–67. Translation of 1973a.

(b) Ed. and Introduction to Murray Edelmann, *Politik als Ritual*, Frankfurt.

(c) *Industry and Inequality, The Achievement Principle in Work and Social Status*, London. Translation of 1970c.

(d) 'Praxisbezüge der Sozialwissenschaft als Krisenwissenschaft', in 'Theorie en praxis in de sociologiese teorie', *Amsterdam Sociologisch Tijdschrift*, Serie A.S.T. Teorie, 1, 38–53

(e) Review of D. Bell, 'The Coming of Post-Industrial Society' and 'Cultural Contradiction of Capitalism', *Merkur*, 9.

(f) Review of R. Mayntz and F. W. Scharpf, 'Policy Making in the German Federal Republic', *Administrative Science Quarterly*, 21 (4).

(g) 'Überlegungen und Hypothesen zum Problem politischer Legitimation', in R. Ebbighausen (ed.), *Bürgerlicher Staat und politische Legitimation*, Frankfurt, pp. 80–105.

(h) 'Wahlen und Wählen', *Links*, 78, 23–4.

(i) With G. Lenhardt, 'Staatstheorie und Sozialpolitik – politisch-soziologische Erklärungsansätze für Funktionen und Innovations-prozesse der Sozialpolitik', in C. von Ferber and F. X. Kaufmann (eds), *Kölner Zeitschrift für Soziologie und Sozialpsychologie*, 98–127, special issue, 19.

(j) With W-D. Narr, 'Was heißt hier Strukturpolitik? Neokorporativis-

mus als Rettung aus der Krise?', *Technologie und Politik*, 6.
(k) With V. Ronge, 'Thesen zum Begriff des "kapitalistischen Staates" und zur materialistischen Politikforschung', in C. Pozzoli (ed.), *Rahmenbedingungen und Schranken staatlichen Handelns*, Frankfurt, pp. 54–70. English version, see 1984a.

### 1977
(a) 'Die kritische Funktion der Sozialwissenschaften' in Wissenschaftszentrum Berlin (ed.), *Interaktion von Wissenschaft und Politik*, Frankfurt, 1977, pp. 321–9.
(b) Introduction to P. Bachrach and M. Baratz, *Macht und Armut*, Frankfurt, pp. 7–34.
(c) Introduction to H. Häußermann, *Die Politik der Bürokratie, Einführung in die Politik der staatlichen Verwaltung*, Frankfurt.
(d) With K. Hinrichs, 'Sozialökonomie des Arbeitsmarktes und die Lage "benachteiligter" Gruppen von Arbeitnehmern', in *Opfer des Arbeitsmarktes – Zur Theorie der strukturierten Arbeitslosigkeit*, (1977e), pp. 3–61.
(e) With Projektgruppe Arbeitsmarktpolitik (eds), *Opfer des Arbeitsmarktes – Zur Theorie der strukturierten Arbeitslosigkeit*, Neuwied.
(f) 'Young Offers known Solutions to unknown Problems', *Zeitschrift für Verbraucherpolitik*, 4, 395–8.
(g) 'Zum Stand der staatstheoretischen Diskussion in der Bundesrepublik', in *Abendroth-Forum, Marburger Gespräche aus Anlaß des 70. Geburtstages von Wolfgang Abendroth*, Marburg, p. 295ff.

### 1978
(a) 'Neukonservative Klimakunde', review of W. Hennis, *Organisierter Sozialismus, Merkur*, 32 (3), 209–25.

### 1979
(a) 'Die Institutionalisierung des Verbandseinflusses – eine ordnungspolitische Zwickmühle', in U. von Alemann and R. G. Heinze (eds), *Verbände und Staat*, Opladen, pp. 72–91.
(b) 'Die Logik des kleineren Übels. Ein Vorschlag an die Sozialdemokraten, sich mit den Grünen zu arrangieren', *Die Zeit*, 9 (46).
(c) 'Entgegnung auf Karsten D. Voigt, *Die Tageszeitung*, 29 November.
(d) Interview in *Arbeitskampf*, 162 (17 September).
(e) Review of A. Wolfe, 'The Limits of Legitimacy – Political Contradictions of Contemporary Capitalism', *Radical History Review*, 22, 117–23.
(f) 'The Future of European Socialism and the Role of the State', in A. Liebich (ed.), *The Future of Socialism in Europe?* Interuniversity Centre for European Studies, Montreal, pp. 67–75.
(g) '"Unregierbarkeit" – Zur Renaissance konservativer Krisentheorien', in J. Habermas (ed.), *Stichworte zur geistigen Situation der Zeit*,

Frankfurt, vol. 1, pp. 294–318. English version, see 1984d.
(h) With R. G. Heinze, K. Hinrichs, H-W. Hohn and T. Olk, 'Arbeitszeitflexibilisierung als beschäftigungspolitisches Instrument – Wirkungen und Grenzen neuer Arbeitszeitpolitik', *Mitteilungen aus der
Arbeitsmarkt- und Berufsforschung,* 12 (3), 276–88.

### 1980
(a) Foreword to H. Kitschelt, *Kernenergiepolitik: Arena eines gesellschaftlichen Konflikts,* Frankfurt.
(b) Interview with Wieland Elfferding, 'Am Staat vorbei? Krise der
Parteien und neue soziale Bewegungen', *Das Argument,* 22 (124),
809–21.
(c) 'Konkurrenzpartei und kollektive politische Identität', in R. Roth
(ed.), *Parlamentarisches Ritual und politische Alternativen,* Frankfurt, pp. 26–42.
(d) 'Politische Folgen reduzierten ökonomischen Wachstums', in T. Ellwein (ed.), *Politikfeld-Analysen 1979,* Wissenschaftlicher Kongreß
der DVPW 1.-5. Oktober 1979 in der Universität Augsburg,
Tagungsbericht, Opladen, pp. 92–108.
(e) 'Sozialwissenschaften zwischen Auftragsforschung und sozialer
Bewegung', in Bodo von Greiff (ed.), *Das Orwellsche Jahrzehnt und
die Zukunft der Wissenschaft,* Free University of Berlin, pp. 98–108.
English version see 1981e.
(f) 'The Separation of Form and Content in Liberal Democratic Politics',
*Studies in Political Economy,* 3, 5–16.
(g) With J. Berger, 'Die Entwicklungsdynamik des Dienstleistungssektor', *Leviathan,* 8 (1), 41–75.
(h) With R. G. Heinze, K. Hinrichs and T. Olk, 'Sind die Gewerkschaften für "alle" da?', in O. Jacobi, E. Schmidt and W. Müller-Jentsch
(eds), *Moderne Zeiten – alten Rezepte. Kritisches Gewerkschaftsjahrbuch 1980/81,* Berlin, pp. 62–77.
(i) With H. Wiesenthal, 'Two Logics of Collective Action: Theoretical
Notes on Social Class and Organizational Form', in M. Zeitlin (ed.),
*Political Power and Social Theory,* 1, 67–115.

### 1981
(a) 'Ausdifferenzierung oder Integration – Bemerkungen über strategische Alternativen zur Verbraucherpolitik', *Zeitschrift für
Verbraucherpolitik,* 5 (1 and 2), 119–33.
(b) 'Recht hat er: "Aussteiger" aussteigen', TAZ, 21 December.
(c) 'Some Contradictions of the Modern Welfare State', *Praxis International,* 1 (3), 219–29.
(d) 'The Attribution of Public Status to Interest Groups: Observations
on the West German Case', in S. D. Berger (ed.), *Organizing
Interests in Western Europe: pluralism, corporatism, and the*

*transformation of politics,* Cambridge, pp. 123–58.

(e)  'The Social Sciences: Contract Research or Social Movements?', *Current Perspectives in Social Theory,* 2, 31–7. Translation of 1980e.

(f)  With U. Berger, 'Das Rationalisierungsdilemma der Angestelltenarbeit', in J. Kocka (ed.), *Angestellte im Europäischen Vergleich, Göttingen,* pp. 39–58.

(g)  With V. Gransow, 'Politische Kultur und sozialdemokratische Regierungspolitik', *Das Argument,* 23, 128 and 551–64.

(h)  With R. G. Heinze, K. Hinrichs and T. Olk, 'Einheitsgewerkschaft – naives Wunschbild oder alltägliche Routine?', Erwiderung auf die Kritiken von C. Deutschmann, A. Deeke und W. Dzielak, *Soziale Welt,* 32 (4), 518–21.

(i)  With R. G. Heinze, K. Hinrichs and T. Olk, 'Einheitsprobleme der Einheitsgewerkschaft. Überlegungen zum Zusammenhang von Arbeitsmarktmacht und organisationspolitischen Vertretungschancen verschiedener Kategorien von Arbeitnehmern', *Soziale Welt,* 32 (1), 19–38.

(j)  With R. G. Heinze, K. Hinrichs and T. Olk, 'Interessendifferenzierung und Gewerkschaftseinheit', *Gewerkschaftliche Monatshefte,* 6, 336–54.

(k)  With R. G. Heinze, K. Hinrichs and T. Olk, 'Verzicht auf "Utopien"', Erwiderung auf die Kritiken von Bischoff, Herkommer und Maldaner, *Gewerkschaftliche Monatshefte,* 32 (12), 757–9.

*1982*

(a)  '"Bewirken" und "Bewahren". Der politische Aufstieg der Grünen signalisiert den Konflikt zwischen zwei konträren Politikverständnissen', *Die Zeit,* 20 August. English version, see 1983f.

(b)  'Countdown für das sozialliberale Regierungsbündnis?', *Links,* 14 (143), 15–16.

(c)  'Kommentierende Thesen zu den Aufsätzen von H. Kohl und W. Streeck', Forschungsintitut der Friedrich-Ebert-Stiftung (ed.), *Analysen,* 101–2, 139–44.

(d)  'Politische Legitimation durch Mehrheitsentscheidung?', *Journal für Sozialforschung,* 22 (3), 311–35.

(e)  Review of U. Himmelstrand, G. Ahrne, Leif Lundberg and Lars Lundberg, *Beyond Welfare Capitalism. Issues, Actors and Forces in Societal Change. Acta Sociologica,* 25 (3), 313–18.

(f)  With J. Berger, 'Die Zukunft des Arbeitsmarktes. Zur Ergänzungsbedürftigkeit eines versagenden Allokationsprinzips', *Kölner Zeitschrift für Soziologie und Sozialpsychologie,* special issue, 24, 348–71.

(g)  With J. Berger, 'Functionalism vs. Rational Choice? Some Questions Concerning the Rationality of Choosing One or the Other', *Theory and Society*, 11 (4), 521–6.

(h) With K. Hinrichs and H. Wiesenthal (eds), *Arbeitszeitpolitik. Formen und Folgen einer Neuverteilung der Arbeitszeit*, Frankfurt.

(i) With K. Hinrichs and H. Wiesenthal, 'Der Streit um die Zeit – Die Arbeitszeit im gesellschaftspolitischen und industriellen Konflikt', in *Arbeitszeitpolitik. Formen und Folgen einer Neuverteilung der Arbeitszeit*, (1982h), pp. 8–31.

(k) With W-D. Narr, 'Zwei Begriffe des Politischen – oder zum programmierten Mißverständnis establierter Politik und sozialer Bewegung', in H. von Kloppenburg (ed.), *Martin Niemöller, Festschrift zum 90. Geburtstag*, Cologne, pp. 142–58.

## 1983

(a) 'Arbeit als soziologische Schlüsselkategorie?', in J. Matthes (ed.), *Krise der Arbeitsgesellschaft?* Verhandlungen des 21. Deutschen Soziologentages in Bamberg 1982, Frankfurt, pp. 38–65.

(b) 'Competitive Party Democracy and the Keynesian Welfare State: Factors of Stability and Disorganization', *Policy Sciences*, 15; reprinted in St Clegg, G. Dow and P. Boreham (eds), *The State, Class and the Recession*, London, pp. 51–71.

(c) Foreword to G. Vobruba, *Politik mit dem Wohlfahrtsstaat*, Frankfurt, pp. 7–12.

(d) 'Ist die Bürokratie unser Schicksal? – Topoi der sozialwissenschaftlichen und der politischen Kritik an der staatlichen Verwaltung', in *Loccumer Protokolle*, (24), 32–9.

(e) 'Perspektiven auf die Zukunft des Arbeitsmarktes', *Merkur*, 5, 489–504.

(f) 'Reaching for the Brake, The Greens in Germany', *New Political Science*, (Spring), 45–52. Translation of 1982a.

(g) 'Stellungnahme zum Beitrag von W. Streeck', in F. W. Scharpf and M. Brockmann (eds), *Institutionelle Bedingungen der Arbeitsmarkt- und Beschäftigungspolitik*, Frankfurt, pp. 199–206.

(h) With U. Engfer, K. Hinrichs and H. Wiesenthal, 'Arbeitszeitflexibilisierung – Alternative zu allgemeinen Arbeitszeitverkürzungen?', *Aus politik und zeitgeschichte*, 34 (27 August).

(i) With U. Engfer, K. Hinrichs and H. Wiesenthal, 'Arbeitszeitsituation und Arbeitszeitverkürzung in der Sicht der Betroffenen', *Mitteilungen aus der Arbeitsmarkt- und Berufsforschung*, 16 (2), 91–105.

(j) With H. Wiesenthal, K. Hinrichs and U. Enger, 'Arbeitszeitflexibilisierung und gewerkschaftliche Interessenvertretung – Regelungsprobleme und Risiken individualisierter Arbeitszeiten', *WSI-Mitteilungen*, 36 (10), 585–95.

## 1984

(a) *Contradictions of the Welfare State*, J. Keane (ed.), London.

(b) 'Korporatismus als System nichtstaatlicher Makrosteuerung? Notizen über seine Voraussetzungen und demokratischen Gehalte', *Geschichte und Gesellschaft*, 10 (2), 234–56.

(c) 'Politische Legitimation durch Mehrheitsentscheidung?', in *An den Grenzen der Mehrheitsdemokratie*, Opladen, pp. 150–83.

(d) 'Ungovernability: On the Renaissance of Conservative Theories of Crisis', in J. Habermas (ed.), *Observations on 'The Spiritual Situation of the Age'*, Cambridge, Mass., pp. 67–88. Translation of 1979g.

(e) With B. Guggenberger (eds), *An den Grenzen der Mehrheitsdemokratie*, Opladen.

(f) 'Zwischenlösung gesucht', *Wirtschaftswoche*, 23, 1 June 1984.

# Index